Empiricist Devotions

*Winner of the Walker Cowen Memorial Prize
for an outstanding work of scholarship
in eighteenth-century studies*

UNIVERSITY OF VIRGINIA PRESS *Charlottesville and London*

COURTNEY WEISS SMITH

Empiricist Devotions

SCIENCE, RELIGION,
AND POETRY IN EARLY
EIGHTEENTH-CENTURY
ENGLAND

University of Virginia Press
© 2016 by the Rector and Visitors of the University of Virginia
All rights reserved
Printed in the United States of America on acid-free paper

First published 2016
First paperback edition published 2023
ISBN 978-0-8139-5071-6 (paper)

9 8 7 6 5 4 3 2 1

The Library of Congress has cataloged the hardcover edition as follows:
Smith, Courtney Weiss.
 Empiricist devotions : science, religion, and poetry in early eighteenth-century England / Courtney Weiss Smith.
   pages   cm.—(Winner of the Walker Cowen Memorial Prize for an outstanding work of scholarship in eighteenth-century studies)
 Includes bibliographical references and index.
  ISBN 978-0-8139-3838-7 (cloth : alk. paper)—ISBN 978-0-8139-3839-4 (e-book)
 1. English poetry—18th century—History and criticism. 2. Literature and science—England—History—18th century. 3. Science and the humanities—Great Britain—History—18th century. 4. Great Britain—Intellectual life—18th century. I. Title.
  PR555.S33S65 2016
  820.9'005—dc23
                                       2015022491

Contents

Acknowledgments   *vii*

Introduction   *1*

1 · Occasional Meditation, an Empirical-Devotional Mode   *33*

2 · Deus *in* Machina: Popular Newtonianism's Visions of the Clockwork-World   *69*

3 · Money, Meaning, and a "Foundation in Nature"   *106*

4 · Empiricist Subjects, Providential Nature, and Social Contracts   *140*

5 · Georgic Realism, an Empirical-Devotional Poetics   *173*

Notes   *211*

Bibliography   *243*

Index   *269*

Acknowledgments

It's a cliché of these acknowledgment pages but not the less true for all that: in the process of writing this one book, I have accumulated an overwhelming number of big and deeply appreciated debts. The project began at Washington University in St. Louis, under the guidance of Wolfram Schmidgen—whose enthusiasms helped give it shape and whose wisdom, rigor, and friendship have made every single page better than it might have been. I aspire to be just such a scholar and teacher. My thanks also to all those who made Wash U such an interesting and lively place to study, including Guinn Batten, Matt Erlin, Derek Hirst, Joe Loewenstein, William McKelvy, Steven Meyer, Nancy Pope, Kathy Schneider, and Steven Zwicker, as well as Joe Conway, Abby Horne, Keya Kraft, Nick Miller, Katie Muth, Emily Smith, and Natalie Spar. Kate Parker and Matthew Augustine have read these pages repeatedly over the years and continue to enrich my thinking about them and much else.

As it happens, I have been doubly lucky in exceptional intellectual communities. I finished the book at Wesleyan University, surrounded by the most wonderfully smart, supportive colleagues. I am indebted to everyone in the English Department and the eighteenth-century group, as well as to the Olin librarians and the fantastic students. Particular thanks go to Kate Birney, Lauren Caldwell, Matt Garrett, Natasha Korda, Sean McCann, Marguerite Nguyen, Joel Pfister, Joe Rouse, Suzy Taraba, and Liz Tinker. I am grateful for Andy Curran's intelligent conversation and indefatigable encouragement. Stephanie Weiner is a generous mentor, perceptive interlocutor, and valued friend—she has made me a better reader of poetry.

Also, I have found the world of eighteenth-century studies to be (almost disarmingly) welcoming. This book has benefited immeasurably from discussions with my fellow travelers in this world, who have asked hard questions, shared their insights and excitements, and commiserated with me over ASECS meals. Among many others who have contributed in formal and less formal ways, Sean Silver and Jess Keiser offered valuable feedback on parts of this project. I'm also grateful for those much better traveled than I, who have gone out of their way to read my work or give advice and encouragement—among them Tita Chico, Lynn Festa, James Force, Kevis Goodman, Suvir Kaul, Jonathan Kramnick, Helen Thompson, my Women's Caucus mentors, and Christopher Fauske and the other "Money, Power & Print" regulars. I would like to thank everyone at the University of Virginia Press, who made the process of finishing this book such a pleasure. Two discerning readers offered sensitive feedback that helped me sharpen the whole, and I was honored deeply by the distinction conferred on my project by the Cowen judges. At every step in the process, I have felt it a special privilege to have such a kind, collegial, and knowledgeable editor as Angie Hogan.

My work has been supported generously by the Olin Fellowship for Women at Washington University in St. Louis, a Dulin Fellowship from the Folger Shakespeare Library, and a sabbatical from Wesleyan University. It has been supported, in a rather different way, by the inspiration provided by all the great teachers whom I have had the good fortune to learn from—including, especially, the sometimes underappreciated ones in my childhood public schools and the dedicated ones responsible for my undergraduate education. Material from the first half of chapter 3 first appeared in *The Eighteenth Century: Theory and Interpretation*, vol. 53, no. 2 (© 2012 University of Pennsylvania Press. All rights reserved); it is reprinted with permission from that journal. Parts of chapter 4 first appeared as an essay and are reprinted with permission from *SEL Studies in English Literature 1500–1900*, vol. 52, no. 3 (Summer 2012).

Finally, my big love goes to my parents, my family, and my friends, who sustain me in more ways than I could ever list. To my people—Tyler, who makes it all possible, and Louisa, who makes it all amazing: I'm devoted, always.

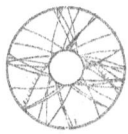

Introduction

> For the Book of Nature is to an ordinary Gazer, and a Naturalist, like a rare Book of Hieroglyphicks to a Child, and a Philosopher: the one is sufficiently pleas'd with the Odnesse and Variety of the Curious Pictures that adorne it; whereas the other is not only delighted with those outward objects that gratifie his sense, but receives a much higher satisfaction in admiring the knowledg of the Author, and in finding out and inriching himselfe with those abstruse and vailed Truths dexterously hinted in them.
>
> —Robert Boyle, *Some Considerations touching the Usefulness of Experimental Naturall Philosophy*

ROBERT BOYLE was an important figure in the emergence of the new science in seventeenth-century England. He was an air-pump experimenter, gentleman chemist, and early Royal Society member. He was also a believer. Boyle believed in God. He believed that God is "Author" of "the Book of Nature" and that humanity has a duty to read the rich "Truths" written in this "Book." He believed that these "Truths" were hard to read and that he would never fully comprehend the unimaginable "knowledge of the Author." Despite this epistemological modesty, he also believed that "Truths" could be at least partially read by scrutinizing "outward objects" and considering their implications (what is "hinted" in them). He believed that such scrutiny could lead him beyond "sense" perception and facts about the physical world, toward insight into nature's "Author." For Boyle, empiricism and devotion were linked intimately, and close, readerly attention to nature enabled glimpses of God's "Truths."[1]

Empiricist Devotions recovers a tradition of empiricist observation and description flourishing in late seventeenth- and early eighteenth-century England that has *this* Boyle as its figurehead and propagandist. My study features a moment before the disciplinary divisions that we inherit today were established. Indeed, in the brand of empiricism that Boyle's "Book of Nature" beliefs encouraged, the techniques and emphases of science, religion, and poetry combined and cooperated. This empiricism was cutting edge in its commitment to particularized scrutiny and epistemological modesty; Protestant in its enabling premises and meditative logics; and earnest in its belief that personifications, periphrases, and analogies were crucial tools for interpreting the divinely written world. Such instrumental use of literary figures is especially significant, for scholars of the period have barely begun to register the extent to which literature and language were caught up in the same project that motivated eighteenth-century science and religion: the search for divine "Truths." In recovering this empiricist tradition, then, *Empiricist Devotions* reimagines the interconnections among science, religion, and poetry in the period.

This brand of empiricism had broad popular appeal and influence. It was closely related to—but distinct from—its more familiar, Royal Society–sponsored counterpart, and it helped motivate and shape the science of the period. Microscopists magnified their objects to learn practical and moral lessons, and Newtonians celebrated how the science of gravity opened up new insights into God's agency in the world. This empiricism was pursued by natural philosophers, Christian meditators, and poets alike. Boyle used it in his experiments, his sister in her prayers and contemporary poets in their nature descriptions. It structured much early eighteenth-century thought. Economists studied the "Book of Nature" as they wrote proposals for governmental action, and political writers engaged with it as they theorized social contract. Alexander Pope and Daniel Defoe wrote conjectural histories in which people scrutinize nature in order to heed its "voice," and it-narratives gave actual voice to nature's particularized "Truths." Georgic poetry dwelled with real specificity on what is "dexterously hinted" in nature. This empiricism motivated Isaac Newton's metaphors, John Locke's narratives, John Gay's prosopopoeias, Joseph Addison's epithets, and Eliza Haywood's descriptive particulars. For many writers at the time, empiricism and devotion were linked intimately, and close, readerly attention to nature enabled glimpses of God's "Truths."

The Book of Nature and an Empiricist Tradition

Boyle's "Book of Nature" beliefs illustrate the contours of this empiricist tradition. The book metaphor was not just a hackneyed convention allowing scientists to gesture politely to God's design before they got on to the work that really interested them, which is how scholars today often understand the new science's treatment of it.[2] Instead, as Karen Edwards argues, in the second half of the seventeenth century this trope was sometimes a well-worn "cliché," but it was also "awakened . . . to new life": it was embraced as a "rationale for observation" and "experimentation" and as a principle motivating the work of serious natural philosophy.[3] Boyle uses it as something even more than "rationale." It is an enabling premise that provides a mandate for minute observation and description. The "ordinary Gazer" is like a childish reader, but proper interpretation requires close reading. People should attend not only to "the great Volume of Nature" but to "each Page" and to the nuances of its language. Here, "Things stand for Words, and their Qualities for Letters."[4] Observers need to cultivate particularity and attend even to things' small bits and "Qualities." These ways of close reading are empiricist. As Joanna Picciotto points out, they could involve things being "sliced open, cut apart, pried into, and put on trial by a 'prying' observer."[5] Proper interpretation demands all the skills of the "Naturalist" or "Philosopher."

This particularity, however, is never an end in itself. Boyle is fascinated by minute particulars but also by what they "stand for." He assumes a providential natural world, a world in which "Truths" and the "knowledg of the Author" are coded into "outward Objects." Provocative recent work by Scott Black, for example, has shown that the metaphor of nature as book allowed contemporaries to bring traditional humanist reading practices to their apprehension of things.[6] Boyle *reads* natural things: he wants to know what they are (their material composition and their "Qualities," say), as well as what they mean in a larger scheme. Nonetheless, the process of reading things for "Truths" remains empiricist. It posits that the specific "Objects" in the external world are the source of understanding, and it requires humble caution in the movement from material fact to speculation on larger meanings.

The most powerful tool in effecting this movement is figurative language. These empiricists use analogies: they scrutinize things and then consider what they are *like*. As Boyle explains, by tropes of likeness such as "Analogy . . . we are, as it were, led by the hand to the discovery of divers useful Notions, especially Practical, which else we should not take any notice of."[7] One plant is like another plant, or a meteorological process is like a biological one. Analogy, here, is a literary technique—something introduced by the language empiricists use to describe things—but it also leads to new ways of seeing: it brings "Truths" to one's "notice." Provisional analogies produce new hypotheses, experiments, and applications. Boyle even asserts that the real difference between the "ordinary Gazer" and the "Naturalist" is the latter's ability to "discern . . . secret Correspondencies and Alliances" between things.[8] Linguistic, imaginative comparisons between things always have the potential to access insight about real, material relationships that pertain in nature. This possibility turns on the precise way that contemporaries understood "Truths" to be coded into "outward Objects": the book of nature is rife with analogies through which the divine "Author" "dexterously hints" lessons to humanity.

These empiricists deploy personification in a similarly instrumental manner. They constantly give nature agency, but this too is no *mere* figure, separate from the real. Rather, like analogy, personification brings "Truths" to one's "notice": it captures and helps us understand what objects actually do. In Boyle's passage above, things act on or "gratifie" the sense; they contain meanings and provoke thought. Personifications also license analogies: the action of the rain in that meteorological process is like the action of the bee in the botanical one. Such materially sensitive personifications work to level the distinctions among humans, animals, and objects in ways that encourage comparisons across species and ontological categories.[9] Empiricists describe things particularly and figuratively, and their rhetorical, even playful figures can illuminate ontological "Truths."

Like other empiricists in this tradition, Boyle believes that the "Truths" accessed through such close attention are remarkably rich. Empiricism helps people understand nature's structure and functioning. It also participates in arguments from design that use natural evidence to "inform Man of Gods Being and Attributes." Importantly, though, Boyle engages substantively with the structures of Protestant meditation as he explains that empiricism can do even more than this. (Much scholarship on the period's natural theology emphasizes design arguments and proofs of God's existence, overlooking a sustained fascination with *what else* nature teaches about God's will for humanity.) Boyle insists that empiricism can also "instruct" "Man" "in his own Duties" in the world.[10] The materially sensitive personifications are crucial here, as the agency of natural things licenses—even prompts—analogies among plants, animals, and people. Just as meteorological processes can be like botanical ones, natural processes can be like human behaviors and religious truths. They can provide meaningful moral exempla or hints for human institutions.

Of course, these empiricist writers realize that such "Truths" are always "vailed" and "abstruse" (from the Latin for "concealed, hidden, secret") and that their conclusions are only ever approximations or guesses.[11] They recognize that their search will never yield complete understanding of God's unimaginable "knowledge." Yet, for all their modest skepticism, they also trust in nature's meaningfulness and their ability to glimpse it. Though the "Truths" are "vailed" and humans struggle to access them, they are *there* for the "admiring" and "finding out." By scrutinizing and analogizing, people can glimpse them in "hints" and fragments, provisional hypotheses and possible applications.[12]

Above all, these empiricist writers want nature to "instruct" them. They want to subordinate their own actions to that of "instructing," "hinting" things. The epistemological stance here is complex. These writers were suspicious of those who claimed to be acting on immediate revelations from God. They knew that providential meanings were difficult to interpret and that human agents must necessarily construct their own moral rules and social institutions. On the other hand, they were deeply uncomfortable thinking about these as products of unfettered, arbitrary human reason. They recognized their agency even as they sought some "Foundation in Nature" (as John Locke put it).[13] They thus studied natural things and tried to understand their physical as well as their moral, social, and political relevance. They modestly understood that they could aim only for approximations of an order encoded into nature, but they tried to develop their science, live their lives, and build even their economic and political institutions in accordance with these provisional approximations. This resonates, to my mind, with their understanding of literary figure: human linguistic constructions could, at best, correspond with and illuminate something fundamental about the structure of the world. These writers wanted *all* human constructs—including economic policies and governmental institutions—to approximate a supra-human order, even as they recognized the difficulty of ever getting it exactly right.

In acts of devotion, these empiricists devoted themselves to close observation and description of nature and to deference for the "Truths" they found there.

Scientific, Devotional, and Poetic Writing

Natural philosophers, Protestant meditators, and nature poets all practiced this brand of meditative empiricism, and therefore fundamental similarities exist in the workings of the period's scientific, devotional, and poetic writing.

These similarities, however, are very different from the ones privileged by the most influential account of the relationships among early eighteenth-century scientific, religious, and literary texts. Since R. F. Jones's work on seventeenth-century prose, we have been taught that the Royal Society's embrace of the "plain style" influenced the prose in sermons and the belles lettres alike.[14] This scholarly tradition privileges Thomas Sprat's ideal for scientific writing: it should be "as near the Mathematical plainness" as possible, "deliver[ing] so many things, almost in an equal number of words."[15] Empiricist description is understood as a basically—and helpfully—reductive project. As Jones explains:

> The new scientists stigmatized the traditional philosophy for being concerned only with words having no concrete significance and representing only figments of the imagination.... Allied to this attitude was the feeling for concrete reality, which naturally eschewed the verbal luxuriance of figurative language and the more subtle effects of imaginative expression. All this led to an insistence upon a direct, unadorned style which should be concrete in idea, and clear and economical in expression.[16]

In this account, a focus on "concrete reality" necessarily led away from "figurative language," which was condemned for introducing confusions and ambiguities. Language was entirely stripped of ornament, as objects themselves were stripped of intrinsic qualities. Scientific language made itself sparer as it tried to reflect things themselves—translating them into stable signifiers, facts, numbers. Jones suggests that other contemporary language followed suit, heeding the new science's stylistic mandates, and scholars since Jones have worked through the connections he first articulated. We are told that Church of England clergy condemned enthusiasts for their wild tropings while developing a "plain style" of their own. Further, "rise of the novel" scholarship has argued that the early novel's formal realism was influenced by scientific attempts "to develop a more factual prose." Both clergymen and novelists deployed the empiricists' particularized, referential, and nonfigurative way of describing.[17]

There are a few problems with such accounts. First, as Tita Chico points out, the arguments of Jones, Ian Watt, and the many, many scholars who have followed in their footsteps privilege the influence of science on literature—"a presumption that places literature at one remove from science, that assumes that science, as the winner of history, was always first and that literature was belated." However, Chico insists that such presuppositions are anachronistic for a period in which "science" and "literature" were not stable, distinctly separate disciplines, a period in which "the practices and protocols of science and literature" were "mutually constitutive."[18] Literature did not come *after* science. Rather, as we will see, lines of influence ran in both directions, as literary language and empiricist method combined and cooperated.

Another "structure of belatedness" motivates the most influential accounts of the workings of scientific language. Chico's phrasing might be reworked to suggest that stories about scientific "plain style" place writing itself at one remove from science, rendering it, too, "belated."[19] Material reality and scientific discovery come first, and then the human act of description that aims to avoid introducing confusions and ambiguities. Even the most influential revisionist accounts of scientific language uphold this "structure of belatedness." Historians of science since Steven Shapin and Simon Schaffer appreciate that empiricist writers were not antirhetorical but rather deployed rhetoric strategically. This tradition argues that scientific prose accumulates complex clauses, vivid details, and active verbs as it encourages "virtual witnessing," a way of capturing a phenomenon in words so as to convince readers of its scientific truth.[20] Here language plays a key role in persuading people of scientific discoveries, but this approach also shares some fundamental assumptions with the "plain style" tradition. These scholars continue to maintain a separation between natural philosophers' rhetorical achievements (including convincing other natural philosophers of the truth of their experiments and propagandizing for the new science) and the scientific work itself. They preserve a realm of the "real" and "scientific" apart from language that, in the end, can reassert traditional accounts of empiricist procedure: when they are not being rhetorical for the benefit of readers, the Royal Society's work has little to do with language. The work of language comes after and is fundamentally separate from experimental science.

Yet, some fascinating recent work bears out my sense that this "structure of belatedness," too, is anachronistic and inadequate to the complexities of the period's empiricist writing. For instance, John Bender and Michael Marrinan's *Culture of Diagram* compellingly argues that the eighteenth-century accumulation of descriptive detail involved an experimental process of discovering correlations between things and putting those things together to create meaning.[21] And Joanna Stalnaker suggests that description could "function as a heuristic device, as a virtual perspective that reveals something about our relationship to objects . . . that we cannot perceive in our everyday experience of them."[22] Science did not simply influence literature, and empiricist language was not distinct from and subordinate to the act of perceiving material reality. The work of description was crucial to the work of understanding nature in the period.

Another problem with accounts linking science, religion, and literature through a notion of "plain style" involves the period's language itself. Empiricist writers did not wholly ban figurative language, nor was figure's "verbal luxuriance" necessarily undercut by a "feeling for concrete reality" (as Jones argues). Certainly, empiricist writers were invested in things over words, experiment over textual authority—"*Nullius in verba*," as the Royal Society motto had it. Their resistance to scholastic Aristotelianism involved a critique of language's confusions and ambiguities, and they expressed opinions about rhetoric and language. As the Royal Society's statutes explained, "In all Reports of Experiments to be brought into the Society, the Matter of Fact shall be barely stated, without any Prefaces, Apologies, or Rhetorical Flourishes."[23] The period's empiricists, then, did suspect ornamental "Rhetorical Flourishes," but they also embraced other kinds of rhetoric or figurative language as crucial tools in their generative, "heuristic" modes of description. An eclectic but steadily growing body of scholarship outside of the "plain style" tradition has demonstrated that figurative language pervades the period's scientific writing and that such language worked in many, overlapping ways. Playful figures of speech captured readers' imaginations, and explanatory analogies enabled them to visualize and understand unfamiliar phenomenon. Other kinds of figurative language were productive of serious science, even structuring the very ways that empiricists observed and described. Tropes helped natural philosophers deal with the unknown and the unseen; provided a key reasoning technique to grapple with induction's overwhelming accumulation of discrete particulars; and suggested new questions, hypotheses, or lines of research. Further, what one scholar has described as "the analogical poetics of ontological speculation" in the period meant that scientific discoveries were *shaped* by an awareness of their analogical applications for humanity.[24] Particularity and figurative language cooperated productively in the search for "Truths" about "concrete reality." In fact, G. A. Starr argues that even Sprat's ideal of one-to-one correspondence between words and things rejects only figurative language used as "mere ornament"—tropes that "obscure" reality—and actually embraces the possibility that tropes such as personification might instead "clarify" nature and assist the scientific project.[25] The meditative empiricism featured in this study turns on just such a possibility, one that has not been properly appreciated. Meditative empiricists embraced a distinctive kind of analogy—often playful and plural, always provisional and unsystematic—that promised to illuminate (at least partially) the physical, moral, and religious meanings encoded in nature. As we will see, their analogizing procedures also often involved other kinds of troping—most important, personification and periphrasis.

Empiricist Devotions offers an account of overlaps among science, religion, and literature very different from the influential one first articulated by Jones (wherein scientific "plain style" influences religious and literary writing alike). Rather, the overlaps have everything to do with the productive potential of description and figurative language, underwritten by a belief in the providential structure of the world. Natural philosophers, Protestant meditators, and nature poets all cultivated empiricist particularity while deploying literary figures in provisional, "heuristic" ways that could lead to real insight.

To better understand how this worked, let's consider three empiricist descriptions that grapple with the same natural principle: that small bodies, in aggregate, can have big effects. In a work of natural philosophy—*An Essay Of the Great Effects of Even Languid and Unheeded Motion* (1685)—Boyle argues that "*Local motions* may perform considerable things, either without being much heeded, or without seeming other then faint, at least in relation to the considerableness of the Effects produced by them."[26] "Observation III" focuses on the motions of "*bodies too small to be visible or sensible,*" especially "little Corpuscles in motion." This is cutting-edge natural philosophy, and it turns on particularity twice over: the argument is *about* the minute particulars that the world is composed of, and it involves Boyle's particularized "heedfull notice" of phenomena others overlook.[27] (Such "heedfull notice" requires both attentive observation and detailed description.) The science itself, though, works through analogies. Boyle begins with analogical "illustrat[ions]" or "gross example[s]" of subvisual processes, so they can be "better conceived" by readers: the workings of corpuscles are like the action of small streams of "wind upon a tree in *Autumn.*" He proceeds by accumulating comparisons that slide smoothly (and unstably) from being explanatory "examples" to "exemplifi[cations]" of the principle: it is also like the way water dissolves sugar, the ability of animal spirits in tiny networks of "Nerves" to move large animals, the power of "Spirit of wine" to corrode metal, and the movement of breath through a blow pipe.[28] This flurry of analogies correlates facts about wind and water, physiology and chemistry—forging links across disparate realms of natural philosophical investigation. The analogies are stated provisionally, with no real need to be reconciled. And Boyle moves only humbly to the ways his accumulation of particulars might illuminate natural truths, both by illustrating a general principle and explaining the individual processes.[29] He also provisionally proposes possibilities for practical applications. For instance, Boyle sees that water particles work most powerfully when they "insinuate themselves every way" into the substance of sugar, and he suggests that such an insight might lead to a refinement of blow-pipe technology: these tools would work even better if the flame could be directed not "onely" to "the surface" but also "every way," even into the innermost parts of a body.[30] Throughout, Boyle's stance is modest: he is describing, comparing, and suggesting, not explaining and concluding. Serious science works though the cultivation of empirical observation, analogical comparison, and provisional application.

Many contemporary Protestant meditations and nature poems work in the same way. In chapter 1, I will show that, in his devotional writing, Boyle uses a similar empiricist process in a meditation on the crucial role of small twigs in enabling a fire to ignite a larger log.[31] His description of the twigs and log is painstakingly particular, and his engagement with the fire itself active, experimental. As in his writings on local motion, he both reaches a conclusion about particular phenomena (twigs will help light fire) and modestly works toward a more general principle (small things have big effects). He again uses analogy to forge links across disparate realms, and here too these analogies access provisional possibilities for practical use. He conjecturally proposes a highly particularized analogy between small twigs and small sins, and then his conditional attitude to the link (they "may" be analogous) slides unstably toward a more serious exploration of how the analogy illuminates truth. Boyle is epistemologically modest as he moves from careful observation of natural fact to the pragmatic application—in this case, a religious not technological application. Just as a fact about water and sugar opened up a lesson about blow pipes, here the workings of twigs and logs leads to the moral truth that "'Twil be but succeslesly, that the Devil can attempt our grand Resolves, till he have first Master'd our less considerable ones" and that we ought to "consider the importance of what such slighted things may, as they are manag'd, prove Instrumental, either to endanger, or preserve." Boyle's position remains humble, his conclusion hypothetical. And the fundamental point is just the same: we need to take "heedfull notice" of small phenomena that others overlook.

Intriguingly, the poet Anne Finch echoes both Boyle's larger point and his specific figures as she likens small streams of wind to small bits of matter and small sins. Digressing from a painstakingly detailed account of the destruction wrought by storm winds in southern England, she explains:

> Those, who but Vanity allow'd,
> Nor thought, it reach'd the Name of Sin,
> To be of their Perfections proud,
> Too much adorn'd without, or too much rais'd within,
> Now find, that even the lightest Things,
> As the minuter parts of Air,
> When Number to their Weight addition brings,
> Can, like the small, but numerous Insect Stings,
> Can, like th'assembl'd Winds, urge Ruin and Despair.[32]

Finch had already been highly particular as she described the natural scene prompting these analogies, and here she even draws on Boyle's corpuscularian vocabulary (mentioning the "Number" and "Weight" of the "minuter parts of Air"). Like Boyle's natural philosophy, this passage is driven by a flurry of analogies that is offered up without any real need for the figures to be reconciled with one another. The "assembled Winds" of a storm are like "the minuter parts" of air, like "small, but numerous Insect Stings," and like small slips in morality (which hardly seem to "reach the Name of Sin"). The general principle she is working toward is also the same as Boyle's: all these small things, in aggregate, "can . . . urge Ruin and Despair." Like Boyle's, Finch's tropes of likeness forge links across disparate realms—from weather and insects to corpuscles and human vanity. Though there is a kind of poetic prowess on display in this dense layering of figures, Finch's analogies also have the potential to lead toward a very real practical application: we, too, should take the occasion of the storm to remember that small things can have big effects (and hence be wary of being "too much adorn'd without, or too much rais'd within"). Like Boyle's lessons, also, Finch's lesson is stated modestly, provisionally. Her poetic medium offers her a freedom to propose and work through a web of connections without dogmatically explaining or univocally concluding. She pursues empiricist observation and description in order to understand what nature means and what we might do with that discovery.

The workings of language are crucial to all of these empiricist descriptions—the science, the devotion, and the poetry. Strikingly, this is perhaps *most* evident in Boyle's natural philosophical text. His tropes of likeness are activated by personifications of a sort, by an awareness of agencies and animation outside the human (particles move, "act" with "force," "carry" and "excite" things), and his analogical procedure is responsive to the metaphorical resonances that inhere in even our "factual" words. For instance, the words "wind" and "blow" offer connections between autumn weather and human breath that seem to motivate his blow-pipe example and application. Scientific, religious, and poetic writings of the period are similar—not because they eschew analogy and personification as they develop highly particularized ways of describing reality but precisely because they embrace both tropes and minute particulars as they seek modestly to illuminate nature "Truths."

However, though these modes of empiricist description work similarly, they are often interpreted in starkly different ways. Scholars approach such descriptions with different assumptions, depending on what kind of text they appear in. When Boyle analogizes the structural principle at work in "Corpuscles" to winds and blow pipes, he gets to be dealing in science, fact, truth. Dedre Gentner and Michael Jeziorski explain that he represents a "modern" scientific understanding of analogy's usefulness: when used with "systematicity" and "firm constraints," careful analogical comparisons are part of a scientific method that underscores "common relational structure."[33] Similar kinds of analogizing, however, are read in completely opposite ways when they depart from what we think of as the truths of science and nature. When scholars approach the moral conclusions that analogies yield in Boyle's devotional writing, they tend to assume that the figurative language leads Boyle to *depart* from science, fact, truth. We are told that his provisional conclusions involve, instead, "personal religious belief," "subjectivity," or "imagination."[34] Or else "expressions of religious belief" are read as "misrecognition[s] of other social or material impulses."[35] This is a far cry from Boyle as "modern" scientist, working with a systematic epistemological tool. Finally, we have been taught to see analogical descriptions in eighteenth-century poetry as the "shriveled offspring" of an older poetics that engaged with the truths of nature and God—the "Renaissance emblem" emptied of its metaphysical purchase and "reduced" to an only mental or linguistic "relation between tenor and vehicle."[36] Alternately, we approach eighteenth-century poems from the anachronistic perspective of a later (instead of an earlier) tradition: we use categories developed around

Romantic poetry and privilege the poet's imaginative or affective work.[37] In either case, Finch's analogies are said to depart from science, fact, truth. They are said to come from the human mind or human language.

In short, when we read natural philosophical texts, we downplay the workings of language, foreground rational human activity, and recognize that the writer seeks truth and fact. Yet, when we read religious nature meditations, we emphasize the subjective and the personal (or the "false consciousness").[38] Also, we assume anachronistically that poetry—quite separate from science—works by loading up a neutral natural world with imaginative or associative meanings. Boyle's analogical insights about wind get to be considered true, but his analogies about twigs and Finch's about air *don't*. All of these, however, work in the same way: they all feature both particulars and figures, both natural facts and provisional play with language, both pragmatic knowledge and creative thought. They should all be read similarly, too—for late seventeenth- and early eighteenth-century natural philosophers, meditators, and poets alike participated in a Christian empiricist tradition.

Rethinking the Stories We Tell about Early Eighteenth-Century England

Empiricist Devotions's foregrounding of the fundamental similarities among scientific, devotional, and poetic language has lively implications for our understanding of the cultural and literary history of early eighteenth-century England. Indeed, taking seriously the meditative empiricism means troubling some of the most influential stories we tell about the period.

First, *Empiricist Devotions* insists on the centrality of religion to the period's empiricist writing. As I have already suggested, science, religion, and literature were not utterly distinct disciplines that should be approached in different ways. Complex interactions across these cultural realms belie the old but still pervasive story about secularization in the period—whereby the rise of science and Enlightenment led inexorably to the decline of religion. There is a long tradition of challenging this commonplace. Scholars like Robert K. Merton and Charles Webster highlight links between Puritanism and science, suggesting not only that dissenting or Puritan-leaning Protestants were overrepresented among early Royal Society members but that their ascetic, utilitarian values and millenarian beliefs were congenial to the development and spread of the new science.[39] The influence of a rather different group of Protestants, Latitudinarian Anglicans, has also been recognized. As John Henry explains, these Christians' "irenic doctrinal minimalism coupled with a liberal scepticism has been seen as going hand-in-hand with a Baconian emphasis upon gathering facts without interpretation, and cautious empiricism without theorizing."[40] Other scholars elaborate on particular ways in which religious thought influenced or interacted with the new science. Amos Funkenstein argues that the medieval "theological imagination prepared for the scientific"—for example, habituating people to modes of counterfactual hypothetical reasoning.[41] Peter Harrison shows that Protestant biblical hermeneutics shaped scientific practices, and Joanna Picciotto recovers a tradition of seventeenth-century experimentalism aiming to restore a prelapsarian understanding of the world.[42] *Empiricist Devotions* echoes such challenges to hackneyed but remarkably persistent stories of secularization and brings their insights to the emerging field of "science and literature"—which has not yet fully accounted for religion as a crucial part of the constellations being studied.[43]

My book also contributes to extant work on science and religion by arguing for the importance to the period's science of providence, an active God, and Protestant meditation. The latter point, especially, resonates with the recent interest shown by historians of science in the period's meditational and devotional practices. There has been a surge of interest in physico-theology, a seventeenth- and eighteenth-century tradition that found, in scientific study of the "*Works of Creation*," "*Demonstration[s] of the Being and Attributes of God*": devotion featured science and helped both popularize and legitimize it.[44] More fundamentally still, Harrison draws on work by Matthew Jones and Sorana Corneanu as he argues that, for natural philosophers like Boyle and Joseph Glanvill, science itself served "as a kind of devotional practice that . . . contribute[d] to the moral and religious formation of the natural philosopher": "Experimental labors constituted a special kind of mental training that more effectively inculcated moral and religious virtues than traditional philosophical exercises."[45] Also, Kristen Girten notes some fascinating formal parallels between meditative and natural philosophical texts, and she stresses the need for more sustained scholarly exploration of "the connections between meditative and empirical practices in early modern Britain."[46] *Empiricist Devotions* takes up this call as it demonstrates some hitherto unappreciated links between meditation and empiricism. The new science provided pious Christians with more than physico-theological arguments from design (proofs of God's existence, wisdom, power, and benevolence). Rather, engaging an established Protestant tradition of occasional meditation, contemporary meditators drew from scientific fact a capacious range of truths: religious but also moral, economic, political, and scientific in our sense today.[47] Further, occasional meditation's enabling logic structured protocols of empiricist observation and description even beyond natural theology, and one of its fundamental presuppositions—that figurative language illuminated the providential natural world—instigated scientific discovery itself (not to mention poetic insight and socio-moral lessons).

Second, I challenge influential assumptions about the impact of science and secularization on language. The usual story is that analogies and other linguistic figures were essential in writing about the natural world *until* science emerged and sorted out the proper differences between words and things, the literal and the figurative. This is said to have happened precisely in the late seventeenth and early eighteenth centuries. For example, Brian Vickers narrates a transition from an "occult tradition" that used analogies as a crucial way of "think[ing] or experienc[ing] the world" to a scientific tradition that distinguished clearly "between words and things and between literal and metaphorical language."[48] However confused premodern writers might have been, new scientists respected distinctions between reality and language, fact and figure, science and literature (giving priority always to the first item in each pair). A related story—that, in an age of science, language was uncoupled from nature—also underpins pervasive ways of understanding the process of modernization. For instance, in his graceful theoretical account of modernization in *The Order of Things*, Michel Foucault argues that sixteenth-century people imagined themselves as part of a world "folded in upon itself" with "the earth echoing the sky, faces seeing themselves reflected in the stars, and plants holding within their stems the secrets that were of use to man." Resemblance was a feature of the world. For Enlightenment man, however, things were "emptied of all resemblances," reduced to mere variables of "form," "quantity," "magnitude," and spatial arrangement. Foucault also suggests that, as things became more unmeaning, people became more powerful. Where one used to wonder about what a sign signified in the grand scheme, one now "began to ask how a sign could be linked to what it signified": "the task of knowledge" that used to involve "dig[ging] out" truth "from" the world came to require a human feat of mastery and synthesis.[49] With the advent of science, similitudes that used to be part of the natural order became products of the creative human minds. Related assumptions motivate the "structures of belatedness" featured in treatments of empiricist language, as well as the very logics underpinning old-fashioned intellectual histories, finely grained cultural and literary histories, high theoretical accounts, and the most recent revisionary work alike.[50]

However, the linguistic complexity, the creatively heuristic descriptions, and the proliferation of figurative language in the empiricist texts I study belie the influential notion that science enforced a strong separation between reality and language, the literal and the metaphorical. Of course, Vickers recognizes that proponents of the new science sometimes used analogies as "explanatory devices" or as "tools to make models," and he rightly notes that they had a different attitude to these analogies than traditions of alchemy, natural magic, and Paracelsianism. Boyle is more epistemologically modest in his analogizing than Paracelsus—more about generating hypotheses or applications. Yet, Vickers further insists that new scientific analogies were "subordinate devices, clearly distinguished from the normal level of discourse, which is nonmetaphorical."[51] He proceeds from an impoverished notion of figurative language as a linguistic construct that comes from human minds and is quite separate from the real. Analogy connects two things by "not a real, but a mental, channel: The gap is sparked by a mental act, but the two poles of the metaphor do not fuse or coincide in reality."[52] This notion reinforces—and presumes—the argument that similitudes migrated from the world into human minds in this period. Contra Vickers (and other modernization stories about language in an age of science), I am not convinced that writers like Boyle made a strong, clear distinction between the literal and the metaphorical. Boyle recognizes that his analogies involve his language and his mind, but, crucially, they do not *only* involve language and mind. At best, they point to things that do in fact "fuse or coincide in reality." Boyle insists that "secret Correspondencies and Alliances" are part of the world and that imaginative analogies illuminate reality *because* "there is so perfect an harmony, and so near a kindred, betwixt Truths, that, in many cases, the one does either find out, or fairly hint, or else illustrate or confirm, the other."[53] Boyle's analogizing, like that of other contemporary empiricists, rests on a conception of a continuous universe that scholars more usually associate with nonscientific forms of Christianity or the occult. In short, Vickers is right that writers like Boyle make instrumental analogies, but he is wrong about the way they understood these analogies to connect to reality. Because the world was a great book written by God, literary figures were human tools that had their counterparts in the structure of nature itself, and even the most "normal level of" scientific "discourse" was driven by a flurry of analogies that might access divine "Truths."

Further, while scholars of the period's science have not fully appreciated figurative language's crucial role in empiricist thought, scholars of its literature have neglected the serious empiricist engagement with nature motivating its richly figurative poetry. Tellingly, a sweeping story of modernization very close to Vickers's and Foucault's structures accounts of eighteenth-century poetry. Earl Wasserman traces the "transition from a world of pre-existent poetic materials to one in which they must be fashioned by the poet."[54] Renaissance poets assumed a "system of analogical correspondences," and their poetry reflected values coded into God's creation. By the end of the eighteenth century, however, "correspondences had become a phase of psychology, not ontology," and poets "had to take the world of things, which science had shorn of all but objective existence, and . . . invest it with values" through an imaginative or "emotive act."[55] Wasserman's work is enormously helpful in insisting that eighteenth-century poetry should be read in the context of "the long Mediaeval and Renaissance tradition that the master key to the total scheme of creation is similitude"; that this tradition was "kept alive" in the eighteenth century "to a degree not usually recognized"; and that it took a distinctive form that fit with the "skeptical, empirical, and anti-mystical climate" of the period.[56] *Empiricist Devotions* owes much to these insights. Yet, as often happens when scholars work with these sweeping accounts of historical change, the seemingly inexorable drive of modernizing currents toward "modern" categories distorts what happened along the way. For instance, Wasserman too easily presumes that science was disenchanting ("the work of science was to sever value from the nature of things") and thus overlooks its influence on eighteenth-century analogizing. He misleadingly suggests that analogies became more "traditional, and general," and he misreads an empiricist posture (the realization that "our knowledge of the total moral scheme must necessarily be as incomplete as our knowledge of the total physical scheme") as a symptom of a crumbling, "outworn creed."[57] Further, where Wasserman sometimes overestimates how far the metaphysical basis for correspondences had withered—hearing in the period's poetic shifts between description and analogue an awkward "grinding of the gears"—work written in his wake has only further back-dated the crumbling of the "creed" and the emergence of the autonomous, meaning-generating human mind.[58] (Remember that poems like Finch's are said to involve the old "correspondences" withered into mere mental "associations.") For meditative empiricists, however, science accessed the "values" encoded in "the nature of things." Analogies—often highly particular—were everywhere, and epistemological modesty was an enabling precondition, not a symptom of decay. Eighteenth-century descriptive poetry was understood to have less to do with a human feat of projection (whether a pre-Romantic associationism or a "grinding," forced attempt at didacticism) than with the ontologically rooted poetics Wasserman outlines earlier: "Mere description would represent only half the divine scheme, and direct moralizing would be contrary to the faculties of man and to God's method of sensory revelation. The didactic passages" are "functional" to this poetry's "total meaning" and "completeness."[59] In allowing poetic analogies to have a purchase on nature—as their authors believed they might—I recover the vital empiricist impulses motivating the period's poetry.

I thereby open up some provocative possibilities for our understanding of literary particularity and realism more generally in the period. Here, my findings run counter to another influential story about modernization: this time, the oft-told "rise of the novel" featured in Watt's *Rise of the Novel* and the tradition of scholars—including Michael McKeon, Nancy Armstrong, J. Paul Hunter, Lennard Davis, and others—who have questioned and confirmed, reworked and extended its critical narrative. This tradition has taught us to understand the realist novel as a literary manifestation of the new scientific prose style: particularized, nonfigurative, referential. It has also taught us to understand the development of this new kind of literary particularity in relation to emerging forces of modernity. In a recent critique of this tradition, Wolfram Schmidgen synthesizes its basic contours. We "place the novel at the literary center of the social, scientific, political, economic, and religious processes that reshaped European societies between 1500 and 1800": "scientifically," "the novel was affiliated . . . with the close observation of particulars"; "socially," "with class mobility"; "politically, with liberalism and individualism; economically with commercial society and exchange relations; religiously with Protestantism." Schmidgen points out that assumptions about the modernity of these "affiliations" all rely on a "paradigm of differentiation": like science, capitalism, and individualism, the novel was modern in its careful differentiations between "nature and society," "persons and things," "public and private," and so on. Further, we are told that another "modern" differentiation is effected by the novel's linguistic particularity: realist detail sets up a distinction between "figure and ground," between "self-possessed individuals" with "clearly delineated contours" and "the settings in which they act."[60] In "rise of the novel" stories, modernizing cultural forces culminate in a literary genre whose techniques of highly particularized, realist description reify the external world and enable the autonomy of the expressive liberal subject. (Note that there is basic congruence between this version of literary history and the influential constellation of assumptions about modernization, human autonomy, referentiality, and figurative language's decline that structures many histories of science.)

Significantly, the realist novel—cast as *the* "modern" genre—is often contrasted to eighteenth-century poetry, with its ornate language and supposedly backward-looking values.[61] However, I trouble this contrast by situating the poetry in relation to the same modernizing forces linked with the novel. Like accounts of the novel's rise by Watt and McKeon, my book charts the influence of seventeenth-century empiricism on eighteenth-century Protestantism (chapters 1–2), on economic developments in the emerging consumer culture (chapter 3), and on political thought about "liberalism and individualism" (chapter 4). And, like this critical tradition, my story culminates with a new kind of literary realism (chapter 5): the realism not of sharply drawn novelistic interiors, however, but of georgic poetry's morally fraught agricultural scene. Similar cultural forces created both the novel and the neoclassical georgic, and realist particularity does not *only* work in the novelistic ways we often consider. Georgic offers a mode of realist description, characterized by highly referential language and the accumulation of sensed particulars. Yet, because of the elaborate, figurative, and patterned ways that it pursues referential particularity, its realist description actually helps access nature's fraught meaningfulness. Particularity and figurative language coexist, and, far from setting the autonomous human self over against nature, empiricist description allows poets to explore the dense meaningfulness of the world. Therefore, while the language of eighteenth-century poetic description is often imagined as highly artificial—its "stock diction" a kind of imposition onto nature—I demonstrate that georgic's careful particularity and ornate figurations offered contemporaries a way of apprehending and understanding nature.

Empiricist Devotions, then, troubles some influential tenets of modernization narratives—about secularization; the separation between language and reality; the decline of figure's instrumentality; the emergence of literary realism and its concomitant, a new kind of individual who could "taxonomize, manipulate, and objectify a newly secular world."[62] More broadly, it challenges the pervasive tendency of scholarship to situate treatments of much early eighteenth-century writing (scientific, religious, poetic, economic, political, etc.) within the inexorable, progressive logics of stories about the emergence of "modern" subjects and objects. Big graceful stories about "revolution" and about the "rise" or "birth" of modernity saturate the study of seventeenth- and eighteenth-century literature and culture—as in our accounts of the "scientific" and "financial revolutions," "the rise of the novel," "the birth of the liberal subject," "the dissociation of sensibility," and "the disenchantment of the world." Some of these stories are indebted to whiggish history, and some to high theory; some to Watt's *Rise of the Novel,* and some to Max Horkheimer and Theodor Adorno's *Dialectic of Enlightenment.* They all, however, offer versions of a graceful historical arc in which empiricism or Enlightenment manifested a human desire to dominate nature and delimit its meanings. It empowered the autonomous, rational subject who no longer existed *in* nature so much as acted *on* it. Whether endorsing or condemning modernity, and whether tracing its influence on science, economics, literature, politics, or religion, such "modernization" scholarship offers a remarkably consistent account of what happened in the period: secular subjects sought mastery over inert objects in a disenchanted world. In stark contrast to this pervasive story—but without denying real change in the period—*Empiricist Devotions* features pious empiricists who cultivated human passivity, affirmed nature's rich relevance, and trusted in figurative language's instrumentality.

My book does more than blur the edges of big stories about secularization and modernization by showing the persistence of older religious ideas in the period. It turns these scholarly stories on their head. Like other work contributing to an emerging "theological turn" or "postsecular criticism," I insist on religion as a force "at the heart of the project of modernity itself, a constitutive element of its very shaping" (in Dror Wahrman's formulation).[63] Faith in the providential natural world and the power of analogy was not a mere lingering remnant of older worldviews—for cutting-edge science offered new, pressing grounds for belief and new, innovative ways to study nature's meanings. Further, I argue that empirical-devotional modes actually encouraged modernizing currents in their moment. People were excited about science because they believed in nature's fraught meaningfulness, and empiricist writers scrutinized nature as they developed "modern" ideas about individuality, consumer culture, and social contract. While the meditative empiricism did not involve autonomous secular subjects, disenchanted objects, or a fundamental separation between words and reality, in its way it *did* help shape the world we inhabit today.

A Note on "Nature"

In his *Free Enquiry into the Vulgarly Reciev'd Notion of Nature* (1686), Boyle laments the overuse of "the too licenciously abused word *Nature*," a word with "very great Ambiguity" and "different Significations" that are not "sufficiently attend[ed] to." While he would prefer the term not be used at all, he acknowledges how "difficult" it is to "Discourse long of the Corporeal Works of God" without it, and he advises writers to at least "add a word or two, to declare in what clear and determinate sense they use it."[64] Good advice.

It is easiest to be "clear and determinate" about what I—and the writers I study—do *not* mean by *nature*. It is not an object, or composed of objects, in the "modern" sense. It is not disenchanted, inert, or reified; it is not totally divorced from either language or God. Helpful, here, are the new materialisms emerging from science studies and philosophy; this work articulates a cogent challenge to influential modern caricatures of nature that are inadequate to the complexity of our world today—and, I would add, that did not pertain in the early eighteenth century. For example, Bruno Latour mocks the way that "moderns" both "tried to become nature's masters and owners" *and* imagined themselves "thrust into a cold soulless cosmos, wandering on an inert planet in a world devoid of meaning."[65] For eighteenth-century empiricists, however, nature was neither as pliable and subordinate nor as hostile and total as these caricatures suggest. Latour's formulations help us see, too, that both the optimistic and the pessimistic caricatures presume that nature is "devoid of meaning"; but for eighteenth-century empiricists it was, rather, rife with "Truths." Timothy Morton condemns modern thought for rendering natural objects as "lumps of blah decorated with accidents" ("like cupcakes decorated with colored sprinkles") or as "featureless chunks of stuff" populating an abstract, totalizing category. Morton also punctures modern pretensions to separateness: nature is neither "something 'over yonder' behind the glass window of an aesthetic screen" nor even a "significant, bounded, horizoning entity," an objectification that helps orient us.[66] We are (part of) it. These challenges to modern notions of nature also often involve challenges to a modern privileging of human meaning-making. For instance, many new materialists reject the Kantian notion that "we cannot think of world without humans nor of humans without world, but only of a primordial *correlation* between the two": the "modern" position doubts whether the world "exist[s] independently of human access" to it.[67] While new materialists imagine a world very different from the meditative empiricists', their critiques of modern caricatures help highlight what nature is *not* for writers like Boyle. It is neither unmeaning nor "over yonder." It surely "exists independently," and its meanings are not determined or limited by human thought.

In contrast to modern caricatures, I use the word *nature* as the meditative empiricists used it, to refer to "the Corporeal Works of God." Or, perhaps better, to refer to material realities created and maintained by God, as well as to the general scheme that these phenomena, considered collectively, comprise or point to. Perhaps this is not entirely "clear and determinate," but neither—as Boyle himself points out—was contemporaneous usage. What Boyle describes as "Ambiguity" in the notion was central to the way nature was understood at the time. Accordingly, my working definition preserves a few fundamental ambiguities.

First, in the late seventeenth and early eighteenth centuries, there were important ambiguities in the relationships among nature, God, and humanity. God made nature, of course, but contemporaries grappled with pressing questions about his continued involvement in it. How active, autonomous, and orderly is nature, really? Is it composed of passive material parts, given agency only through the direct interposition of God (or some spiritual intermediary)? Or are material processes and active principles *part* of nature, maintained by him only at arm's length? Are the laws that seem to pertain in nature entirely fixed, or can God intervene to alter or suspend them? What is the exact relationship between second causes and the divine first cause? The boundaries among nature, spirit, and God were blurry. Human involvement with nature was also complex. These empiricists sometimes rendered "Nature" (capital *n*) as a passive female, just waiting to be penetrated (or raped), but on close encounter it never really seemed so stable, monolithic, or obedient to human seductions: air pumps were leaky, what worked on one field didn't on another, storm winds razed buildings. Instead, particular things could be male or female, active or passive, eager to "hint" and give up secrets or devastating in their resistance. Further, in eighteenth-century usage, nature was that which is not made by humans—the "natural" contrasted with the "artificial"—but human activity was part of nature too. For instance, nature included things untouched by us (wild expanses) but also things that, while made by God, are the result of all sorts of human activities (such as experimental findings, which require human manipulation to get at nature's truths, or agricultural crops, where human cultivation is understood as helping to actualize the nature of things). Finally, humanity was included in the term *nature*: we too are creatures made by God. This means that the meditative empiricists sometimes pit humanity against nature, or suggest that God designed nature *for* us, or render parts of it as distanced objects of study; but at the same time there is a kind of modesty or humility, an awareness that humanity is situated within nature (and under God) and that there is no way to ever transcend this embeddedness.

Other important ambiguities have to do with the way the term refers to both parts and wholes. In the moment (as now), *nature* signified particular things and processes—and even the specific "properties of any thing, by which it is discriminated from others"—as well as the larger scheme that these particular things all participate in.[68] Most eighteenth-century nature talk vacillated between these two significations; indeed, such talk often involved meditation on how parts relate to wholes. The meditative empiricists were fascinated by the whole—*system, order,* and *design* are keywords—and their use of the general noun *nature* signaled an ambition to know something of the broader scheme. Yet, these empiricists also recognized they would never comprehend the totality, that mortals will only ever deal in parts. Nature is a book written by God, but its / his meanings are "abstruse and vailed," only ever "dexterously hinted"; they exist prior to and exceed human attempts to define them. Far from being discouraged by this realization, empiricist writers refined sophisticated techniques in the search to understand how parts *comprise or point to* the whole. Things were parts, hints, illustrations, exemplifications, symbols, indexes, analogues, metonyms, and more. Samuel Johnson's *Dictionary* definition preserves something of the provisionality and the awareness of human involvement that thus attached to attempts to comprehend: *nature* and the *natural* refer to material realities as well as to human approximations of what is "Consonant," "conformable," or "adapted to" those realities.[69] Further, the scheme thus "hinted" was physical (as in the laws of nature or the established course of nature), but it far exceeded the physical. Lorraine Daston and Katherine Park point out that, in the early eighteenth century (as in the centuries prior), "the natural order was also a moral order in the broad and somewhat old-fashioned sense of moral as all that pertains to the human, from the political to the aesthetic."[70] It is "unnatural" both for a rock to fall upward and for a son to murder his father. But there is "Ambiguity" here too, for how exactly does one heed the normative force of nature when it is unclear exactly how the physical links up to the moral order? And while in the moment nature-as-norm was used in worrying ways to marginalize or disempower those of other genders, races, and cultures, in meditative empiricist writings "nature" was less a complacent coherent category to be used confidently (against others) than a problem one could only humbly attempt to solve. Studying nature in its particulars was the way to glimpse anything of the whole—material or moral—and partial, provisional glimpses were all that were available anyway.

When I say *nature*, then, I refer not to a stable, discrete, fully comprehensible entity but rather to what these writers are trying to comprehend, despite the ways they were caught up in it. I refer to something that shifts unpredictably between and among being active, passive, pliable, devastating, us, them, pure, mixed, legible, illegible, particular, general, physical, moral, a thing, a collective, a code, an approximation, a norm. These writers speak frequently of "following nature," or of designing institutions that have their "Foundation" there, or of letting nature "instruct" them, but they never forget that their notions are, at best, provisional approximations of a scheme that is complex (and never totally knowable) in just these ambiguous ways.

Toward a Hermeneutic of Provisional Trust

Empiricist Devotions also has notable methodological implications, for our usual ways of reading presuppose anachronistic "modern" caricatures of nature and anachronistic divides between subjects / objects and language / reality.

We too often approach eighteenth-century texts through the postures and practices of "the hermeneutics of suspicion." As Paul Ricoeur explains in his diagnosis of such reading practices, this hermeneutics seeks "unmasking, demystification, or reduction of illusions."[71] Intriguingly, Latour helps us see that suspicious reading often relies on a rather tidy ontological bifurcation. Critics presuppose a fundamental distinction between objects and subjects. They "purify by separating natural mechanisms from human passions," nature from society, the real from the constructed, phenomena on the object side of the divide from that on the subject side. Then they denounce "illegitimate mixtures" lying anywhere between these poles.[72] Latour offers a lively exaggeration of how this can work out in contemporary cultural critique: critics revel in demonstrating that, while "naïve believers" think that their behavior is autonomous and free, it is really "entirely determined by the action of powerful causalities coming from objective reality" (e.g., "genes," "social domination," or "economic infrastructure"). Reversing course, in a way that is especially influential in readings of eighteenth-century religion and poetry, critics also insist that what these "believers" "are doing with objects is simply a projection of their wishes onto a material entity that does nothing at all by itself."[73] The hermeneutics of suspicion delights in puncturing illusions: the behavior of subjects is *really* objectively determined, but depictions of "objective" nature are *really* subjective constructions. A similar ontological bifurcation and a similar urge to purification underwrite our reading practices more generally, even when we are not in an explicitly critical mode. They encourage us to try to see *through* a text's appearances and to explain its hidden depths. As Susan Sontag once mocked this impulse, "The interpreter says, Look don't you see that X is really—or, really means—A? That Y is really B?"[74]

While suspicious postures can certainly be used with sensitivity and care, scholars have tended to deploy them in an especially blunt, especially intense manner when interpreting texts about nature and texts about religion. For instance, Lorraine Daston and Fernando Vidal underscore a problematic critical procedure often brought to descriptions of nature. Critics assume that statements about nature's meanings work by "smuggling certain items . . . back and forth across the boundary that separates the natural and the social"; and "critics, like customs inspectors, return items to their rightful categories, extraditing the natural from the social, and especially, the social from the natural."[75] Further, Misty Anderson points out that related reading methods are doubly problematic when brought to "expressions of religious belief." These are often not allowed to remain on the side of the real, and—by "extraditing" them to the other side of an ontological divide, by interpreting them as "misrecognition[s] of other social or material impulses"—scholars affirm "in advance" "always-already secular categories."[76] Because meditative empiricist analogies intertwine religious belief and concern with nature (and in the process use language that has seemed to later readers overly ornate or artificial), recent scholars tend to deploy suspicious reading methods with special vigor, creating distinctive distortions. When empiricists access meanings in nature that do not square with our contemporary understandings of science and nature, critics deny that the meanings are from nature at all. They "return items" to what they understand as "their rightful categories." Boyle's Protestant meditations and Finch's poetic meditations are *really* about "personal religious belief," "subjectivity," "Imagination," the mind's "associations," or linguistic constructs. Or, more cynically—making the "always-already" secular move that Anderson decries—their claims about nature are ideological "mystifications of economic, political, and social conditions and relationships."[77] When empiricists say they are "finding out" moral lessons *in* nature, scholars assume that they are really projecting meanings *onto* nature, "misrecognizing" their own desires, or cunningly conscripting nature's authority to serve interested ends. These readings prevent us from understanding meditation and poetry as earnestly engaged with nature—despite what eighteenth-century writers repeatedly say.[78]

Such reading methods also influence treatments of science itself. As I have suggested, perceptive work in the history of science recognizes that some early Royal Society members used tropes as epistemological tools that could illuminate nature. Often, however, scholars do not seem to know what to do with such figurative possibilities, and their ways of managing the problem are motivated by suspicious critical postures. Some, like Gentner and Jeziorski, reinforce the ontological bifurcation by downplaying the role of language: analogy is treated as a methodological or epistemological procedure akin to induction or deduction. It becomes a technique of knowledge production that has little to do with rhetoric, a technique truly belonging on the "science" or "nature" side of the divide. Other scholars treat specific examples of the stranger figurative possibilities rather as they treat devotional and poetic instances: suspecting them. These possibilities come to seem anomalous—a personal idiosyncrasy of a particular writer or a departure from the real work of science.[79] Perhaps the most influential strategy, though, involves situating such possibilities within a big story about modernization and then relegating them to a mere lingering persistence of modes on their way out.[80] Vickers provides an interesting instance of this. He clearly aligns his own "modern" presuppositions with the scientific mentality. He assumes (and assumes that seventeenth-century natural philosophers assume) that human minds should have control over language. Starting from this "modern" notion, he proceeds to show the many ways that the backward-looking occult tradition gets it wrong. For instance, he judges occult writers for mistakenly, misguidedly, failing to "use[ ] analogies"; rather, they are "used by them." Vickers's anachronistic assumptions then lead him to complex confusions, for he insists—in spite of his sources—that scientific writers keep figurative language "subordinate" and separate from the "scientific argument" and that everyone else is not really scientific.[81] In other words, he takes a suspicious approach that privileges the autonomy of the human mind.

Clearly, such cultural and literary interpretations rely on separations between language / reality, society / nature, and especially subjects / objects. Scholars distrust claims about nature's lessons because they privilege the human mind and neglect the material world as a source of meaning. They posit a manipulative distance between the meaning-generating writer and the world described. Language (a product of the human mind) is something added on top of—but fundamentally separate from—the realities of nature. It is subordinate, secondary, belated. These, however, are anachronistic "modern" notions that simply did not pertain to the late seventeenth- and early eighteenth-century world.[82] And the reading practices based on these "modern" notions are totally inadequate to understanding the meditative empiricism. Most problematically, these practices presume a total separation between language and reality that denies the meditative empiricism's central premise: these writers recognized the work of their minds and their language, even as they humbly hoped that their figurative language would illuminate a creation encoded, analogically, with "Truths." Instrumental analogies could approximate and elucidate the real. "Modern" reading practices also carve up the world into mutually exclusive categories of social and natural, precluding another of the meditative empiricism's central premises: nature contained "Truths" that could enrich society, morality, even government and economics. Of course, I recognize that representations of nature have very real ideological implications and that writers' minds and experiences play a crucial role. Yet, the critical tendency to dissolve all claims for the material into the ideological, imaginative, or linguistic goes against the very purpose of an empiricist mode motivated by the possibility of glimpsing God's "Truths" *in* creation. From such suspicious critical postures, we will never fully appreciate these writers' commitment to nature: they will seem silly or wrong, projectors shooting meanings onto a blank screen or constructors building them out of unbiased facts. In fact, my cultural-historical arguments function as arguments for the inappropriateness of the suspicious approaches that have often been brought to eighteenth-century nature texts. Meditative empiricist writers did not understand themselves as the sole actors involved in the work of creating meaning: God remains active in and through nature; things "hint" and teach, and figurative language assists in the work of illuminating truth.

These realizations should inform our methodologies, which could do a better job grappling with such complexity. They inform *my* methodology, which tries to respect seventeenth- and eighteenth-century empiricism's own interpretative dynamics.[83] Writers like Boyle looked closely at objects. They cultivated a mode of active attention that also involved passivity, openness to the ways that things "instruct" and literary figures prompt. They trusted in nature's fraught meaningfulness, but not naively. And they recognized that specific interpretations of an object neither exhaust all of its meanings nor substitute for its material reality. These empiricists were self-aware and skeptical, never dogmatic about their version of "Truths." They instead preferred to focus on provisional but usable applications of their discoveries.

Empiricist Devotions proceeds in a somewhat similar manner. I look closely at empiricists looking closely at nature—painstaking attention is the sine qua non of my readings (as it was of theirs). Always, though, I allow their engagements with nature to be real engagements with nature, even if they have a different sense of nature's possibilities than we do. I maintain an openness to the logic of their descriptions on their own terms. This rather modest interpretative posture involves a provisional suspension of anachronistic assumptions about fundamental divides between people and things, language and reality. It involves a willingness to take seriously the way that humans, things, God, *and* words could all contribute to the creation of meaning.[84] I trust what empiricists say, but not naively. For instance, I can trust that Boyle took a lesson about small sins *from* close attention to a fire without sharing his period-specific Christian worldview or even affirming his specific conclusions. And I can recognize the sociopolitical or personal implications of nature descriptions without rendering them entirely ideological or subjective, without reducing them to products of the merely human.[85] Specific interpretations of an object never exhaust all of its meanings, so I resist making confident, univocal claims about what descriptions *really* mean. I thereby open up some usable insights.[86] By respecting the way empiricists imagined their own project, I suggest, we can better understand how and why they spent time observing and describing natural things—what their motivations were for turning to nature in the first place. And we can better appreciate the complex, robust relationships that existed in the moment among science, religion, and poetry. Indeed, in the spirit of an empiricism that uses analogies instrumentally, my book heeds throughout unexpected likenesses. Far from "extraditing" texts into their "rightful" sides of an ontological divide or "rightful" disciplinary categories, I explore similarity and commonality (without denying difference). Here is a tradition that motivated the shared energies in personal devotions, scientific treatises, economic proposals, and conjectural histories, in it-narratives, sermons, and georgic poetry. In sum, *Empiricist Devotions* proceeds in a spirit of provisional trust that owes something to the sophisticated interpretative dynamics of eighteenth-century empiricism.

The book opens with a cultural history of the meditative empiricism. Chapter 1 examines the Protestant genre of "occasional meditation," which began to accommodate a new empiricist precision in the second half of the seventeenth century. In Boyle's hands, the genre provided a way of reading the Book of Nature. This devotional practice was prevalent and influential in the late seventeenth and early eighteenth centuries. It was also an *em-*

piricist practice: observers scrutinized particulars, made provisional analogies, and modestly sought nature's larger implications. They trusted in the meaningfulness of created things even as they skeptically embraced the limits of human knowledge. This empiricism's close relationships with its Royal Society–sponsored counterpart help reveal an underappreciated logic crucial to the period's scientific scene. Empiricist scrutiny was often coupled with wide-ranging, creative analogizing. In Boyle's meditations and Robert Hooke's experiments, in the writings of Anglican preachers and innovative agriculturalists, figurative language was a key resource in the search for truth.

The following chapters, then, trace occasional meditation's eighteenth-century afterlives. Or, rather—since there was no death or decline to initiate an afterlife—I demonstrate that the meditative empiricism was a viable mode throughout the early eighteenth century. It exerted influence across our anachronistic disciplinary divisions: writers turned to nature to make sense of physical, religious, economic, political, and moral issues.

In the second chapter, for example, I explore how popular Newtonianism deployed the meditative empiricism. I read responses to the science of gravity in the decades after Newton's *Principia* (1687), including pop-science poems, the correspondence between Samuel Clarke and Gottfried Wilhelm Leibniz, and scientific sermonizing in the influential Boyle Lectures. These early Newtonian texts took Newton's science as empirical proof that God was the constantly acting cause of gravity, and their writers used this discovery to rework the conventional metaphor of the world as a clock: God himself spun the wheels of the grand clockwork. In my account, this reworked clock figure structured Newtonian meditations on nature; falling clock-weights and rocks enabled empirically proven glimpses of divine agency and active guidance in moral and political matters. These texts therefore provide a paradigmatic example of how scientific scrutiny and mathematical sophistication, far from making the world more abstract, rationalized, or mechanical, helped contemporaries comprehend nature's moral meaningfulness and catch sight of God's agency.

The third chapter focuses on empiricist attempts to make sense of new economic realities. It establishes that the meditative empiricism enabled the discovery of pragmatic, secular, and forward-pointing "Truths." Economists including John Locke and William Lowndes investigated the particular properties of bullion as they reacted to the recoinage crisis of the 1690s. In fact, some advocates of all three main positions on the recoinage—the conservative position privileging bullion, as well as the more innovative proposals that are often read as proto-capitalist—scrutinized nature as they attempted in their policy proposals to approximate a supra-human order. The second half of the chapter treats Charles Gildon's *Golden Spy* (1709) and Joseph Addison's "History of a Shilling" (1710) as literary manifestations of the same basic logic. Complicating an emergent critical consensus that associates the newly canonical genre of it-narratives with modernization, capitalism, and commodification, I argue that Gildon and Addison are interested in what the natural world tells them about proper human behavior in consumer culture. Their talking coins dramatize the meditative empiricism's belief that nature offers supple resources for guidance, even as they show the complex ways that human agency is involved in the process of accessing such guidance.

My fourth chapter turns to empiricist engagements in debates about politics and government, and especially about social contract and the origins of civil society. While scholarship has found in eighteenth-century contractarian thought a model of the autonomous rational subject, I show that the selves featured in some of the period's important social contract stories actually behave more like occasional meditators than democratic citizens. In different ways, John Locke's *Two Treatises of Government* (1689–90), Daniel Defoe's *Jure Divino* (1706), Alexander Pope's *Essay on Man* (1733–34), and Lord Bolingbroke's *Fragments* (published posthumously in 1754) made close attention to nature a crucial engine of social progress. These conjectural histories gave consenting individuals agency and gave contract transformative power even as they maintained that God's creation offers clues about how societies should work. According to these stories, people scrutinized fish, metals, animal claws, and their own bodies as they tried to build governments in approximation of an always inaccessible order. I therefore contend that the individual at the heart of some eighteenth-century social contract stories used figurative logics to understand the providential natural world, and I bring this insight to a reconsideration of the period's empiricist thinkers, moral agents, and human selves more generally. This is the climax of a set of arguments about modernization and human agency foregrounded in *Empiricist Devotions*'s middle chapters, which focus on aspects of the period often praised as inaugurating a newly secular modernity: Newtonian science, money, consumer culture, and social contract theory. In these chapters especially, I show that the meditative empiricism's humble, pious, nature-oriented postures helped access some strikingly "modern" ideas.

The final chapter furthers another of this book's overarching arguments: that figurative language and literary genres were understood as powerful instruments of empiricist apprehension. Not only do I recover the productive role of tropes like analogy, personification, and periphrasis in seventeenth- and eighteenth-century empiricist thought; I show that literary forms were deployed as tools in a related way. Throughout, this book features the genres that were created or repurposed to encourage meditative-empiricist thinking (the occasional meditation and the it-narrative, for example). Chapter 5 argues that georgic poetry offered contemporaries an especially apt generic vehicle for empirical-devotional modes of observing and describing. Writers like Pope, Addison, John Philips, and John Gay used georgic to refine minutely particular techniques of empiricist description that fostered the discovery of practical, political, and ethical meanings *in* nature. I suggest that georgic's close links with the meditative empiricism help explain the poetic genre's immense popularity in the early eighteenth century—a phenomenon that has often puzzled scholars. These links also shed light on the genre's formal workings. Challenging an influential account of the genre's "heightening" language, I insist that its personifications, periphrases, and metaphors constitute a serious engagement with nature and science and that particularized description and poetic periphrases are both part of georgic's *realist* project. Georgic became the mode, par excellence, of empiricist devotions.

This book recovers modes of observing and describing that helped people—as Boyle said—go about "finding out and inriching" themselves "with those abstruse and vailed Truths dexterously hinted in" nature. In the following pages, I will ask: How did this work? What "Truths" did they learn, and what did they do with them? What can *we* learn by taking seriously such empiricist devotions?

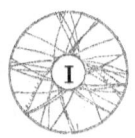

Occasional Meditation, an Empirical-Devotional Mode

ROBERT BOYLE wanted to popularize empiricist attention and description. He thought that all kinds of people should scrutinize nature: "the Learned" and "the Devout," "Gentlemen, and Ladyes," "Inquisitive Persons of several Kinds & Conditions."[1] His most resonant popularizing attempt was his *Occasional Reflections* (1665), which brought together serious science and Protestant devotional techniques to forge an empiricist method for reading "the Book of Nature." As Boyle explained, this method of "attentive observation" to "a multitude of particulars" in nature could offer the observer "some new practical consideration" (a fundamental aim of the new science), but it could also offer "Examples to imitate, *or* shew him the Danger, *or* Unhandsomness, *or* Inconvenience of some thing that he should avoid, *or* raise his thoughts and affections Heaven-wards" (32, 41). Empiricist scrutiny led the observer to implications that are scientific in our sense today, involving insight about natural laws or possible practical applications in medicine. But it also led to social exemplars, moral warnings, and religious encouragements. Indeed, Boyle thought "Inquisitive Persons of several Kinds & Conditions" should look closely at nature *because* of how very much they stood to learn from it. Close attention to nature accessed both physical facts and clues about God's will for humanity.

This chapter examines this empirical-devotional engagement with nature, a brand of scrutiny that aimed to access the capacious meaningfulness of nature's "Book." Against a scholarly tendency to dismiss this mode as

Boyle at his least scientific and most religious, or to downplay the earnestness of its engagement with nature, I insist that it became a real brand of empiricism, a way of looking closely at particulars and modestly seeking their larger implications.

Lorraine Daston provides a helpful starting point for understanding the workings of empiricist observation and description in the period. She explains that such attention was "pointillist" and "magnifying": "Visually and intellectually, the observer pulverized the object into a mosaic of details." It was also "deliberately repetitive"—the observer noticed particulars and returned to them again and again, "picking out different details, different aspects each time, and multiply confirming what had already been observed." The aim was to get from these particulars to broader truth, but the humble observer proceeded through inductive accumulation and provisional hypotheses about application. He or she used "comparisons and cross-correlations" to help identify "patterns and regularities" or to articulate hypotheses that could prompt new observations, experiments, and uses.[2] Close attention "pulverized" things into particulars and sought to put them back together into partial, modestly inductive meaning. This is how Boyle's air-pump experiments and Robert Hooke's microscope investigations worked, for example.

This is also just how occasional meditation worked. *Occasional Reflections* opens with a how-to guide in which Boyle explains the method.[3] It begins with "pointillist" and "magnifying" close attention: as Boyle instructs, observers should "pry into the several attributes and relations of the things," "to obtain the greater plenty of particulars" (32). They should show a "heedfulness to circumstances" and "display and consider the minute particularities" (32, 12). Boyle insists that this empirical attention and description are "the Ground-work of all the rest," but they are not ends in themselves. They should be followed by an "Application" that shares the spirit of Daston's "comparisons and cross-correlations": the observer should "reflect on" the object's "properties and circumstances . . . and thereby observe[ ] the relations of things to one another" (37). They should make "an Application of what" they are "taking notice of" (15). Boyle calls for a rich analogical sensibility—a willingness to consider how things are *like*. He was interested in likeness between physical things but also between physical and ethical or religious truths. A specific animal behavior, for example, can be like a related process in plants, but it can also be like something people should do or not do (it could provide an "Example to imitate" or "something" to "avoid"). This "Application" step involves creativity, and—as scholars have pointed out—the genre of occasional meditation is allied closely with the "literary traditions of the bestiary, the herbal, the fable, the emblem, the proverb," as well as humanist traditions of reading, rhetoric, and natural history.[4] But Boyle did not understand the "Application" as a departure from empiricism. He explicitly maintains that the lesson should not be *merely* rhetorical or imaginative, "*far-fetch'd*" or forcefully "*strain'd*," and he stipulates that it should be "rather suggested *by* the Occasion, than barely applied *to* it" (13, 35). Boyle also maintains an empiricist skepticism in pursuing the "Application." The observer should state it only provisionally and license it by "repetitive" empiricist observation. He or she should work modestly toward broader truths by fleshing out the analogies with more empirical particularity: "prosecut[ing] the Resemblance through all the particularities," "Insist[ing] on their particular Circumstances" (11). And the meditator should keep returning to the object, "as its several Attributes may be differingly consider'd" under different circumstances and at different moments (43). Boyle concedes that he doubts the products of "these kinds of Reflections would endure a rigorous Philosophical Examen," even as he continues to evince a real trust that he could access—not systems, absolute truths—but provisional hypotheses and pragmatic *uses* (111). Ideally, for Boyle, once all the "particularities" have been explored, the reflector should end up with a lesson that directs human behavior. For instance, close attention to a dog's feeding habits reveals how people should behave to God; the colors visible in clouds put him on guard against vanity and pride; and differing soil consistencies provide an object lesson in how humanity receives and retains information.

Occasional meditation's brand of empiricism differed from the Royal Society–sponsored brand that our cultural histories usually privilege—differed importantly, in the explicitness of its commitment to a Christian ontology and in its exuberant embrace of the multiple meanings and capacious kinds of knowledge that might be extrapolated from nature. A single object, fully considered, could "require above fifteen," or even "twenty," "differing Meditations" (11).[5] But occasional meditation worked like the Royal Society–sponsored empiricism: "magnifying," "pulverizing," repeating, "correlating," hypothesizing, and skeptically seeking applications. Moreover, the two brands of empiricism both deployed analogy as a crucial tool and understood its explanatory power in relationship to Christian beliefs about the structure of the world. Boyle practiced this empirical-devotional mode in both *Occasional Reflections* and his canonical scientific writings, and a whole slew of other contemporary scientific texts, including Hooke's

Micrographia (1665), feature the same meditational mode. The relationships between mainstream new science and the meditative empiricism are enormously complex.

My recovery of this other empiricism—related to but separate from its more familiar Royal Society counterpart—has far-reaching implications for our understanding of the period's scientific scene. It suggests that we can uncouple our accounts of empiricism from the influential modernization narratives that structure many assumptions about how it worked and why it was exciting to contemporaries. Empiricism influenced—and was influenced by—Protestant meditation. The realization that natural things were made of mere corpuscular matter did not preclude the possibility that they contained clues to religious and moral truth. And observers did not want to assert mastery and dominance over nature; they attempted to subordinate themselves to truths and dictates encoded, but only ever glimpsed, there. Freed from powerful critical associations among science, modernization, and secularization, we can see that empiricism actually cooperated with the spiritual beliefs it is supposed to have undermined; that the empirical subject could be humble and pious, seeking subordination instead of mastery; that tropes like analogy were central to the new science's logics; and that people scrutinized nature in pursuit of both scientific *and* moral or religious truths.

This chapter opens with a consideration of the mental work and formal structures central to occasional meditation, as well as the ontology underpinning its practice. I trace its development from the widespread Protestant practice of "occasional meditation" into a popular and influential way of apprehending nature. The second and third sections then turn to recovering its close relationships to the new science it developed alongside in the later seventeenth century. A short closing section demonstrates the robust presence of occasional meditation in early eighteenth-century England—laying the foundation for the rest of the book, which will explore the surprising and widespread ways such habits of empiricist devotion structured early eighteenth-century thought.

What They Are, How They Work

Boyle thought that all kinds of people should practice this method of reading God's great book—and many did. Recently, Joanna Picciotto, Raymond Anselment, Kristen Girten, Scott Black, Cynthia Wall, J. Paul Hunter, and Marie-Louise Coolahan have done valuable work recovering this "hugely popular and accessible mode" in seventeenth-century England.[6] They show that there was a lively print market, an eager audience, for such texts, and manuscript evidence attests to its popularity even among private individuals with no intention of publishing.[7] Of course, Boyle hoped that occasional meditation could be more than a thriving genre—he repeatedly cast it as a "*way of thinking,*" "a general and habitual attention," or "a Disposition and a Readiness" to explore "things" and their "uses" (16, 32, 52). Scholarship corroborates this as well. Occasional meditation was important in the period as a mode of both written devotion and thought more broadly.[8]

This popularity had everything to do with the exciting possibility of accessing a rich variety of truths about nature, society, morality, and God. In one of the most insightful treatments of the genre, J. Paul Hunter argues that its appeal lay in its very capaciousness. Hunter points out that neither Boyle nor any other contemporary offered a mechanism for testing the validity of truths gleaned from such meditation, but the truths nonetheless retained "a certain epistemological status." The genre turned on trust—trust that it was possible to glimpse meaning in nature and trust "that opening up meaning was more productive than shutting it down."[9] People practiced occasional meditation because they *wanted* to "open up meaning."

Significantly, the genre—and the very possibility of "opening up meaning" from nature—was underwritten by a belief in nature as God's great book.[10] In *Occasional Reflections,* Boyle exclaims that "the World is the great Book, not so much of Nature, as of the God of Nature, which we should find ev'n crowded with instructive Lessons, if we had but the Skill, and would take the Pains, to extract and pick them out" (39). Boyle firmly links "God" with both "Nature" and the "instructive Lessons" that it contains; and God secures the very possibility that meaning can be extrapolated from nature. In the literature of occasional meditation, the sentiment echoes and resounds: readers are told that they have access to "that *great Book* of the whole Creation, all the *several, most stupendious, and glorious* Works of God"; that they should "take and look over all the *guilded leaves,* and there to meditate on wonder after wonder"; and that the world is "ten hundred *thousand books,* for every Creature is as it were a book." This point was made frequently across the later seventeenth century—these are the voices of Nathaneal Ranew in 1670 and Edward Calamy in 1680, respectively.[11]

Recognizing the Book of Nature trope, scholars have explored how the reading process worked—how the mind moved from "minute description of the landscape" to "a search for its significance to the self," how meditators pursued an "analogical progression from material details" to broader concerns of "human experience" and "humanity's relationship to God," how each "engage[d] the book of the world as a reader and a potential author."[12] Rather paradoxically, though, this emphasis on reading "the book of the world" often leads scholars to downplay the genre's ontological grounds, the sincere belief in the bookish nature of the world that made such reading possible. Much of even the best work on occasional reflection privileges the subjective and imaginative, refusing to take the genre's engagement with nature entirely seriously. For instance, while Hunter importantly shows that the genre turns on trust in "opening up meaning" and gives these meanings "a certain epistemological status," he also somewhat undercuts this "status." He claims that not only is there no test of truth, but "the grounds of understanding are seldom addressed." Hunter privileges, instead, human imagination, creativity, and subjectivity.[13] These emphases threaten to empty out the genre's ontological grounds. They make meaning the property of the individual mind—and this cuts against the very purpose of a genre based on the desire to know God's nature, God in nature.

In a suggestive recent discussion, Joanna Picciotto goes further than Hunter in this vein. Picciotto's *Labors of Innocence in Early Modern England* recovers among early Royal Society members a tradition of "*imitatio Adami,*" an "experimentalist" tradition aiming to at least partially restore an innocent, prelapsarian experience of the world. (This tradition represents another rich way that science, religion, and literature interacted in the period.) Picciotto's treatment of *Occasional Reflections* compellingly explores its intellectual and religious contexts and emphasizes the complexity of the actual thinking process. Yet, in treating Boyle's practice, Picciotto seems to undercut some of the radical religious-ontological possibilities that the rest of her book foregrounds, for she explicitly questions the genre's ontological grounds: "The occasional reflector does not pursue his craft with any trust that the book of the world is really a semantic web of knowledge designed for his lectorial convenience."[14] Even more than Hunter, she takes the fundamental draw of the genre to be the way it "empowers" and "composes" the self. The meditator does not need so much "trust" in the bookish nature of nature, because the "wondrous God-given capacity of the mind to operate on the world is the real object of Boyle's celebration." The genre becomes one of subject formation, self-fashioning: "Boyle makes writing a personal book of the self synonymous with reflecting on nature's book."[15] Both Hunter and Picciotto, then, manage their otherwise insightful treatments of how occasional meditation works by downplaying possibilities that truth comes from the material instead of the human mind.

In less sensitive readings than these, such emphases are linked to the big modernization narratives that have meaning shift from being a property of the world to a power of the human mind in precisely this period. They also conjure the related argument that modernization led the "book of nature" idea to modulate into a "respectful trope" or rhetorical flourish.[16] However, the genre's form, its popularity, and its fundamental presuppositions all tell against these critical assumptions. This section recovers occasional reflectors' very earnest and reasoned notions of the bookish nature of nature, of the ways things communicate truths. I heed contemporaries' claims to have discovered lessons in nature as I aim to secure a fuller understanding of how occasional meditation worked, of how and why people scrutinized objects in the period.

First, the genre's very existence belies any notion that the "book of nature" had become mere trope, flourish, or polite commonplace. Occasional meditation was a serious devotional practice, not an appendage to the scientific process. It grew out of Catholic, Ignatian meditational techniques seeking to involve the mind and the senses in the act of devotion. In the early seventeenth century, English Protestant divines sought to rework these traditions in accordance with their own faith and beliefs. Resisting a Catholic emphasis on icons and the individual creative faculty, they rooted their practice in the external world, twice over. Instead of meditating on imaginative pictures or visualizations, as Ignatians did, Protestants focused on something outside the human mind, one of God's three books—scripture, the self, or nature. These meditations could also be either set and formal (the usual Ignatian form) or occasional ("Extemporall, and occasioned by outward occurrences").[17] Directing attention "outward" by privileging both nature and extemporality, believers attended to something produced by God, not men. To be sure, this practice drew on ancient, medieval, and early modern ideas about nature's ordering, but it brought to these age-old ideas some quintessentially seventeenth-century Protestant emphases. As Barbara Lewalski and Picciotto demonstrate, the English practice drew on the "application" fundamental to the structure of contemporary Protestant sermons, and it privileged things above pictures, progress over statis, and outward facts instead of inward imaginations.[18]

The practice of occasional meditation began to gain real popularity with Bishop Joseph Hall's *Occasional Meditations* (1630). One advantage of this practice was its accessibility: Boyle pointed out that even the young, female, or uneducated could look closely at nature and make an "Application" that accesses meaning. In a similar spirit, the practice was pitched especially to people on the lower end of the social spectrum, including husbandmen, sailors, weavers, and tradesmen. Such popularizing attempts assumed that these people were already handling objects in God's creation, and so the aim was to get them past mere materiality to spiritual truths. The book of nature was not a "respectful trope" but an enabling premise. Divines worked (as the subtitles of volumes for husbandman and weavers promise) to "Direct[ ]" people "how they may be Heavenly-minded while about their Ordinary Calling" or to "instruct[ ]" them "how to raise *Heavenly Meditations,* from the several parts of their Work."[19] The genre aimed, not for greater knowledge of nature (with a polite but insincere nod to God), but for real knowledge of God in and through his creatures.

Furthermore, occasional reflectors deliberately located meaning in nature, not in human minds. "The grounds of understanding"—far from being "seldom addressed"—were constantly affirmed, in as many ways as practitioners could. For one, the possibility of "opening up meaning" from God's "Book of Nature" was underwritten by contemporary science's ideas about the natural world. As Karen Edwards points out, in the second half of the seventeenth century the "Book of Nature" trope was embraced as a "rationale for observation" and "experimentation" and as a principle motivating the work of scientific discovery.[20] As I suggest in the introduction, even cutting-edge empiricists in the moment upheld a notion of nature that assumed "vailed Truths dexterously hinted in" its particulars.

Empiricists like Boyle also enlisted Scripture, ancients, and church "Fathers" to license their faith in nature's meaningfulness. They repeatedly declared that nature is a glass, a pair of wings, a school, or Jacob's ladder ("whereof *though the foot lean'd on the Earth, the top reach'd up to Heaven*") (53). They also gave nature a voice. Alluding to the Book of Job, 12:7–8, Boyle proclaimed that occasional reflections "turn not onely Birds and Beasts, but all kinds of Creatures in the world, as well mute and inanimate, as irrational, not onely into Teachers of Ethicks, but oftentimes into Doctors of Divinity" (28), and another practitioner, Ralph Austen, wrote that "The Creatures of God do all of them speak out the Praises of God," that they "call aloude unto Man, and instruct, and teach him, what he ought to do."[21] Austen's explanation of this as something more than a figure illustrates the way the idea worked in these seventeenth-century texts. Austen conceded that of course creatures do not have an "articulate voyce," but they do "speak plainely to us, and teach us many good lessons": when we "consider, and meditate of them, when we search out their vertues and perfections which God hath put into them, when we pry into their natures, and properties, *that is speaking to them*." The fruit trees answer back, then, "when we (after a serious search) do make some use and result of what we see in them, when we collect something from them concerning" either "*God*, or our duty to God."[22] There is a very real way, Austen believed, that empirical attention and description activate the creatures' voices.

Another crucial contemporary explanation of nature's meaningfulness relied on the Bible: occasional meditations worked for the same reason biblical parables did. Parables were everywhere cited as models and examples for occasional meditation. In fact, occasional meditators read parables *as* meditations: the ox and ass shadow forth loyalty; the stork, crane, turtle, and swallow are all exemplary in recognizing that God has "appointed times" for certain things; ravens are an occasion to preach God's care for man, and lilies, his beneficence.[23] Much more than rhetorical flourishes, these citations speak to the very possibility of the genre. Humans could learn from God's creatures because God created them thus. One occasional meditator, seventeenth-century minister Richard Steele, explained that parables and meditations represent God "making use of this world to instruct us about another," and an object can function as a "Sermon" because "*God* himself hath taken the text."[24] God created the world like a meaningful book, and it is God here "taking the *Text*," giving the sermon through and about the world he created. We should not underestimate the seriousness—the ontological seriousness, even—of these appeals in the deeply religious culture of the period. Interpretations of the genre that emphasize the subjective and imaginative would, I think, have made practitioners like Steele, Austen, or Boyle deeply uncomfortable.

While Boyle appeals to parables and likens nature to a book, a ladder, and a glass, he also provides a special case illustration of how contemporary writers conceived of the ontological grounds. For instance, he provides Edwards's example of a serious approach to the "Book of Nature" trope. Further, J. R. Jacob argues that most of Boyle's oeuvre proceeds from his deeply held conviction that "the study of nature offers insight by turns into morals, politics, and divinity."[25] Jacob demonstrates that Boyle believed such possibilities were licensed by the nature of the world. Influenced by hermetic texts and the writings of J. A. Comenius, Boyle theorized "the harmony between truths and the interrelation between different spheres of reality," "physical, moral, political, and spiritual." Jacob then shows that this fundamental ontological tenet—this belief in "the underlying unity of reality"—enabled Boyle to ponder the moral implications of natural facts in both his meditational treatise and his more straightforwardly scientific texts.[26] While Jacob's arguments about Boyle's ideological contexts have been controversial, these basic points have not been challenged. For his part, Boyle is quite explicit in *Occasional Reflections:* "there is so perfect an harmony, and so near a kindred, betwixt Truths, that, in many cases, the one does either find out, or fairly hint, or else illustrate or confirm, the other" (30). Boyle's philosophically reasoned conviction, then, suggests that—whatever we might think about the nature of nature—we cannot truly appreciate how and why people meditated in the period without at least recognizing their urgent belief in the possibility of extracting meaning from nature.

Of course, Boyle was not naïve. He never confirmed anything like the total system of meaning characteristic of medieval or Renaissance cosmologies, instead focusing empirically on particulars and aiming humbly to achieve only glimpses or guesses at truth. He recognized that he had no real way of testing a particular conclusion's validity, and, as we have seen, he admitted they might not "endure a rigorous Philosophical Examen." However, he then immediately continued to insist that, though these meditations may not "work Conviction in an Infidel," he believed they could "excite good thoughts in a Believer" and possibly access a partial glimpse into the layered nature of reality (111). After his skeptical concessions, Boyle was left with the kind of trust that Hunter outlines—a trust in nature's meaningfulness and the human ability to access it that is accompanied by a sense of human limits, of our irredeemable inability to ever pierce beyond the veil.

This trust was central to the ways Boyle theorized occasional meditation. In his introductory discourse, Boyle emphasized the way that meaning is generated by the confrontation between the pious observer and inherently fraught nature; it is neither subjective nor wholly objective. External reality is both the source of and the prompt to meaning: "our Instructions are suddenly, and as it were cut of an Ambuscade, shot into our Mind, from things whence we never expected them" (27). The morals come from outside, into the human mind. This possibility turns, I think, on Boyle's trust in two kinds of providence: God's general providence in creating a meaningful natural world and his special providence in actively guiding this world (so that occasions always fall out for a reason). These religious beliefs enable Boyle to trust, and this trust seems always to be confirmed. He continues: "the Informations we receive from many Creatures, and Occurrences, are oftentimes extremely distant from what, one would conjecture to be the most obvious, and natural Thoughts those Themes are fitted to present us, though, when the Circumstances are throughly examin'd, and consider'd, the Informations appear properly enough" (27). The "one" here represents the unassisted human mind—the subjective, imaginative mind. What this "one would conjecture" is not what happens, though. Rather, the reflector "receives" an insight, an idea for an application from the object. And these insights are confirmed by close empirical attention to both the particular "Circumstances" and the parallel being developed. Boyle's careful skepticism allows him to say only that this process "oftentimes" works like this. It is not infallible, but it works. Believers could foster the process by looking closely and thinking carefully. Boyle outlines something similar to Austen's sense that trees talk when we scrutinize them: by "examining" and "considering" objects and the "Informations" they shoot into our minds, people can better comprehend the world. Throughout his introduction, Boyle continually reinforces this point by giving objects impetus in the encounter, while still acknowledging a crucial human role. It is "the Thing it self, which sets a mans thoughts a-work," and skill in occasional reflection means "being able to find the latent resemblances betwixt things seemingly unlike" (15, 39). Also, "since attention, like a magnifying glass, shews us, even in common Objects, divers particularities, undiscerned by those who want that advantage, it must needs make the things he is conversant with, afford the considerer much more of instruction than they obtrude upon the ordinary regardless beholder" (32–3).[27] Humans "find" and "discern," their minds are "a-working"; but the objects activate thought, contain "latent resemblances" that guide the reflection, and "obtrude" truths on the careful "considerer."

The limited, self-aware trust and the complex encounter between person and thing that Boyle outlines in theorizing the genre also structure his actual practice of meditation. For instance, Boyle begins his meditation on a fire that will not light as Daston's account suggests all empiricist observations begin, by "pulverizing" the object into particular concrete details: "'Twas not . . . the Greenness of this Wood, that made it so uneasie to be Kindled; but, 'twas alone the greatness of the Loggs, on which the Fire could take no hold, but by the intervention of such smaller Sticks as were at first wanting here: Witness, that I had no sooner laid on a little Brush-wood, but the Flame, from those kindled Twiggs, invading and prevailing on the Billets, grew suddenly great" (85). Like the good seventeenth-century empiricist he is, Boyle includes concrete details ("Green" wood, large logs, "Brushwood" as kindling, and so on); he even precisely dates the observation. He focuses on the "attributes and relations" of these particulars as he pursues pragmatic problem solving. Carefully considering various reasons why the fire will not light, he soundly rules out one possible cause (that the problem is the "Greenness of this Wood") before determining the real reason, "the greatness of the Loggs." He is sure, for he withholds his experimental intervention—placing "smaller Sticks" just so—until the appropriate moment, and the effects bear out his working hypothesis. Also, as he crams concrete particulars into his sentence's accumulating clauses, Boyle eschews reliance on authorities or recourse to ornamental figures of speech. He even deploys the rhetoric of "virtual witnessing" or *enargeia* that recent scholars have prized in his scientific writing.[28] He invites his readers to "Witness" what happens when he lays kindling on the fire and dramatizes the effects: the "smaller Sticks" catch flame and go about "invading and prevailing" on the larger logs, until the fire rages with a life of its own, leaping ever larger. Boyle looks closely, considers causes, and communicates the facts.

While Boyle might seem here to be set over-against nature—manipulating it, capturing it in prose—his position vis-à-vis the fire becomes more complicated as he seeks the broader implications of the phenomenon. He makes the turn into the "Application" by asserting, "Me-thinks the blaze of this Fire should light me to discern something instructive in it" (85). He recognizes his own creativity and observation—"Me-thinks," he says, he should "discern" a lesson. Yet, he also gives the object agency. The fire activates his interest ("should light" him) and contains the lessons (there is "something instructive *in* it" that he can "discern"). Meaning comes from the confrontation between attentive observer and meaningful nature. He at once recognizes, limits, and disavows his agency in creating meaning as he develops the analogy:

> These Blocks may represent our Necessary, these Sticks our less important, Religious practices, and this aspiring Flame, the subtile Inhabitor of that of Hell. 'Twil be but succeslesly, that the Devil can attempt our grand Resolves, till he have first Master'd our less considerable ones. . . . Our more neglected and seemingly trivial Affections, having once receiv'd his Fiery impressions, do easily impart them to higher Faculties, and serve to Kindle solider Materials. (85)

Natural processes are like spiritual ones: Boyle's difficulty lighting the large log without first lighting smaller sticks resembles the way the devil works in human lives, only gaining traction once he manages to tempt people to neglect little things. Boyle of course recognizes that this spiritual lesson is not "in" the fire in the same way as, say, quickly moving corpuscles. True to his humble empiricism, he carefully uses two conditional verbs as he makes his turn into the application: the fire "should" teach him a lesson, and his spiritual analogue only "may" correspond to the natural phenomenon. Even as he notes that it is he—the observer—doing the "discerning," however, he evinces a remarkable faith that the lesson comes from the fire. He seems to trust implicitly in the moral lesson, as his conditionals give way to a more confident impersonal third-person voice: first with a future-oriented claim ("'Twil be but succeslesly, that the Devil can attempt our grand Resolves" without first getting our small ones) and then a confident declaration of fact—small sins "serve to Kindle solider Materials." This confidence is bolstered by the process of "prosecut[ing] the Resemblance through all the particularities." Fire is like the devil in its "aspiring" tendency, its "subtil[ity]," its ruinous tendency, the way it must make smaller "Fiery impressions" before it can "Kindle" larger ones. The distinction between the fire and the devil collapses somewhat. Both wood and human souls can receive "Fiery impressions," and Boyle slips smoothly between natural and devotional registers as he observes how "solider Materials" receive fire.

By the end of the passage he is urging his provisional point as a forceful practical conclusion that could direct human behavior. Because fire/the devil makes its first "impressions" on "seemingly trivial" "Materials," "It is therefore the safest way, to be faithfull ev'n to our lesser Determinations, and watchfull over our less predominant Passions, and whensoever we find our selves tempted to violate the former, or neglect the latter . . . to consider the importance of what such slighted things may, as they are manag'd, prove Instrumental, either to endanger, or preserve" (85). Careful attention to kindling leads Boyle to the conviction that he must emphatically refuse little sins, so that the devil never gets traction to tempt him to larger transgressions. The moral here is stated confidently but without any claim for absolute truth; it is merely provisional, "the safest way." And this specific moral itself confirms Boyle's self-aware trust in nature's meaningfulness. It is about small, "slighted things," and the genre of occasional meditation heeds this lesson more generally. It is premised on "considering the importance" of "slighted things," the "Instrumental" truths that particular objects teach.

Such a trust in the "Instrumental" nature of things enabled meditators to accumulate empirical facts and "prosecute the Resemblance through all the particularities" to almost extreme lengths. What Anselment says of one occasional meditator was true more generally: "Though the spiritual meaning is paramount, she does not sacrifice the literal for the figurative."[29] A trust in the confrontation between attentive observer and meaningful nature allowed these writers to slip easily between the literal and spiritual, even speaking of both simultaneously. Another writer actually formalized the way that meditations shift smoothly back and forth between and among parallel or simultaneous registers that are both of real interest. Each of the meditations in John Flavel's popular *Husbandry Spiritualized* (1669) begins with an empirical description of natural fact that draws on Boyle's "virtual witnessing" techniques. This is followed by an innovatively structured "application," in which Flavel outlines his central analogy and develops it with several "particulars." Each "particular" begins with a new, accumulated natural fact that further enriches the lesson. For example, Flavel's meditation "Upon the winnowing of corn" focuses on the idea that "Men have their winnowing dayes, and God hath his"—the divine husbandman intends to sort the sinners from the elect.[30] After detailing the winnowing process and posing the parallel, Flavel offers "seven particulars" (167). The fact that "the stalk bears up the ear, and the chaff covers the grain, and defends it from the injury of the weather" while the corn is in the field helps Flavel make sense of the presence and function of sinners in this world. ("Thus," he says, "wicked men" sometimes serve to "support and protect" the pious [168].) He similarly accumulates meaning by focusing on how chaff and wheat grow "upon the same root and stalk," the way the different materials fall when blown by the winnowing wind, and what happens to each after the process is completed (167–69). By the time Flavel reaches the "reflection" and poem concluding each of his meditations, the boundaries between the natural and spiritual, between sinner and chaff, have somewhat collapsed. He prayerfully debates with himself whether he is corn or chaff: he will prepare for "fanning time" by "sift[ing]" his own heart to see if there is something "solid . . . that will abide the tryal" (169–70). Flavel is talking about corn, and he never really neglects to focus on these "particulars," but simultaneously he is talking about sinners and saints, about a future "trial" during which God will, in a very real way, winnow the one from the other. Like Boyle, he trusts that such shifts between registers of truth work because there is a "harmony" or "latent resemblance" between them, because God created them accordingly. (This particular "resemblance" is also licensed by Scripture.) These shifts are not only possible but desirable, for they help the meditator refine his understanding of both the physical and the moral truth.

Occasional meditation, then, required a sincere belief that the world contains prompts to meaning and an earnest trust in the power of analogy. Hunter, of course, rightly points out that Boyle's "blissful vagueness" about how to test the validity of these truths proceeds from his commitment to "opening up meaning." Picciotto extends this intriguingly, exploring the tension between the observer's desire to receive nature's "Ambuscuade" passively and the careful habits of empirical attention, the "effort and skill" required to put oneself "in the line of fire."[31] This section has argued that we can affirm these insights about the complexity of the reading process without limiting meaning to the human mind—a notion Boyle and company would have rejected. While it requires supple, flexible mental work, occasional meditation is not fundamentally about imaginative or subjective meaning-making. Again and again, occasional reflectors insisted they got their lessons *from* nature. They were looking closely at nature, in the first place, because they wanted such lessons. Yet, they also accepted that they would never be able to see God's total plan—only the glimpses, fragments, and clues encoded in nature. The genre required a rather sophisticated epistemological stance: meditators trusted in the meaningfulness of created things even as they skeptically recognized their own fallibility, their own necessary distance from comprehending divine truth. They, therefore, scrutinized particulars. "Slighted things" could be "Instrumental" indeed.

An Alternate Empiricism

Occasional meditation was not only a Protestant practice—it was a scientific one. Scholars have identified several ways that the genre was influenced by the new science and, further, have shown that practices of science and meditation overlapped and interacted in the period. Other work compellingly argues that occasional meditation was a popularization of a new empiricist mode: "a sort of non-equipment-based microscopy" for the people, as Cynthia Wall has it.[32] I agree on all counts. In this section and the next, I extend these insights by exploring complex intersections between the two modes in the period. Here, I argue that occasional meditation constitutes, in itself, a very real brand of empiricism—one as devoted to an empiricist epistemology, techniques of close attention, experiments, plain style, healthily skeptical notions of human knowledge, and generative uses of analogy as the kind theorized by the Royal Society's canonical texts. Of course, the meditative empiricism differed from its counterpart in the explicitness of its commitment to a Christian ontology and in the exuberance of its fascination with how particulars point to interpretations that go far beyond the "physical" (to the "moral, political and spiritual"). But it is my contention that contemporary meditative and scientific practices obey *the same logic*. They work the same way: "magnifying," "pulverizing," repeating, "correlati[ng]," hypothesizing, and skeptically seeking applications.

Early occasional meditations were often very conventional, based on well-known emblems or scriptural passages (betraying no sense that real objects were involved). For instance, ants were among the most common examples of meaningful creatures. In Proverbs 6:6, Solomon sends the sluggard to the ant to "consider her ways"—the ant's hard work and prudence in saving up for winter—"and be wise." This could be worked into an extremely conventional meditation: humans ought to be similarly industrious in providing for the future. Yet, as it developed throughout the later seventeenth century, the genre of occasional meditation increasingly incorporated the premises and practices of cutting-edge new science. As other scholars have noted, the meditative practice turned on empiricist premises shared by the Royal Society: that knowledge comes from outside the human mind and is accessed by painstakingly close observation of small, mean, particular things. Meditators were encouraged, too, to take an "experimental relationship" to the object (as in carefully adding kindling at the proper time); and they cultivated a rhetoric of precise description, eschewing the excesses of rhetorical elegance while forging techniques of precise *enargeia*.[33] These empiricist premises fundamentally transformed the older meditative practice. Thus, when Edward Bury meditated on an ant in 1677, he heeded Boyle's prescriptions for empirical precision—meditators should "pry" into "minute particularities." The biblical commonplace from Proverbs served its most important role in prompting Bury to go outside and look at a colony of ants. He even tried an experimental intervention—disturbing the colony with his foot—and carefully observed the results, which inspired lessons: about what we should do when our souls are under attack, why we should distrust the "hurlyburly" of the busy world, and how we ought to always work for the "publick benefit."[34] Occasional meditation incorporated close attention and experiment.

The new empiricist spirit also motivated meditations performed on specific, unconventional objects in specific places and times: on a dirty sieve laid under a pump; on a particular hen owned by a friend; "*Upon a Crum going the wrong way*" down the throat; on uprooting a leek; "upon the heaveing wormes in my gums, and the takeing them out."[35] Other meditations focused on new scientific objects and discoveries.[36] For example, both Mary Rich, Countess of Warwick (Boyle's sister), and Samuel Purchas wrote occasional meditations to make sense of the newest scientific discoveries about bees.[37] While both recognized that bees are conventional emblematic objects, Rich drew on her experience seeing "a glasse bee hive"—a scientific instrument used by the likes of Samuel Hartlib and John Evelyn—and Purchas derived meditations from his own experiments with bees. Rich and

Purchas also observed with real specificity, noting the surprising discovery of "blake, dry" combs where honey ought to be and the bees' techniques to keep warm in winter, or experimentally observing their behavior when closed up in their hives.[38] Actual objects were scrutinized with the kind of empiricist attention that "magnif[ied]," "pulveriz[ed]," and repeated.

Even as occasional meditators aimed to draw rather wide-ranging and far-reaching truths from their observations, they continued to uphold an empiricist epistemological modesty. For one, they respected the new scientific critique of occult qualities that put moral agency in nature, "such as the 'fear of the void' associated with Aristotle."[39] Boyle did not explain the fire process *by* moral qualities—it is not that the twigs kindled the log through some kind of occult process of sympathy. Rather, while allowing for properly corpuscularian notions of causation, he believed that something moral could be extrapolated *from* the process. Nature is nature, but it is also a book that can be read. The resulting knowledge was provisional yet anchored in precise attention to material processes. Meditators were also good empiricists who recognized that knowledge is always more limited than system-building rationalist thinkers like Spinoza or Leibniz would have it. Like (and sometimes *as*) Royal Society members, meditators were after—not systems or absolute truths—but working hypotheses they could act on. It did not matter if the kindling existed in order to send a message about Satan so long as the meditator profited practically from the message.

Importantly, meditators maintained an empiricist attitude even as they moved from particulars to larger meanings. Standard Royal Society rhetoric claimed that natural knowledge should be actualized in practical applications. Occasional meditation simply extended this: it accessed not only nature's practical or technological but also its religious and moral applications. The same word—*application*—is used to describe the meditator's moral lesson and the natural philosopher's hypothesis for pragmatic use. In both cases the application is stated provisionally, with an eye especially to its possible usefulness in the world. The same crucial tool, analogy, motivates the "application" in both modes. Where Daston emphasizes "comparisons and cross-correlations," in *Occasional Reflections* Boyle asserts that by tropes of likeness such as "Analogy . . . we are, as it were, led by the hand to the discovery of divers useful Notions, especially Practical, which else we should not take any notice of" (39). Like other kinds of empiricist attention, occasional meditation used "magnifying" and "pulverizing" visual scrutiny to find "patterns and regularities," and it worked skeptically from these to provisional hypotheses or "Practical" applications.

Occasional meditation offered a way to scrutinize particulars and provisionally seek their larger import. That's empiricism! It is a distinctive, seventeenth-century kind of empiricism even. Daston and Katherine Park helpfully distinguish "the new empiricism of facts" emerging in the period from earlier empiricisms by its attitude to interpretation. Whereas "the texture of Aristotelian empiricism," say, "was smooth, fusing particulars into the universals," the new science made a "sharp distinction between a datum of experience, experimental or observational, and any inference drawn from it."[40] This is not to say that new scientists did not offer inferential theories or conjectures; they certainly did. Yet, their empiricism "was grainy with facts" and gaps, as they flagged the distance between particular and inference and embraced an epistemological modesty about the status of the latter.[41] So too the meditative empiricism: granular in its particulars and cautiously provisional in its interpretations. The meditative empiricism differed from the more canonical empiricism, however, in more eagerly emphasizing the importance and the appeal of the inferential interpretation. If empiricist writers in the mainstream Royal Society mode scrutinized things and then considered what they are like and how they might be applied, empiricists in the meditative mode simply pursued the likeness and the application with more exuberance (though with no less epistemological modesty).

This way of thinking about the relationship between the meditative and the more canonical brands of seventeenth-century empiricism resonates with the contemporaneous suggestion that meditation offered a version of and a step beyond science, a way of replicating and then fully actualizing its logic. For example, George Swinnock outlined three approaches to nature: (1) "*Ordinary and vulgar persons*" who see only "*rudely and superficially*"; (2) "*Schollars and Philosophers,* who go a step higher" and see things "somewhat exactly"; and (3) "*Christians* and *spiritual* men, who move above the Philosopher and most skilful Naturalists in their own *sphere*." These are listed in terms of ascending sophistication, so that the Christian supplements the philosophical "exactness" of the second step with a fuller sense of nature's stakes. As another contemporary meditator put it, "It is good to be a naturall Philosopher, but better to be a supernaturall, a Christian Philosopher, that whiles we intentively observe the creature, we may attentively serve the Creator."[42] Meditators managed this actualization of scientific discoveries not by departing from the logic of empiricism but by completing it. Occasional meditation was a kind of empiricism that functioned in the same way as its Royal Society–sponsored counterpart; it just went further, opening up more meanings.

That Boyle's practice of occasional meditation replicates the logic of his natural philosophy—even that meditation replicates and *completes* the logic of natural philosophy—is borne out by his statement of method in *Occasional Reflections:* meditators should "make of the Objects they contemplate not onely a Theological and a Moral, but also a Political, an Oeconomical, or even a Physical use" (30). Boyle here expands the possibilities for meditation beyond the theological and the moral. Scholars identify this as his innovative contribution to the occasional meditation form as he received it in the work of Bishop Hall, but they usually imagine the innovation in the "Political" or "Oeconomical"—Boyle's lessons are novel for not only focusing on God.[43] However, Boyle also asserts that close attention accesses possibilities for "Physical use." By looking closely and entertaining analogical insights, he might learn about theology, morality, and politics or discover something of practical or scientific use. Similarly, we have already seen Boyle affirm that occasional meditation makes things yield not only "Examples to imitate" and prompts to "raise his thoughts and affections Heaven-wards" but also invitations to "some new practical consideration." Boyle treats scientific ways of thinking as just one part of broader and more flexible habits of mind at work in meditation. While elsewhere acknowledging that meditation's applications might not pass a "rigorous Philosophical Examen," Boyle here proposes a real "Philosophical" possibility: if people "were sollicitous to apply" their empirical observations "to the discovery or illustration of Oeconomical, Political, or Physical matters, it would . . . possibly conduce to the improvement of those parts of Knowledge themselves" (30). Practicing meditation can "conduce" to the "improvement" of science and society. Boyle does not simply suggest here that empiricism influences meditation. He renders Royal Society–sponsored empiricism—often duly focused on the physical and practical—as a small subset of *occasional meditation*'s logic.

Boyle helpfully illustrates the continuities and the differences between the two modes. A consideration of his career suggests that the Royal Society subset differed from the broader meditational mode in offering slightly less room for explicit interpretation mongering (however empirical, provisional, and modest). Boyle's intellectual trajectory has been traced carefully, and there is some consensus that his writing and thinking shifted from an overriding focus on moralistic and religious concerns in the 1640s to the fascination with natural philosophy and experiment that marked his work from the 1650s onward.[44] As Lawrence Principe notes, Boyle's later work evinces "an interest in science *qua* science" that manifested in an increasing restraint about moralizing in his scientific work and increasing precision in distinguishing between his "Philosophical" and "Theological" modes.[45] Boyle's response to critics of his *Occasional Reflections* illustrates some of this increasing caution. He seemed shaken by the criticism of "three or foure Learned Men" who criticized his meditations not "for their owne sakes, but for" Boyle's, "pretending That Composures of that Nature might well have been spar'd by" a man who was also "a Philosopher." This criticism led Boyle to warn another natural philosopher-cum-meditator to publish separately the experimental and meditational parts of a text.[46] My sense is that Boyle here capitulates to critics, who would enforce a very nascent notion of disciplinary divisions that does not structure his own thinking.[47] And Boyle is all the more willing to capitulate because meditations (including his own) include the exploration of political meanings, which could be seen as contradicting the way that Restoration science was billing itself—as safely focused on things themselves and not on contentious, divisive political interpretations of them.[48] To be politically palatable in the wake of the turbulent middle decades of the seventeenth century, the new science remained rather quieter about possible applications that could not "endure a rigorous Philosophical Examen."

Being "rather quieter about possible applications" does not mean, however, that the urge to apply went away. For one, the "analogical poetics of ontological speculation" remained robust in Boyle's writings and in the new science more generally. Margaret Jacob, John Rogers, and Wolfram Schmidgen have done invaluable work showing that realms of natural philosophy and politics were understood as intertwined, such that "the scientific figuration of physical motion spoke throughout this period to the nature and scope of human action, while the figurations of systems routinely inscribed the contemporary concerns with political order" (as Rogers puts it).[49] Further, as I will show in the next section, what we might call the "analogical poetics" of empiricist scrutiny more generally remained robust in the new science: applications far exceeded the physical and technological.

Further, there are remarkable continuities in Boyle's thought from his early moralistic concerns to his later science. Boyle practiced the new science and meditation side by side. He began writing occasional meditations in the late 1640s and continued to work on the project at least until he published *Occasional Reflections* in 1665—after the establishment of the Royal Society and Boyle's rise to being a key figure in the English scientific scene.[50] Also, as we have seen, J. R. Jacob demonstrates that Boyle's writings across realms ("physical, moral, political, and spiritual") proceed from the same ontological assumptions. Other crucial continuities in Boyle's methods have to do with his ways of applying and interpreting particulars. Scott Black argues that "a skill of attentive reflection that is construed as reading"—a skill "evolved out of a humanist practice of reading"—"serves as a hinge between Boyle's moral and natural philosophy."[51] Relatedly, Principe insists that Boyle deploys fundamentally similar assumptions and techniques as he moves from examining Scripture and the "book" of his conscience to the book of nature: "The mental process is identical; the difference lies in text to be glossed." Principe further suggests that, even as later in life Boyle showed increasing caution about moralizing, the "meditative habitude of thinking ... drawing out unseen implications from observables" might well have "carried over unchanged as a crucial part of Boyle's mature experimental career."[52] Lotte Mulligan helps confirm this possibility, arguing that Boyle's methods are fundamentally similar in his "writing about metaphysics, ethics, or natural philosophy": "Meditating closely upon the problems presented in nature, giving them close 'attention,' led to these unexpected flashes in which the true connections between things were perceived through appropriate analogy."[53] Principe's possibility is further confirmed by the fact that Boyle was still sounding similar themes in his *Christian Virtuoso* (1690).[54] Jacob, Black, Principe, and Mulligan all support my sense that meditation is the broader category, and Royal Society science a slightly more limited subset.

Occasional meditation drew energies from the Royal Society's more rigorously limited brand of empiricism. And in itself it offered an empiricist approach to things, a way of "magnifying," "pulverizing," repeating, "correlati[ng]," hypothesizing, and skeptically seeking applications. It just sought *all* the fraught meaningfulness of nature's book.

Empiricisms, Interacting

Meditation and cutting-edge natural philosophy did not just offer separate, parallel brands of empiricism. There was real traffic between the two modes—they overlapped, interpenetrated, and combined. As I have been arguing, Royal Society science was understood as a subset of the meditational mode, with the broader category offering rather more room for provisional interpretation mongering. In this section, I show that these crucial links have implications for our understanding of both meditation and science itself.

Clearly, the new science influenced the practice of occasional meditation, but the relationship between the two modes is not simply a matter of one-way influence (as it is often described). For Boyle, the modes overlapped. In one of *Occasional Reflections*' recurring tropes, Boyle contrasts the perspectives of uninformed and scientific observers. For example, he says that someone "ignorant" of how distillation and alembics work would think he ruins the rose whose perfume he seeks to preserve; but those who understand "this Artificial way, that Chymists take" realize the wisdom of his procedure (54–55). He likens these two perspectives, respectively, to those who think the charitable man profligate and those who recognize that, by giving away, he actually preserves his soul. Knowledge of chemical processes opens up religious insight. Boyle takes this trope further in a meditation where the contrast is not between the uninformed and informed so much as between the irresponsible and the diligent scientific practitioner. He depicts a natural philosopher watching "*the Quenching of Quick-lime*": "He that should see only the Effect of the first Effusion of cold Water upon quick Lime, would think, that by a kind of Antiperistesis, the Internal heat of the Lime is rather encreas'd than suffocated by the Coldness and Moisture of the Water" (134–35). This observer is onto something: it does seem like antiperistasis, a force of resistance or opposition. Yet, the effects of the experiment, which a diligent practitioner would have "the Patience to stay a while" for, belie the initial impression, for the quicklime eventually lies "quench'd" underwater (135). This opens up a moral on how devout men behave among sinners— what they pridefully think will happen at first versus what actually falls out. Boyle's search for both scientific and meditative understanding here works through a process of observation, provisional comparison, and possible application. Quicklime in water seems like a chemical process of antiperistasis, but it is actually more like a slowed-down process of quenching; quicklime in water is also like a pious person among sinners, and this too has practical applications. It is significant, too, that in meditations like these, Boyle dramatizes and popularizes scientific objects and methods. Similarly, Rich's and Purchas's reflections on cutting-edge discoveries about bees demonstrate that occasional meditations provided textual space for seeking to understand and popularize new scientific objects and discoveries. As Purchas's meditations were published within a long factual account of bees, we can see that occasional meditators slipped into and out of a straightforwardly "scientific" mode.

Moreover, in their interest in technical processes and trades, occasional meditators obliquely participated in some of the Royal Society's Baconian early projects: their call for a collaborative natural history of trades and the surveying done by its "Georgicall Committee." As Michael Hunter explains, the early Society desired "information about technical processes" used by tradesmen, mechanics, and farmers "for its value in its own right and as a potential source of data for scientific hypothesis, while, through collation and comparison, it was also hoped that improvements noted in one area could be introduced in others."[55] (Note again a comparative impulse at the heart of the Royal Society's projects.) Meditators happily participated in this drive to collect and popularize practical knowledge, focusing on specific technical processes and exploring their implications in especially broad terms. For example, John Collinges's occasional meditations described and meditated on the precise details of weaving: the way *"the Weaver fasteneth the Warp unto his Beam, and divideth it"*; how *"his filling Boys prepare the Yarn, for the Woof, winding it on quils or pieces of reed, which he afterwards puts into his Shuttle in order to his Work"*; and the complex simultaneity of the actual process (the weaver *"swiftly throw[s] his Shuttle with one hand, which he catcheth with the other,"* and *"In the mean time his Feet are moving the Treddles, which raising the heavels do part the Warp, and are continually making a new room for the Shuttle,"* and again *"In the mean time a pair of Temples spread upon the Web, keep it fixed and extended,"* and so on).[56] Of course, as he collected details, he learned from them: the shuttle is swift like the days of our lives, and, as weaving involves the worker's whole body, so should Christianity engage the believer's whole soul. This is meditation, but it also explored and popularized a technical process. It heeded the Royal Society's call.

Perhaps most important, meditational meanings were crucial to the contemporary appeal of the new science—even when such meanings were not explicitly spelled out. Boyle again is symptomatic. Meditation sparked his early interest in science. The text that historians of science agree represents the turning point in Boyle's scientific thought, "Of the Study of the Booke of Nature," was intended (as its subtitle indicates) "For the first Section of my Treatise of Occasionall Reflections."[57] The significance of this is explained by a letter that Boyle wrote to his sister, Katherine Jones, Lady Ranelagh, in August of 1649: Boyle details how "transported and bewitch'd" he was with his early chemical experiments—delighting, in particular, in "the Theologicall Use of Naturall Filosophy" and in "those Morall speculations, with which my Chymicall Practises have entertained mee."[58] Science was exciting *because* of the "Theologicall" and "Morall" meanings it opened up.

The meditative empiricism and its Royal Society–sponsored counterpart were two modes that writers could slip easily between, and if meditation participated in and encouraged science, so too did the most serious science in the period have a place for meditation. As the Purchas example suggests, sometimes occasional meditations were published with or in experimental science. Ralph Austen's *Treatise of Fruit-Trees* (1653) is another case in point. Austen was a horticulturalist and member of the influential Oxford and Hartlib circles. His *Treatise* was cutting-edge husbandry, described by one historian of science as "the most systematic and detailed treatment of this subject yet published in England" at the time.[59] Its ninety-seven pages of experimental husbandry are punctuated with forty-one pages of occasional meditation on "*the Spirituall Use of an Orchard.*" For Austen, the second part was not an afterthought or an apologia. In fact, when he published an expanded edition in 1657, he signaled the importance of the second, "Spirituall" part by making it substantially longer than the "naturall."[60] The relationship between the two parts is interestingly complex: he saw them as complementary, and the most "scientific" parts could be those most closely linked with meditation. For instance, one of Austen's groundbreaking discoveries was his argument against the descent of sap. Many, including Francis Bacon, believed that leaves fell in the autumn when sap began to descend from the branches to the root. Drawing on experiments and "Twenty yeares" experience, Austen demonstrated that "*Sap* in Trees never *descends,* but alwaies *ascends,*" and leaves fall when "*Sap ascends not to them,* sufficient to nourish, or feed them any longer." In the second part of his book, he cited these arguments and moralized on the experimentally corrected mistake: as the root always gives nutrients and moisture to the branches, and never vice versa, so God gives us everything. We *"are continually receiving new supplyes from him"* (but are wrong if we think we *"adde"* anything to him).[61] Experimental science opened into and popularized meditation.

The meditative empiricism was also featured in even more canonical new science. We can see this especially in the branch of natural philosophy dedicated to looking closely at the world: microscopy. Girten has pointed out that the very form of early microscopy texts—their titles and vignette structuring—is indebted to meditational ones: "Compare," she says, Robert "Hooke's 'Observ. XVI. Of Charcoal, or burnt Vegetable' with [Joseph] Hall's 'XXXVII. Upon a Coal Covered with Ashes.'"[62] I would add that both of microscopy's two pioneering English texts—Henry Power's *Experimental Philosophy* (1664) and Hooke's *Micrographia* (1665)—also slipped sometimes into a meditative-empirical mode. Power, for example, went beyond both Proverbs and Bury as he scrutinized an ant under the microscope, noting with precision its "large and globular" head and its eye, "of a very fair black colour, round, globular, and prominent, of the bigness of a Pea, foraminulous and latticed like that of other Insects."[63] From the beginning, however, Power's interest in the ant was motivated by an awareness of broader possibilities for truth: his description situates the insect as a "Pattern of Industry and Frugality," cites the Proverbs passage, and explains that "in those virtues" the ant excels other animals and "most men." Because Power introduces other facts about the ant within this moral paradigm, the reader is invited to extrapolate further moral and social meaning from factually stated (but always at least potentially analogical) details: the ant is also notable for its "strength of its body, that it is able to carry its triple weight and bulk"; for the "Agility of its limbs, that it trips so nimbly away . . . without any fits or starts in its Progression"; and even for the mechanism of its "pincers," which can be used as both weapon and means to carry "eggs . . . for better security." Readers learn facts about the ant but are subtly encouraged to learn yet more—the value of strength, agility, constancy, and concern for their children.

Hooke similarly employed this brand of empiricism, going beyond conventional meanings when closely viewing a common emblematic object like the bee. Hooke was highly specific, focusing only on the bee's sting and featuring a detailed visual image (in which the tiny object is rendered over five inches long) (fig. 1). In his account, Hooke minutely describes the sting's mechanism, even keying the particulars to the image. After forcing the sting into another animal's skin, the bee tries to pull the sting back into its "sheath"; it "draws . . . the top of the sheath (*t s r v*) into the skin after it," and "the crooks *t, s,* and *r, v*" are "entred," and so on.[64] This precise description shows how the sting manages to "pierce the toughest and thickest Hides," and Hooke attests to the success of this clever mechanism: in this way the bee "put[s] to flight a huge masty Bear." He continues to find a human analogue for this mechanism. The functioning of the sting as it punctures a bear "thereby shew[s] the world how much more considerable in Warr a few skilfull Engineers and resolute soldiers politickly order'd, that know how to manage such engines, are, then a vast unweildy rude force, that confides in, and acts onely by, its strength" (164). Hooke analogizes here—the sting is like an "engine"—and the analogy implicitly contains a moral: clever "engine-making" and "politick ordering" are more desirable than "rude," brute force. He concludes with a social application: we should fight wars thus. Microscopy enabled meditative truths.

Significantly, the analogy that gets Hooke from bee sting to the social application is just one among many, many analogies that crowd the *Micrographia*'s pages. There are playful analogies aiming to spark the reader's

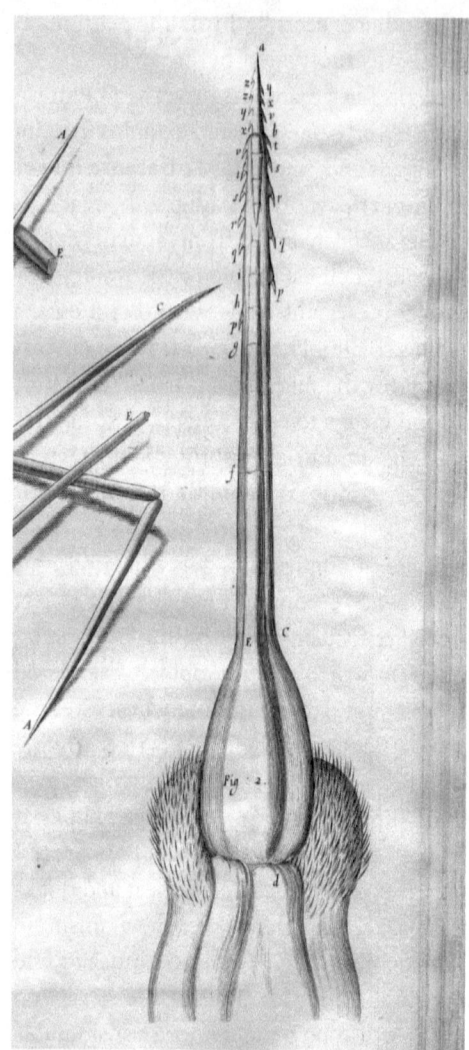

FIGURE 1. *Micrographia: Or Some Physiological Descriptions of Minute Bodies Made By Magnifying Glasses*, detail from scheme XVI, Robert Hooke (London, 1665). (Reproduced by permission of Special Collections, Wellesley College)

imagination (a printed period under a microscope is "like a great splatch of *London* dirt") and explanatory analogies meant to aid reader comprehension (the jointed legs of microscopic mites are like more familiar "Crabs and Lobsters legs") (3, 214). There are, too, foundational analogies that enable Hooke's very project (nature is like a machine) and more local analogies that serve a generative scientific purpose—as in his frequent analogical applications yielding ideas for practical use, akin to Boyle's suggestion for innovating on the blow pipe (discussed in the introduction).[65] Hooke might revel in such proliferating analogies more than many, but he only highlights a strategy central to the new science more generally. The presence of occasional meditation's brand of analogizing within the *Micrographia* can help us better understand the complex relationships that existed in the period among rhetorical, explanatory, and scientifically productive analogies, as well as among analogies that yield physical, technological, moral, and social insight. Hooke helps us see that analogy—understood in a capacious way that includes both rhetorical play and moral implications—was a crucial tool of empiricist epistemology, even of science at its most "Practical."

It is worth insisting on the centrality of analogy to the new science, for it is too often overlooked—a victim of outdated commonplaces about the new science's hostility to rhetoric and literary figure. Somewhat perversely, such neglect has been reinforced by promising work recovering figurative language's importance to science in other periods. For instance, Brian Vickers recovers generative uses of analogy in sixteenth- and early seventeenth-century occult science, but draws a strong contrast between the occult embrace of figure and new science's rejection or subordination of it.[66] And Peter Reill's work on Enlightenment vitalism has demonstrated that, in the second half of the eighteenth century, analogies were used to "discover similar properties or tendencies between dissimilar things that approximated natural laws without dissolving the particular in the general"; this technique required, at once, "a close investigation of empirical phenomena" and "the cultivation of creative imagination." Yet Reill too contrasts this embrace of provisional, creative analogy with the mechanical new science of the late seventeenth and early eighteenth centuries, which (in his rather straw-man version) rejected the instrumentality of figure as it aimed for "the reduction of things to fixed, logically coherent principles inspired by mathematics' simplicity and elegance."[67] Late seventeenth- and early eighteenth-century science, we're told, banned figurative language. It aimed to mechanize and rationalize the material world, to subject it to human scrutiny and control.

However, a scattered but steadily increasing body of work helpfully contradicts these commonplace assumptions. J. E. McGuire's groundbreaking work demonstrated that Isaac Newton's *Principia* (1687) upheld a "metaphysics of analogy"—its "Third Rule of Philosophizing" even providing theoretical justification for analogies between the essential qualities of observable and unobservable things.[68] More recent scholarship extends McGuire's insight, exploring multiple and overlapping ways that the period's empiricists emphasized likeness as they tried to understand nature and act in the world. For instance, Alexander Wragge-Morley demonstrates that analogy served crucial explanatory purposes in seventeenth-century natural history (and that this possibility was licensed by a contemporary understanding of how brains worked).[69] James Elkins's study of "visual desperation" reveals that early eighteenth-century microscopists faced with the unknown used analogies to enable them "to see bodies where" they might have only "see[n] meaningless aggregates, formless matter of 'substrate.'" Only through analogy making were scientists able "to keep looking" at new things, to keep attempting to place them in a larger scheme. (Were spermatozoa like worms? Or like machines? Or like spirits?)[70] And, while Gentner and Jeziorski contend that analogy was a crucial methodological tool for Boyle, James Bono argues that metaphor functions "constitutive[ly]" and "generatively" in science still today. Insofar as metaphors "direct scientists to explore links that would otherwise remain obscure," they "can prove enormously productive of theoretical advances and empirical observations," and insofar as they "forge links" with extra-scientific discourses, they can "shift the import of key theoretical terms." (For instance, the comparison of our brains to computers enables an interaction between neuroscience and computer science that opens up new lines of research and impacts both fields, and our cultural connotations are also invited into the messy mix.)[71] Such scholarship provides a helpful context for understanding the functioning of analogy in both the meditative empiricism and its Royal Society–sponsored counterpart. These two modes share a distinct kind of empiricist analogizing that is distinguished by five important characteristics. Their analogies (1) access usable truths (including ones that move science forward) and (2) work by linking disparate realms of experience—physical, religious, moral, social, and so on. The analogies have real relationships with both (3) the structure of the world and (4) the play of language, and they are (5) often unsystematic and multiple.

First, for empiricists of all stripes in the period, analogies were not mere decorations or after-the-fact appeals to the reader. Rather, they accessed real knowledge, generating new links, questions, and applications. The best work on new scientific analogy—by McGuire, Elkins, and Bono, as well as William Lynch, Claire Preston, and Geoffrey Cantor—recognizes that figurative language is integral to science and productive of new discoveries.[72] For example, Lynch argues that the *Micrographia* "aim[ed] to build theoretical understanding upon a dynamic process of observation, speculation about causes making use of analogy, and subsequent further observation" or "investigation."[73] Note the similarities between Lynch's description of Hooke's method and Boyle's how-to guide for occasional meditation.

And Boyle himself is quite explicit about this characteristic of meditative-empirical analogizing: he celebrated the way that figures of speech like analogy "led" him "by the hand to the discovery of divers useful Notions" that he otherwise "should not take any notice of."

Second, in both, the analogical impulse extended beyond the material world to encompass moral, political, and theological truths. Meditative empiricist writers like Boyle took quite seriously the possibility that they might "make of the Objects they contemplate not onely a Theological and a Moral, but also a Political, an Oeconomical, or even a Physical use." While these writers might be more exuberant about such possibilities than writers of Royal Society–sponsored texts, the two (overlapping) groups of empiricists share a belief that such realm straddling is both possible and desirable. As I have pointed out, the work of Jacob, Rogers, and Schmidgen demonstrates not only that realms of natural philosophy and politics were intertwined but also that the scientific speculations of mechanists and vitalists alike—Boyle and William Harvey—were *shaped* by an awareness of their analogical applications for humanity.[74] Empiricist analogies far exceeded the physical and technological.

While Bono compellingly shows that figurative language functions "generatively" in science today, such possibilities worked in distinctive ways—and were especially influential—in an age that believed in the "metaphysics of analogy." Hence the third distinctive characteristic I want to underscore: in the late seventeenth and early eighteenth centuries, the structure of the world licensed the possibility that analogies could access truth. McGuire helpfully explains that Newton's "Third Rule" was underpinned by an ontology that combined atomism and Christianity to affirm (in Newton's words) "the analogy of Nature, which uses to be simple, and always consonant to itself."[75] The *Micrographia* turns on a similar logic; as Hooke puts it, "Nature does not very much alter her method" from phenomenon to phenomenon (153). Because nature is like a machine (its various objects made in fundamentally like ways by God-the-mechanist), Hooke can assume the essential sameness at the core of quite different objects, and for this reason analogies can enable insight into the structure of the world. Further, McGuire shows that Newton's practice also involves a conviction that different planes of reality are harmonious or parallel. McGuire even contends that an "inter-relatedness among all realms"—not just "physical" but "moral, spiritual"—is "implicit" throughout Newton's works.[76] Similarly, for practitioners of the meditative empiricism, different cultural or metaphysical realms (the "physical," "moral," and "spiritual") were not understood as any more stably distinct than different realms of nature (the biological, chemical, and meteorological, for example). Boyle reminds us that "there is so perfect an harmony . . . betwixt Truths." The world was created in such a way that analogy could offer glimpses of insight not otherwise available to the limited human intellect.

Fourth, for writers like Boyle, Hooke, and Austen, the serious scientific insight that figurative language could access retained an important relationship to the workings of rhetoric. This aspect of new scientific analogizing has often been neglected. As I suggest in the introduction, there are crucial divergences in the way recent scholarship treats figurative language in scientific texts. Historians of science like Gentner, Jeziorski, McGuire, and Lynch tend to treat analogy as a disciplined methodological or epistemological procedure that has little to do with rhetoric. Other scholars recognize playful, ornamental, or strategic use of literary figures in the new science but imagine these as attempts to convince or popularize that came *after* the work of real science.[77] The scholarship that is most helpful in understanding the meditative empiricism, however, refuses too tidy distinctions between language and the real, between playful and scientifically productive figurations. John Locke provides the theoretical underpinnings for such collapsing of distinctions (a fact that will come as a surprise only to those entrenched in the "plain style" tradition that overemphasizes his famous comments distrusting rhetoric). As Peter Walmsley has demonstrated, Locke knows that analogies and metaphors can be playful (associated with wit) and lead the judgment astray; but he also sees them as "the best help we have in coming to a comprehension" of a world that will always elude total human comprehension. Locke recognizes that "hypothesis proceeds by way of analogy, drawing disparate experiences together in an attempt to construct the world that lies beyond our senses," even as he remembers the necessary—and necessarily fallible—role of human minds and human language in the process. "*Analogy*," Locke writes, "in these matters is the only help we have, and 'tis from that alone we draw all our grounds of Probability."[78] In a similar spirit, writers in the tradition of meditative empiricism take an essentially comparative approach to things—an approach that is propelled by the proliferating tendency of their tropes. They trust, even revel, in the way imaginative or explanatory figures can slide unpredictably toward illuminating scientific fact.

This distinctive attitude toward rhetoric is made possible by a fifth characteristic of empiricist analogizing. Both new scientific and meditative empiricist writers treat their analogies as provisional and contingent, allowing them to work in unsystematic, loose, and capacious ways. Much of the scholarship cited above treats analogy as a systematic epistemological tool or limits the category of scientifically productive figuration to a very specific subset. (For instance, analogies are allowed to be generative only when they link observable and unobservable essential qualities of things or known and unknown causes of mechanical phenomena, or only when natural philosophers treat things impossible to be seen or encounter an epistemological crisis in the face of the unknown.) Yet, within empiricist texts of both the canonical and the meditative varieties, these various kinds of analogy bump up into one another, and they are joined by other kinds still—playful, pedagogical, and biblical tropes, as well as analogies between various known and seen things or between different realms of experience. In these texts, analogies of all kinds could be thrown out, toyed with, and either set aside or expanded upon. There was no need to reconcile a flurry of analogies among themselves—any analogy was interesting so long as it was helpful in "opening up meaning." Elkins describes this as the "propaedeutic function of analogies" in the period, their status not as "permanent insights" but rather "as heuristic devices that" could be "constructed in order to be discarded."[79] Of course, from our twenty-first-century vantage point, it is tempting to distinguish between analogies linking specific natural phenomena (sugar in water and breath through a blow pipe, or wet quicklime and antiperistasis) and those between cultural realms (small twigs and small sins, or material and political orders). Or among playful, explanatory, and generative analogies. Such an impulse, however, leads to a misleadingly tidy account of the scientific scene, for part of the draw of analogy in the period was its very capaciousness and slipperiness. At the time, the term *analogy* was flexible enough to cover a large spectrum from a precise relationship existing in objects without human involvement (as in "analogy" in mathematical proportions or Newton's "analogy of nature") to an inexact general relationship suggested by human fancy (as in "analogy" as ornamental rhetorical device).[80] Empiricist analogizing was thus realm-straddling in more ways than one. And the remarkably flexible and provisional attitude that empiricists exhibited toward their figures means there is less contrast than Reill imagines between "mechanist" natural philosophers and the Enlightenment vitalists who encourage, at once, "a close investigation of empirical phenomena" and "the cultivation of creative imagination" that works heuristically, provisionally, "without dissolving the particular in the general."[81]

Hooke's *Micrographia* illustrates such analogizing at work in mainstream science of the period. It is driven by analogies, and his meditative (warmongering) application is not his only observation about what the bee sting is like. Hooke also notices that the sting emits "corrosive and poisonous liquor" that causes pain, and he refers readers interested in this process to his "description of a Nettle and of Cowhage" (164–65). There, he uses analogy to make sense of the various parts of a nettle. The nettle's point is "shaped very much like a round Bodkin," and it is attached to a solid base that "looked almost like a little bagg of green Leather" (143). Hooke's analogical language here is explanatory, almost playful, but it allows him quite seriously to conjecture function. The point that looks like a "Bodkin" probably has an offensive purpose, and the "bagg" does seem to be a receptacle. Hooke confirms this by stabbing himself with the bodkin point and watching what happens with spectacles attached to his face. For Hooke, analogies can slide from rhetorical gambits into epistemological tools and ontological facts. The functional principle he discovers—the "corrosive penetrant liquor" held in the bag finds a "deep passage into the skin" via the sharp weapon—works in fundamentally like ways in nettles and bee stings. Analogy helped Hooke see how the world works.

Once he established the principle of injecting liquid into skin, Hooke analogized to make productive use of his discovery. The same principle, he suggests, might explain why mineral baths work or why toads die when salt is put on their porous backs; and someone knowledgeable about dyeing might usefully apply the principle to that art. He also points out that "'tis not unlikely, but the Inventors of that Diabolical practice of poisoning the points of Arrows and Ponyards, might receive their first hint from some such Instance in natural contrivances, as this of the Nettle." Poisoned swords work because they allow the passage of poison deep inside of human bodies, and their invention "might" have been an application of the nettle's mechanism. Hooke then redeems this "Diabolical" use by recommending "a good as well as an evil application of this Principle": he outlines the invention of medicinal injection by syringe into human skin. Natural philosophers—like occasional meditators—used analogy to move from particulars to the "applications" that they prompt. As in occasional meditation, Hooke stages the confrontation between attentive observer and meaningful, active nature ("Inventors . . . might receive their first hint" from nettles [144–45]).

Of course, bee stings and nettles are like in a different way than bee stings and syringes or than bee stings and war strategies. But, like Boyle's meditations, Hooke's microscopy aimed to put objects in complex patterns of meaning that stretch from plants to God and from the practical to the moral. He wanted to collect facts, to perceive webs of likeness, and to speculate on how these help him understand the world.

The close, vital links between meditation and cutting-edge science highlight the real importance of analogy in the period's science. They also confirm that part of the draw and the excitement of empiricism in the period was the way it opened objects outward into manifold meanings. Far from always wanting to assert control or fix meaning, people sometimes scrutinized nature because they wanted it to explode into multiple analogues and applications: bee stings teach about nettles, toads, poisoned swords, syringes, wars, and God.

Into the Eighteenth Century

Thus far, this chapter has considered the widespread practice of occasional meditation in the second half of the seventeenth century. The question for *Empiricist Devotions*, which will trace the continuing influence of such habits of mind, is: What happened to this empirical-devotional mode in the early eighteenth century? Few scholars pursue occasional meditation's influence beyond the turn into the eighteenth century, and some even explicitly incorporate its decline into a story of modernization or secularization.[82] J. Paul Hunter is less sure. He leaves the question open, suggesting that "Boyle's kind of meditation flourished at least through the 1680s, perhaps well into the eighteenth century"; and Hunter's own early work on Daniel Defoe's "emblematic method" reinforces this possibility.[83] In concluding this chapter, I warn that assumptions about the genre's definite decline in this period are misleading—as misleading as commonplaces about the Book of Nature becoming mere "respectful trope." Occasional meditations continued to be written and read in the period. Their brand of empiricism remained compelling.

We know that people continued to care about occasional meditation in the early eighteenth century because they continued to read and discuss these texts. Jonathan Swift read Boyle's meditations aloud to Lady Berkeley during his regular visits to Berkeley Castle, even playfully perpetrating a prank. Swift read his own squib, "A Meditation upon a Broom-Stick" (wr. 1702), as if included in Boyle's book. Tellingly, the trick was discovered when Lady Berkeley praised Swift's mock meditation to her friends, who laughingly informed her "that they had never heard of such a Meditation before."[84] This anecdote indicates a rather broad public awareness of occasional meditation, of Boyle's particular collection even, in the early years of the century. There is less anecdotal proof, as well. A thriving market for the genre persisted throughout the first half of the century. Popular seventeenth-century texts were often reprinted: between 1690 and 1740, Flavel's meditations came out in at least fifteen editions.[85] New meditations were also published. Interesting instances include *Travelling Spiritualized* (1700), a dialogue "About Natural Things Spiritualized" (1720), and Isaac Watts's meditations on thunderstorms and hornet nests (1734).[86]

The techniques of occasional meditation were also adapted into new forms for different kinds of readers. For one, John Bunyan—who featured occasional meditation in his *Pilgrim's Progress* (1678)—reworked the genre into a popular children's book that introduced this mode to new generations. His book was reprinted frequently throughout the eighteenth century, often with a title, *Temporal Things Spiritualized*, that underscored its relation to Flavel's books.[87] Occasional meditation was also adapted for polite readers lulling in their gardens or cultivating their sensibilities. James Hervey's *Meditations and Contemplations* (1746; 1748) drew on the tone and stylistic features of the *Spectator* and contemporary poetry (John Milton, James Thomson, and Edward Young are frequently cited).[88] However, the basic impetus of occasional meditation—scrutinizing objects and letting them prompt analogical meanings—was unchanged, and much of what Boyle theorized about the practice was repeated. Hervey's book was enormously popular: it ran through about fifty editions by the end of the eighteenth century and inspired other meditators as well as poets and novelists.[89]

Occasional meditation also endured as do-it-yourself science. Hervey experimented with and meditated on scientific objects, such as the instinctive motions of the "*Sensitive Plant*"; and he encouraged his readers to do the same, viewing even mundane objects "with an Evangelical *Telescope* (if I may be allowed the Expression), and with an Evangelical *Microscope*." Echoing his seventeenth-century predecessors, he described this "Train of Thinking" as "the Christian's *Natural Philosophy*."[90] Eliza Haywood's *Female Spectator* brought this encouragement to an audience of women. As Girten has shown, Philo-Naturae, a possible Haywood persona, wrote a series of essays in 1744–46 exhorting women to scrutinize small things in the world around them. The project deployed the structures of occasional meditation as it linked empirical scrutiny with broad implications: "Contemplation . . . on the Works of Nature affords not only a most pleasing Amusement, but it is the best Lesson of Instruction we can read, whether it be applied to the Improvement of our Divine or Moral Virtues." Philo-Naturae offered examples more and less conventional (bees teach people to "regulate their Passions," and the manner in which "latent Sap" emerges "from the Roots of Vegetables" can influence our ideas about death).[91] Later in the text, Haywood's narrator herself goes out into the field, using a microscope and observing the behavior of caterpillars to prove the fundamental point: "the Study of *Nature* is the Study of *Divinity*."[92] Throughout the first half of the eighteenth century, then, occasional meditation still thrived. People scrutinized nature to access the rich meaningfulness of things.

The rest of this book traces occasional meditation's less organized and often even more empirical eighteenth-century afterlives. We have already begun to see that these habits of empiricist devotion trouble pervasive assumptions about science and modernization. A usual story of secularization simply does not make sense of these texts: science and Protestant meditation informed one another, and scientific scrutiny of nature was motivated by religious devotion and literary figure. This meditative empiricism also opens up new ways to think about what science did to the fundamental categories of person and thing. Far from empowering the self who asserts mastery over the external world, the meditative empiricism featured humble human subjects searching nature for lessons to obey. A desire to subordinate oneself to a supra-human order motivated constant talk in occasional meditations about heeding the "Voice of the Nature," about letting flowers and clouds become our "Teachers of Ethicks" and "Doctors of Divinity." One of the most common themes in such meditation involved the chastening of human pride and ambition, the recognition that brutish creatures and small contemptible insects do better than erring humans. (The orbital regularity of planetary motion prompted Hervey to exclaim, "if *all*, ALL" of "material Nature" is "*obedient* to the Divine *Command*," then "*shall Man* be the only *Rebel*?")[93] Empirical selves could be pious and humble, and their ways of engaging with nature could involve providence, passivity, and literary figure.

Further, empirical attention did not necessarily disenchant or rationalize the world. Certainly, when its particulars were scrutinized, "Nature" seemed less a stable singular standard to be wielded as weapon or a passive feminized victim giving up her secrets than a shifting multiplicity that might be active or passive, male or female, normative or cautionary, copiously legible or resistant to understanding.[94] Close attention "pulverized" objects "into a mosaic of details," and new science's ontology "pulverized" the world into atoms and corpuscles, without in the least interfering with nature's ability *to mean*. Its meanings were just only accessible in bits and fragments—hard earned through painstaking scrutiny and humble, partial, and provisional inference.

The early eighteenth-century empiricist devotions explored in the following chapters actually bear out what Boyle saw as a distinctive promise of occasional meditation: that close attention to objects could lead to "discovery" of "a Theological and a Moral, but also a Political, an Oeconomical, or even a Physical" truth. We will see early eighteenth-century empiricists searched nature to better understand science and religion, but also ethics, economics, and politics. They scrutinized nature as they tried to understand how best to *be* in the world.

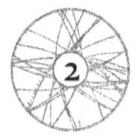

Deus *in* Machina

Popular Newtonianism's Visions of the Clockwork World

> The best Image or Idea we could frame of the *System* of the Universe was, as of a *noble* and *immense Machin* . . . whose Springs are an immaterial Principle (if I may so call that of *Gravitation*), which animates the whole and all its Parts; an Original Impress, or a constant efflux from the Divine *Energy.*
>
> —George Cheyne, *Philosophical Principles of Religion, Natural and Reveal'd*

SEVENTEENTH- AND eighteenth-century science is full of clocks. Natural philosophers used the clock as a powerful metaphor that helped them understand the world: nature was a great clockwork machine, a complex system of wheels and weights and matter and motion. Daniel Tiffany explores such clock talk as a paradigmatic example of how figurative language can structure and further scientific inquiry. Like poetry, he suggests, natural philosophy proceeds "in part, by making pictures of what we cannot see . . . by attributing corporeal qualities to inscrutable events." Seventeenth-century mechanists' "conception of matter" "depende[d] on" the "unsubstantiated pictures" developed in their clock talk. It depended, in short, on tropes.[1]

Scholarship on the new science's clock talk has approached the fundamental arguments of *Empiricist Devotions*, as it shows that figurative language played a constitutive role in science, as well as that contemporaries took a notion from the material world and thought through its applications in other realms. Historians of science tell us that clocks provided a figure for new science's ontology as well as its theology and methodology. Their world was a clock, and their God was a divine mechanic who had increasingly little to do with his machine after he contrived it. Further, since the world was a clock (mechanical, rational, and open-able), these new scientists could analyze, pick apart, and experiment in order to understand and replicate its regular workings. The clock was *the* figure for seventeenth-century science.

Even more provocatively, scholars have shown that the clock metaphor was crucial to contemporary understandings of the deep links between science, politics, and religion. Margaret Jacob's work on Newtonianism is exemplary. Traditional scholarship holds that Isaac Newton's discovery of laws of motion and the theory of universal gravitation added complexity and mathematical rigor to the contemporary understanding of the ordered mechanism of the clock world. This is part of an oft-told tale in which Newton is the triumphant climax of seventeenth-century mechanism. Jacob extends this by insisting that the Newtonian notion of a law-governed natural system had real ideological stakes. The Newtonian understanding of the clockwork world was promulgated to a wide popular audience in the first decades of the eighteenth century through Anglican sermons that used it to legitimate the Whiggish constitutional settlement. The law and order, the balance and stability, of the Newtonian world was deployed as a model that (naturally) endorsed constitutional monarchy, fixed social hierarchies, and the public function of the church.[2] Jacob compellingly confirms this book's argument that many contemporaries turned to nature as a source of knowledge about human institutions.

As I explore the logic and central terms of popular Newtonianism in this chapter, I embrace these insights about mechanism's figurations and the implications of natural philosophy for politics (and vice versa). Yet, I point out that Newtonian clock figures were often rather stranger than is usually allowed. There is a pervasive, if usually implicit, assumption that the clock metaphor is only compatible with a rationalized universe and a distanced creator-God.[3] For instance, claims about Newton as the climax of seventeenth-century mechanism often feature a straw-man "Newtonianism," emblematized perfectly in the clock as an ur-figure for a rationalized world and a rationalized God, for a rationalizing, reifying, and quantifying approach to the world.[4] Moreover, like a majority of scholarship, even Jacob's more sensitive work on Newtonian natural theology focuses rather exclusively on the design argument—whereby the complex mechanism of the finished clock implies an in-the-beginning clockmaker—and assumes that Newtonians posited a clock-making, law-giving God invested in "stability and order."[5] The problem is, Newton did not necessarily represent for his contemporaries the apotheosis of the clock figure as a finished, rationally ordered mechanism. This chapter argues that, as his science of gravity first was popularized in the decades following the publication of the *Principia* (1687), Newton actually encouraged a radical revision of the metaphor of the world as a clock. Providing contemporaries with arguments that God was the constantly acting cause of gravity, Newton's science suggested that God himself spun the wheels of the great machine: God was the clock's crucial power source. This chapter recovers a rich tradition of popular early Newtonianism, immensely influential from the 1690s until the early 1730s, that celebrated God's action inside his clock.

I draw on some of the most important scholarship on Newtonian natural theology: Alexander Koyré's masterful exploration of Newton's metaphysics, Steven Shapin's nuanced account of the social and political stakes of one Newtonian's clock figure (in which, contra Jacob, God is maintenance man), John Brooke's discussion of "divine activity in a mechanical universe," and James Force's work on providence and prophecy among those in Newton's circle, for example.[6] I bring this refined understanding of how contemporaries understood Newton's science of gravity to an oft-considered question: What did Newtonianism mean for ways of looking at nature? Popular Newtonianism provides a rich example of how scientific scrutiny—far from making the world more abstract, rationalized, or mechanical—instead helped contemporaries access (as Boyle said) "knowledg" of the Book of Nature's "Author" and "those abstruse and vailed Truths dexterously hinted" in the text. After tracing the development of a Newtonian version of God inside his clock, I recover the different ways that Newtonians used this figure to access "knowledg" and "Truths." The world, approached through this reworked version of the clock figure, offered glimpses of the kind of moral and political lessons explored in the last chapter, as well as a quite empirical (even physical) experience of God's agency in the world. Put another way, Newton enabled his contemporaries to affirm nature's moral meaningfulness and the divine's constant activity in precisely the place where we might expect the opposite: clock talk.

Newtonian Clock Figures

G. W. Leibniz and the Newtonians disagreed. There were many points of contention—who first invented calculus, whose physics and metaphysics were more convincing, whether a continental, Cartesian scientific tradition was better or worse than an empirical English one, and so on. The scuffle was increasingly rancorous and public, and the political and national stakes were lively, especially in the wake of the Hanoverian succession in England.[7] Amid all the careful polemic and stinging critique, however, was a recurring and wide-ranging discussion about the clock as a metaphor for the world. Leibniz argued that God, the master clockmaker, designed a perfect clockwork world that worked mechanically according to a "beautiful *pre-established* Order." He suggested that the Newtonians, by contrast, made God into a second-rate mechanic and the world into a faulty clock:

> According to their Doctrine, God Almighty wants to *wind up* his Watch from Time to Time: Otherwise it would cease to move. He had not, it seems, sufficient Foresight to make it a perpetual Motion. Nay, the Machine of God's making, is so imperfect, according to these Gentlemen, that he is obliged to *clean* it now and then by an extraordinary Concourse, and even to *mend* it, as a Clockmaker mends his Work: Who must consequently be so much the more unskilful a Workman, as he is oftner obliged to mend his Work and to set it Right.[8]

Leibniz's use of the clock as a vehicle to express his objections to Newtonianism was savvy, but not in the way this is often understood. It was savvy in that Leibniz opened up the conversation to a wider audience by deploying a figure conventionally useful for rendering scientific ideas accessible to a more general public. But he was not—as scholars sometimes suggest—craftily exaggerating the logic of Newtonianism by foisting the clock on Newtonians who, at their most serious, anxiously avoided the figure.[9] Rather, Leibniz's critique of Newtonianism drew on a rich Newtonian tradition of featuring God's actions inside the clock. Leibniz said that the Newtonian God needs to "*wind up* his Watch," "*clean*," and even "*mend it*"—this all would have seemed quite familiar to English readers of, say, George Cheyne's work on Newtonian natural theology (published in its second edition in 1715, the same year as Leibniz wrote these words). Cheyne insisted that God performs chores, as it were, inside of his clockwork world: the "winding up of the Spring or Weights" and the "removal of those Obstructions and Disturbances, time and the frail Nature of material Organs must bring upon it." Cheyne even asserted that, if God's power were withdrawn for a single moment, the whole "would become a lifeless unactive heap of matter"—"cease to move," in Leibniz's words. For Cheyne, the world is an *"immense Machin"* with a divine power source ("Springs").[10] Leibniz did not delight in a Newtonian discomfort with a figure he had cunningly imposed on them but rather faithfully summarized an apologetic tradition that was already well established by 1715. God was inside the clock, keeping it ticking and giving it power. Significantly, moreover, this Newtonian model might have been *more* intuitive to contemporaries than Leibniz's suggestion (and our anachronistic assumption) that clocks do not need constant upkeep and do not register external forces. The opposite would have been a daily experience for the owner of a timepiece in this period: clocks were wound and reset about every eight days; gears needed occasional repair; friction affected the time in unpredictable ways; and the metals and oils swelled and contracted with the weather, telling literally different times at different times of the year.[11]

This section recovers the Newtonian tradition of the world as a clock that needs some divine assistance. It shows that the early Newtonians were not limited to a rationalized version of the clock figure. They were not consistently uncomfortable with the metaphor, nor did they—as some scholars, taking this assumption to its extreme, have suggested—"b[reak] the spell that the clock metaphor had held over Europe for many generations."[12] Rather, Newtonians eagerly and frequently affirmed God's constant activity in his clockwork. I focus on three influential versions of the metaphor—one by Newton himself, one by Richard Bentley (an early popularizer), and one by Samuel Clarke (the philosopher who formally defended Newton from Leibniz's attack). These texts also demonstrate the *popularity* of the God-inside-his-clock figure, challenging scholarship that understands Newtonian natural theology as difficult and "eminently nonpopular."[13]

Before turning to Newtonian clock metaphors, we need to understand why Newtonian thinkers disagreed with Leibniz's version of a perfect, wholly mechanized world. Clarke, who offered the "official" Newtonian reply to Leibniz's critique, explains the problem quite clearly: "The Notion of the World's being a great *Machine*, going on without *the Interposition of God*, as a Clock continues to go without the Assistance of a Clockmaker; is the Notion of *Materialism* and *Fate,* and tends (under pretense of making God a *Supra-Mundane Intelligence,*) to exclude *Providence* and *God's Government* in reality out of the World" (1:14). Newtonians argued that the world is emphatically not like a clock if we believe that clocks "continue without the

Assistance of a Clockmaker." The analogy has a dangerous tendency: just as a clockmaker is no longer involved in his clock after he finishes building it, God would have no need to intervene in his world after Creation. It is an easy jump from here, Clarke suggests, to "*Materialism* and *Fate*" or outright atheism, the belief that everything is merely matter and mechanism and that there is no God at all. Clarke here takes a standard early Newtonian position: the world is not a clock in a Cartesian, Leibnizian, or deistic sense, in *any* sense that makes God into little more than a distant first cause. These versions of the clock figure threaten to "exclude Providence and *God's Government* in reality out of the World." With a bit of fear mongering, Clarke puts his point another way. If a king had a kingdom in which everything ran perfectly without him ever doing anything, men would be tempted to "set the King aside" (1:4). Anarchists, atheists, mechanists—Clarke argues that it is Leibniz's system, not Newton's, that truly demeans God.

The Newtonians rejected Leibniz's completely mechanized clockwork model, but they were not out to kill the clock figure. Rather, they offered a competing version of the clockwork world, one that includes the "Assistance" of the divine clockmaker. First, the Newtonians insisted that God played maintenance man. Both Leibniz's "mending" accusation and Cheyne's affirmation of God's occasional chores refer to Newton's belief (stated in the *Opticks*) that the gravitational action of comets and planets on one another introduce some "*small irregularities*" that will continue to increase until "*the present System of Nature shall want to be anew put in Order by its Author.*"[14] This defense of cosmic irregularities was important to the early Newtonians, but it was only one part of their clock thought.[15] Newtonians also downplayed the negative connotations of words like "mending," "cleaning," and "irregularities" as they offered a more positive paradigm for God's activity in the clock. God quite literally spins its wheels.

Their version of the clock figure rested on an invitation that the Newtonian understanding of gravity offered. In fact, when Newton used the clock metaphor in an unpublished 1712 manuscript, he dwelled on gravity's workings inside it. He did this in order to address one of Leibniz's most potent accusations. Newton had discovered the existence of universal gravitation and detailed the laws it followed, but he refrained from authoritatively explaining its cause. His usual solution to the problem was to say that he had no solution. "*Hypothesis non fingo*," he famously asserted in the *Principia*.[16] With these words (a promise to "feign" no hypotheses), Newton claimed that when he speaks of forces he refers only to observable and quantifiable effects from a mathematical point of view. Leibniz, however, thought that this solution begged the question: "Is it God himself that performs" the perpetual miracle of gravity? Or "some spiritual Rays, or some Accident without a Substance, or some kind of *Species Intentionalis*, or some other *I know not what*"? (5:118–19). Leibniz bemoaned Newtonian gravity as a backward step, a deus ex machina, or a slyly reinvented piece of scholastic jargon that makes God into a bungling mechanic who has to constantly come back into his machine to keep it moving. Leibniz thought that Newton was inappropriately using magic or mysticism to explain the workings of his clock.

In the 1712 manuscript, Newton tried to justify himself against this criticism; he resourcefully used the clock figure to reinforce his point that he "meddle[s] not" with the question of cause but only asserts the verifiable fact that gravity actually does affect all the planets. He continued, "to understand this without knowing the cause of gravity, is as good a progress in philosophy as to understand the frame of a clock and the dependence of the wheels upon one another without knowing the cause of the gravity of the weight which moves the machine is in the philosophy of clockwork."[17] Of course, as the paradigmatic mechanical object, the clock was assumed to be fully understood. By the time Newton wrote this, the "philosophy of clockwork" was considered a quite developed science (with what has been called the "Horological Revolution" well under way). Newton, however, highlighted limits in the understanding of clocks. No one knows "the cause of the gravity of the weight which moves the machine." His point is obvious. Contemporary science was in exactly the same position regarding planetary motion as it was regarding clockwork. It knew that planets orbit and, with some precision, what paths they follow and what laws they obey. It did not know the cause of the gravity that keeps the planets in these orbits, but this boots nothing, he suggested. Clockmakers functionally understood a clock's mechanism without knowing the cause of gravity; Christaan Huygens had harnessed the force of gravity on a pendulum to achieve unprecedented accuracy in his clocks and yet knew no more than Newton about the cause of the gravity that makes the pendulum swing with isochronic regularity. Newton effectively put *"non fingo"* brackets around the cause of gravity, but these brackets did not require a return to occult qualities or at all interfere in continued clock building and orbit measuring. They simply marked the limits (for now at least) of what his brand of careful inductive empiricism could explain.

An older tradition of scholarship privileged *"non fingo"* moves like these as evidence of Newton's scientific modernity, rendering him the prototype of the positivist scientific genius.[18] More recent research into Newton's many, many manuscripts, however, has undermined these arguments. This fascinating work shows that Newton spent his career wrestling with the ontological problem of the cause of gravity. These scholars chart Newton's changing beliefs as he attempted in his laboratory to verify conclusions cobbled together from a whole variety of philosophies, from alchemy and Arian theology to Cambridge Platonism, neostoicism, and the thought of ancients like Thales and Pythagoras.[19] They have concluded that, for some period between 1687 and about the middle of the first decade of the eighteenth century, Newton entertained the idea that God was the direct cause of gravity. As he planned on putting it in a revised corollary to an aborted second edition of the *Principia* in the 1690s, "There exists an infinite and omnipresent spirit in which matter is moved according to mathematical laws."[20] Yet scholars have shown that, at other times, Newton also considered the possibility that God would use some sort of intermediary—spiritual or, more problematically, material (or more problematically still, composed of a substance somewhere about the middle of an alchemical spectrum between spirit and matter). In the final decades of his life, he published speculations that a strongly elastic subtle aether was the cause of gravity. Newton's understanding of gravity's cause, therefore, is notoriously complex. Sometimes it was divine; sometimes it was not.

However, because Newton was secretive about these changing beliefs as he continued to "*non fingo*" in public, it has been tempting for scholars to depict the Newton of the private manuscripts as the last of the magicians while, as a public figure, he remains the first of the true scientists. Even as they delightfully demonstrate how alchemical spirits, plastic natures, created divinities, and allegorized myths guided Newton in his study and his laboratory, these scholars stop short of a similar revisionary treatment of Newtonian*ism*. They often continue to assume that his science was popularized in accordance with some progressive conception of science: reason, math, measure, order.[21] Yet, such a clean separation of public and private or science and magic is simply untenable. First, Newton's private beliefs were not always a well-kept secret. For example, in 1701 Nicolas Fatio de Duillier declared that Newton "would often seem to incline to think that Gravity had its Foundation only in the arbitrary Will of God," and one of Newton's colleagues reported in print in 1727 that Newton was "firmly persuaded" that gravity "Was deriv'd from the immaterial Presence and Power of the Deity."[22] More important, though, this scholarly separation between public and private ignores the ways contemporaries picked up and used Newtonian science. While most early supporters did not grasp all the nuances in Newton's bricolage of sometimes obscure ontological systems, they embraced in particular the aspects of Newton's work that allowed glimpses of divine agency.

Newton's pseudo-positivist public stance did not quash the discovery of the divine—far from it. His contemporaries interpreted this agnosticism as expressing and protecting the possibility that an omnipresent God constantly moved matter. In other words, the very move now privileged as evidence of Newton's scientific modernity—his causal agnosticism—actually enabled a radical celebration of divine agency for his contemporaries. Newton's version of the clock figure makes this connection quite clear. In comparing celestial science to the "philosophy of clockwork," Newton made both a methodological and an ontological point: by bracketing the cause of gravity, Newton's figure undermined—or at least questioned—the ontology of total mechanism emblematized by conventional and Leibnizian uses of the clock figure. In the context of seventeenth-century science, the stakes of this ontological question were quite high. Throughout the seventeenth century, scientists used mechanism to banish occult qualities, substantial forms, and magic from the material world. Yet this always threatened to go too far toward matter. As Clarke insisted in his response to Leibniz, to account for everything by mechanics and matter was to deny spirit or the divine a role in the world. It was, in effect, "to exclude Providence and *God's* Government" from his clockwork. This problem vexed the early Royal Society. At times, English corpuscularians like Boyle opposed traditional scholastic philosophy by arguing that corpuscles composed a divine clock that kept ticking away without any magic or nonmechanical forces whatsoever: God's "Machine" can "perform all those many things which he design'd it should, by the meer contrivance of Brute matter, managed by certain Laws of Local Motion." At other times, though, the same virtuosi entertained the possibility of spiritual and divine agencies, worrying that a "Law"-driven world of "Brute matter" reduced the world to "meer" matter and motion and relegated God to the position of a passive spectator a la Hobbesian materialism.[23] In one sense, then, Newton's "*non fingo*" effected a kind of temporary solution to this problem. It allowed Newton and his followers to affirm the rational, clockwork nature of the world while protecting the possibility that spirit or God could act: "the dependence of the wheels upon one another" remains, but we just do not know what causes "the gravity of the weight which moves the machine." It might well be divine, not mechanical.

Newton's "*non fingo*" resonated far beyond this rather lame *possibility* of a saved space: the early Newtonian God was more than a God of the Gaps.[24] Of course, Newton never publicly professed that God or some divine emanation is the motive power that drives the clock. Instead, he ostensibly gave other scientists leave to explain gravity "mechanically or otherwise." However, the *Principia* contains powerful arguments that gravity could not have a material, mechanical cause in any traditional sense, and Newton's early followers rehearsed these arguments again and again. Here, in the voices of popularizers writing in the first three decades of the eighteenth century, are the reasons Newton provided for why gravity must be extra-material, nonmechanical. First, Newton showed that Descartes's mechanical account of gravity was wrong. As a 1708 popular encyclopedia explained, it "implies a kind of Contradiction" for upward-moving subtle matter to be responsible for forcing objects downward.[25] In his 1715 primer, Cheyne also pointed out the contradiction involved in a substance without gravity being the cause of universal gravity (1:36). More fundamentally, unlike Cartesianism, Newton's physics required the existence of some nonmechanical force. Newton focused on this argument in the final queries to the *Opticks* (1718), his most popular, vernacular explanation of his system. The laws of mechanism are "passive Principles" only: bodies continue in their state of motion or rest until acted upon, they react in proportion to the force affecting them, and they tend toward inertia.[26] Left to themselves in a world of diminishing motion, these "passive Principles" could not stop everything from grinding to a halt—thus, the need for some sort of (nonmechanical) active principles to make up the constant decay, to conserve motion. There was also the more concrete consideration that gravity did not behave according to the rules of mechanism. First, as a 1728 encyclopedia explained, gravity is "always proportionable, not to the Surfaces of Bodies or Corpuscles, but to their solid Quantity and Contents." This means that whatever causes gravity is capable of "penetrating the very solid, and intimate Substance" of bodies, but mechanical causes—one body knocking another into motion—act in proportion to external surfaces and could never pervade a body's innermost parts.[27] Also, as William Whiston asserted in 1717, mechanical causes affect moving and resting bodies differently—"A Body in Motion impels another at Rest with its whole Force; but one in Motion, with only the Excess of its own Velocity above the others"—but gravity affects all bodies equally. Finally, Whiston continued, gravitating bodies seem to act on each other at a distance (the ocean gravitates toward the moon), which is simply impossible by any mechanical or material means.[28] While Newton did not know the cause of gravity, therefore, he did know that the passive movements of mechanical causation could take him just so far. They could never move the weight that moves the machine.

Later in his career Newton entertained some kind of non-Cartesian, quasi-electrical aether as a candidate for this cause, but the aether (although it became increasingly important in the 1730s and 1740s) confounded his contemporaries, who usually ignored or dismissed it out of hand. It smacked of a worrying return to Cartesianism. For them, delighting in frequent recitals of the early proofs, Newton's causal agnosticism did engage to revise conventional mechanical philosophy. His reworking of the clock figure left a mysterious, nonmechanical, extra-material (and possibly spiritual, omnipresent, and all-powerful) agent lurking inside of it. One of Newton's colleagues reported a conversation in which Newton suggested that these arguments for God-as-cause are actually latent in the *Principia*. Newton said "that 'He saw those Consequences: but thought it better to let his Readers draw them first of themselves.'"[29]

Readers certainly did "draw" these consequences. Some even promulgated them in print, publicly praising God's activity inside his clock. Popular interest in this figure was sparked by the earliest popularization of Newton's science. As Jacob's work has taught us, Richard Bentley's 1692 sermons at the inaugural Boyle Lectures—a lecture series established by Robert Boyle's will as a public forum against atheism—were a crucial early attempt to explain Newton's discovery of universal gravitation to a popular audience. Bentley, who corresponded with Newton as he grappled with a relationship between cutting-edge physics and Anglican theology, also offered the first public exposition of the reworked Newtonian clock figure. Bentley began with a scientifically sophisticated version of the conventional design argument (the argument that Jacob highlights). He also supplemented the idea of the world as a finished mechanism with a "new and invincible Argument for the being of God."[30] This "new" argument started with the Newtonian understanding of gravity as something more than mechanism acting in a mechanical world: "Universal Gravitation, a thing certainly existent in Nature, is above all Mechanism and material Causes" (7:32). There is something more than matter and motion at work in the world, and Bentley did not stop with the Newtonian agnosticism that one early textbook described as "the deficient Cause of Gravity."[31] Bentley happily filled in the blank with a cause that seemed quite sufficient to him: God. He continued, gravity is above all mechanism "and proceeds from a higher principle, a Divine energy and impression" (7:32). "Gravity do immediately flow from a Divine Power and Energy" and is "the immediate *Fiat* and Finger of God" (4:6).

Significantly, even as Bentley used Newtonian gravity to celebrate divine agency, he retained a vital sense of the clockwork nature of the world. The world, for Bentley, is a clock that God acts within: "Gravity, the great Basis of all Mechanism, is not it self Mechanical," and "all the Powers of Mechanism are intirely dependent on the Deity," on an active God whose "Power and Energy" is at work in his clock world (4:6, 5). Such arguments seem to have pleased Newton, who confided to Bentley that he wrote the *Principia* with "an eye upon such principles as might" convince "considering men" to believe in "a Deity & nothing can rejoyce me more than to find it usefull for that purpose."[32]

In the first decades of the eighteenth century, Newton's friends and followers repeated, time and again, the fill-in-the-*non-fingo* that Bentley influentially espoused (and that Newton, at least for some period, secretly believed). For example, in *Lexicon Technicum* (1708), an early scientific encyclopedia, John Harris began in true Newtonian form by establishing the reality of universal gravitation as a phenomenon, whatever its cause, and explaining the inadequacies of material and mechanical explanations. Then, he cited the "Learned Mathematician Capt. *Edmund Halley*," Newton's friend, who, aware of such proofs, "owns Gravity to be an Effect unsolvable by any Philosophical Hypothesis." Material and mechanical explanations fail, but Harris and Halley have an idea of an actor adequate to fill the mysterious role of gravity causer. Harris continued, Halley "Modestly and *Religiously* resolves it into the immediate Will of our All-wise Creator."[33] In his expansion of Harris's entry in his *Cyclopaedia* (1728), Ephraim Chambers let this sentiment reverberate. After establishing the Newtonian bracket as to the cause of gravity, Chambers quoted a whole chorus of scientists who, by 1728, had enacted this "immediate Recourse to the Agency of the Almighty." Halley was echoed by Clarke. Chambers also cited William James 'sGravesande, a Dutch scientist and mathematician and an early proponent of the Newtonian system, as he repeated this sentiment: since "the Cause of Gravity is utterly unknown," "we are to look on it no otherwise than as a Law of Nature, originally and immediately impressed by the Creator, without any Dependance on any Second Law or Cause at all."[34] When material explanations of gravity failed—and they always failed these early Newtonians—they were happy to have "Recourse to the agency of the Almighty" to account for the mysterious nonmechanical and extra-material agent lurking inside of the clock. Not being able to prove the cause of gravity is not the same as not knowing it. Newton taught his contemporaries that God is at work.[35]

Often such arguments were made popularly, with more exuberance than scientific sophistication. However, the figure could be offered in the most serious science and philosophy, as it was by Clarke in his extended and wide-ranging correspondence with Leibniz. Clarke's Newtonian credentials were impeccable: he had provided the then-standard Newtonian annotations for the Cartesian textbook used at Cambridge (1697), translated Newton's *Opticks* into Latin (1706), and drawn on Newton's science in two well-received Boyle Lectures (1704–5) as well as in a famous controversy with the free-thinker Anthony Collins (1706–8).[36] He was among the most influential early Newtonian spokesmen, and his correspondence with Leibniz became the most famous philosophical debate of the early eighteenth century.[37] In the debate, Clarke offered a philosophically acute exploration of God's activity inside his clock, one that helpfully demonstrates the motivations and worries of the early Newtonians.

Clarke's response to Leibniz's clockwork critique was twofold. First, as we have seen, he rejected Leibniz's clockwork-without-assistance model, and he reinforced this point throughout the debate by insisting that the world is not "*mere absolute Mechanism*" (5:93–95). Clarke, however, continued to outline his own alternative paradigm.[38] He recognized God's maintenance-man intervention into the cosmic system, and then—like other early Newtonians—he shifted the focus to a more positive paradigm: God provides the clock's motive power. Clarke made this point by differentiating between the work of the human and the divine clockmakers. The human clockmaker's skill "consists only in composing, adjusting, or putting together certain Movements, the *Principles* of whose Motion are altogether independent upon the Artificer: Such as are *Weights* and *Springs*, and the like; whose forces are not *made*, but only *adjusted* by the Workman." Yet, the divine clockmaker's role is different, for "*He* not only composes or puts Things together, but is himself the Author and continual Preserver of their *Original Forces* or *moving Powers*" (1:4). For Clarke, God not only builds the machine. He also provides the "*moving Powers*" that keep it running; he is the "Author" of the "*Forces*" that pull the weight downward. Clarke thus gestured to the usual Newtonian suggestion that God causes the "gravity of the weight that moves the machine." In his other writings, Clarke evinced real excitement about this version of the clock figure. He rehearsed the standard Newtonian arguments, moving swiftly from gravity's nonmechanical nature to its divine source. And in his Boyle Lectures, he explicitly asserted that gravity—which is caused by an "Immaterial Power" that is "*perpetually and actually exerting itself every Moment in every part of the World*"—provides "a very noble Idea of *Providence.*"[39] In his debate with Leibniz, Clarke seemed to want to use gravity similarly, as a concrete instance of God's power exercised constantly inside his system. Clarke even argued that God's role as "Author"-of-forces ensures "that *nothing* is done without his *continual Government* and *Inspection*" (1:4). Clarke obliquely suggested that the cause of gravity, which is "*invisible* and *intangible,* and of a different nature from mechanism,*"* is divine (4:45).

Leibniz fiercely attacked this idea: "invisible, intangible, not Mechanical. He might as well have added, inexplicable, unintelligible, precarious, groundless" (5:120). Leibniz then offered the critique we have already seen Newton address, that gravity is a "Chimera," perpetual miracle, or deus ex machina. Clarke's reaction to this attack is intriguing. He backed down but did so in a way that shows how strategically Newton's "*non fingo*" could be used. Clarke responded to Leibniz by asserting that Newtonian gravitation is "a *Phenomenon,* or *actual Matter of Fact,* found by *Experience.*" This fact "is all that is meant" when he speaks of gravity, and he knows nothing of the cause, "be it *mechanical,* or *not mechanical*" (5:118–23). Clarke rehearses a causal agnosticism coupled with a strong assertion of the experimental validity of the facts, and several scholars have taken him at his word here.[40] Yet, this agnosticism is unexpected, to say the least, from a man who elsewhere celebrates gravity as solid proof that God and angels are among us. With something less than good faith, Clarke ventriloquizes a version of Newton's causal agnosticism that lets him have his cake and eat it too. It provided strategic cover from Leibniz's criticisms even as it worked as it did for Newton: protecting the possibility that something more than mechanism could work in the clockwork world. There might well be something non-mechanical, even divine, lurking inside the machine.

Yet, Clarke also offered a more positive defense of his version of God acting inside the clock. Throughout the correspondence, Leibniz affirmed the doctrine of the conservation of force. For him, God's clock is perfectly orchestrated so that "the *same* Force and Vigour remains always in the World." One clock part communicates its motion to another part, and the clock keeps ticking away in "perpetual Motion," without any need for the clockmaker to wind it back up (1:4). From Clarke's point of view, however, this was a worrying feature of Leibniz's "*mere absolute Mechanism.*" With the conservation of force, Leibniz denied the possibility that anything ever influences the clock once it is set a-ticking; any intervention into the preordained mechanical order would change the amount of force in the system, which he denies is possible. Clarke's earlier argument clearly applies here: a world in which no force is ever created or lost, in which motion passes from one part of the clock to another in a perfectly preordained pattern without anything external ever intervening, is an atheist world (a "great *Machine,* going on without *the Interposition of God*"). Against this, Clarke wanted to affirm gravity as a concrete instance of God's "*Interposition,*" but in the face of Leibniz's attack he shifted focus to a more fundamental tenet of Newtonian physics: there must be forces lost or gained in the world. Drawing on Newton's argument that the laws of mechanism are merely "passive Principles," Clarke maintained that matter is "*lifeless, void of Motivity, unactive* and *inert,*" its force constantly diminishing. It is, therefore, entirely dependent "upon some *other Cause* for *new Motion*" (5:100–102). For Clarke, Newton's physics *require* that some extra-mechanical force must sometimes intervene into the world.

As Clarke continued to insist on such a nonmechanical force, he helps us understand all that was at stake for the early Newtonians in keeping God's action inside of the clock. He argued: if "everything be not *mere absolute Mechanism,*" "if *God* or *Man,* or *Any Living* or *Active Power,* ever *influences* any thing in the *material World,*" "there must be a continual *Increase* and *Decrease* of the *whole Quantity of Motion in the Universe*" (5:93–95). If forces are never lost or gained, Clarke argued, nothing can ever affect the clock once it starts ticking. God cannot perform miracles or use his special providence, and humans cannot exert their free will—they are mere cogs in the machine. Clarke, by contrast, contended that the Newtonian physics require some kind of extra-mechanical force. He privileged this extra-mechanical force, for he saw that it rendered a complete reduction of phenomenon to mere mechanism impossible. In upsetting Leibniz's thoroughgoing mechanism, this force quite literally saved a space for the possibility that "*God* or *Man*" could "*influence*" the world.

Throughout the correspondence, Clarke drew on this logic. There is something more than matter and motion at work inside of God's mechanism (forces are lost and added, after all), and this something more saves a space for miracles. Clarke accused Leibniz's understanding of miracles of excluding God from "the *Governing and Ordering* of the *Natural* World" and placing an unacceptable limit on the ways God can exercise his power (2:12). Instead, Clarke affirmed God's ability to perform miracles, to come adjust the machine, any time, all the time. Similarly, this something more saves a space for human agency. Clarke—whose grasp of Leibniz's system, with its monads and *praestabilita harmonia,* was admittedly imperfect—also countered Leibniz's insistence on the purely mechanical motion of human bodies in the material clockwork world with another affirmation that forces are constantly lost and added and thus that humans can have free will.⁴¹ Finally, this something more ensures that God designed the world in whatever way he chose. While Leibniz affirmed the intellectualist belief that the world must be the best of all possible worlds, Clarke took the voluntarist position that the world was made according to God's contingent and utterly free will. Drawing on a longstanding association between a voluntarist theology and an affirmation of human liberty, Clarke made human free will a kind of analogue for God's free will.⁴² The force that God adds to the universe by causing gravity occupies the same saved space as the force that he adds when he performs miracles and that humans add when they move their bodies. And this saved space ensures that even the in-the-beginning design of the world was utterly dependent on God's free will. The forces at work in the clock preserve the possibility that "*God* or *Man*" can "*influence*" the world.

Clarke, then, repeatedly resisted Leibniz's reduction of phenomena—the world, humans, God himself—to "mere" matter and motion, and his critique was motivated by his own, competing conception of the clock figure: a clockwork world made, driven, and constantly "assisted" by God. The revised Newtonian clock figure allowed Clarke to affirm constant divine action in the world without letting go of the idea of the world as a clock. Throughout the correspondence, Clarke's language balances these two extremes: God not only made "the Frame of things" ("Frame" is the technical word for "the Out-work of a Clock or Watch") but can at any moment effect whatever "*Alterations* he is pleased to make in the Frame" and is responsible at every moment for the "*continuation* of it" (3:16).⁴³ For Clarke, God is clockmaker *and* clock owner. He is crucial, constantly, to keep the machine running.

Leibniz died before the correspondence could properly conclude, but the Newtonians, reveling in their bias, were sure that their clock figure won. Newton joked that Leibniz died of heartbreak about losing the philosophical battle. Even Princess Caroline, who initially sided with Leibniz, finally came over to the Newtonian side; she realized the virtues of a worldview in which (as she had put it by way of accusation years earlier) God continually "reanimate[s] his machine."⁴⁴ More broadly though, the figure of God acting inside his clock achieved real popularity in England between Bentley's 1692 sermons and the ascendency of aetherial explanations in the 1730s. A gravity-causing God crucial to the clockwork world was honored, for example, by John Keill in 1700, Samuel Colliber in 1718, and Stephen Hales in 1727. In this period, these suggestions were made by the English and the Dutch, by Americans and Scots. They could be found in religious treatises, natural histories, medical textbooks, and popular science classes. Benjamin Worster taught the students in his London Academy that the cause of gravity "is altogether immechanical and independent from Matter, and can only proceed from the first Cause and Author of all things." In a piece of literary criticism, William Warburton took occasion to announce that the new science of gravity "considered that property in matter, as something extrinsical to it, and impressed immediately by God upon it. Which fairly and modestly coming up to the first Cause, was pushing natural enquiries as far as they should go." And a later Boyle lecturer, citing Clarke, preached that God constructed the clockwork world, "still continu[es] constantly to repair the weakning by Time of the first Impression of Motion," and "still watches over his Workmanship, repairs any Failures in it, and continues it in its State as long as He thinks fit."[45] In fact, given the surprising number of clock metaphors featuring God's action in the earliest popularizations of Newtonian thought, I suspect that it was among the first ideas that the average English person understood and associated with Newtonian science.

Of course, Newton's "*non fingo*" deliberately left room for interpretation, and the gravity apologetic could take slightly different forms in these different texts. The most significant divergence involved the precise role of second causes. Many Newtonians imagined God's immediate action in the world, but Clarke conceded that God might appoint angels to do the acting. Bentley seemed to vacillate between focusing on God's immediate action ("Gravity do immediately flow from a Divine Power and Energy") and recognizing a "secondary Agent" used by the "first and real Cause" (4:5–6).[46] Despite these differences, however, all the Newtonians decried John Toland's brand of out-and-out atheism. In 1704 Toland perversely twisted Newton's findings into an assertion that gravity is essential to matter (and that God does not interpose in his world and might not actually exist). The early Newtonians all assumed that Newton's discoveries about "the cause of the gravity of the weight which moves the machine" established a God who *continuously* acts in the world. For example, although Bentley sometimes seemed to gesture to a kind of superadded "secondary Agent," he left no room for anyone to doubt his understanding of the first cause's continual activity: gravity proves "That the Frame of the present World could neither be made nor preserved without the *Power* of God" and "that an immaterial living Mind doth inform and actuate the dead Matter, and support the Frame of the World" (8:3, 7:30). God did create, but he does continue to concern himself with his creation. He "preserves," right now, "informs," "actuates," and "supports."

Clearly, for the early Newtonians, God was inside his clock. The Newtonian science of gravity provided concrete, positive proof that God not only created but continually re-creates the material world—he recreates inside of it. He moves "the weight which moves the machine."

Of Gravity, Morality, Politics

In the last chapter, I argue that seventeenth- and eighteenth-century empiricists thought analogically—applying scientific findings to other realms, physical, religious, moral, and political. Early Newtonians confirm this insight, as they were deeply interested in the analogues of gravity's force. Not only does gravity work on earth as it does in heaven (affecting both falling rocks and orbiting planets). Clarke suggested that God's gravity-action occupies the same saved space as—is fundamentally *like*—his providence and his power to work miracles. Clarke also explained that the way gravity involves God at work in the mechanical world is a close analogue to the way human souls work in and on our mechanical bodies, and this was especially influential in the period.[47] Joseph Addison wrote a *Spectator* essay adding animal instinct as an analogue: it functions like "the Principle of Gravitation in Bodies" (and "is not to be explained . . . from any Laws of Mechanism, but, according to the best Notions of the greatest Philosophers, is an immediate Impression from the first Mover, and the Divine Energy acting in the Creatures").[48] Early Newtonians were clearly interested in analogizing gravity, and they did not stop at the physical. They eagerly speculated on what the Newtonian model of God acting in the clockwork world meant for human institutions. Clarke, for example, argued that Leibniz's metaphysics demean both God and king.

Some intriguing scholarship on popular Newtonianism has focused on such broader possibilities. Jacob conclusively shows that the Newtonian system of the world had political applications, and other scholars explore the eighteenth-century desire for a "Newton of the moral world."[49] This work, however, usually focuses on aspects of Newtonianism other than its model of God inside the clock: Jacob is interested in the design argument, and scholars of Newtonian moral philosophy often treat "Newton" as an emblem for a certain kind of method or systemization. This section supplements such research by focusing on how contemporaries applied the reworked Newtonian clock figure. I feature three exemplary contemporary explorations of this model's human implications: George Berkeley, George Cheyne, and J. T. Desaguliers each offered a thoughtful treatment of the moral, religious, or political lessons the clockwork world could teach.[50] These writings demonstrate that mechanical figures for the world did not necessarily rationalize or disenchant. In the hands of early Newtonians, the clock figure was comfortably consistent with an understanding of the world as providentially coded with moral and social meanings. These Newtonian explorations attest to the robust presence of the meditative empiricism in the eighteenth century.

In order to understand the implications of Newtonian science, some contemporaries engaged thoughtfully with the genre of occasional meditation. The form offered both an ontological warrant and a formal structure for pursuing such implications. The idealist philosopher and Irish clergyman George Berkeley wrote one such Newtonian occasional meditation. In 1713, not yet thirty years old, Berkeley was in London, moving among a fashionable circle of writers and thinkers that included Jonathan Swift, Alexander Pope, Joseph Addison, and Richard Steele; through Addison, Berkeley also met Newtonian advocates like Clarke and Princess Caroline. Around the same time, Berkeley became a contributor to the *Guardian,* and, in August, just after Newton published the second edition of his *Principia,* Berkeley contributed to the periodical a thoughtful consideration of the moral implications of Newton's science of gravity.[51]

Berkeley's essay begins with an explicit statement of the ontology from which he precedes. While in his philosophical writings Berkeley famously argued against the independent existence of matter, here, in a popularizing mode, he remains quiet about this aspect of his thought. Instead, he simply posits that "a certain Correspondence," "a Similitude of Operation," or "Unity of Design" structures the entire universe—"the Moral and Intellectual, as well as the Natural and Corporeal."[52] He insists that "Divine Power" has "ordained" "Laws" that guide both the material and moral realms and that there is often an analogical correspondence between the laws of the different realms (152). This is precisely the kind of assumption that enabled the opening-outward procedures of the meditative empiricism.

Berkeley continues in the form of occasional meditation. He offers a highly detailed, scientifically acute description of gravity as a natural phenomenon. Berkeley's treatment of gravity engages the tradition of God inside the clock. Universal gravitation exists: "there is a mutual Attraction between the most distant Parts at least of this Solar System" (152). It is a "secret, uniform, and never-ceasing Principle," and he later identifies its cause with God's "immediate Operation" (152, 154). After a detailed treatment of Newtonian gravity, Berkeley then draws the kind of moral "Parallel" characteristic of occasional meditation. He invites the reader to "carry" his or her "Thoughts from the Corporeal to the Moral World," where "a like Principle of Attraction" is evident. There is a kind of social "Attraction": humans "are drawn together into Communities, Clubs, Families, Friendships, and all the various Species of Society" (152).[53]

Berkeley develops this analogy with five particulars. (1) Both gravity and human benevolent instincts should be explained by God's "immediate" action (154). More specifically, though, the two work in similar ways. (2) As gravity exerts the most powerful force when bodies are closer together, "so it is likewise" for humans—social bonds operate most powerfully to draw us to our "Family," "Friends and Neighbors" (152–53). (3) Despite the special pull of close bodies, however, in the solar system all bodies, no matter how distant, attract one another. When nearer bodies are removed, more distant bodies will start to exert stronger pressure. Again, this "holds with Regard to the Human Soul": when in Rome, a British person feels close to another Briton, though a stranger, and, if humans ever visited Mars, an Englishman would bond with a Chinese man (because both are human in an inhuman place) (153). (4) Further, planetary bodies are kept in orbit and prevented from rushing together into a central giant "Mass" through the strong centripetal force of gravity, by the planets' tendency to continue still in their "rectilinear Motions"; so too the attractive principle in humans is countered by the "private Passions and Motions of the Soul" (153). (5) And, finally, gravitation can explain "innumerable" celestial and terrestrial "Effects" in bodies (154). Like many early Newtonians, Berkeley uses the fundamental principle of gravity to account for several analogically functioning phenomena: gravity explains why planets stay in their orbits about the sun, why moons continue to circle their planets, and why the globes themselves cohere into a spherical shape. Similarly, Berkeley says, "the corresponding Social Appetite in Humane Souls" explains many human feelings: sympathy, parental love, international awareness, concern for the future (154). In all these carefully detailed ways, "the Analogy of Nature" holds (155).

In true occasional meditation form, then, Berkeley concludes his short essay by distilling the moral point, the way this analogical insight might direct human practice. Because attractive "social Inclinations" are a basic and ordained force in the moral world, "it is the Duty and Interest of each Individual to cherish and improve them to the Benefit of Mankind" (154). In other words, the way planets are pulled toward the center of the solar system suggests that humans ought to live their lives in a "Spirit of Love, Charity, and Beneficence to all Mankind" (155). For Berkeley, the divine force at the center of the Newtonian universe taught something fundamental about human society.

George Cheyne's *Philosophical Principles of Religion Natural and Revealed* (1715) proceeds from a similar analogical insight as Berkeley's text but goes much further. We have already seen that Cheyne delighted in the Newtonian figure of God's action inside the clock. In his book, Cheyne exuberantly and repeatedly affirmed this model, while corralling all the usual proofs to demonstrate that the "Universal Law of Gravitation . . . cannot be *Mechanically* explain'd" (1:37). Even while praising the clockwork world, however, Cheyne also insisted that it is providentially designed to be meaningful—it is loaded with moral and spiritual lessons for humans. He explains, over and over again, that natural and moral systems are powerfully linked via their shared creator: "There is in all the Works of Nature, a *Symmetry,* and *Harmony,* running on in a perpetual *Analogy*" (2:36). Further, this "*Analogy of Things*" means that "The *material* world is an Image of the *spiritual* World" and the "*Visible* and the *Created,* are *Images* of the *Invisible* and of the *Increated*" (2:116). God continually intervenes in his machine, and the machine itself was designed to constantly teach about God.

Cheyne brings the two points together. In one powerfully recurring line of argument, his book offers a thoughtful attempt to understand what Newtonian gravity means for human behavior. He is quite explicit about the basic analogy: as gravitation constantly pulls material bodies toward the sun (the center of the system), so there is a "*Principle* of *Action* in intelligent Beings, *Analogous* to that of *Attraction* in the material *System,*" that constantly pulls human souls toward God (2:85). He calls this attractive force "the *Principle of Reunion.*" It is a force at work in human hearts that prompts us instinctively to "an *infinite Love* of the *supreme Being:* And . . . of all his *Images* in proportion to their *resemblance* of Him" (2:93). The parallel is thoroughgoing. For example, gravitation and reunion are "the *Active, Cardinal,* and *Energetick Principles,* of either *Systems* respectively" (2:78); and both, if allowed to work without obstruction, produce the beauty God intended: "this *Principle of Reunion,* if attended to, duly Cultivated, and Expanded, wou'd as certainly bring about, the Temporal and Eternal Happiness of all intelligent Beings, in the *spiritual World;* as that of *Attraction,* brings about the Comely and *Harmonious* Motions, of the *great Bodies* of the *material World*" (2:90). The moral lesson for humans, then, is that we should "duly Cultivate" this natural instinct. We must block all the forces that pull us in different directions—toward carnal desires, for example—and dedicate our lives to obeying the dictates of God in our hearts, to worshiping God and showing kindness to his creatures. This is closely related to Berkeley's findings (especially insofar as loving God's creatures requires "*Benevolence*") but played out in a slightly more mystical, God-oriented key (2:74).

Yet, Cheyne also goes much further than Berkeley. He spins out this insight into an entire moral system. He explains that he can "derive[ ]" "the true and genuine Nature, of *Moral Good* and *Evil*, and of all the Moral Virtues, and *Social* Duties of Life" from this spiritual force: "Whatever retards, or opposes this *Reunion*, in intelligent Beings, is to them *Moral Evil*; whatever promotes, or advances this *Reunion*, is to them *Moral Good*" (2:91). The system is startlingly simple. Carnal desires are bad, and actions like worshipping God and showing charity to his creatures are good. Cheyne dwells the longer on this system, because it allows him to get around a common bind for moralists at the time. His system is emphatically "not founded on *Interest*, or the *views* of *Rewards* and *Punishments*," and "neither" is there "any room for *Contracts*, or *Pactions*, between the *supreme Being*, and his intelligent Creatures" (2:94, 96). Moral truths are, then, neither human constructs nor the products of an impossible, enthusiastic communication with God. I will return in the fourth chapter to some of these pressing contemporary problems about the grounds of morality, but here I simply note that Cheyne is clearly pleased at having developed a system rooted in creation—in an instinct that "flows naturally from" a desire "*implanted*" in us by God—but also requiring continuous human activity to maintain (2:94). For Cheyne, the Newtonian model of the clockwork world contains moral and religious imperatives. Far from making God into a distant first cause, this clock figure features a God who is constantly at work in both the material world and human hearts.

One final example of the creative ways that the Newtonian science of gravity was deployed in the period will suffice. J. T. Desaguliers's poem *The Newtonian System of the World, The Best Model of Government* (1728) brought the reworked Newtonian clock figure to an explicitly political question. Desaguliers—an influential Newtonian known for his coffee-shop lectures, as well as his roles as Newton's assistant and the Royal Society's curator of experiments—had more scientific expertise than many popularizers.[54] In his poem's prefatory materials, he interestingly confirms that Newtonianism had lively political implications by assuming that his natural knowledge qualified him to speak on political issues. He says forthrightly: "among my Philosophical Enquiries, I have consider'd *Government* as a *Phaenomenon*, and look'd upon that Form of it to be the most perfect, which did most nearly resemble the Natural Government of our *System*, according to the Laws settled by the *All-wise* and *Almighty Architect* of the Universe."⁵⁵ His "Philosophical Enquiries" are scientific—he elsewhere describes his Newtonian lecture series as *A Course of Experimental Philosophy*. By imagining "Government as a Phaenomenon," as a thing or occurrence, to be empirically "enquired" about, studied, and explained, Desaguliers implicitly posits a continuum between the natural and the moral systems. He even explicitly links the two, asserting that the best human governments are those that "most nearly resemble" God's government of the "Universe." There is a kind of imperative to this way of imagining the relationship between realms. Humans ought to "Model" their governments after God's, to study God's "Universe"—its "Laws" and forms—in order to approximate it in their institutions. Scientific knowledge leads to political truth.

Desaguliers structures his poem accordingly: a detailed examination of the Newtonian universe opens into explanation of the political system it suggests. In his depiction of the Newtonian system, he insists on the centrality and active force of gravity: "By *Newton's* help, 'tis evidently seen / Attraction governs all the World's Machine" (153–54). In Desaguliers's hands, God's immediate action as the cause of gravity is more muted than for many popularizers, but the possibility lingers—he explains in footnotes that gravity cannot be mechanical in the Cartesian sense and must be "continually acting" (128n).⁵⁶ After carefully explaining the structure of celestial system, Desaguliers then happily "draw[s] the Parallel" (156). The Newtonian system of the universe turns out to be a nice model for the British system of limited monarchy. As the sun's gravity pulls planets toward the center, so "MAJESTY diffusive Rays imparts, / And kindles Zeal in all the *British* Hearts" (181–82). And as gravitation exerts centripetal force while allowing planets to continue in their rectilinear motions—the "Pow'r, coerc'd by Laws, still leaves them free, / Directs but not Destroys, their Liberty"—so the king exerts his power on his subjects even as "all the Powers of Throne" continue "to maintain our *Liberty*" (130–31, 183–84). The English limited monarchy of George II, Desaguliers suggests, contains all the features that empirical study of the celestial world suggests it ought: subjects experience a powerful and constant draw toward their king, while remaining free to continue in their individual courses, and laws structure and control the whole. For Desaguliers the Newtonian system does not have as its political analogue a system notable for its preordained law-and-order stability. Rather, it depends on constant spiritual movement: "diffusive Rays," zealous hearts, continuous human "Liberty" to act as one pleases. The Newtonian clock allows for divine agency in the universe and suggests a political system turning on the constant action of both king and subjects.

Of course, these examples were not the only possible applications of Newtonianism. In other hands, Newton's science could endorse radically different political systems, for example. Yet, these writings compellingly demonstrate both the cultural reach of the reworked Newtonian clock figure and a widespread contemporary willingness to engage the meditative empiricism's habits of mind. Contemporaries thought about science, as well as about what science meant for religion, morality, and politics. They brought the Newtonian notion of the world as a clock with a divine power source to their understanding of other systems—physical, moral, and political. Because God acts in his clock, humans should show kindness to others, commune with God in their hearts, and praise the benevolent sovereignty of George II.

How to See God in Action

The meditative empiricism, we remember, accessed the "Truths" encoded in nature but also "knowledg" of their "Author." Popular Newtonianism embraced both of these possibilities. Not only did it help contemporaries glimpse particular moral and political lessons in the clockwork world; it helped them see, in real time, God still at work in the clock world he had built. If—as generations of scholars have assumed—the wholly mechanized clock is the exemplary object of attention for a mechanical philosophy that analyzes, experiments upon, and mimics the regular workings of the material world, the reworked Newtonian clock is exemplary for a way of discovering divine immanence or efficacy in the orderly material world.[57] In recovering this possibility, this section starts with William Whiston, who designed an innovative map to help his popular audiences visualize God's activity in the solar system. I then treat two texts that go further in cultivating modes of vision adequate to this kind of clockwork world: Cotton Mather and Andrew Baxter each invited their readers to see—even to experience physically—material order and divine activity simultaneously. Finally, I turn to the poetic panegyrics written upon Newton's death in 1727. These eulogies reveal that among the most important and exciting of Newton's insights for contemporaries was a way of seeing God in things, a way to discover and celebrate constant divine action in the world.

William Whiston was among the reworked clock figure's most exuberant and influential proponents, as well as a fascinating character in his own right. He was a Boyle Lecturer, popular coffeehouse scientist, errant prophet, and altogether eccentric. He was Newton's chosen successor and, then, annoying antagonist. (Newton arranged for Whiston to succeed him in his Cambridge chair in mathematics, but—displeased with Whiston's public avowals of a heretical Christianity and subsequent removal from the Cambridge chair—Newton then successfully plotted to exclude him from the Royal Society.)[58] In Cambridge classes, coffeehouse lectures, and printed primers, Whiston rendered Newtonian arguments in scrupulous detail. He invited contemporaries to glimpse God's constant agency everywhere in the clockwork world.

For example, Whiston's *Astronomical Principles of Religion, Natural and Reveal'd* (1717) stresses the reworked clock figure. Whiston recasts the Newtonian argument about the physics of force into clockwork terms. It is nonsense, he argues, to believe that a "Clock or Watch will of it self go forever": there is "such wearing of the Wheels and Pivots, such decay of the Spring and such Rust and Foulness over the whole (besides the Necessity of its being wound up every Revolution) as must, by Calculation, put a Stop to its Motion in twenty Years time."[59] That the world still smoothly runs demonstrates, for him, that the God who ordered things in the beginning continues to adjust the order and add forces. Whiston supplements this argument with the Newtonian understanding of gravity. He offers all the usual arguments to support his claim that gravity "is entirely Immechanical, or beyond the Power of all material Agents whatsoever" (27). Gravity "is not strictly speaking, any Power belonging to Body or Matter at all" (46). Rather, "God, the Creator of the World, does also exercise a continual *Providence* over it, and does interpose his general, immechanical, immediate *Power*, which we call the *Power of Gravity*" (111). For Whiston, Newton discovered the "Secrets of that Contrivance, with that universal Power of Gravitation, by which the whole Machine has all along been upheld" (254).

In *Astronomical Principles,* Whiston uses this figure to help readers imagine God's activity in the world around them. For example, he links Newtonian gravity to traditional ideas of God's omnipresence. He draws on his understanding of gravity as an exertion of God's "immechanical" and "immediate Power" to suggest that universal gravitation provides a lovely instance of God's power "continually exerted throughout the whole Universe." It is a simple scientific fact that no agent "Acts *where* it is not." Therefore, Whiston explains, everywhere gravity happens, there God is. He is "every where substantially and really *present* through the whole" (120). The gravity that we can see "throughout the whole Universe" provides Whiston with a constant reminder of God's presence all around us.

Whiston brings a similar desire to help his audience cultivate an understanding (even the sight) of God's constant activity in the world around them to his other popularizing attempts. He actually designed a visual aid to encourage such an understanding. Developed in collaboration with mapmaker and engraver John Senex, Whiston's *Scheme for the Solar System* (1712) (fig. 2) is a large, detailed map of the planets and comets. As Stephen Snobelen has suggested, the *Scheme* "epitomizes Whiston's genius as a popularizer": Whiston presented it to the Royal Society, where it was hung prominently on the wall, and he apparently used the broadsheet engraving to dramatic effect during lectures at places like Button's coffeehouse. Joseph Addison, for example, praised the map, and Alexander Pope wrote about how Whiston's popular astronomy captured the imagination.[60] The drama of the *Scheme* is the way it invites viewers to visualize both the intelligent design of the solar system and God's constant role in keeping it going.

At first glance, the *Scheme* demonstrates the majestic order of the universe. It shows the relative size of the planets, their paths around the sun, the way the comets intersect planetary orbits in strange paths, and so on. In the text surrounding the outside of the large circular illustration of the system, Whiston emphasizes the providence of in-the-beginning order: the world is God's great clockwork. Whiston's accessible explanations of this order conclude (at the bottom right of the page) with a design argument: "O Lord, how manyfold are thy Works! In Wisdom hast thou made them all!"

While emphasizing God's intelligent clock-making around the edges of the system, however, Whiston has a rather different focus in the text circles that float inside of the solar system illustration. He there privileges the way God continues to work *inside* the clock. Whiston's map thus recognizes the conventional clockwork of the design argument but quite literally centers on the reworked clock figure. For example, one ball of text in the center of the map offers a version of the Newtonian argument for God as maintenance man. Whiston notes "a few irregularities" in God's otherwise excellent "Order"—"irregularities" caused by the gravitation of planets and comets. Whiston cites Newton as he argues that these "irregularities" "probably may" intensify "till at length this frame of Nature comes to want a mending hand." God will step in as clock repairer to maintain the beautiful order clearly displayed on the map.

Whiston further privileges the more positive paradigm for God's activity inside his clockwork. Three of the other balls of text pictured floating be-

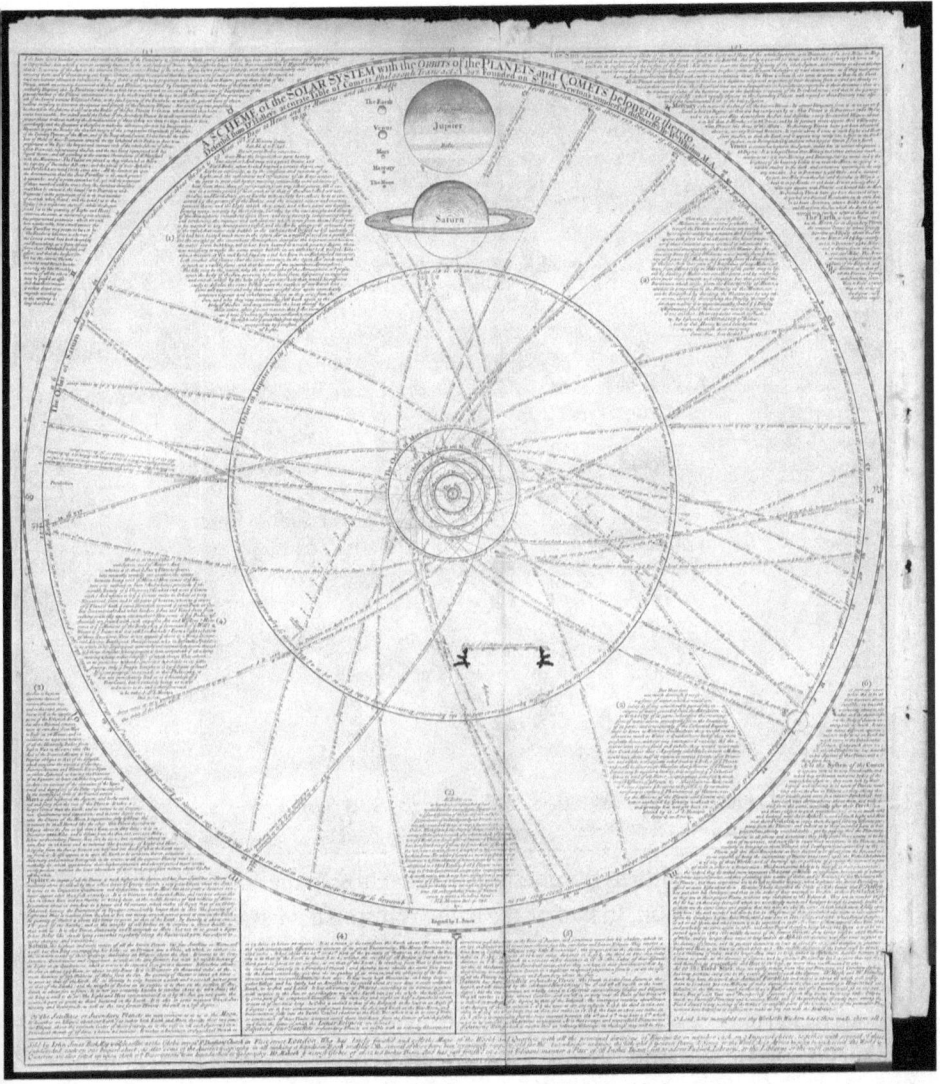

FIGURE 2. *A Scheme of the Solar System with Orbits of the Planets and Comets Belonging Thereto*, William Whiston (London, 1712). (Reproduced by permission of the Albert and Shirley Small Special Collections Library, University of Virginia)

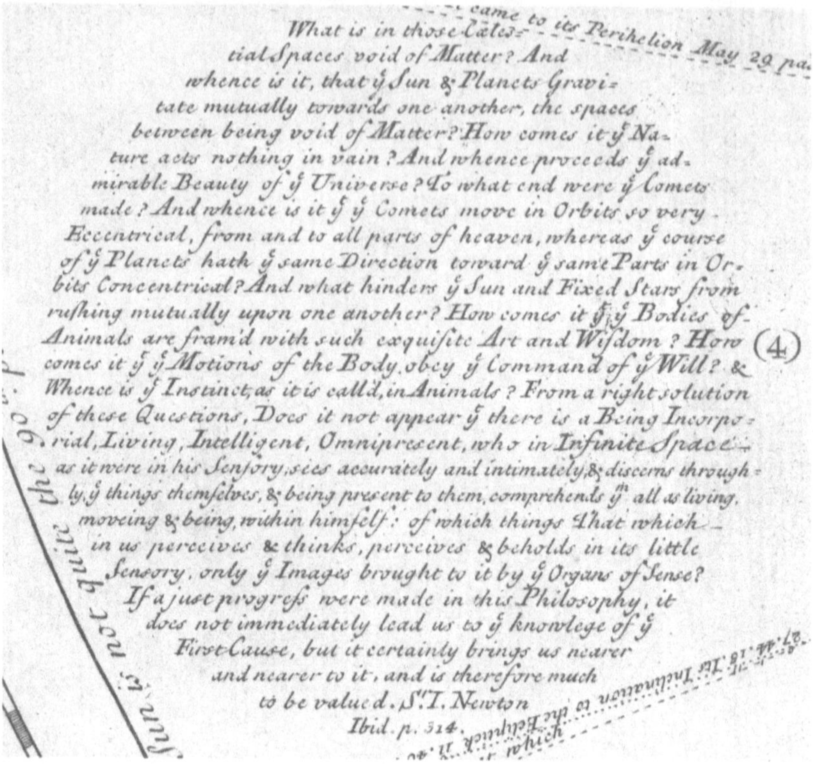

> What is in those Caelestial Spaces void of Matter? And whence is it, that ye Sun & Planets Gravitate mutually towards one another, the spaces between being void of Matter? How comes it ye Nature acts nothing in vain? And whence proceeds ye admirable Beauty of ye Universe? To what end were ye Comets made? And whence is it ye Comets move in Orbits so very Eccentrical, from and to all parts of heaven, whereas ye course of ye Planets hath ye same Direction toward ye same Parts in Orbits Concentrical? And what hinders ye Sun and Fixed Stars from rushing mutually upon one another? How comes it ye Bodies of Animals are fram'd with such exquisite Art and Wisdom? How comes it ye Motions of the Body, obey ye Command of ye Will? & Whence is ye Instinct, as it is call'd, in Animals? From a right solution of these Questions, Does it not appear ye there is a Being Incorporial, Living, Intelligent, Omnipresent, who in Infinite Space, as it were in his Sensory, sees accurately and intimately, & discerns throughly, ye things themselves, & being present to them, comprehends ym all as living, moving & being, within himself: of which things That which in us perceives & thinks, perceives & beholds in its little Sensory, only ye Images brought to it by ye Organs of Sense? If a just progress were made in this Philosophy, it does not immediately lead us to ye knowlege of ye First Cause, but it certainly brings us nearer and nearer to it, and is therefore much to be valued. S'. I. Newton
> Ibid. p. 314.

FIGURE 3. Detail of William Whiston's *Scheme of the Solar System*

tween the planets address the question of what fills up the space that they occupy in the illustration. In two of the balls, Whiston develops the Newtonian argument against any kind of aether and cites Newton to suggest that the solar system's vast spaces are empty, "void of all Matter." The third ball of text (see fig. 3) clinches the argument by explaining what, exactly, viewers should imagine in these empty spaces: God. Whiston begins to offer this solution with a series of questions: "What is in those Caelestial Spaces void of Matter? And whence is it, that ye Sun & Planets Gravitate mutually towards one another, the spaces between being void of Matter? How comes it yt Nature acts nothing in vain? And whence proceeds yt admirable Beauty of ye Universe?" Beginning with two questions that many natural philosophers had asked seriously *as* questions, Whiston then shifts to related questions whose answers philosophers were more comfortable answering with an appeal to God. With this strategic series of questions, Whiston slowly reveals his belief in a divine answer for *all* these questions. As if to underscore gravity's key role in this argument, Whiston mentions it once more in the questions that follow: "And what hinders ye Sun and Fixed Stars from rushing mutually upon one another?" He concludes this questioning with another speculation about the source of the "exquisite Art and Wisdom" evident in the creation, before offering the solution that is obviously implicit in the reasoning that drives the above questions: "From a right solution of these Questions, Does it not appear yt there is a Being Incorporial, Living, Intelligent, Omnipresent, who in Infinite Space—as it were, in his Sensory, sees accurately and intimately, & discerns throughly, ye things themselves, & being present to them, comprehends ym all as living, moveing & being, within himself."

While continuing in the interrogative mode ("Does it not appear"), Whiston is pretty unequivocal in his belief that the "right solution" to all his questions is God. God is "Living, Intelligent," and "Omnipresent" throughout the entire system. He is the source of "yt admirable Beauty of ye Universe," the reason that "Nature acts nothing in vain," and even the cause of the "Sun & Planets Gravitat[ing] mutually towards one another" without "rushing" into one big clump. With his last phrase—God "comprehends" all things "as living, moveing, & being within himself"—Whiston explicitly invites the audience to fill up "the spaces between" the planets that are "void of Matter" with God, God's action. The balls of text literally float in the area of "Infinite Space" that God fills up.

Whiston confirms his argument with Scripture: his insistence that God "comprehends" "all as living, moveing & being within himself" is a paraphrase of Acts 17:28, "For in him we live, and move, and have our being." Nearly every Newtonian text I have discussed to this point cites this scriptural passage, which Newtonian gravity was understood to have vindicated. Clarke cites Acts against Leibniz, Bentley against atheists, and Newton himself cites it in his *General Scholium* (1713).[61] Over and over again, early Newtonians affirmed that what the Apostle taught, the *Principia* confirmed. Whiston's map helps viewers to see that God is "*in*" everything. He fills up the frame and spins the wheels of this clock world.

Whiston's *Scheme* emblematizes the logic of much early Newtonianism. It features a real scientific emphasis on order, accuracy, and measurement. Whiston very precisely delineates the solar system, offering loads of particular facts: Venus, for example, is "7,906 miles" in "Diameter," located "59,000,000 Miles from the Sun." Yet, such scientific scrutiny of the solar system actually opens up possibilities for worship. As Whiston puts it in one ball of text, citing Newton again, natural philosophy might "not immediately lead us to" divine truth, "but it certainly brings us nearer and nearer to it, and is therefore much to be valued." The *Scheme* invites viewers to enact this logic. It suggests that it is God who keeps the planets and moon circling in their orbits as they ought and that it is God who fills up the 59,000,000 miles of "Celestial Spaces" between Venus and the sun. The viewer is invited, as he or she learns about the precise patterns of planetary orbit, to imagine God's hand moving the bodies along, to visualize God at work inside of his machine.

Other Newtonians explored the implications that Newtonian gravity had for ways of seeing God at work in the world around them. For example, Cotton Mather's *Christian Philosopher* (1720) developed a Newtonian understanding of God and gravity in the clock world as he encouraged readers to experience God visually, even physically. Though Mather was an American (influential in bringing British New Science to American culture), he was also a Fellow of the Royal Society of London. His book is modeled after the work of British physico-theologians like John Ray and William Derham and steeped in a British Newtonian tradition: on gravity, he cites Clarke, Halley, and Cheyne, as well as John Keill and David Gregory. As it was published in London in 1720, *The Christian Philosopher* is itself very much a part of this tradition.[62] For Mather, the fundamental discovery of the Newtonian science of gravity was God's activity inside the clock. Newtonians demonstrate that gravity is a nonmechanical, divine force. They teach, therefore, that "the Great GOD not only has the *Springs* of this immense *Machine,* and all the several Parts of it, in his own Hand, and is the *first Mover,* but that without His *continual Influence* the whole Movement would soon fall to pieces."[63]

Mather argues that this understanding of God's gravity in the clock world provides "a continual Opportunity for a considerate and religious Man, to have a *Sense* of a Glorious GOD awaken'd in him!" (86). It enables an actual perception of the divine agency of this "Glorious GOD": "*He is not far from every one of us.* When I see any thing moving or settling that way that its *heavy Nature* carries it, I may very justly think, and I would often form the Thought, *it is the Glorious GOD, who now carries this Matter such a way!* When *Matter* sinks *downward,* my Spirit shall even *therefore* mount *upward,* in acknowledgement of the God who orders it" (86). This is remarkable. Mather sees every little falling thing as a wheel in the clock that God powers. Every falling thing is moved by God, and thus people can literally see God in motion. Mather goes further. The experience of gravity makes possible a physical sensation of God's agency: "I *perceive* Him in the *Weight* of every *Matter....* I see Him *at work,*" "I feel it in *my own*" body (87, 86). Mather is unusually explicit, even ebullient, in his treatment of gravity as an experience of the divine, but he is far from idiosyncratic. For example, he concludes his treatment of gravity by paraphrasing the crucial Bible verse for the Newtonians: "*Great GOD . . . I acknowledge in Thee we move and have our Being*" (88). For Mather and his readers, Newtonianism provided scientific license for a quite physical experience of divine agency.

Similarly, Andrew Baxter—whose *Enquiry into the Nature of the Human Soul* (1733) was a kind of *summa* of the reworked Newtonian clock figure and a conduit for bringing early Newtonian arguments and ideas to later generations—further developed this tradition's implications for ways of looking at the material world.[64] Baxter's explanation of the Newtonian clock figure is very accessible. Newton asserts the need for active principles on the grounds that the quantity of motion in the world is always decreasing; in other words, the "mechanism of all the parts of the world" could not continue "a going" without some immaterial infusion of "motive power."[65] In a primer he wrote for young boys, Baxter developed this worldview into an invitation to glimpse divine agency: "we can neither turn our Eyes nor our Thoughts to any one Object in all Nature, where the Power of the Deity is not the first . . . Thing that occurs to us. The Thought is awful and ravishing!"[66] This invitation is closely related to Mather's. In the *Enquiry*, Baxter makes a related point with a stronger emphasis on the way this insight helps him revise traditional ideas about nature. Like other Newtonians, Baxter affirms the traditional Christian tenet that the material world is corrupt and fallen. He asserts that matter is "*a powerless, dead substance,*" in itself capable only of a negative or passive inertia (36). God's mechanism would grind to a halt if left to itself. Yet, this inert matter is for Baxter only a small part of the experienced natural world. For one, the "*dead substance*" of the world evinces God's wisdom and design. Further, Baxter says, God is constantly at work on "*dead*" but perfectly contrived things: there is "*a constant and universal Providence in the material world, extending to the minutest things,*" and God's "invisible Hand" gives them life (36, 42). Baxter couples these two points. "[E]very thing to which we can turn our thoughts or eyes" features both God's design and perpetual activity: "The admirable mechanism discovered in the structure of a plant or animal, is not only the effect of his wisdom and skill in the first contrivance, but the minutest office in the oeconomy is *incessantly performed* by his almighty finger. His power is still working *near* us, *round* us, *within* us, in *every part* of us" (81, 45). Baxter couples local evidence of design with a more pervasive sense of God's activity. We can see sophisticated contrivances everywhere, but we can also see that God is "*near,*" "*round*" and "*within.*" "His almighty finger" performs "*incessantly*" even the "minutest office"—God is "wisely, knowingly... *pushing, ordering* every particle and every atom" (45). Where Mather encourages a visual and physical experience of God at work in his clock, Baxter uses a similar insight to revalue the natural world. Just look around, Baxter invites his readers: God is at work everywhere "we can turn our thoughts and eyes."

When Newton died in 1727, a flood of poetic panegyrics celebrated the man and his accomplishments—and many emphasized, in particular, how Newton enabled the mode of vision that this section recovers. Scholars have tended to emphasize the way these panegyrics commend Newton's sight for enabling an almost sexual domination of nature or a superhuman control over it. These tropes of deification are fascinating but have unfortunately led scholars to neglect the ways that early poets also insistently praise, not Newton's power, but God's.[67] Many Newtonian panegyrics praised Newton for offering a way of seeing God's work inside the contrived order, a way of achieving exhilarating glimpses of God in action.

For example, James Thomson's "Poem Sacred to the Memory of Sir Isaac Newton" (1727) glorifies Newton's sight: his "All intellectual eye," "well-purg'd" (literally, spiritually purified) "penetrative eye," and "amazing mind," "Deep-searching."[68] While Newton's sight sometimes is described as "subdu[ing]" nature and mastering it (he "bound" planets to orbits and "Untwisted" white light), Newton is above all celebrated for finding God in nature (37, 17, 98). The poem opens by describing Newton's achievement: "while on this dim spot, where mortals toil / Clouded in dust," Newton attended to "*Motion*'s simple laws" in famous observations of how lead weights fall faster than feathers and how slings hold buckets in orbits (13–14). These scientific experiments led him to a discovery: he was able to "trace the secret hand of *Providence*, / Wide-working thro' this universal frame" (15–16). Near the poem's end, Thomson repeats this logic, this vision that sees through the mechanical and experimental to the divine. Newton's understanding of the material world led straight to God: his "*Devotion* swell'd / Responsive to his knowledge!..." (137–38). Thomson continues:

> ... for could he,
> Whose piercing mental eye diffusive saw
> The finish'd University of things,
> In all its order, magnitude, and parts,
> Forbear incessant to adore that *Power*
> Who fills, sustains, and actuates the whole. (138–43)

Thomson praises Newton for his way of looking—his "piercing mental Eye"—and he again has Newton look at the mundane materials of natural philosophy. Earlier, it was the laws of motion, but here the objects of Newton's observation become even more conventionally mechanical. Newton observes the "University of things" in corpuscular terms of number, size, and texture—he sees the various parts that make up the machine that God has "finish'd." Thomson then continues to detail what Newton's "Eye" allowed the scientist (and by extension the poet and his readers) to see. In the physics of material things, Newton glimpsed an active "*Power.*" Thomson draws on the language of early Newtonian apologists as he explains how this works. While Bentley had God "actuate the dead matter," and another Newtonian imagined him to "Pervade and Comprehend as wel as to Sustain the Universe," Thomson speaks of a God who "fills, sustains, and actuates."[69] Thomson draws on Newtonian tradition to stage a discovery of God's constant, everywhere activity within the order of the world. Newton sees that the "order" of the "whole" material world—the laws of motion or the textures of corpuscles—is a product of the continuing action of God's "Wide-Working" "Hand" (filling, sustaining, actuating).

Interestingly, Thomson's version of Newtonianism underwrites his work on vision in the slightly later "Hymn to the Seasons" (1730)—a poem whose natural religious aspects are often linked with Shaftesbury instead of Newton.[70] In the "Hymn," Thomson contrasts an everyday unthinking vision of the world with a Newton-esque vision:

> wandering oft, with brute unconscious gaze,
> Man marks *Thee* not, marks not the mighty hand,
> That, ever-busy, wheels the silent spheres;
> Works in the secret deep....[71]

Some look at the world and do not see God inside of it. The project of Thomson's poem (like the project of Newtonianism in his earlier poem) is to correct this "gaze." Thomson's own alternate brand of "gaze" illuminates precisely what its unthinking counterpart cannot see—exhilarating traces of divine action. It does so, moreover, in a manner indebted to the reworked Newtonian clock figure. Thomson's gaze glimpses the "Work"ings of a particularly active ("ever-busy") and powerful ("mighty") "hand," and there is a relationship between this "hand" and the "secret hand of *Providence,* / Wide-working," that Newton discovered in Thomson's earlier poem. Thomson's gaze in the "Hymn" also discovers a way in which something divine acts on or in a mechanical universe. God "wheels the silent spheres"—one imagines an orrery, a scientific mechanism that models the solar system, being wheeled about by the hand of a scientist. Further, Thomson's vision of the Grand Mechanist moving his great orrery (a discovery clearly related to, say, Clarke's recognition of God driving the weights and springs of the clockwork world) is no isolated vision in the poem. It provides a paradigm for the "gaze"—the direct opposite of that "brute unconscious" one—that keeps on discovering God at work. As the poem continues, Thomson's gaze glimpses God's immanence in all different seasons and natural phenomena: "The rolling *Year* / Is full of" him, and he inspires the winds, bids the sea to roar, "Flings from the sun direct the *flaming Day*," and generally "sustains, and animates the whole."[72] Newton, in effect, taught Thomson to "mark" that "mighty hand" that "wheels" the planets about.

Like Thomson's, many of the poetic panegyrics written upon Newton's death in 1727 celebrate the ways Newton allowed contemporaries to see God constantly at work. Samuel Bowden's "Poem Sacred to the Memory of Sir Isaac Newton" (1733) offers an interesting example, as he seems in the beginning of the poem to depart from the reworked Newtonian clock figure in conceiving of gravity as some sort of second cause. Bowden explains that matter is passive, "And when no foreign Energy's imprest, / Is still alike inclin'd to roll, or rest."[73] As he treats gravity, however, Bowden (like Bentley) seems a bit unclear whether this energy was "imprest" in the beginning or is continually infused. He praises gravity as a "Power" on its own terms, without attending to its cause:

> A wondrous Power he saw diffus'd o'er all,
> Which unremitting governs every Ball:
> He saw perpetual *Gravity* obtain,
> And o'er the System hold coercive Reign (23–26)

The poem progresses, then, through Newton's particular discoveries about the role of gravity in the orbits of the moon and in the rhythms of the tides. Bowden narrates as Newton pursues his discoveries toward their final object: we see Newton "step by step th'harmonious Chain pursue, / Till Nature's Secrets open to his View" (185–86).

The secrets he learns?

> on their *latent Cause Effects* depend,
> That unseen Cause which agitates each Sphere,
> Pervades the Mass, and rules the circling Year. (192–94)

Here we can again hear resonances of the verbs associated with the tradition of God inside his clock. God is the "unseen Cause" that "agitates," "pervades," and "rules." This debt becomes even starker as Bowden elucidates the highest level of Newton's upwardly aiming search for truth:

> Still rising, he adores the *Power* which reigns,
> Supreme o'er all, and every part sustains.
> For *Newton* saw, fair Stamp of Hand divine,
> With conqu'ring Beauty o'er Creation shine;
> He saw a mild Omnipotence preside,
> And Deity diffus'd the System guide. (203–8)

True to the tradition in which he works, Bowden recognizes both God's role as Creator (he "Stamp"ed matter with beautiful wisdom) and his continuing action in the world. Bowden describes a God, familiar to us now, whose "Hand" is active and who "every part sustains."

Yet, the most notable verbal echoes in Bowden's description of God are not to the Newtonian clock tradition per se but to his own earlier description of the power of gravity. Wonderfully, these echoes make the reader rethink the causal agency behind gravity. Bowden introduced gravity earlier in the poem by asserting that Newton saw a "wondrous Power . . . diffus'd o'er all" that "governs" each planet. In this later passage, he repeats all of these points. There is a "Power" acting "o'er all" as governor or king. In both cases, he speaks of its "reign" over "the System," and he uses language that evokes the image of Thomson's divine Hand in the grand orrery (the power "steer[ed]" the system earlier and, here, "guide[s]" it). In both cases also, the power is "diffus'd" across this system. However, in the second passage the "wondrous Power" becomes explicitly God, "Deity diffus'd." Bowden invites his readers to revisit Newton's starting point in the contrived order of the world—the "Balance," the "*mechanic Laws*," the world that was ruled by gravity as a power seemingly without a cause—but they are now armed with the true knowledge of the constant cause of the balance, laws, and power (40, 45). God *does* gravity, and in gravity Newton was able to see God everywhere acting. Clearly, when Bowden talks of laws and order, he does not refer to the kind of static, designed order of clockwork conventionally understood. Bowden's version of Newtonian order is given life, constantly, by guidance from God.

The Newtonian clock figure enables a vision of God's "Order" that was simply more alive, more present and active, than a conventionally clock-obsessed or design-oriented tradition allows. This realization can help us read the frequent contemporary mentions of Newtonian order as richer and more capacious in their reference than has been realized. For example, Jane Brereton captures the early Newtonian discovery of God's immanence in a 1735 poem: Newton "Th'established Order, of each Orb, unfolds, / And th' omnipresent *God,* in all, beholds."[74] God is "in all," and Brereton obliquely invites her contemporaries, with Newton, to "behold" an "Order" "in all." To be sure, this "Order" was "established" in the beginning, but it also is revived continually by a God who is literally and actively "omnipresent." ("*In him*" they were living and moving and having their being.) Like Bowden, Thomson, Baxter, Mather, Whiston, and Newton himself, Brereton invites contemporaries to "behold" something beyond God's in-the-beginning ordering intelligence. With Newton, they could see and even feel that God was *in* action. Clearly, Newton was not a closet magician and public mathematician. His science, rather, both privately and publicly promoted the discovery of a mystically active and immanent (not merely utilitarian) order in the world.[75]

When early Newtonians looked carefully at the natural world, they did not find—as one Cartesian put the discovery of generations of "mere" mechanists both before and after Newton's time—that it was only "Wheels and Weights that cause the movements."[76] Theirs was not the "brute unconscious gaze" that Thomson describes, nor was it the rationalizing and demystifying "gaze" that conventional clockwork is supposed to have encouraged. They did not see only an order of fixed and inflexible laws. (Too much work on Newtonian natural theology dwells on design and a clockwork Creator, emphases that represent only one of the many ways that Newtonians understood God to be involved in his clock world.)

Instead, when early Newtonians looked at the world, they could see the heavenly "Hand" moving his grand orrery, or the divine mechanic constantly caring for his clock and causing the gravity of the weight that moves it. As Cheyne put it in the passage that stands as epigraph to this chapter, the world was "*a noble* and *immense Machin,*" a machine "whose Springs are an immaterial Principle . . . an Original Impress, or a constant efflux from the Divine *Energy*" (1:159). For Cheyne and his contemporaries, Newton's science encouraged not a sharpened sense of stable cosmic law and order but a capacious set of moral and political truths based on constant divine activity and a new and robust feeling for God's immanence. This feeling resonated, restructuring understandings of the natural world. The world was a noble, worthy place, an exciting place to look at. God was everywhere diffused throughout it, everywhere acting inside of it. It had order, but this order only happened as God moved about his machine. God was close—as Cheyne proposed—allowing the clock "Parts" to tick away, "regularly constantly and harmoniously to attain their destin'd Ends and Purposes" (1:160).

Praise be to the *Principia*. When Isaac Newton came along, he enabled a vibrant vision of the divine acting in the clockwork world.

Money, Meaning, and a "Foundation in Nature"

People in late seventeenth- and early eighteenth-century England were concerned about money and about the new consumer culture that money was enabling. They needed to decide how they wanted to order their quickly changing economy, how they should deal with new economic realities like paper money, credit, and structurally permanent national debt. They wanted to figure out how people should behave amid the new social realities of a world where the use of money had personal, national, and even international stakes, where the merchant classes were rising quickly, and where the right clothing purchase could seemingly transform one's social status.

This chapter demonstrates that many writers addressed these pressing problems by scrutinizing the created natural world for clues about God's will for human society. That is, they addressed these problems by deploying the postures, practices, and logics of the meditative empiricism. Like other meditative empiricists, these writers wanted their money and their economic and social systems more generally to have (as John Locke put it) a "Foundation in Nature."[1] They assumed that empiricist observation of nature's particulars—for instance, the weight, durability, malleability, ductility, or color of bits of silver and gold bullion—could help access hints about how human institutions should work. True to their tradition, too, they modestly recognized that attempts to articulate an order that has its "Foundation in Nature" were provisional and approximate, at best. They were modest and humble but earnest in their attempts to search nature and to try to understand the ethical and social guidance it offered.

The presence of the meditative empiricism in economic writing is significant, for it troubles the usual scholarly tendency to treat the changing English economy within sweeping stories of modernization. English money and markets are often taken as early sites of modernity's new understanding of humanly instituted (as opposed to inherent) value, as early sites of modernity itself. Such scholarship often assumes—as both liberal and Marxist narratives of modernization also assume—that, as the English economy became more modern, it increasingly lost touch with nature, and it was built increasingly on the products of human minds. The solid, inherent value of bullion gave way to immaterial human constructions of paper, credit, and debt. Consumers asserted their own self-interest as they navigated economic institutions understood as built by and for humans, and their own agency confronted them in the mystified form of the commodity. Or so the usual stories go.[2] The texts featured in this chapter, however, belie any notion of a move away from nature: economic writers scrutinized nature's particulars as they tried to articulate policy proposals that would have their "Foundation" there. These texts confirm the central insight of the exciting recent work that attempts to do economic history as history of science: in Margaret Schabas's words, "Until the mid-nineteenth century, economic theorists regarded the phenomena of their discourse as part of the same natural world studied by natural philosophers."[3] These texts also illustrate the complex role of human agency involved in the process of treating economic matters "as part of the same natural world studied by natural philosophers."

The presence of the meditative empiricism in economic tracts is significant, too, for it demonstrates how widespread such practices were. Certainly, not all participants in economic debates of the time turned to nature in ways indebted to the meditative empiricism; it was not the only available way of thinking through economic problems. Yet, it was a thriving, viable mode in economic discourse, and—as we will see—writers from across the political and ideological spectrum did draw on it. Clearly, the meditative empiricism was not the lingering remnant of a waning worldview or merely a conservative crutch for those who would resist economic progress. In fact, in showing that both liberal and conservative thinkers turned to nature, my book spins stories about modernization on their heads. Not only was the meditative empiricism brought to the most "modern" of problems in the period; it led to the most "modern" of possibilities. It enabled quite secular, pragmatic, and even forward-pointing kinds of knowledge.

This chapter features two kinds of writing about money. The first part focuses on the debates surrounding the English recoinage crisis of the 1690s. English currency was alarmingly scarce and debased by the middle of that decade, and the pamphlets and polemics addressing this problem constituted what was, in the words of one historian, "the first major concentrated burst of development" for modern economic thought—a debate about the very nature of money, happening at the height of the "Financial Revolution."[4] Empiricist scrutiny of natural clues helped many participants in the recoinage debates articulate economic and political systems that approximated a decidedly supra-human order. The second part, then, shifts focus from economic policy to popular writing that grappled with new problems that everyday people faced in the emerging consumer culture. I feature Charles Gildon's *Golden Spy* (1709) and Joseph Addison's "History of a Shilling" (1710), fictional texts that inaugurated the popular genre of it-narratives. These texts' talking coins gave a literary form to some of the meditative empiricism's key tenets: they dramatized the possibility that nature offered supple resources for guidance, if humans could only manage (skeptically, analogically) to heed its prompts. In the period, money's matter *mattered*. People modestly scrutinized coins and metals as they attempted to understand this relevance, to figure out what it meant for the ways their economies and societies should work.

Economists Turn to Nature

By the mid-1690s, the English were very worried about the metal in their money.[5] For one, they were concerned about a general shortage of silver. Recent scholars interested in the interconnectedness of the period's global markets help us see that this concern proceeded from a fundamental worry about England's place in an international economy.[6] Contemporaries often measured England's wealth by its accumulation of treasure: silver and gold bullion. Therefore, all bullion exports could be understood as economic losses, provoking anxiety about even the potentially lucrative trade opportunities offered by the English East India Company, for example. There was no real demand for English products in Indian and Asian markets, and so—in order to import the exotic luxury items that English people wanted—the East India Company needed to export significant amounts of gold and silver bullion. These exports sparked decades of debate on whether the Company was hurting the English economy. Second, at the moment, the Nine Years' War was disrupting English trade, and England's need to fund troops caused another serious drain in available bullion.[7] Further, since the English Mint undervalued silver, it struggled to attract new resources of bullion to coin. Arbitrageurs could turn a profit by melting English coin into bullion and exporting it. In part because of these anxiety-producing drains on the bullion supply, there was just not enough available silver coin in circulation to conduct everyday trade. People worried about the metal in their money and the metal in their nation's coffers.

The problems caused by this shortage were exacerbated by the terrible condition of the little silver coin that remained in circulation. As one popular broadside put it in 1696, the "Lamentable Confusion . . . of the People of this Land" was due to "the badness of the Coyn."[8] For centuries, the Mint had used a traditional hammering process that produced coins containing a proper amount of silver but with uneven stamps and jagged edges. Clippers exploited this, cutting off the exposed edges of these coins and melting the excess silver into saleable bullion. After 1662 the Mint adopted new technology that successfully guarded against clipping by giving coins a milled edge. The problem was, the new milled coins weighed precisely the amount in silver that their stamp promised while most other coins weighed dramatically less and still circulated. Savvy people eager for a quick profit turned this to their advantage by hoarding or melting the "heavy" coins. Counterfeiting was also rife, and the bad clipped or counterfeited money drove the good money out. By the last decade of the seventeenth century, then, circulating coins were hard to come by and about 50 percent lighter than they should have been—some were nearly a century old. This "badness" threw trade into disarray, and the sense of crisis was only heightened by the dramatic, unsettling inflation in the price of the gold guinea. (It skyrocketed from 22s. 9¼d. in January 1694 to 29s. 9¾d. in July 1695.) People craved any kind of stable store for value. The secretary of the treasury described the contemporary situation: "great Contentions do daily arise amongst the King's Subjects, in Fairs, Markets, Shops. . . . Persons before they conclude in any Bargains, are necessitated first to settle the Price or Value of the very Money they are to Receive for their Goods."[9] The English worried about the metal in their money—they haggled over it in "Fairs, Markets, Shops."

Because of this widespread concern with the metal in money, by the mid-1690s most economic thinkers agreed that all the English clipped silver money should be melted down and recoined into full-sized money with milled edges. The crux of the problem, however, was more fundamental: about how money was supposed to work, how the economy ought to be ordered. As English economic thinkers addressed these problems, they continued to evince concern with the metal in money. For many writers, this metal was important for more than its monetary value; it was important because it was material, natural, created by God. They assumed that it might thereby contain clues that could help them figure out how to structure the economy. I argue that some advocates of all three main positions on recoinage turned in this manner to nature, to the natural properties of metal—though they focused on different natural facts, used different techniques in moving from nature to its human implications, and came to different conclusions.

The meditative empiricism motivated (1) proposals for restoring the coin to its original purity outlined by John Locke, rehashed in countless popular pamphlets, and eventually adopted by Parliament. These writers assumed that the economic order was embedded in a larger natural order and that monetary and material value were intricately interconnected. Many allowed for a complex (sometimes providential) process in the past whereby humans recognized a value in silver, but they all agreed that, in their here and now, an ounce of silver equaled another ounce in such a way that governments could not alter the value of money legitimately. Intriguingly, empiricist habits of mind also guided some of those advocating the opposite policy position— including (2) the proposal offered by the secretary of the treasury to raise the value of the coin to correspond with the fluctuating commodity value of the silver bullion it contained. Advocates of this position understood the natural world to provide an intractable fetter on economic decisions, even as they too recognized the human work of approximating supra-human clues and maintaining economic systems. The meditative empiricism also influenced (3) more innovative proposals for raising the coin offered by the most lucid of Locke's critics, like Nicholas Barbon and James Hodges.[10] Barbon and Hodges freed economic decisions from what they saw as material fetters, but they still found it important to keep them in tune with a cosmic order. Hodges even deployed the structures of occasional meditation in his reasoning. These policy proposals were offered by thinkers across the political spectrum and with varying degrees of good faith; for example, Locke believed deeply in his cause, while some projectors were self-interested. All of these proposals, however, were enriched by close attention to natural things and their implications. They were all articulated as provisional approximations of a supra-human order.

Moreover, in showing that an engagement with nature could motivate both conservative and more forward-thinking policy proposals, I upset our usual ways of thinking about meaning, materiality, and modernity. Work in "the new economic criticism" affirms the modernization narratives that posit a move away from natural order in this period. These scholars are "fascinat[ed] with debt," "credit," and paper money and with the processes by which the economy was loosened from its natural material base and built instead on imaginations and a play of signifiers.[11] For example, with historical and theoretical nuance James Thompson traces the cultural processes by which eighteenth-century England shifted "from realist to nominalist conceptions of [monetary] value, in a dematerialization from metal to paper medium," and Sandra Sherman and Colin Nicholson investigate how the resulting new sense of money's insubstantiality and instability (even fictionality) affected contemporary writers.[12] Of course, new economic critics also recognize that some contemporaries made sense of these developments by appealing to the material world: land. In this, they are good students of J. G. A. Pocock's influential work on civic humanism. Pocock argues that civic humanists of the "Country" party in early eighteenth-century England resisted the corruptions of a new finance by grounding the political personality in land. Land quite literally connected the owner to the country and its ancient customs, enabling him to contemplate public good free from that corrupting mix of human fantasy, appetite, and self-interest characteristic of emergent commercial society.[13] Much scholarship associates Pocock's argument that civic humanism could be used as "the vehicle of a basically hostile perception of early modern capitalism" with Isaac Kramnick's treatment of the *Politics of Nostalgia*. Scholars thus recognize both a new money culture and a deeply conservative eighteenth-century reaction against it.[14] Novelty, credit, the City, and Daniel Defoe are on the one side, and a conservative "Country" tradition, land, bullion, and Lord Bolingbroke on the other. Of course, the best new economic critics argue that these categories were contested late seventeenth- and early eighteenth-century constructs. And they recognize that at any given moment economic thought proceeded from a messy mix of "the residual" and "the emergent."[15] Still, most scholars assume that weirdly material appeals to nature, land, or bullion belonged to hostile conservative or "residual" backward-looking forces in this cultural moment.[16] Yet, I contend that what might seem like a "residual" approach to economic problems—one committed to close attention to the natural world and to developing its implications for human institutions—could open up even the most "emergent" and proto-capitalist of possibilities.

An engagement with the natural world as a source of ethical and social guidance is most obvious in the conservative position that won the day in the end.[17] Advocates of this position, including most famously John Locke, fervently resisted proposals for "raising the coin"—in other words, for retaining each coin's customary value while coining it with less than its customary amount of silver (in effect, a devaluation). Instead, they suggested that every coin be reminted to contain the precise amount of silver that its customary denomination declared it to contain. The coin needed to be "restored" to its proper weightiness, so that the stated monetary value was backed up with metal.

Many advocates of this position shared with empiricists like Boyle an assumption that there is "so perfect an harmony" between "Truths" in different realms. For them, the physical and the economic were closely interconnected, even almost identical. Locke articulated what one in his cohort called the "Fundamental Axiom" of this position: "an equal quantity of Silver is always of equal value to an equal quantity of Silver" (2:411).[18] Locke argued that, since silver's substance constitutes its value, it is nonsensical for one ounce of silver coin to have a different value than an identical ounce in bullion. An ounce of silver "is, and eternally will be" equal in value to another ounce, and changing the name of a coin does nothing since "Sounds" do not "give weight to Silver" (2:416, 451). Such arguments were motivated by anxiety about unfettered human agency in the workings of money, an anxiety only compounded by reports of the terrible consequences attending changed denominations of French and Spanish coins.[19] Locke was also acutely aware of an international marketplace in which symbols or "Sounds" decreed by English people would not magically become "weight" or value in Holland, for example. He insisted that the physical and the economic are overlapping realms and that value is a material phenomenon, to be measured on both English and Dutch scales.

Similarly, the author of two popular letters (1696) appealed to "Rules of Equity" that are at once material and moral.[20] In the most literal sense, the "Rules of Equity"—like Locke's "Fundamental Axiom"—bring the force of a new scientific obsession with number, weight, and measure to a purportedly obvious, empirically verifiable proposition: an ounce of silver is equal to an ounce. Clipping violates these "Rules of Equity" as it produces an "inequality in the Intrinsick Value of different pieces of our Coin, which passed still under the same Denomination."[21] A full-weight crown with milled edges worryingly could buy as much as a crown that had half of its silver clipped off—half the amount of silver buys as much as the whole. The writer exclaims, this is "An Absurdity," "A Force upon Nature which could not hold."[22] It perverts the natural, material value of silver. "Equity" more broadly, though, conjures connotations of justice, and the author plays up these connotations as he condemns schemes for raising the coin with the same moral outrage popularly directed toward clipping. Stealing grains of silver from current coin was thought of as stealing from the nation; it was a treasonous crime punishable by death. Like Locke, the letter writer suggests that proposals for raising the coin are just a form of clipping writ large. When the government assigns a denomination that is not backed up by weighty silver, it creates a similar "inequality" between the intrinsic value of the silver and its denominative value as money, and it too violates the nature of things in an "absurd" or dishonest way. Of course, the writer allows that governments are involved in coining money, but he insists that kings merely certify with a stamp that a coin contains silver of a said weight and fineness. Stamps vouch for—instead of generate—value, and there is a firm link between money's matter and its worth, between signified material and signifying stamp.

I want to underscore the importance of the material here. Robert Markley has suggested that Locke has silver provide a "tangible guarantee" of the use value of money—with the "tangible" nature of the "guarantee" guarding against certain kinds of human interference and ensuring the "stability" of basic "systems of value."[23] To Markley's emphasis on the ways that bits of silver incarnate the use value of money, I add that many arguments like Locke's were underwritten by a conviction in a meaningfully designed natural world, a "tangible" world that God created such that it could prompt insight into the best kinds of economic order. For both Locke and the anonymous letter writer, material things provide a kind of ethical guide, a source of knowledge about what should or should not be done with financial systems. It is morally suspect to assign names that are not backed up by material value in silver. Interestingly, the letter writer even describes the material-moral "Rules of Equity" as sacrosanct: they are eternal and "unalterable," even "Sacred."[24] These popular pamphlets nicely represent the conservative position for restoring the coin. Their writer attempts to ground the value of money in a natural world that is part of a larger moral order. Nature provides clear parameters for Parliament's decision concerning recoinage: to mess with money was to mess with the nature of things.

There was a problem with this position, however—a problem posed by human agency. Sometimes this problem was expressed in terms of the ancient diamond/water paradox: if value is intrinsic and based on usefulness, why are metals like gold and silver more valuable than goods like corn or water that support human life? Humans *must* have been involved in some way in the process of valuation. Locke wrestled with this problem in interesting ways. In his *Some Considerations of the Consequences of the Lowering of Interest and Raising the Value of Money* (1692), he conceptualizes monetary value as a product of human consent in the past, and yet he clearly wants to make it a material phenomenon in which kings cannot meddle. He is led into some conceptual acrobatics. Intrinsic value is "nothing else but" silver's "Durableness, Scarcity, and not being apt to be counterfeited," but it is also "not natural" and "only in the Opinion of men consenting to it."[25] Silver's value is material like leather but also a construction of human "Opinion." Intriguingly, Locke develops a powerful strategy for reconciling material and humanly instituted value: an appeal to the nature of things, even possibly to God's design for his creation. For example, he addresses the problem by explaining that silver's distinctive material properties motivate human consent. Men "consented to put an imaginary Value upon Gold and Silver by reason of their Durableness, Scarcity, and not being very liable to be Counterfeited" (1:233). Value might be "imaginary" for Locke, but it is not random or arbitrary. In his mind, this motivated consent is underwritten by God's providential design of metals. This becomes clear in the explanation that Locke submitted to the government: "The *intrinsick value* of silver considerd as money is that estimate which for its fitnesse, common consent has placed on silver" (2:374). "Common consent" does not arbitrarily assign value to silver. People value silver because of its "fitnesse"— the way its material qualities make it peculiarly apt to function as money.

Fitness was a key word in contemporary arguments about God's design, and it recurs several times in Locke's monetary writings as a reason why silver and gold are valuable. He asserts in *Some Considerations* that "*Silver*, for many Reasons, is the *fittest* of all metals to be this measure [of commerce], and therefore generally made use of for Money" (1:326). And, years later, the "fittest for" use as equivalent "of all other, is *Silver*"—"because it decays not in keeping, and never sinks much in its value," because it can "be divided, and keep [its] value," and because there is the proper amount of if distributed throughout the world (2:423–24).[26] Locke justifies and even motivates man's choice with an appeal to silver's "fitnesse." (Note that he presumes that valuation involves people paying close attention to silver's particular properties.) Locke also evokes the inevitability of silver's choice as standard, arguing that silver has "been thought the fittest Material[ ]" in "almost all Ages, and parts of the World" (1:323). He "need not" mention the "many reasons" silver is "fittest" because "It is enough that the World has agreed in it, and it is their *common Money*" (2:423). Locke also clinches his most considered statement of intrinsic value (1695–96) with an appeal to Ecclesiastes 10:19: "And thus as the Wise Man tells us, *Money answers all things*" (2:410). Conjuring a sense of inevitability and confirming it with scripture, Locke accentuates silver's material properties as he suggests that silver's special "fitnesse" directs the human decision to value it. Consent seems to bubble up spontaneously around a peculiarly "fit" material. Locke's arguments here share energy with the meditative empiricism: he renders nature's particulars as meaningful in themselves but assumes that attentive humans must access and actualize their truths. The resulting meaning is neither subjective nor wholly objective—it is a human approximation or realization of dictates encoded in creation. In this way, Locke allows that humans assigned value to metal while insisting that the resulting monetary systems still "have their Foundation in Nature" (2:403).

Locke's approach was not unusual. Advocates of the conservative position everywhere pointed out that to make an ounce equal more than an ounce was a perversion of a natural order. And Jacob Viner and Louis Landa have shown that other commercial apologists in the period often turned to particulars of the natural world to find justification for the mercantile economy: the providential design of rivers and oceans invited men to navigation, and God's choice to have different countries produce different products constituted his approval of international trade.[27] The anonymous *Some Observation's on our Trade, and on the Use of a Standard* (1701?) developed such logic at length. The author argues that the silver standard was designed by God such that silver's material properties would invite human consent. The author dwells on the ways that the material properties of silver peculiarly suit it to function as a standard. The material acting as standard, he suggests, must be "durable," nonperishable, and "Malleable"; it must be divisible into smaller pieces and "have a natural intrinsick value." Finally, it must be available "Sufficient in quantity to do the service in all parts, and yet not so much, as to make it Cheap, common, or despicable."[28] *Some Observation's* then makes the bold claim that only silver fits all of these criteria—other metals are either too scarce (gold) or too prevalent (lead). Therefore, while humans esteem silver, its function as a monetary standard is determined by material properties that specially suit it for the job. The author continues, "we may conclude that Silver, made its own way, and got into this post by its merits and qualifications" (22). He enacts a transfer of agency from people to the metal in his very syntax. The silver jumps to life with his active verb—it "made its own way." In something quite like the meditative empiricism's encounters between attentive observer and meaningful nature, here silver elicits, and human consent is guided by the imperatives inherent in it.

The author of *Some Observation's* goes even further in situating money in a natural moral order much larger than commerce itself. In the opening pages of his book, he makes the striking claim that careful study of the economy is actually "more capable to create a just Admiration of the goodness, as well as power of the Deity, than enquiries, about single Atoms, Insects and Vegetables" (6). He engages with a physico-theological tradition that loved to find evidence in the clocklike nature of the world for the existence of an intelligent clockmaker up above. He offers a twist on this logic, asserting that the commercial system is a divine creation as marked with evidence of God's purposive design as the plants and animals that were featured in countless popular design arguments. The author leaves no room for anyone to mistake his meaning: "Commerce and Trade are . . . Essential to the subsistence and preservation of mankind," and "they have their Foundation in the Divine Institutions and are a part of the Laws of Nature" (2). He depicts a complex commercial machine designed by God for the good of man. Money has a critical role in this machine: "that Specie, that passes as the Standard, is the chief *Spring or Pendulum*, which by its co-operation with such endeavours, procures the good effects expected; if that be not kept true and steady, there will be jarring and confusion in the whole body of Trade" (153). The silver standard helps ensure the steady functioning of the system God designed, and the human work of preserving a "true and steady" silver standard becomes the best way humans can preserve God's designed order in the world. According to this logic, though humans of course formalized value arrangements, the intrinsic value of silver money is natural, even ordained—for that metal is the only material fit to be a standard. *Some Observation's* emphasizes this: "as *Truth ever was and will be Truth*, notwithstanding any false representations, so weight, finess, or intrinsick value, will be the Standard, in despight of all endeavours to the contrary" (154–55). Truth, God's design, and intrinsic value: all the more reason why humans should not meddle with money any more.

Many advocates of restoring the coin attended to silver's natural material properties as they devised policy proposals that they understood as approximations of a divinely ordained order.[29] Indeed, the urgency with which Locke, the letter writer, and their cohort rigidly limited the possibility of human intervention into the workings of money helps us appreciate the broader philosophical stakes of the recoinage. Debates about money participated in a cultural crisis about value: Is it coded into nature or constructed by humans? Hobbes was the boogeyman, raising for contemporaries a deeply worrying specter of the arbitrary constructedness of all values and institutions. The recoinage debates constituted an especially fraught arena for such larger questions to play out, as money seemed particularly and problematically linked with human decisions, human institutions. As Jose Torre aptly puts it in his treatment of the eighteenth-century American economy, "If economic value in money was not a 'real' objectively knowable standard dictated by the supreme deity, was moral value also arbitrary—a function of men's belief"?[30] Some of those for restoring the coin drew on the logics of meditative empiricism as they managed to uphold seemingly contradictory positions: they recognized human valuations and institutions alongside a natural notion of value, a sense of God's design of even the economic realm.

Interestingly, however, they were not the only ones who explored material particulars as they articulated monetary systems, not the only ones who wanted to retain some kind of "Foundation in Nature." Some of those making the opposite policy recommendations also turned to nature as a source of guidance in monetary matters. The single most influential proposal for raising the coin, Secretary of the Treasury William Lowndes's *A Report containing an Essay for the Amendment of the Silver Coins* (1695), is a case in point. Scholars have located in this devaluation proposal an important precursor to dematerialized and nominalized notions of value and to modern capitalism generally. Thomas Levenson's work on Isaac Newton's time at the Mint provides a symptomatic discussion. Levenson suggests that at the heart of proposals for devaluation like Lowndes's is "a radically modern thought: the King's imprimatur was a mere fiction" and not a guarantee of "the absolute worth a given piece of silver." Levenson asserts that this leads Lowndes to another "modern thought," that "money need not be seen as merely a thing, a tangible object jangling in one's purse. It could be understood as a term in an equation, an abstraction."[31] Levenson is quite right in one sense—Lowndes argues that the king should use his imprimatur to alter the value of money and that value need not be fixed and absolute. Yet, Levenson's emphases on "fictions" and immaterial "abstractions" are retrospective "modern" emphases that most advocates of raising the coin would not have shared. Lowndes manages this "modern" insight by attending carefully to the nature of metal. He shares with advocates of restoring the coin a belief that economic institutions ought to respect, even approximate, a natural order, and he affirms a concomitant notion of value that is anything but nominal.

Lowndes begins from an assumption that he shares with Locke and the letter writer: governments cannot just conjure up imaginary value by their own authority. Lowndes asserts forthrightly "That if the Value of the Silver in the Coins should (by any Extrinsick Denomination) be Raised above the Value, or Market Price of the same Silver, reduced to Bullion, the Subject would be proportionably Injured and Defrauded" (78–79). Value is not an arbitrary construct for Lowndes. Yet, while advocates of "restoring" the coin tended to understand the value of silver as fixed since the beginning of time (or at least since a long-ago human decision), Lowndes sees that the value of silver is its value in the current international "Market." Lowndes widens his notion of monetary value to consider the commodity value of money. This is an aspect of value that we today tend to conceive in terms of fluctuating human demand but that Lowndes imagines in more material terms, as a result of the amount of silver available in the world. As a contemporary put it in a pamphlet also paid for by the Treasury, this value is "Real" and "adherent to the Species, with respect to time and place."[32] Lowndes describes this "Real" value in stubbornly material terms; it is the value of the silver that a coin contains when "reduced to Bullion" or when considered "in Mass" (78, 87). This notion of value considers an individual lump of bullion in relation to the precise amount of bullion available in the world at that moment. Lowndes then suggests a devaluation—the government should lighten current coins by 20 percent—that would merely bring coins' value in line with this "Real" value. His proposal for raising attempts to reckon with the shifting scarcity and plenty of silver without ever leaving the material ground. This position incorporates human desire in the marketplace into monetary value *and* emphatically refuses the possibility that humanity or human institutions can intervene deliberately to alter this value. Lowndes articulates a natural limit for how governments can and should alter the value of money, insisting that to push prices beyond this limit would be morally suspect. It would "Injure and Defraud" the English people.

Historians have now established that Lowndes might have been ambivalent about his devaluation proposal: he might have been acting as the representative of the Treasury, presenting ideas that he did not himself endorse.[33] Still, other writers earnestly affirmed Lowndes's position. They expressed a similar desire to keep money and the economy grounded (in Lowndes's words) on a "true Foundation" (79). John Briscoe, whose "Discourse of Money" (1698) advocated Lowndes's position and was influenced by Lowndes generally, voiced this desire. Of course, endorsing devaluation, Briscoe allows the value of silver to fluctuate in a way that thinkers like

Locke do not. Yet, Briscoe insists that its value remains firmly tethered to a "Real" value, a value that shifts only according to "the general scarcity and abundance of the Species of Gold and Silver."[34] The value of silver, considered in terms of its relative scarcity in the world, provides a natural tether for monetary value.

Briscoe offers an origin story for value that demonstrates how this natural tether serves a concrete political end. He suggests that monetary value in metals originated in a reaction against ad hoc currencies generated by local governments. Subjects quickly learned that they needed a measure of value that could not be altered by "emergencies of State, or caprice of Princes" (12–13). If money does not have an intrinsic value, kings can alter its value as they desire. France and Spain haunt the discussion as Briscoe argues that it is a "sign of Slavery" to live under a government in which value is "capriciously" changeable (18). Briscoe's account of the origins of monetary value both acknowledges human agency and works to make it disappear. He says that "no sooner" had men recognized this need, than "their choice of the Matter whereof to make" money "fell inevitably on Gold and Silver" on account of their natural properties (40). Here again the confrontation between attentive observers and meaningful nature yields a truth that is neither an immediate revelation from God nor a mere human construction. Briscoe later speaks freely of "the Reasonableness, or Necessity, or both, of the choice Men made of Gold and Silver" (42). He also insists that value in gold and silver is international and "universal"; it is "solid," not constructed by human caprice or conferred by human institutions (20). Because silver money has such an intrinsic value, it provides a curb for royal prerogative. Briscoe's sense of the political stakes is not unusual. Lowndes points out that corruption of the coin is the result of an undue exercise of sovereign prerogative that is a sure manifestation of the corruption of the state; the best examples, in Lowndes and everywhere, are King Henry VIII, who debased the coinage, and Queen Elizabeth, who virtuously restored it.[35] Arguments for the restoration of the coin are suffused with a similar sense that preserving the monetary standard preserves the property of subjects from abuses of royal prerogative. We saw hints of this, for example, in the anonymous letter writer's suggestion that kings who raise the coin are just clippers writ large. Supposedly backward-looking appeals to the materiality of value could actually serve quite progressive political purposes. They could protect the property and the rights of the subject against the crown. Clearly, for all these writers, the natural, material world had implications for politics.

If Lowndes and some advocates of his position proposed a devaluation that continued to engage with silver as a material entity, other contemporaries offered even more innovative proposals—proposals that seem to make a leap into a kind of "modern abstraction." For example, in the most complete and compelling contemporary critique of Locke's arguments, James Hodges sees quite clearly how arguments for restoring the coin try to exclude governmental involvement in monetary systems by insisting on the material nature of value. Against this, Hodges repeatedly and urgently affirms "the just Right" and "Power of the Government" to determine the value of money "as is seen most convenient for the publick and private Circumstances and Interest of the Nation, without any Obligation to the contrary from any thing that is to be considered in the Substance of Money, or Quantity of Silver in it."[36] Hodges's language is telling. He suggests that these writers use the "Substance of Money"—that is, the "Quantity of Silver in it," understood as containing a natural, unalterable intrinsic value—to try to put an "Obligation" on the monarch to order it in certain ways. Hodges points out that this position, in equating value with silver's material properties, holds that humans "can no more alter" the value of money than they "can make an Ounce of the same Bread as nourishing as two Ounces" (267). Hodges ridicules the assumption made here that "Silver had in its natural Substance some such real Worth and Virtue, as Bread hath for nourishing" (264). He argues, instead, that kings are under no "Obligation" whatsoever; they have an "unlimited Right and Power to put what Value they please upon Silver in Money" (278).

Nicholas Barbon's *Discourse concerning Coining the New Money Lighter* (1696) provides the theoretical underpinnings for this critique. Barbon—insurance man, sometime "slumlord," and schemer extraordinaire—was not the most disinterested of writers, but his insights point forward to a more modern economics.[37] Barbon attacks the popular notion of intrinsic value, the idea that money "has its sole Value from the Quantity of Silver in each piece of Coin."[38] Most basically, he distinguishes between "Vertues" and "Values." Things can have intrinsic virtues: the loadstone, for example, can "attract Iron" (16). Yet, these natural "Vertues" should not be confounded with economic value, an entirely different creature. Value springs not from the natural properties of things but from the wants of humans. It depends on time, place, and circumstances, on the ebb and flow of fashion and desire in the marketplace. Barbon argues that there is no such thing as an intrinsic fixed value, and he does not except the value of silver bullion from this blanket conclusion. Silver has "no Certain or Intrinsick Value" but varies according to its "Plenty or Scarcity" and the human desire for it (17).

Silver, in other words, is a commodity with a fluctuating value, and such an uncertain value simply cannot "be a certain Measure of another Value" (17). Further, he argues, "Money has its *Value* from the Authority of the Government, which makes it currant, and fixes the price of each piece of Metal"—the government intervenes to give value to money and to assign arbitrary denominations (56). For Barbon, these instances of human involvement in the creation of value license human activity in the continued workings of the monetary system. Since humans and their governments gave value to silver in the first place, they are free to alter it: "For, the Authority being the same, the *Value* will be the same" (56). Here, Hodges and Barbon seem to be proto-capitalists, new economic men comfortable with human fictions and dematerialized signs.

Scholars have focused on such embraces of human fictions. Yet, the resulting critical narratives about dematerialization and modernization overlook an interesting aspect of these arguments: like other contemporaries, Barbon and Hodges wanted to maintain some kind of "Foundation in Nature" for monetary systems. Intriguingly, recent work has suggested one way that Barbon, who arguably goes further than any of his contemporaries in emphasizing the driving force of human desire, continued to have economic systems respect the natural world. He continued to search nature for clues about how economies could work. As Barbon rejects the idea that monetary value is linked with bullion, he also rejects the very idea of value on which notions of intrinsic value and balance of trade are based. He is guided, in this, by his own ontological convictions. Markley and Andrea Finkelstein argue that Barbon's position relies on his belief in the "infinite" fertility and "bounty of nature," in "an essentially organic and fecund universe" with "inexhaustible" resources.[39] This belief is prompted by an awareness of natural realities like "Beasts," "Fowls," "Fishes," "Plants and Fruits," and "Minerals"—and even of cutting-edge science about these creatures.[40] As Finkelstein explains, Barbon believed in the infinite productive potential of the natural world evidenced by these things, as well as in humanity's infinite productive potential and infinite desires. Therefore, an economic system fixated on the balance of trade—and thus on a notion of value as limited by a finite amount of bullion moving about in a zero-sum game—disrespects natural realities, the natural order. Barbon has the plenitude of the natural world underwrite the infinite nature of supply and demand, and he argues that money must be able to fluctuate to accommodate such infinite productive potential. In his own peculiar way, then, he has his economic system approximate a natural order. Carl Wennerlind's *Casual-*

ties of Credit extends this insight as he argues that proposals for even that most immaterial kind of money, credit, were shaped in the later seventeenth century by scientific and alchemical beliefs about nature's "abundance" and possible "improvement."[41]

Hodges's *The Present State of England, as to Coin and Publick Charges* (1697) provides another example of how the innovative argument for devaluation could engage thoughtfully with a supra-human order. Throughout, Hodges insists that kings can alter value however they like—his argument for devaluation is also a strong affirmation of royal prerogative. Even as Hodges affirms this royal prerogative, however, he remains invested in some kind of nonhuman source for silver's value as money. This works in two ways. First, Hodges never forgets that the king's actions participate in an order larger than even the international economy. Where the author of *Some Observation's* appealed to a divine order designed by God and encoded in his creation, Hodges approaches the possibility of a divine order in a different manner. He denies outright the possibility that the natural world contains intrinsic monetary value but repeatedly suggests that the human circumstances and kingly discretion that determine value are subject to the workings of God's active providence. Hodges both begins and ends his book by invoking God's guidance of kingly discretion: he "pray[s] God to direct our Rulers" to effect a recoinage that is best for the public (340, xv). It is tempting to read these as commonplace or throwaway references to providence, except that Hodges includes providence in his theoretical anatomy of value.

In this anatomy, he explains the "six several sorts of Values in Silver considered as Money." First, Hodges recognizes a limited notion of the "Intrinsick Value" of silver closely related to Barbon's "Vertue" (270). Like Barbon, Hodges insists that this has nothing to do with the value of silver qua money. He continues, then, to undercut any sense that governments are somehow obligated by the nature of silver in their decision making as he catalogs the many ways humans create and maintain monetary value: people gave an original consent to value silver, their governments fix monetary denominations and mint current money, and individuals can confer a more idiosyncratic value on the coins in their pockets.

Hodges's remaining category of value is the most vexed. He explains that silver has a "Figurative Value, which also is intrinsick in its Substance and natural Constitution; yet so as it is alike in all its Parts, and maketh not a greater Quantity preferable in Value to a lesser on that account." Here, he "refer[s]" a fuller explanation of this value to "another occasion, seeing it would take more room than is proper to be allowd at this time" (270). Unfortunately, he never gets back around to this explanation, but earlier in the book he offers some preliminary and highly suggestive comments on this value. He explains that silver is "esteemed above" other metals "on the Account of the Value providentially put upon Silver in Money" (147). He describes this as an intrinsic value that is "only figurative, and respecteth the Providence whereby Mankind hath been determined to put a Value upon it, without seeing or regarding that Cause" (146). Of course, as he catalogs kinds of extrinsic value, Hodges is quite clear that silver became the standard or equivalent by the "common Consent" of "Nations and People." Hodges argues emphatically that the "general Value, which for Convenience of Foreign Commerce" is put on silver bullion, is "altogether Extrinsick, and not Intrinsick" (270). His remarks on figurative intrinsic value, however, add a caveat of sorts to this. Hodges suggests that there is some unseen "Cause" directing or "determining" this choice: providence guided men to choose silver, and their valuations approximate the providentially plotted order. Crucial to Hodges's argument is his insistence that such figurative value is intrinsic, but not in the way that intrinsic value is usually understood. He points out that arguments for restoring the coin imagine value annexed to each grain of silver, such that "a greater Quantity" of intrinsically valuable silver is "preferable in Value to a lesser" quantity. Hodges's figurative intrinsic value, however, is "alike in all its Parts"; it belongs to silver as category of substance without inhering in individual bits of silver (270). Providence can guide humans to silver without obligating them in any way to it. Like the author of *Some Observation's,* Hodges locates the silver standard in a divine order, but he chooses to emphasize—instead of an inherently meaningful natural world—a continuously acting providence whose hints humans heed. The notion of figurative value allows Hodges to retain a lively sense that economic systems are divine institutions that receive divine guidance while simultaneously embracing the complex ways humans participate in these systems.

Hodges posits a continuing, providential guidance over the world that replaces the injunction against meddling that advocates of restoring the coin found in nature. While preferring to emphasize a constantly active order over a static one that binds kings and governments, Hodges also finds it useful to turn to the material world for knowledge about monetary systems. He just finds in it a very different lesson than his opponents did. He discovers in "the very Substantial Nature of Quantity in Silver" a way to "refute[ ] demonstrably" their position that kings should not meddle with money.

His argument draws on the analogical logic of the meditative empiricism. Hodges explains that silver has a "ductile Nature": "by beating out it may be made a fifth part larger" or "a fifth part broader ... without the least Alteration of, or Addition to its Quantity and Weight" (301–2). Materially, silver is always subject to contraction or expansion. Its length and width are never fixed. Thus, he concludes, "the very Nature of Silver it self seemeth to teach and direct us to consider, if it ought not, or may not be so ordered in Money, as that in the same Quantity and Weight, it may be commensurate to, and serve larger, broader, and longer Necessities and Occasions, as well as it is capable to do in Bullion" (302). In true occasional meditation form, Hodges asserts that the material properties of silver "teach" and "direct us" as to the proper way of managing monetary systems. In the stretchiness of silver, Hodges discovers a kind of sanction ("ought"), or at least a provisional natural invitation ("may"), for governments to stretch a finite amount of silver out over a larger amount of money. His conclusions are buttressed by faith that the natural world participates in a divine order, that it contains hints and prompts. The natural properties of silver are conceived of as the source of a supple, rich variety of meaning. It is not just that equity applies both physically and morally but that the fact that an ounce of silver can be stretched to be longer than an equal ounce of silver has a sociopolitical application.

Scholars have long recognized that a hostile conservative reaction to new economic developments distrusted humanly constructed economic value and appealed to the natural world. I have established that writers across a much broader spectrum of policy proposals and political affiliations proceeded on startlingly similar assumptions. These writers participated in the meditative empiricism as they scrutinized natural particulars for ethical guidance and allowed for the complex human task of approximating divine hints about how the economy ought to work. While not all contributors to the recoinage debates turned to nature in this way, it was a viable move for proponents of every position. For some advocates of restoring the coin, natural facts about silver's durability, weight, and divisibility licensed its monetary value. Whether the material substance was ordained to be inherently valuable or somehow elicited human valuation, an ounce of silver equaled an ounce of silver in such a way that governments simply could not mess with monetary value. Advocates of raising the coin instead affirmed the government's ability to alter value. Yet, proposals like Lowndes's continued to maintain that the natural world provided a fetter on economic decisions. Extrinsic value could be altered only to correspond with "real value"—an understanding of value that took into account how many grains of silver were scattered throughout the world. A related turn to natural facts as a source of economic guidance motivated the arguments of more forward-looking innovators, as well. Barbon understood value in relation to the robust productive capacity of the natural world, while Hodges conceptualized an interventionist providence and found analogical sanction in silver's ductility. While proposals for devaluation seem to twentieth- and twenty-first-century scholars to contain a "radically modern" dematerializing force, they could be offered up by thinkers genuinely concerned to have economic systems respect and approximate a natural order.

My treatment of the recoinage debates therefore complicates usual ways of understanding late seventeenth-century English economic thought. First, the political affiliations of the writers we have looked at do not map as the new economic criticism's binaries teach us to expect—with Whiggish, moneyed men comfortable with "paper credit, volatile signifiers, and increasingly immaterial forms of property" on the one side and "Country" conservatives embracing land and bullion on the other.[42] Locke, for example, was a Whig, and his powerful Whig friends like Lord Keeper John Somers and Edward Clarke endorsed his position. On the other hand, Hodges clearly had royalist sympathies, and Barbon was active in "Country" and Tory politics. Without broaching the whole potent set of issues about war, foreign marketplaces, government intervention, the domestic economy, royal succession, and religion that determined political identity at the moment, I want to point out that these affiliations seem somewhat counterintuitive in terms of the usual binaries: Whigs insisted conservatively on bullion, while their political opponents were quicker to embrace human agencies in the functioning of money.[43]

More generally, advocates of all three major positions on the recoinage could pay close attention to the natural world, and especially to the natural properties of metals, as they tried to figure out how the economy should work. This shared interest in nature upsets the tendency of the new economic criticism to relegate engagements with the natural world to a "residual" or hostile conservative reaction against new money culture. It also disturbs the powerful critical narratives that imagine modernization as a steady process of dematerialization, as a steady movement away from the natural. It is not just that "residual" ideas about nature's meaningfulness persist into new money culture. Even the more "emergent," dematerialized notions of value were worked out by thinkers who found guidance, logical principles, and political hints in the natural world—in silver itself.

Consumers Turn to Nature

The first part of this chapter has focused on the ways that people turned to natural things as sources of economic and social information. In Charles Gildon's *The Golden Spy* (1709), the possibility that things have answers is realized as gold coins grumble to life to teach their owners a lesson or two. The next year, Addison's *Tatler* #249 (1710) similarly featured a living, loquacious shilling. These founding texts sparked a fashionable subgenre, and by the end of the eighteenth century not only every kind of money, from bank notes to rupees, but all sorts of trinkets, clothing objects, and animals had leapt to life to tell their tales.[44]

These strange stories have received much scholarly attention of late, as texts participating in and commenting on an emergent consumer culture in England. Certainly, the genre engaged this culture's new possibilities and mobilities. In story after story, people at court are corrupted by bribes; gamblers are punished for using money irresponsibly; ladies are condemned for selling themselves for money or on the marriage market; and religious hypocrites are exposed for valuing cash over piety. The genre also celebrates and even formally enacts circulation within contemporary consumer culture. Gildon's coins boast of their vast "Experience and Knowledg" and large acquaintance—one trumpets that he has "belong'd to several great Politicians, Favourites and Courtiers," as well as kings, gamesters, clergymen, vain ladies, whores, actresses, poets, and chemists.[45] Addison's shilling seems to proximate the logic of the general equivalent as it chronicles its "ramble[s] from Pocket to Pocket": an "Apothecary gave me to an Herb-Woman, the Herb-Woman to a Butcher, the Butcher to a Brewer, and the Brewer to his Wife," and so on.[46]

Scholars propose a more fundamental relationship between the genre and emergent consumer culture. It is no accident, they point out, that some of the earliest and most popular it-narratives feature money objects. Money represented not only new mobilities but an odd new kind of agency first made possible in eighteenth-century consumer culture. They suggest that money-agency has something to do with ascendant human agency, with the way human projections and fictions were displacing a natural order. It-narrators become early manifestations of Marx's commodity fetish. For example, Christopher Flint argues that the genre plays up the "commodity nature of money"—its "dematerializing power," its exchange value, and its symbolic representation of the "social contract." The genre "reveal[s] in a particularly distressing way what Marx calls the 'definite social relation between men' that governs all commodities."⁴⁷ According to such readings, when money talks, its agency is more closely linked with human fictions and fetishisms than with nature. Similarly, the eighteenth-century texts are said to register an increasing alienation between people and their things, and their active things actually diminish humans. As Aileen Douglas puts it, the genre expresses the "fear" that "people have become enthralled to things."⁴⁸

However, the genre-forging it-narratives by Gildon and Addison do not stage the emergence of a deeply worrying commodified object agency, a nascent fetishism that mystifies the natural and signals the alienation of people from their things. For one, the best recent work on it-narratives points out that it is anachronistic to read eighteenth-century it-narrators as commodity fetishes (a notion developed around a distinct class of nineteenth-century products). As Lynn Festa explains, "The world that Marx's commodity inhabits is not yet fully realized in these books" or in the world in which these books were written.⁴⁹ Jonathan Lamb's provocative *The Things Things Say* goes even further, challenging common assumptions about the ontological emptiness of objects that underwrite commodity readings. (Similar assumptions also underwrite another scholarly interpretation, emphasizing sentimental human projections onto things.) Lamb helpfully distinguishes between two kinds of things and, by extension, thing-narratives. Some eighteenth-century objects function like property—safely subservient to the humans who circulate them, use them for self-expression, or project moral meanings onto them. Lamb, however, also highlights things "no longer owned or ownable," things that are unaccommodated into human schemes, disinterested in or downright hostile to humans.⁵⁰ Lamb's account is exemplary in the way he takes seriously not just thing agency created or projected by humans but also an agency that confronts humans as fundamentally separate. He offers a salutary rejoinder to scholars who assume that thing agency is a mystified manifestation of human agency—through the process of commodity fetishism or even imaginative or sentimental projection. Things exist and mean *in themselves*.

Lamb emphasizes the "hostility" of such recalcitrant things. For example, he cites a rich passage from Gildon's *Golden Spy* in which the human narrator explains that "the Mysteries" that his coins "reveal'd are like those . . . which are not be expos'd to unhallow'd Eyes, for fear the Sense of Things should destroy all confidance betwixt Man and Man, and so put an end to Humane Society" (116).⁵¹ Lamb associates this "secret held by money so devastating it threatens the basis of civil society" with "hostility," "outrage," or "disapproval" about human nature, with the "radical challenge[ ]" to humanity offered by Gulliver after his time with the Houyhnhnms. Things refuse to approve human malfeasance; they sit in silent judgment even as people try desperately to appropriate or accommodate them. Of course, Lamb is quite right that it-narrators take on agency to point out the "mercilessness, greed, and inhumanity of human beings," but—departing from his emphases—I want to insist that these critiques can unfold from the things' place in a providential natural order.[52] The civilization-destroying secret in Gildon's book, for example, is about the way corrupt humans *deviate from* nature: the coins know of "such villainous Designs," "such Monstrous Vices," even "to the confounding of Sexes and Nature" (116). The things things know might threaten civil society (as the narrator gets a glimpse of how terribly people can act and loses faith), but they also offer an ethical guide that constitutes and maintains society ("Nature" un-"confounded" as ethical standard). Recalcitrant things, fundamentally separate from us, can still mean something *for* us. Just as occasional meditators constantly insist that instinctive animals are superior to erring humans, Gildon's coins pop to life to show how badly humans sin. They earnestly attempt to set humanity aright, to reinstate a correspondence between "Nature" and human nature.[53]

Gildon's "golden spies" and Addison's chatty shilling bespeak the possibility that the natural world is full of hints and prompts; they even speak out specific hints and prompts. These early, genre-forging it-narratives deploy meditative-empiricist assumptions about the agency and import of natural things—the same assumptions that allow Hodges's ductile silver to "teach and direct" people to knowledge about proper human behavior within the contemporary economy. As we have seen, contemporaries believed that they could extrapolate rich meanings from nature, though only in fragments glimpsed through skeptical, self-effacing attention. The it-narrative's supple generic form enacts and explores this process. It gives articulate (though fictional) voice to the meanings available, if humans could only manage to heed nature's prompting. The form also deploys personification and analogy as instrumental tools that—provisionally, even playfully—help access such meanings; and it thereby generates a unique kind of didacticism that does not have to be explicit, that works through implicitly encouraging analogical meditation on particular things.

Both it-narratives situate their talking things within a natural order understood to contain messages and morals. Addison, for example, emphasizes his coin's natural origins and materiality. "I was born," the coin explains, "on the Side of a Mountain, near a little Village of *Peru*" (269–70). Addison moves rather quickly from the coin's birth, through mention of its specific material forms ("Ingot," then Queen Elizabeth shilling), to an insistence on its "natural Disposition": "I found in me a wonderful Inclination to ramble," or, slightly later, "we Shillings love nothing so much as travelling" (270). What is at stake in this move from material nature to "natural Disposition" is clarified by Addison's willingness, elsewhere, to explicitly develop the kind of argument that found economic hints in the providential natural order. In his famous praise of the Royal Exchange in *Spectator* #69 (written about six months after the shilling essay), Addison turns to nature to find a mandate for global trade. He explains, "Nature seems to have taken a particular Care to disseminate her Blessings among the different Regions of the World." He suggests that this was done, providentially, "with an Eye to this mutual Intercourse and Traffick among Mankind, that the Natives of the several Parts of the Globe might have a kind of Dependance upon one another, and be united together by their common Interest."[54] In having different material products exist only scattered across the globe, "Nature" facilitates global "Dependance" and world peace. Material realities—the particular ways that God distributed products in nature—contain clues for humans. England without trade is a "barren uncomfortable Spot of Earth," and, by enriching it with products from all over globe, English merchants are fulfilling a providential decree encoded into nature. Addison's it-narrative dramatizes this providential prompt. In order for Peruvian silver to function as English coinage, people had to heed the providential exhortation to "Traffick" internationally, and the coin itself speaks the "natural Disposition" encoded into it: "I found in me a wonderful Inclination to ramble." The way Addison situates his treatment of circulation within a providential natural order problematizes the common argument that it-narratives' privileging of circulation comes from emergent capitalist society, that the money's desire to circulate is linked with its identity as nascent commodity. The natural context also sheds interesting light on both the coin's syntax ("I found *in me*") and the significant fact that it is most material in the moment it begins to speak its lessons: "the Shilling that lay upon the Table reared it self upon its Edge, and turning the Face towards me, opened its Mouth" to speak "in a soft Silver Sound" (269).

Gildon's text also firmly situates his speaking coins and their desire to circulate within the natural world. From his opening pages, Gildon goes out of his way to link the agency of the talking coins to the created material world. The narrator opens the book by signaling his interest in science—in "noble Enquiries into the hidden Secrets of Nature"—and by evincing pride in England's marked dedication to the scientific project. The scientific hypothesis that especially interests him is the heterodox one that holds that things "which we generally not only esteem mute but inanimate" might have "*Sensibility,*" "Rationality," and even "Reflection." In discussing this possibility, the narrator cites occult sources that teach of animate matter: he has read Campanella's "*de Sensu Rerum*"; he knows "of the *Soul of the World*, and of Maxims that hold ev'ry part of the Universe to be compos'd of animal sensible, and perhaps rational Particles" (2). The agency of the material world was an active concern in cutting-edge natural philosophy, and earlier in Gildon's career he had written on both sides of the controversial question of "whether Matter and Motion think."[55] Here, posing the possibility only playfully, Gildon nonetheless deliberately links coin agency with material realities.

Gildon's treatment of circulation also engages with another heterodox scientific tradition: alchemy (or perhaps more generally the web of analogies characteristic of early modern thought, in which the macrocosm had its microcosm, and each element had its corresponding planet). Gildon's gold coin insists on a relationship with gold's traditional-alchemical analogical counterpart: the sun. The first coin to speak—a French "half *Louis d'Ore*"—repeatedly voices its love for the sun, its passionate desire to "behold the glorious Light of the Sun" (5, 7). We get an intriguing idea of what the gold/sun link might have to do with circulation by looking at another near-contemporary text that deployed the logic of meditative empiricism. In an edition of Aesop's *Fables* (1708), Joseph Jackson discovers guidance on consumer behavior in the metal's materiality. He opens by positing an ontological link between gold and the sun:

> Gold it's Original takes from the Sun:
> As such the Sire, let th'Off-spring like himself,
> Around the World, it's shining Circle run. . . .[56]

The sun is the "Original" and "Sire" of gold. This traditional association is powerfully reinforced by the shared coloring of the sun and gold, as well as by the still-current belief that metals grow underground as they are warmed by the sun. Jackson then proceeds to moralize on this natural fact. Gold is like the sun, and so the behavior of the "Sire" elucidates the proper behavior of "th'Offspring." The sun seems to circle the earth constantly. Jackson does not worry too much about the outdated astronomical facts he works from (the sun, of course, was no longer understood to "run" in a circle around the earth). He simply accepts another traditional cosmic association. The implicit reasoning continues: because the sun is constantly moving about the sky, gold ought to be allowed to move freely and constantly. Jackson usefully underscores the way that natural fact generates a human imperative: "As" the sun, we ought to "let" gold behave in this natural way—to "run" a "shining Circle." As his moralizing continues, Jackson applies the natural mandate contained in gold more directly to human behavior. "Misers" who "heap" up gold or "hid[e]" it underground do something unnatural and morally problematic to it.[57] They ought to heed the instructions encoded in the material world. Gildon's text similarly moves from the ontological link between gold and the sun to the economic imperatives it generates: gold desires to behave like the sun. The French coin voices its abhorrence of consumers who lock up coins in hoard-prisons, for (it explains) its remarkable powers of speech are entirely lost when a miser "shut[s]" the coin "up in his Coffers." Its powers are "only maintain'd by an absolute Freedom of circulating with the Sun about the World" (7). This mandate even manifests itself physically, as Gildon depicts the French coin losing some of its powers when confronted with the threat of dark imprisonment (in the narrator's actions that "seem to confess the Miser") (7).[58] Like Addison's shilling, Gildon's gold voices the providential prompts encoded in it.

Early it-narratives thus give fictional, personified form to the logic that motivates the meditative empiricism. They assume that the natural world contains hints and prompts to meaning, and they give voice to those meanings. Furthermore, they deploy the meditative empiricism's distinctive kind of personification. For example, Robert Boyle insists that occasional meditators "can (as it were) make the World vocal, by furnishing every Creature... with a Tongue to entertain him with... and the very Flowers of his Garden, read him Lectures of Ethicks or Divinity" (22). This formulation foregrounds the complexity of the personification. Most important, Boyle registers a very real way in which things act; he is quite serious about this passage's general argument that meaning comes from the natural world. Of course, he also recognizes the human agency involved in this process, for a certain kind of empiricist scrutiny is required before things "can" teach lessons in "Ethicks and Divinitie." Like the silver that "made its own way" in the anonymous pamphlet, the personification figures the very real way that things assert themselves, while allowing for the necessity of human attention, inference, and action. Meaning is created in the confrontation between prompting thing and observant human. Finally, Boyle's parenthetical "(as it were)" recognizes and flags something playfully figurative in his formulation; of course, birds and flowers do not *really* lecture. Boyle is self-aware, here, about the figurative status of the personification, but even this more exaggerated possibility is licensed by scripture: "But ask now the beasts, and they shall teach thee; and the fowls of the air, and they shall tell thee: Or speak to the earth, and it shall teach thee: and the fishes of the sea shall declare unto thee. Who knoweth not in all these that the hand of the LORD hath wrought this?" (Job 12:7–9). Boyle's personifications register the agency of humans, nature, and God; they are at once figurative and truthful.

Intriguingly, Gildon and Addison might have gotten the central idea of the it-narrative form—the idea of using sustained personifications of this sort to allow things to speak in urgent (if also fictionalized and playful) attempts to voice nature's particular dictates—from the occasional meditators. Ralph Austen provides a fascinating example. We saw in chapter 1 that Austen concluded his cutting-edge scientific work on fruit trees with meditations titled *The Spirituall Use of an Orchard* (1653, 1657). Years later, Austen recast his meditational work on fruit trees into *A Dialogue (or Familiar Discourse) and Conference between the husbandman and fruit-trees* (1676). In this proto-it-narrative, personification is licensed by—and personified things give voice to—the truths of creation: the trees promise, "we are continually speaking to men, and are never weary, of instructing, and teaching man his Duty towards God, our Creator."[59] Austen also intriguingly underscores the complexity of his personifications. They are rooted in a Christian ontology and sensitive to a highly particularized, even scientific understanding of natural realities. They are also somewhat figurative. He explains that things speak "very *intelligibly*," when activated by empirical attention, "though not with *an articulate distinct voice*": "to *confer, and discourse with Fruit-trees*" is "to *consider them, and dive, and search into their Natures, and Properties*"; "And then the making of *right conclusions, upon such Considerations,* those are the *Answeres, Teachings, or instructions of the Fruit-trees.*"[60] Austen recognizes that trees do not really talk at the same time that he insists that the personifications figure the very real possibility that meaning comes from nature. He assumes that these meanings are accessed through the human work of paying painstakingly close attention to nature and making inferences, applications, or analogies. When these inferences are "*right,*" meditators access the truths that the creatures are trying to communicate. Meaning is neither wholly objective nor wholly subjective. In Austen's hands, the notion of a "dialogue" is especially apt. The trees and husbandman engage in a continual back and forth that illustrates the way that things can prompt but also resist or refine human attempts to understand them.[61] The personified trees "continually speaking to men" featured in his dialogue, then, approximate and give voice to natural truths, while their animation remains somewhat playfully figurative, and their specific conclusions remain always possibly fallible approximations filtered through the person who writes them up.

It is in a similar spirit that Gildon and Addison have coins speak. Whereas occasional meditators have to draw the conclusions themselves, the it-narrative allows the thing to speak, and even enact, what Addison calls its "natural Disposition." The dream of the genre is the dream of unmediated access to providential meanings, the dream of a morality that comes straight from nature without the corruptible influence of a human mediator. Yet, the form presents the very serious possibility of accessing natural truths in a playful way. It is acutely aware of the figurative, fictional status of its talking objects. Addison's coin talks in a dream, literally, and Gildon can personify coins without insisting "That Matter and Motion Can Think"—fiction offers an attractive kind of provisionality that attaches to both the personifications themselves and the specific lessons they express. As we will see, both texts also feature human attempts to make sense of things, and both leave room for play, even punchlines. These texts therefore allow for the inherent meanings of things, the human work of accessing such meanings, and the somewhat exaggerated figurations involved in writing it all up. This complexity was, I think, crucial to the genre's appeal for contemporaries: it-narratives' speaking things promised unmediated access to truths encoded in nature—even if this access was of course mediated, approximated, provisional, and fictionalized.

The influence of the meditative empiricism's personifications is perhaps clearest in the way Addison manages the it-narrative form. Addison's text sets up an analogy between coins and people. In the story's deliberate framing device, Isaac Bickerstaff reports a conversation that passed the night before between himself and a friend. The friend points out "That it required much greater Talents to fill up and become a retired Life, than a Life of Business," and he "rallied very agreeably the busie Men of the Age, who only valued themselves for being in Motion, and passing through a Series of trifling and insignificant Actions" (269). The conversation is about human worth or value. Fashionable men "valued themselves" according to the bustle and business of their lives. But, as Bickerstaff's friend notes, quick motion does not necessarily entail value. Instead, he says, men who can "fill up" and "become" a quiet life away from the bustle have real "Talents," real value. It is in pursuit of this point that Bickerstaff's friend—"In the Heat of his Discourse, seeing a Piece of Money"—makes the comparison between money and men: "I defie (says he) any of these active Persons to produce half the Adventures that this Twelvepenny-Piece has been engaged in, were it possible for him to give us an Account of his Life" (269). He posits that the real "value" of human beings corresponds to the real value of money, and movement in both cases boots nothing. This analogy chastens fashionable people who pride themselves on something in which they are surpassed by mere shillings. Addison poses a problem of insides and outsides, of how and why value is conferred. The question is about circulation and about how real value "fills up" its vehicle.

The story then continues: Bickerstaff admits that his "Friend's Talk made so odd an Impression" on him that he fell asleep and had a vivid dream in which the coin offers an "Account of his Life and Adventures" (269). Thus, the coin's "Adventures" in valuation are from the beginning linked to the problem of human worth. While the dream vision contains an extended history of the coin, the essay invites readers to think about the different ways they value coins in a meaningful analogy with the ways they value people. The moral flipside, as it were, always remains. The frame of course endorses a real value apart from circulation: it takes more "Talents to fill up and become a retired Life" than a life of mere "Motion." (Note the pun on "Talent," as both a feature of the human personality and a biblical economic unit.) This affirmation of real value is reinforced by the climax of the coin's narrative. It expresses shame and anger at being clipped: a clipper "with an unmerciful Pair of Sheers cut off my Titles, clipped my Brims, retrenched my Shape, rubbed me to my inmost Ring, and, in short, so spoiled and pillaged me, that he did not leave me worth a Groat" (272). The coin acknowledges that this was a "general Calamity," and all its friends were similarly "curtailed and disfigured." The coin, however, gets a happy ending. It is thrown into the "Furnace" "and (as it often happens with Cities rising out of a Fire) appeared with greater Beauty and Lustre than we could ever boast of before" (272). Like London rising from its ashes, the coin is restored to greater beauty and greater value. It is happy in its newfound weightiness, its real value. The moral, then, is that something real and weighty is needed, for both an adequate coinage and a "retired Life." Addison suggests that bits of metal can teach us a lesson about solid insides. Put another way, he believes that the way coins move through the world can teach something about how we ought to move through the world.

It is telling that Addison's it-narrative features the same moral conclusions that a contemporary occasional meditator found when scrutinizing silver. In the immediate wake of the recoinage controversy, one anonymous sermonizer turned to bullion for economic and moral guidance, and he found that the crucial bit of moral knowledge that coins illuminate has everything to do with intrinsic value. The sermon opens with a scriptural analogy that Jeremiah constructs between corrupt men and *"Reprobate Silver"*—a biblical passage that would have structured contemporary understandings of Addison's people/coin analogy too. The sermonizer then proceeds to establish and explicate a much more thoroughgoing analogy between *"the degeneracy of the People"* in a Church and the *"debas*[ement] *of the Coin"* in a country.[62] In practice, this means the writer scrutinizes, in extraordinary detail, the techniques of the (successful, he thinks) recoinage to see what lessons they might hold for those interested in a restoration of the religious and moral purity of England. His central theme is that his country and his congregants should resist all sorts of "disagreements" between "the right Stamp" and weight in metal, between name and thing, appearance and reality, public and private, "outward Professions" and inner reality. The fundamental moral lesson he takes from the recoinage debate can be summed up in an imperative: "See that in your whole life and course you be according to the *Standard,* and full Weight."[63] Advocating a kind of moral "restoring the coin," this sermonizer worried about a discrepancy between "Value" and "Vertue," and he solved the problem by insisting on a correspondence between stamp and weight, outside and inside. For Addison, as for the occasional meditator, scrutiny of silver money teaches the importance of solid human insides.

Provocatively, Gildon reaches the same conclusion. Gildon's coins are observers who can see through human corruptions and hypocrisies. They insist that words be backed up by things, titles be grounded in substance, appearances correspond to truths. While boasting of the many intriguing stories it can tell, Gildon's first, French coin underscores this particular moral issue: "I have been in every station of Life, from the *Prince* to the *Peasant,* and can unfold all the Mysteries of Iniquity, that in all Nations have always enrich'd Knaves, impos'd on Fools, and baffled Men of Sense" (14). It has traveled, and it can expose the hypocrisies and corruptions happening behind the scenes. But it does not say "hypocrisies and corruptions." It says "the Mysteries of Iniquity," and the narrator repeats this phrase shortly thereafter, preferring "to know the Mysteries of modern" (as opposed to ancient) "Iniquity" (30). "Iniquity" can refer to injustice or unfairness generally, functioning as a kind of blanket accusation of corruption. Yet the word comes from the Latin *aequus,* meaning "even, just equal," and the word echoes the recoinage writers' concern with the material/moral "Rules of Equity." Gildon's coins underscore these connotations as they focus their moral indictments on problematic disjuncts, inequalities. They insist on the importance of insides, weighty moral cores.

Gildon, however, manages the it-narrative form rather differently than Addison. In *The Golden Spy*'s frame stories, the analogy between coins and people is less striking than analogies between incidents that happen to the coins and to the human narrator in the day between each night's storytelling session. Gildon's text nonetheless works to generate morals by inviting readers to think analogically about coin agency. He just achieves this by drawing on another technique evident throughout the occasional meditation on coin (and available in occasional meditations more generally): a predilection for punning. The sermonizer repeatedly uses words that apply both to money and men—"reprobate," for example. He even flags this technique in 2 Corinthians 13:5, which includes the exhortation to "*Examine*" and "*prove your own selves.*" The sermonizer explains that the "Apostle" here "useth a word"—*prove*—"that is also made use of for the Tryal of Metals of which Money is made."[64] Such words (like Addison's "Talents") somewhat collapse the distance between money and men, between the monetary and the moral. Gildon similarly toys with money language to render the "iniquities" problems of value that coins are peculiarly suited to explain. In one of the text's many plays with "value" and valuation, a coin describes a young spark whose "Person was extreamly charming, but his ignorant Education denied him those few Qualities of Mind that are more valuable" (54). Real value is the solid moral core that ought to back up appearances. In another story, a poor young woman is forced to promise a corrupt suitor sexual satisfaction in order to help save her beloved. The guinea points out, she "never design'd to comply with his lewd Desires, yet she had found, that Sincerity was of no use in a Court, where false Promises are current Coin" (105–6). Sincerity, inner worth—constituted by a refusal to say one thing and be another—are not valued, but lies and flattery are accepted as valuable, as "current Coin." Courts value the wrong thing and neglect real value, inherent moral worth.[65]

Gildon also plays up the theme of "currency" that the corrupt "current Coin" in this woman's story suggests. In money talk of the time, a clipped coin that was accepted "passed" as current. Gildon repeatedly uses this language of "passing" to stage his "iniquities," repeated disjuncts between outside and inside, between what people value and what is properly valuable. His coins describe religious hypocrites who "play the Devil" but "pass for Saints," an unfaithful young wife who "disguis'd her Disgust so artfully, that it pass'd with" her old husband "for a sincere Tenderness," a nonsense trumpeter in fashionable society who "pass[es] for a great Master of Music, and

Eunuchs" who "palm on the Town Grimace, and Action for Harmony and Voice" (44, 54, 13). Especially in the last example, where bad musicians turn master counterfeiters as they both "pass" and "palm" their talents on the public, Gildon brings a concern with "currency" to human valuations. That all this talk of "passing" is crucially involved with discourses of money is underscored by Gildon's last use of the term in his book. In a discussion of the dangers of love intrigues, the guinea tells of a typical "bad Woman," the dangerous sort only after money and her own, licentious pleasure: "Nature had given her a Person extreamly Charming," and this "pass'd for Wit and Truth, and every thing else, of real Value" (233). Like the young spark, this woman has an attractive appearance, and—to use moral language that itself elides distinctions between social legibility and concern with coinage—this "face value" proclaims inner virtues that she simply does not have. Gildon's text also puns on "Base" repeatedly and, once, on "Talent."[66] Like Addison's "Talents," Gildon's puns link money and people. And like Addison's frame story—though in the absence of an explicit analogy—they encourage readers to think about monetary matters in meaningful relationships with human morality. It is no accident that Gildon's coins end up somewhere quite close to the occasional meditator scrutinizing silver: they condemn those who do not live "according to the *Standard,* and full Weight."

Gildon also thematizes the process of meditating upon nature to understand its moral dictates. He does this, first, by taking advantage of the room for play that his sustained fictional personifications offer: he toys with character. Giving anti-Catholic prejudices free reign, he depicts the "*Roman Crown*" as a bad coin whose moral code is not to be trusted. It has taken on too much of the tincture "of the Court of *Rome,*" which "calls[ ] Vice *Virtue,* and Virtue *Folly*" (39, 125). Accordingly, the Roman coin offers a perverted, corrupted sense of "Nature"; for instance, it justifies love intrigues by making the libertine argument that "Nature has given such Desires" to humans to act on (149).[67] Yet, the stolid English guinea is there to speak for uncorrupted nature. It draws the proper morals—here: avoid whores—and insists that "If the Practice of Virtue is not so general as it might be, yet all" in its less-corrupted domains "allow the Excellence of it" (155). (The French coin has a more complicated status; through most of the book, it is basically good—if a bit too chatty; however, when talk turns in the final night to "Peace *and* War," it becomes the mouthpiece for corrupt French policy.) Gildon's sustained personifications demonstrate—and comment reflexively on—good and bad appeals to nature. Gildon further encourages his readers to meditate on both the coins' stories and nature itself by providing a positive human model for meditation within the text itself. Twice the human narrator spends part of the day between nighttime storytelling sessions meditating during "a Walk into the Fields." The first time, he ponders how corrupt humans deviate from nature—"degenerat[ing], not into Brutes, but into Divels." He draws an analogy between women's beauty and men's minds, on the one hand, and, on the other, the natural things he "behold[s]" in the "Fields": "how soon" each of these "fades and changes from all its Beauty with deformity and dissolution." "Lord," the narrator piously thinks, "what a Mystery is not only Man, but the whole Creation!" (145–46). His second meditation underscores even more emphatically that the corruption the coins speak of functions to strengthen, not undercut, the need for religion and morality: the fact that humans are hypocritical even in "Religion, the most Sacred Tye of Humane Society," serves the narrator as "a stronger Proof of its"—religion's—"Excellence, and only an Evidence of the Extraordinary Wretchedness of Mankind" (275). The coins' critiques of humanity preserve a larger providential order.

The talking coins of Gildon and Addison do address issues of a newly consumerist economy. Avarice and iniquity are seen as pressing problems, for example. But they do not represent proto-commodities first made possible by this economy, and their agency does not signal a move away from the natural toward human fictions. In fact, for Gildon and Addison, things speak in an attempt to keep human constructions and institutions in touch with nature. There was something desirable—and not just, as in commodity fetishism, deeply worrying—about thing agency and human subordination: to act in accordance with the dictates of the material was to act as a God-obeying subject. Of course, those very dictates were always rather hard to come by. People could only access partial, provisional glimpses of larger truths, and at best the resulting meanings involved a confrontation between prompting thing and observing, approximating human. It-narratives negotiate this problem of human agency in complex ways. On the one hand, these texts—like many contemporary monetary arguments—were born from a nervousness about human intervention and a belief that the material world offers supple resources for guidance. The genre's earliest instantiations proceeded on a conviction that things can teach moral lessons and limit human behaviors in desirable ways. The idea of a thing directly espousing a providential moral code was enticing, if impossible. On the other hand, these fictional stories worked through sustained personifications that were clearly figurative—coins do not really speak. Humans approximated the natural prompts and wrote up the stories in which things speak them. The form of the it-narrative actually encouraged the human work of thinking analogically about coin movements.

Clearly, in the period money's matter mattered.[68] Writers of economic proposals and it-narratives alike engaged the meditative empiricism as they tried to understand how this mattering worked. Indeed, they dreamt of the possibility that things mattered "in the active voice," without the problematic but necessary mediations of human agency.[69] Silver "made its own way" and could "teach and direct us"; money talked, literally and loudly.

Empiricist Subjects, Providential Nature, and Social Contracts

BOYLE THOUGHT THAT THE meditative empiricism could lead to "discovery" of "Physical," "Theological" "Moral," "Oeconomical," "but also a Political" truth. This chapter demonstrates its workings in the realm of the "Political." Particularly, the meditative empiricism's postures and logics featured prominently in some important theories about social contract and the origins of society. Many eighteenth-century writers assumed that their historical predecessors must have scrutinized nature and approximated its meanings as they constructed moralities, societies, governments, and institutions. This assumption confirms the arguments of chapter 3, that the meditative empiricism accessed pragmatic, secular, and forward-pointing kinds of truth.

This assumption also raises some far-reaching questions about the human individual in the period. Social contract theories are often thought to privilege a quintessentially modern understanding of the human: autonomous liberal individuals supposedly broke from nature and tradition to construct governments by and for themselves. Interestingly, this oft-told tale about autonomous political subjects has been challenged by recent scholarship that insists on the limits of individual autonomy even in the period's thinking about contract—see, for example, Victoria Kahn's treatment of contract theory's close relations with theological notions of covenant and cutting-edge psychologies of the human passions, or Sandra Macpherson's argument against the prevailing assumption that eighteenth-century governments and domestic relationships were both "organized around the freedom of persons to choose their associations." Like Kahn's embodied subjects and like Macpherson's bundles of "matter in motion" obeying a tragic logic, the political individuals featured in this chapter are less autonomous and more closely connected to the material world than scholarship usually allows.[1]

I argue that, in some key texts, the individual making social contracts looks less like a democratic citizen today than like an occasional meditator. Eighteenth-century writers could give consenting individuals agency and contract transformative power even as they insisted that God's creation offers clues about how societies should work. They could draw on the meditative empiricism as they depicted human agents scrutinizing the natural world and trying—meditatively, analogically—to access its social and political truths. The social contract stories that I explore in this chapter share with the meditative empiricism a distinctive understanding of the human individual: people act but act in attempts to subordinate themselves to a supra-human order encoded, but only ever glimpsed, in nature. These social contract stories also feature a helpfully reflexive awareness about the implications of this understanding of the human. Meditative empiricists were suspicious of both the constructions of unfettered human agency and claims for immediate revelation from the divine. Societies should be made by and for humans, but they should not be merely arbitrary human constructs. Nature mediates between God and humanity, and painstaking empiricist attention to it in the articulation of human institutions ensured the presence of important links between nature and convention.

While the meditative empiricism did not motivate all accounts of political individuality and social contract in the period, I insist that it was a viable, influential mode in some key ones. I focus on four richly complex stories about the origins of society offered by four eighteenth-century writers: John Locke, Daniel Defoe, Lord Bolingbroke, and Alexander Pope. As in chapter 3, I demonstrate that the meditative empiricism influenced thinkers from across the political spectrum—Locke and Defoe are Whigs, and Bolingbroke and Pope Tories—and I thereby upset usual ways of thinking about materiality and modernity. Where new economic critics pit proto-capitalists and dematerialized money against conservatives' land and bullion, an influential scholarly tradition has liberal Whigs making a modern break from a natural political order, while conservative Tories "nostalgically" hold onto it. For example, Isaac Kramnick renders the party divide symptomatic of two diametrically opposed notions of the individual. He argues that Whig thought featured a new "bourgeois, liberal, and individualist" political agent who "stood alone, creating and shaping his own world and his own destiny."[2] This new kind of individual was theorized by Locke, featured in social contract stories, and celebrated by Defoe ("the lyric poet" of the emerging economic society). For their part, we're told, conservatives like Pope and Bolingbroke worried that this individual played "too great a role in manipulating his own world, interfering too much in a divinely ordained hierarchy and nature"; they instead affirmed a more traditional idea of the individual embedded in a natural patriarchal order.[3] I argue that such a strong contrast is untenable and instead recover fundamental similarities in these writers' assumptions about nature, human agency, contract, and the mechanics of progress. Both Whigs and Tories could assert the "modern" idea inherent in contract, but both could also continue to believe that nature provided conceptual resources for government-building individuals.[4] None of these writers wanted humanity to "interfere too much" with a providentially plotted order.

In thus following the influence of the meditative empiricism into "Political" thought, this chapter (like the previous one) highlights what contemporaries understood as very real—even *natural*—links among science, religion, and society. It also underscores another set of disciplinary links, those between political theory and poetry. My strategy of reading philosophical writings by Locke and Bolingbroke alongside poetry by Defoe and Pope is a corrective to old-fashioned readings that have the poets merely paraphrasing or "proselytiz[ing]" philosophical work by others; I take the poets seriously as thinkers in their own right.[5] I take seriously, too, lines of influence running in both directions between political theory and poetry. For instance, social contract theories work through what political theorists today call "genetic arguments": they derive in-the-moment political obligations from stories about origins. Poets were uniquely equipped to contribute, here. They had ready to hand some powerful myths of origins, and they drew on resources hard to translate into prose: narrative nuance, allusive awareness of precursors and influences, and ways of respecting and foregrounding the complexity of agency.[6] Clearly, the disciplinary divisions through which we traditionally approach these texts (is it science or politics? serious philosophy or imaginative poetry?) do injustice to their complexity.

Bolingbroke and Pope

I begin my exploration of the ways eighteenth-century writers problematized a liberal, contractarian political agent in precisely the place where we most expect to find such problematizing: in the works of conservatives like Alexander Pope and Henry St. John, First Viscount Bolingbroke. Though both figures had famously complex politics—witness Bolingbroke's alleged "political opportunis[m]," or Pope's identification in recent scholarship with both crypto-Jacobitism and the Whig Opposition of the 1730s—they indisputably shared strong Stuart and Tory commitments and an inveterate hatred of Robert Walpole's Whig regime.[7] In accordance with our expectations, Pope's *Essay on Man* (1733–34) and Bolingbroke's *Fragments or Minutes of Essays* (published posthumously in 1754) do offer stories about the origin of societies and government that complicate any sense that governments are the autonomous constructions of rational agents. Yet, rather more surprisingly, these same stories also affirm the "modern" idea inherent in social contract—that people construct governments by and for themselves. This section will explore these writers' investments in providential order *and* human construction. It will also demonstrate the influence of the meditative empiricism's humble turn to nature for guidance on social and political issues.

Pope and Bolingbroke developed their origin stories for society alongside one another. Pope was working on the *Essay* at the same time (and sometimes under the same roof) as Bolingbroke wrote his epistemological, ethical, and political essays, and they worked out their ideas in conversation with one another. Pope hails Bolingbroke in the *Essay* as his "guide, philosopher, and friend," and Bolingbroke describes the *Fragments* as his contributions to discussions with Pope.[8] Yet, they are each offering their own ideas, and—far from mere mouthpiece for Bolingbroke—Pope was grappling with big questions in ways that would later be praised by philosophers like Voltaire, Rousseau, and Kant.[9]

Still, the two thinkers do share real conceptual ground, most strikingly in their treatment of how human nature conduces to society. For example, Brean Hammond demonstrates that Pope's history of society shares with Bolingbroke's an argument about "the origins of civil society in self-love and instinctive sociability."[10] In the *Fragments,* Bolingbroke argues that an instinctive self-love "made the union of man and woman" and "that of parents and children" (3:401). Compare this with the beginning of Pope's origin story, as narrated in the *Essay*'s third epistle. He considers "How far SOCIETY [is] carry'd by INSTINCT":

Each loves itself, but not itself alone,
Each sex desires alike, 'till two are one.

> Nor ends the pleasure with the fierce embrace;
> They love themselves, a third time, in their race. (3:121–24)

For both Pope and Bolingbroke, self-love activates sexual and parental instincts that naturally lead to society. Pope's lines actually perform this dialectical coming-together, as the antitheses smooth out. The two men also share more than a general interest in instinct as a fact of human nature. At moments, they use the same language: where Pope has his couple "love themselves" "in their race," Bolingbroke restates his point about self-love as a motor to family by explaining that parents are "prompted by self-love . . . to love themselves in their children" (4:43).

Both Pope and Bolingbroke link this instinct to a created order, to God's will. Earlier in his third epistle, Pope draws on a widely available Augustinian understanding of instinct as he privileges it over reason. Instinct is the realization of God's will in his creatures: "In" instinct "'tis God directs, in" reason "'tis Man." God guides animals directly "To shun their poison, and to chuse their food"; to build the habitations that best suit them; and to act in ways that encourage their survival (3:98–108). Relatedly, Bolingbroke repeatedly insists that the will of God—the law of nature—can be glimpsed in the created world and that instinct is one of the most important "promulgations" of this law, available "immediately and universally" (4:8). By having instinct, understood in this way, "carry" people into society, Pope and Bolingbroke suggest that God himself encourages society. Humans form natural societies because God made them thus.

Pope and Bolingbroke continue to tell their origin stories in parallel, with an emphasis on created human nature. For Bolingbroke, "Self-love begat sociability; and reason, a principle of human nature, as well as instinct, improved it. Reason improved it, extended it to relations more remote, and united several families into one community" (3:401). Using the same language of "improving" and "extending," Pope asserts that "love" does not end as children become capable to stand on their own: "Reflection, Reason, still the ties improve, / At once extend the int'rest, and the love" (3:134–35). Pope goes further than Bolingbroke in insisting that the whole range of human mental faculties conduce to strengthen instinctive sociability: humans require "longer care" in infancy, and this "contracts more lasting binds"— habit and time strengthen the bond between parent and children (3:132). (Pope's invocation of "contracting" in this emphatically natural context is telling.) Sympathy contributes too, as do thankfulness and charity. Children grown see their parents "helpless" in age and feel even further compelled to care for those who cared for them: "Mem'ry and *forecast* just returns engage" (3:141–43). God-given instincts and God-given mental faculties conspire to encourage people to join in societies. In fact, as Hammond further points out, both Pope and Bolingbroke have these faculties conspire to encourage *political* society.[11] Pope dramatizes this: little naturally formed family groups conglomerated into larger groups: societies grew "and join'd"; and political society emerged from the "draw" of "Love" and "Nature" (3:207–8). It is at its start patriarchal: "The same which in a Sire the Sons obey'd, / A Prince the Father of a People made" (3:213–14). Human nature guides people into families, communities, governments.

This part of their stories seems conservatively pitted against any sense of government as a human construct, but Pope's and Bolingbroke's stories also share features with narratives of social contract. Bolingbroke insists that "Nothing but consent can form originally collective bodies of men" and that governments are "of human institution, established by the people, and for the people" (3:405, 4:65). Pope also features a contractarian sense that people create governments by and for themselves—the poem stages two separate instances of human government construction—and he unequivocally endorses John Locke's argument against Filmerian divine right theories: "Nature knew no right divine in Men" (3:236). Howard Erskine-Hill emphasizes Pope's challenge to distinctions between culture and nature, even provocatively suggesting that Pope insists on a crucial overlap between the two. The human consent to society staged in the *Essay on Man* is "a stage in a process rather than a start on a totally new foundation."[12] Some critics have read this dual emphasis on nature and culture as involving a polite nod to contract theory. For example, Erskine-Hill asserts that Pope gestures to social contract theory (he is "sometimes close to specific passages in Locke"), but he "does not centrally affirm the Lockeian myth of contract," the Lockean myth of "a clean break between man's original condition and the beginning of civil society."[13] Others see this dual emphasis on human instinct and social contract (nature and culture) as a mark of Pope's confused thinking.[14] All this scholarship perceptively points to Pope's blurring of boundaries, but—following the work of Tom Jones—I argue that the blurring is, not polite or accidental, but deliberate.[15] For both Pope and Bolingbroke, it is the *point* of the origin story. They want to feature heroes who build societies in an approximation of an order glimpsed in nature. The basic logic here resonates with the model of the human at the heart of the meditative empiricism: people act but act in attempts to subordinate themselves to a supra-human order encoded in nature (here, in human instincts and human family structures).

Helpfully, Bolingbroke offers a reflexive discussion of the stakes of such origin stories—that also functions as a discussion of the stakes of the meditative empiricism's model of human agency. (Isaac Kramnick's nuanced discussion of Bolingbroke's conjectural history remains the most useful scholarly treatment of these issues.)[16] Most pointedly, Bolingbroke asserts his version of an origin story with created human nature as cause against Hobbes's account of political origins, with its alarming privileging of human agency. Bolingbroke explains: for Hobbes, society and even morality are "nominal natures, dependent on the will of man" (3:409). They are mere names, products of arbitrary human agreements, and therefore there is no ultimate sanction for law or morality outside humanity and its constructs. Against this, Bolingbroke wants to insist that the foundations of morality and government are something more than mere human whimsy, human agreement. He has nature anchor and inspire society or morality. For example, he attempts to render Hobbes's position absurd by comparing morality and mathematics as parallel cases. He notes that mathematicians formulate principles and axioms, but, he asks, who would ever imagine that these principles are true only "because mathematicians have made an agreement or compact to proceed upon them" (3:397–98)? This is nonsense, Bolingbroke points out, because the truth of the principles of mathematics *precedes* human recognition and institutionalization of them. So too, he argues, the principles of morality and social institutions. When people make covenants and laws, they make them as formalized "glosses" of natural truths that precede and license them. For Bolingbroke, then, Hobbes "confounds" laws of nature—products of God's will—and the human laws "made to explain and renew" them (3:406, 408). He wrongly attributes to the will of man what ought to be attributed to God's plan (though available only through human approximations). Bolingbroke associates Hobbes's extreme position with the work of more moderate thinkers like Richard Hooker and John Locke who "reason about the institution of civil [society], as if men had been then first assembled in any kind of society" (4:66). Bolingbroke contends that—by downplaying any kind of preconsensual natural society—these thinkers also seem to suggest that society is based on human agreements or conventions. (This reading of Locke is a bit unfair, for Bolingbroke elsewhere recognizes that his account shares some common ground with Locke's.)[17]

Bolingbroke also takes on writers like Robert Filmer, who go to the other extreme. If Hobbes and social contract theorists threaten to make government a product of mere human agency, royalists like Filmer make it into an immediate divine order presided over by a king who is but a proxy for God. Bolingbroke widens his critique of Filmer to include any position that makes sovereignty a direct gift from heaven, "a sort of divine emanation, from God" (4:64). Bolingbroke spends less time refuting this position, because it is so manifestly ridiculous in his eyes. Governments do not descend entire from heaven. They are necessarily "established by the people, and for the people" (4:65). For Bolingbroke, people try to realize a supra-human order in "establish[ing]" their institutions, but, with a kind of empiricist humility, he remembers that their access to this order is only partial, through God's works—nature and human nature.

Bolingbroke concisely summarizes the thrust of his account of origins: "nature begets natural law, natural law sociability, sociability union of societies by consent, and this union by consent the obligation of civil laws" (4:9). This is wonderfully put, for Bolingbroke articulates a set of causal links that forge a close relationship between nature and human institutions. He brings the two within one sentence that has "nature" as its first agent. In its way, "nature begets" civil society. But there are many links in the causal chain, and human "consent" is directly responsible for political "obligation." Bolingbroke also remains aware that this process of "begetting" is fallible, prone to bad approximations, backslidings, and corruptions as much as steady development. For Bolingbroke, this means that the progress of society happened in many stages; it was necessarily a *process* because political authority did not happen in an absolutely transformative Hobbesian moment of irrevocable consent, nor did it come in a thunderbolt direct from God to Adam. God works through created instincts and human mental faculties to pull people into society, and humans do the work to formalize the arrangements. The resulting societies are approximations of a providentially encoded plan. Throughout his discussion of the conceptual stakes of origin stories, Bolingbroke is quite clear that his position steers a sensible middle course between extremes. Bolingbroke keeps society and its institutions in touch with nature without ever conflating the two: "the foundations of civil or political societies were laid by nature, tho they are the creatures of art" (4:40). "Nature begets," humans approximate.

Like Bolingbroke, Pope distrusts arguments that make society into a pure product of human construction. Most directly, Pope engages with Lucretius's version of this argument in *De Rerum Natura*'s account of the origins of society, the classical poetic set piece that clearly inspired the *Essay*'s parallel account. In Lucretius's version of the history of society, instinctive sexual and parental drives draw people together, and individuals strengthen these associations by self-interestedly entering into ad hoc compacts. Pope agrees with Lucretius on the role of instinct in history, but with a difference. For the ancient Epicurean, instinct is an accidental product of the fortuitous combination of atoms. God is emphatically not directing the show. In a late seventeenth-century translation of *De Rerum Natura* (1682), Thomas Creech explained the resulting problem: Lucretius's ideas about the origins of society are "pernicious" in suggesting that societies "are founded on Interest alone" and that "self-preservation is the only thing that obliges Subjects to Duty."[18] Pope guards against the implication that there is no ultimate sanction beyond human caprice on which to ground authority, law, and justice by making instinct a manifestation of God in his creatures, by making the decision to come together into society the natural unfolding of God's plan expressed in creation. Pope—like Bolingbroke, uncomfortable with the "pernicious" drift of arguments that foreground human agency or accident in the formation of society—gives God and God's creation an important role to play in the process. Like Bolingbroke, Pope insists that society is neither mere human construct nor an unmediated divine order. He manages to suggest that people come together to construct governments by and for themselves, while maintaining that society has some reassuring supra-human foundation. Pope, too, is explicit that this process happens gradually, in stages over time: "See him from Nature rising slow to Art" (3:169).

When Bolingbroke talks of nature, he emphasizes human nature (instinctive drives, mental faculties, family arrangements), and recent scholarship interested in an overlap of nature and convention in Pope's *Essay* has focused on these evidences. We have, however, only glimpsed one small part of Pope's origin story, and he is far from finished thinking about the created realities that encourage people to political societies. The *Essay* continues to feature episodes—links in the chain of "begetting"—that have no analogue in Bolingbroke. It is not just human nature but nature itself that serves to mediate in this process. Whereas Bolingbroke asserted that people can glimpse the divine truths still available in nature "By employing our reason to collect the will of God from the fund of our nature, physical and moral, and by contemplating seriously and frequently the laws that are plainly, and even necessarily, deducible from thence" (4:34), Pope suggests people collect the will of God from the "fund of nature" writ large. In so doing, Pope directly engages the meditative empiricism, which of course also insists that "Nature begets" and humans approximate. Pope's origin story depicts our ancestors (like occasional meditators who turn to nature to access moral truths or like economists who heed clues in the natural world as they try to write policy) being prompted by nature and using analogy to approximate its meanings as they come into societies and create governments. Of course, true to his middle way between Filmerian divine right and Hobbesian conventionalism, Pope recognizes that the interpretive process is fallible and vulnerable to corruption, but he insists nonetheless that people ought to look closely at nature as they try to realize God's will in their institutions. Pope makes the meditative empiricism's brand of close attention—a close attention premised on a trust in the meaningfulness of things and the power of analogy yet always aware of the limits of human knowledge—crucial to the formation and maintenance of society. Scrutiny of fish, bees, plants, and planets actually directs the development of civilization.

After Pope's mythical civilization builders instinctively and naturally move from the state of nature to patriarchal communities, they continue to progress by attending to clues in the external world. At the dramatic center and philosophical heart of the *Essay*'s third epistle, Pope has the "voice of Nature" rise up in a tour de force monologue that gives voice to the ways nature helps direct people to social institutions (3:171). This passage is often ignored altogether or dismissed as "childish," "unsatisfying," or silly, but Pope quite seriously delineates his understanding of a relationship between the natural world and government-building individuals.[19] Pope suggests that "observant Men" manage to get into civil society by heeding clues encoded by God into "Great Nature" (3:199). They sometimes get it wrong, but good societies can be constructed by looking carefully at bees, birds, and atoms.

Pope's "voice of Nature" is a reworking of *De Rerum Natura*'s famous personified Nature. When Nature speaks in Lucretius's Epicurean poem, however, it is nature imagined as an accidental combination of atoms, as the frailty of matter and the mortality of all things in a world without God. Pope departs from his poetic predecessor by emphatically Christianizing "Great Nature."[20] Pope's "voice of Nature" begins her monologue by speaking in the language of the scripture. In Proverbs 6:6, Solomon exhorts, "Go to the ant, thou sluggard; consider her ways, and be wise." As we have seen, this is a key biblical precedent for the idea that nature provides clues for how people ought to behave: ants teach us to be provident. Pope's "Nature" stays close to the syntax of the Proverbs passage and renders its point as a general rule: "Man" should "Go, from the Creatures thy instructions take" (3:171–72). The personification here shares energies with Boyle's lecturing flowers, Austen's talking trees, and it-narratives' chatty coins. Pope's "voice of Nature" speaks of the complex ways that creation bespeaks its creator's will.

Pope then allows the "voice of Nature" to specify these "instructions":

> "Learn from the birds what food the thickets yield;
> Learn from the beasts the physic of the field;
> Thy arts of building from the bee receive;
> Learn of the mole to plow, the worm to weave;
> Learn of the little Nautilus to sail,
> Spread the thin oar, and catch the driving gale,
> Here too all forms of social union find,
> And hence let Reason, late, instruct Mankind:
> Here subterranean works and cities see;
> There towns aerial on the waving tree.
> Learn each small People's genius, policies,
> The Ant's republic, and the realm of Bees;
> How those in common all their wealth bestow,
> And Anarchy without confusion know;
> And these for ever, tho' a Monarch reign,
> Their sep'rate cells and properties maintain." (3:173–88)

Nature's monologue expresses the key tenets of the meditative empiricism: "Go," scrutinize nature, and use analogy in attempts to glimpse its practical, moral, and social lessons. The passage even dramatizes the way that nature directs and humans approximate, thus affirming Pope's middle way between government as arbitrary human convention or unmediated divine message. Nature is an agent, two times over. Nature's "voice" is all imperatives—"Go"—and nature (lower-case) contains hints and clues that get a more subtle kind of instructive agency. "The birds" and "the beasts" teach what foods people should eat and which plants work as medicines. Bees, moles, and worms provide lessons in "building," "plowing," and "weaving." Political systems come from insects. Nature provides these insights, so the resulting society has a foundation in God's plan for creation. Humans play a role as well, but when all is working according to God's design, as here, nature is doubly active, and humans are doubly subordinate. People passively receive orders to actions that require them again to subordinate themselves. They "take," "learn," "receive," "find," and "see," but, in all these actions, they get their "instructions" "from" and "of" natural processes. They find them in nature.

Pope reinforces this distinctive relationship between people and nature at the passage's conclusion: "Great Nature spoke; observant Men obey'd; / Cities were built, Societies were made" (3:199–200). "Men" necessarily play a central role in "building" and "making" communities. In fact, Pope recognizes a real degree of latitude in human decisions by allowing for a plurality of possible "Societ*ies,*" possible approximations of nature's instructions. God does not prescribe institutional arrangements but offers several models for "forms of social union." Bees exemplify an ideal monarchy where individual liberties and property rights are respected ("tho' a Monarch reign, / Their sep'rate cells and properties maintain"), while ants provide a useful model for a republic, "Anarchy without confusion." In the lines that follow this passage, Pope has these societies slowly "join" together in ad hoc agreements that climax in a moment of formal social contract: "common int'rest plac'd the sway in one," who is chosen for his "VIRTUE" (3:202, 210–11). Yet again, human agency is elided in a curious way. The moment of social contract occurs in obedience to nature's commands, and political agents do not even get active verbs: "Cities were built, Societies were made." When Pope allows people the agency necessary to form a social contract, then, once more it is only in "observing" natural world and "obeying" its analogical dictates. God offers hints and clues, mediated through nature. People pursue such hints as they try to order their societies.

Pope insists that people get closest when they are "observant." He here embraces a contemporaneous emphasis on empiricist precision. Pope imagines his ancestors looking closely, empirically, at the canny mechanism in the feet of nautilus fish, the geometry deployed in beehives, the way the mole's snout digs into the ground, and the "policies" governing anthills. For Pope, such close attention works like Boyle's applications or Hooke's analogies—to open up technological, practical, and even political information. Interestingly, Pope treats this possibility in an expansive and creative manner that reveals its rich intellectual underpinnings. For one, his treatment suggests that the meditative empiricism is part of a larger seventeenth-century tradition. That great propagandist of science, Francis Bacon, provides a precedent for Pope's passage, as he suggests that *"Beasts; Birds; Fishes; Serpents, rather than Men"* ought to be considered "the first Doctors of Sciences."[21] Pope's interest in animal behavior is also indebted to an even older tradition: an ancient one found in the work of Lucretius, Cicero, and Vitruvius that has civilization emerging from primitivism slowly, through attention to nature.[22] Pope gestures to this tradition in his treatment of the nautilus fish. His lines propose that the nautilus offers humans a model for sailing: it provides analogues for the "oar" and the sail that can "catch the driving gale." His note on these lines refers to Oppian's *Halieutica*, a georgic poem on fishing that is firmly within the ancient primitivist tradition.[23] Pope's note, though, explains in properly empiricist detail how the nautilus fish provided a natural prompt toward navigation. Nautilus fish "swim on the surface of the Sea, on the back of their Shells, which exactly resemble the Hulk of a Ship; they raise two Feet like Masts, and extend a Membrane between which serves as a Sail; the other two Feet they employ as Oars at the side" (3:177–78n). Pope here brings a contemporary emphasis on scientific precision to the ancient tradition.

If Pope's "observant Men" evince a remarkable trust in the dense significance of things, the poet also carefully maintains his middle course between nature and convention by remaining alive to the possibility of human misinterpretation. Drawing on Michel de Montaigne's skeptical essays, in which many of the animal examples in his passage can also be found, Pope has Nature close her monologue by chastening human pretensions, asserting a firm sense of the limits of human knowledge and urging humility before God.[24] Man is invited to "Mark" the beautiful regularity of the world, "Laws wise as Nature, and as fix'd as Fate" (3:189–90). Pope underscores that humans ought to try but will always fail to approximate this exemplary regularity. The Voice of Nature exclaims, "In vain thy Reason finer webs shall draw, / Entangle Justice in her Net of Law"; human approximations of "right, too rigid," will "harden into wrong" (3:191–93). Human knowledge is fallible, human nature limited. People try their best to be "instructed by" nature, by animal "*Instinct* in the Invention of ARTS, and in the FORMS of *Society*" (as Pope's paraphrase puts it), but they always miss the mark at least a bit (3:169n).

Thus, in this extended passage, Pope draws substantively on the meditative empiricism, as well as on traditions of thought about natural law (about both patriarchal kings and social contract), an ancient belief in the social potential of natural observation, and a skepticism insistent on the limits of human knowledge. He sees no contradiction in these assumptions, using them to forge an origin story that turns on "observant" people heeding hints in "Great Nature" and trying to construct governments accordingly.

Pope's *Essay* continues to trace this process, even highlighting the fallibility of human approximations by offering three conjectural possibilities for the origins of religion. The best-case scenario is realized when natural objects prompt men to love the force at work behind them. Faith springs from an awareness of God as Creator, and humanity never strays from the light of truth: "simple Reason" saw "The worker from the work distinct," and "Man, like his Maker, saw that all was right" (3:229–30, 232). Another possible scenario ends with "TRUE RELIGION" but acknowledges the possibility of human error. The naturally ordained leader of each little society cares for his people, who in turn love him immoderately and revere him as a god magically in control of nature. At some point, however, the people recognize the leader's mortality, and they then see what they missed before: they, "looking up from sire to sire, explor'd / One great first father, and that first ador'd" (3:235n, 225–26). In this scenario, fallible people stray from the truth, but circumstances and the wisdom everywhere manifest in created realities lead them back. Finally, Pope acknowledges the possibility that people fall from truth altogether, perverting true religion and government. "SUPERSTITION" and "TYRANNY" happen when people turn their backs on nature and let their "FEAR" guide them in constructing churches and societies. These people "invert the world, and counter-work its Cause" (3:235n, 244). Pope's explanation of false religion and government accounts for these historical facts without taking away any of the divine sanction from true religion and government.

At this point in Pope's origin story, humanity is in a precarious position. The worst in people, their fear and cowardice, has obscured the dictates of nature and God. Pope's story then concludes with a second moment of voluntary government construction; in this doubling Pope clearly recognizes social contract theory's point that people retain the power to resist and restructure their governments. Pope insists, though, that the moment of consent to institutionalized society is motivated by nature:

> 'Twas then, the studious head or gen'rous mind,
> Follow'r of God or friend of human-kind,
> Poet or Patriot, rose but to restore
> The Faith and Moral, Nature gave before. . . . (3:283–86)

Pope asserts that society is the work of men, but the work of men in approximating an order that has somewhat faded. As "observant Men" "obey'd" the voice of Nature's "instructions" earlier, here the "Poet or Patriot" mimics an order that "Nature gave before." Men exert themselves—they "rise"—but only to "restore" natural religion and morality. They "Relum'd" nature's "ancient light, not kindled new," and "If not God's image, yet his shadow drew" (3:287–88). True statesmen reilluminate the spark of this flickering order or retrace its outline as they construct societies.

Pope then focuses on another clue that "Nature" offers government-building individuals. He explains that governments should be instituted such that "jarring int'rests of themselves create / Th'according music of a well-mix'd State." In this, they mimic "the World's great harmony, that springs / From Order, Union, full Consent of things!" (3:293–96). This description closely echoes his prior descriptions of nature and of the state of nature. The reader who has reached this point in the *Essay* has already been introduced to "Union" as an ontological principle that structures the universe. Pope invites his readers to "behold the chain of Love / Combining all below and all above" (3:7–8). "Union" or "Love" occurs at every level of reality. "Union" draws "single atoms" together—each is "Form'd and impell'd its neighbour to embrace." "Union" even happens over time: matter blossoms then decays but in decaying gives life to other forms (3:10, 12, 15–18). In his origin story, Pope extends his ontological principle into a social one, describing the state of nature as a naturally peaceful expression of the universe's underlying principle: "Union" is "the bond of all things, and of Man" (3:150). Importantly, then, when humans construct their social institutions, they try their best to recreate the order of the created universe. The proper human government should preserve some semblance of the "chain of Love" that binds men together with each other and with the universe as a whole, that "Nature gave before."

Pope's origin story gives real agency to individuals. They build cities and make societies: they "join" together, "place" power, and "draw" out the contours of the "State." The third epistle also concludes with a strong affirmation of human agency in the day-to-day workings of political institutions: "contest[s]" about the most efficient and virtuous "Forms of Government" are naïve if they do not consider which are "best administer'd" (3:303–4). Pope's entire conjectural history to this point, however, is a chronicle of how "Nature gave" these political, administering individuals a "Faith and Moral" and even a politics—of how government-building agents find rich resources in the natural world. God gives his creatures instinctual powers that guide them directly into society. Nature exhorts people to pay attention, and particular natural processes give them clues to the proper order. Natural realities direct people to true religion, and "the chain of Love" provides a model for "Th'according music of a well-mix'd State." Pope finishes off his origin story with two more natural things that provide analogical prompts to good behavior. "Man," Pope says, is "like the gen'rous vine": "The strength he gains is from th'embrace he gives." And he is like a planet spinning on its "Axis" as well as "run[ning]" around the sun (3:311–15). As the planet regards at once its own circular motion and its place in the whole, so each person ought to regard self and whole. Pope offers concrete analogies between the natural world and human behavior, but these are more than figures. The great "Chain of Love" connects all things, from atoms to plants to planets. All of nature exhibits this fundamental "Principle": the vine that leans toward its neighbor and the spinning planet are just obeying a truth of nature that people ought to heed as well. Society, Pope insists, should be constructed by "observant" humans such that it "restores" what "Nature gave before."

Pope offers a version of social contract that requires the meditative empiricism's distinctive brand of close attention, which couples a firm sense of the limits of human knowledge with a conviction that nature contains ethical, social, and political clues.[25] Moreover, Bolingbroke helps highlight the stakes of a nature orientation of this sort. By showing that created things play a formative role in society, both Pope and Bolingbroke embrace a degree of human autonomy and remain skeptical about the infallibility of any human construct even as they insist that nature (and the God who stands just behind it) anchor society and morality. Pope extends this, narrating the history of civilization by dramatizing a logic we have met with repeatedly in this book. Human subjects have real agency to construct governments, but that agency is best used when people follow hints in particular things as they attempt to approximate a divinely ordained, naturally manifest order.

Locke and Defoe

In blurring the boundaries between nature and convention such that "nature begets" humanly constructed governments, Pope and Bolingbroke usually are understood to be rejecting John Locke and Whiggish social contract theory more generally. In fact, they are usually understood to be rejecting the new, autonomous individuals who make a "clean break" from nature in order to construct institutions by and for themselves.[26] Certainly, Locke and Defoe differed politically from Pope and Bolingbroke. Locke made his career in the service of the arch-Exclusionist the first Earl of Shaftesbury, and, as we have seen, his economic thought structured Whig policy in the recoinage debates. His *Two Treatises of Government* (1689–90) is considered "something of a blueprint for the Whig political project" in the late seventeenth and eighteenth centuries.[27] Daniel Defoe's political career was famously full of intrigue and strategic posturing, but he was a fervent supporter of King William and the post-1688 settlement. From 1704 to 1713, he consistently advocated Whig, Dissenting, and City interests in the *Review*, and his twelve-book epic poem *Jure Divino* (1706) vigorously attacked high

Tory, high Church doctrines of divine right and passive obedience.[28] The differences between the Tory and Whig thinkers, then, are stark, especially insofar as the latter aimed to bolster personal sovereignty against the right of kings in sometimes radical ways. Yet, I argue that—far from featuring fundamentally opposed notions of the political individual—important "liberal" social contract theorists actually shared with "nostalgic" or "conservative" thinkers a way of imagining the political individual engaged with a providential natural order. Both Locke's *Two Treatises* and Defoe's *Jure Divino* emphasize contract and consent even as they offer (in parallel to Pope's story) original accounts of the ways particular natural objects prompt people to political truths. Across the political spectrum, some key social contract theorists drew on the meditative empiricism. They underscored links between nature and convention as they insisted that the best societies are formed when individuals subordinate themselves to a suprahuman order encoded, but only ever glimpsed, in nature.

For the last few decades, historians of political thought have been challenging the caricature of Locke's modern subjects who break decisively with nature and tradition. Scholars like John Dunn, James Tully, Gopal Sreenivasan, and Ross Harrison argue that, "contrary to common misunderstandings," Locke treats political man not as an "isolated individual" but "in his various relations with other men and with God." Locke believes that humans are God's "Workmanship."[29] Because of this, he reasons, people are obligated to preserve themselves and others; they also have an obligation to use reason and nature to understand how God wants them to conduct themselves. Locke thus provides a compelling model for the nature-culture overlaps of Pope and Bolingbroke: Locke suggests that, since God "Judge[d], it was not good for" man "to be alone," he "put him under strong Obligations of Necessity, Convenience, and Inclination to drive him into *Society*."[30] Locke acknowledges natural communities born of instinctive sexual and parental drives: "God Planted in Men a strong desire also of propagating their Kind, and continuing themselves in their Posterity," and the "Obligations" extend from a society "between Man and Wife . . . to that between Parents and Children" (1:88, 2:77). Finally, Locke proposes that natural familial arrangements provided a useful model for rudimentary monarchies (2:75–76, 105–7). The Lockean individual is made by God to live in society. Locke proceeds from a set of empirical facts about created humanity as God's "workmanship" to determine natural laws founded in the nature of things, and he insists that human institutions try to mimic and formalize these laws. As Tully puts it, each government should "embody in its fundamental constitution an approximation to the normative structure of natural law," but Locke allows some "degree of 'latitude' between natural law and its application."[31] Locke also recognizes that some institutions "approximate" this normative structure more successfully than others, while some succumb to corruption and tyranny. The distinction between natural and conventional is therefore quite blurry. Lockean individuals strive to construct societies in "approximation" of an always-just-inaccessible divine plan. Intriguingly, then, Tully's Locke is quite similar to Kramnick's Bolingbroke and Tom Jones's Pope.

Though recent work has challenged the old commonplace that Locke was *the* central Whig voice in the early eighteenth century, his understanding of contracts and human nature was not anomalous among Whigs. Daniel Defoe made related arguments in *Jure Divino*, the epic poem defending the 1688 settlement that scholars understand as "the most complete statement of Defoe's political and ethical philosophy."[32] Manuel Schonhorn points out (citing Kramnick), that "for Defoe, as for Bolingbroke, 'there is no initial coming together of all to form a political community'; king and community exist as a natural and God-given phenomenon"; and Schonhorn also underscores that Defoe allows for both human and divine agency "in the origin of political authority and the determination of the king."[33] For example, in *Jure Divino*, Defoe is quite clear that humans construct societies. He begins by acknowledging that God prescribes moral rules (the "Knowledg first infus'd by Providence"), but he insists that "as to Government," God "left" people "Free," left them "wholly to their own Choice."[34] Governments are human constructions, but they are not—or should not be—arbitrary constructions, mere productions of human fancy. Defoe continues immediately from his assertion that God "left" humanity "Free" on questions of government to assert that the "Rules of Politie" were "Needless to Dictate" because "Reason" and *"Nature directed"* (2:198–99).[35] He then tells a story that should be familiar to us now: people use their God-given mental faculties to figure out how societies should work—"Reason the easy Methods did contain" (2:201). (In dedicating his poem to "LADY REASON," Defoe celebrates this faculty as "The Almighty's Representative and Resident in the Souls of Men.")[36] Further, "directed Nature knew its Law" and knew that "faithful Instinct wou'd Performance draw" (2:207–8). Thus *"Necessity* with Nature *joins"* to push people into societies (2:83).[37] These societies then transform into "Patriarchal" governments; the family structure is "*A Sketch of Monarchy*" given to man so he will know "What Methods of command he shou'd pursue" (2:7, 9–10). Finally, people are "united by consent," "Compact and mutual Treatises of Accord, / Between a willing People and their Lord" (2:56, 58–59). Humans form contractual governments, but only after being "infus'd" with morality, "directed" to society through reason and instinct, and prompted to monarchy by the "*Sketch*" of government inherent in natural family relations.

Like Bolingbroke, Pope, and Locke, Defoe wants to inhabit a compromise position between Filmerian divine right and Hobbesian conventionalism. Defoe features natural prompts to government alongside social contract, providential order alongside human constructs. Like the others, also, Defoe depicts the process of government building as prone to both pious progress and corrupt backsliding. As Katherine Clark insightfully puts it, Defoe imagines the history of mankind as "an epic drama in which, guided by reason, man's better nature struggled against his proclivities for sin, passion, and folly."[38] Humans sometimes heed reason, instinct, and nature in order to glimpse and actualize God's intended order on earth, but they sometimes ignore nature and act in corrupt or sinful ways that pervert God's design. Governments form naturally; craven and ambitious men start to corrupt them; the people insist on their God-given power and further formalize laws. The resulting governments "bear the Image of Divine Authority" when they protect the people (3:358). Even in the case of the best laws and systems, however, Defoe insists that a careful balancing of divine and human is involved: "The *High Original* from Heaven was sent; / *Fix'd in the Minds of Men*, from thence they flow" (3:364–65). Truths are "sent" from heaven, but laws are at best "Images," approximated by and "flowing" from men. Defoe features an awareness of government's origins in both nature and human agency, as well of its possible corruptions through history.

Despite their different party politics, then, Bolingbroke, Pope, Locke, and Defoe all believed that God creates humans in ways that conduce to society: instinctive drives lead into communities, and natural family relations encourage government. For all, these natural societies are formalized by crucial moments of contract, and the progress of society beyond the moment of consent is "slow," prone to human corruptions and backslidings as much as progress. What is more, like Pope in *Essay on Man*, both Locke and Defoe engage with the meditative empiricism. They suggest that the external world contains meaningful hints and prompts to society, encoded by the God who created nature. They too believe that the political individual should try to subordinate himself to a supra-human order by heeding prompts discovered by scrutinizing small things.

Locke develops this possibility most fully in treating the creation of money in the *Two Treatises*' famous chapter on property. For Locke, "the *Invention of Money*" is a crucial moment of human consent: "Fancy or Agreement hath put the Value on [these metals], more then real Use, and the necessary Support of Life" (2:36, 46). Many scholars understand the creation of money as the paradigmatic moment of consent in Locke's story. C. B. Macpherson reads this agreement as an instance of the autonomous individual ordering his world to suit his interests, and even scholars like Tully suggest that money enables an "unnatural" accumulation that disrupts God's plan for humanity.[39] At times, Locke supports this reading, asserting forthrightly that "Riches and Treasure . . . are none of Natures Goods" (2:184). Yet, while Locke allows that the creation of money involves a new degree of human involvement in the social order, he does not believe that this consent involves a "clean break" from nature. In the chapter on property, Locke problematizes this interpretation. He insists that, even if money is not one of "Natures Goods," nature still played a role in its creation. He retains a divine sanction for economic society while allowing for human corruption.

Locke's story begins with individuals happily coexisting in a state of nature. This state features a rudimentary form of private property. In the beginning Nature belonged "to Mankind in common," but God also gave each man power over his own person, labor, and the products of labor (2:25). For Locke, the same law of nature that gives this property also bounds the property that each person can justly appropriate: "As much as any one can make use of to any advantage of life before it spoils; so much he may by his labour fix a Property in. Whatever is beyond this, is more than his share, and belongs to others" (2:31). The acorn that an individual gathers and the land that he tills belong to him, just as long as they are used to further God's intention to preserve mankind. Locke suggests that people could have lived happily in this state ad infinitum were it not for the emergence of money.

Locke even describes a strange utopia in which this state does continue forever. He imagines "an Island, separate from all possible Commerce with the rest of the World, wherein there were but a hundred Families." This island has plenty of animals, food, and land. However, there is "nothing in the Island, either because of its Commonness, or Perishableness, fit to supply the place of *Money:* What reason could any one have there to enlarge his Possessions beyond the use of his Family . . . ? Where there is not something both lasting and scarce, and so valuable to be hoarded up, there Men will not be apt to enlarge their *Possessions of Land,* were it never so rich, never so free for them to take" (2:48). People here remain forever in a happy community, everyone assured of more than enough. Because everything decays, there is nothing "fit to supply the place of *Money*" and therefore no possible "reason" for men to hoard or to exceed the natural bounds of use. There is nothing to make men "apt to enlarge their *Possessions*." The social inequalities that lead people to create civil society would never be introduced.

The real world differs from this utopian decaying island in one essential respect: there is something "lasting and scarce, and so valuable to be hoarded up." As we saw in chapter 3, Locke's economic writings repeatedly underscore the "fitnesse" of gold and silver in ways that resonate with contemporary design arguments: people value silver or gold "for its fitnesse," and these metals have "been thought the fittest Materials" in "almost all Ages, and parts of the World."[40] This language of "fitnesse" also resonates with Locke's own understanding of the providential natural world. In his early *Questions Concerning the Law of Nature* (1664), Locke argues that the natural world exhibits marks of its creator's intentions: God ordained laws of nature that he wanted men to use as "the rule of our conduct and life"; he "published" these laws in nature and gave men the mental faculties to discover them.[41] Using the idiom of design, Locke suggests that God made gold and silver such that they are especially "fit" to be used as money.

This providential-economic argument relates interestingly to Locke's description of the rotting island. In the real world, there is something "fit" to be money. And, in its negation, Locke's passage suggests that the existence of such a thing provides a "reason" for men to enlarge their possessions. It actually makes men "apt" to do so. In concluding his discussion of the example, Locke further underscores the inexorability of the connection between the nonperishable thing and its employment as money: "Find out something that hath the *Use and Value of Money* amongst his Neighbours, you shall see the same Man will begin presently to *enlarge* his *Possessions*" (2:49). Locke suggests that human attention to the properties of metal actually encourages a different kind of community. Because gold and silver exist, men are "apt" to make them valuable so they can enlarge their possessions. They "will" heap up goods in a way unimaginable if a nonperishable, somewhat scarce substance did not exist.

Of course, Locke follows his emphasis on the inexorable connection between nonperishable thing and its use as money by again asserting that money "has its *value* only from the consent of Men" (2:50). Consenting individuals play a crucial role in constituting value and governments, but these individuals are not entirely autonomous or separated from nature. Instead, people manage to create a community by discovering and heeding prompts contained in the providential natural world. Their consent to value is "voluntary" but "tacitly"—even pushed forward by mindful attention to metallic substances (2:50). The community-forming power of bullion functions in Locke's argument as an analogue to those "Obligations of Necessity, Convenience, and Inclination" that God put men under "to drive him into Society." For Locke, God's providential care of placing men into families is matched by his creation of gold and silver as instruments encouraging men to enter political society.

These prompts to society do not disturb the fundamental truths that government is humanly constructed, that monetary value is conventional. People make the choices, and their choices are sometimes misguided (at one point Locke condemns a kind of fall by which "vain Ambition, and *amor sceleratus habendi*, evil Concupiscence, had corrupted Mens minds" [2:111]). Yet, at best, individuals attend to material realities as they try to realize a supra-human order. Locke wants to keep society and its institutions in touch with nature without conflating the two: individuals make governments, but nature itself encourages human contracts, human economic and social arrangements. Nature "begets," but humans approximate—and they pay close attention to the properties of bullion as they approximate.

Defoe imagines his ancestors paying similarly close attention to natural objects as they try to realize God's order in political society, but his version of this story emphasizes animal biology: the body parts and abilities that God gave each particular creature when he created it. Defoe's *Jure Divino* is preoccupied with tyranny and with what Defoe understood as its contemporary manifestation in doctrines of "*Passive Obedience and Non-Resistance.*"[42] These high Church, high Tory doctrines privileged the power of kings over the personal sovereignty of their subjects, holding that subjects should passively submit to the will of the king (however right or wrong it may be).[43] Defoe's argument against these doctrines starts from his belief, shared with Locke, that one of the most fundamental "Laws of Nature" is the law of "*Self-defence*" or "*Self-Preservation*" (3:240, 242, 243).[44] Defoe's presentation of this idea draws on the logic of Locke's "workmanship" argument. God made us, and so a person who destroys himself "*betrays* the High Orig'nal *Trust*" and "Contradicts the Ends of Providence": "what Heaven gives, *it binds him to enjoy*" (3:293, 296, 300). Defoe points out that contemporary "*Passive Obedience*" doctrines tend to violate this natural law. A man who takes these vows seriously must be ready to "resign" "His *Wife, Life, Land,* his *Sword* and *Gun*" to his king, effectively destroying himself

(3:277). Defoe explicitly describes this as a perversion from a divinely decreed and naturally manifest order: this man *"Rebels against his Reason,"* "Contradicts the Ends of Providence," and even (in a rather strange personification) *"puts out Nature's Eyes"* (3:296–98).[45]

It is not just "Nature" (with a capital *n*) that plays a role in the argument against passive obedience. Defoe supplements this logic with an assertion that particular natural objects provide prompts and proofs for the truth of his position. After outlining the natural right of "Self-defence," Defoe turns to animals:

> The meanest Creature is upon *its Guard*,
> By Nature *Guided*, and in part *prepar'd;*
>
> There's *not an Animal*, a Life of Sense,
> But has *some Native Weapon* for defence;
> Nature provides Oppression to oppose,
> And Nature *all the Rules and Method* shows;
> Instinct the needful Force of Skill supplies,
> By this *he fights*, or else by that *he flies*. (3:247–54)

This argument turns on a reasoned awareness of animal biology and behavior, and Defoe glosses it with two empirically minded footnotes. First, he asserts that, though animals "have no Reason, yet by the Power of Sense diligently defend their Lives, and provide for their own Safety" (3:243n). Echoing Pope's Augustinian understanding of instinct, Defoe suggests that animals instinctively protect themselves; they never fail to confront their enemies ("fight") or else retreat quickly ("fly," either literally or figuratively, with wings or feet). Further, "Most Creatures have some Weapon given to them for their Defence, against Common Injury; and Nature directs them how to make use of them to that end" (3:248n). Cats have their claws, bees their stings, spiders their webs, snakes their venom, sharks their teeth, and so on.[46] The generalizations in these footnotes are empiricist—seeming to spring from an awareness of particular wings, feet, claws, and teeth and moving toward a larger claim that never reaches the universal ("Most Creatures").

The empirical observations, however, are used to make a very *political* point. Humans rule over animals. Since the Bible explicitly decrees this, animal subjection is much more thoroughgoing and divinely sanctioned than any human power arrangements: it is "ne're to be retriev'd," as Defoe puts it (3:256). This is the context for Defoe's interest in the ways animals instinctively and naturally incline to self-preservation and violence. His empirical facts demonstrate that animals "may"—and do—"oppose what they cannot prevent" (3:264). Defoe glosses this in a footnote: "they are not bound to be Passive under all his [man's] Oppressions, and are allow'd to resist Force with Force" (3:257n).[47] Animals are designed both to be subject to humans and to resist this, to "Take Arms against his *Lawful Government*" (3:263). Defoe then moves toward the application of these empirical facts: mankind should mimic the animals. A human is also "a Life of Sense," and the notion that people should not protect themselves, even against an unjust, unnatural oppressor, involves "Laws that Nature *never saw*" (3:274). Humanity, too, should resist when oppressed; we too should "take Arms." Just as nature guides animals through biology and instinct, "Nature Tells" humans "how" to react to oppression: "With *Hand and Tongue* his Life he shou'd maintain, / Or else his Hands and Tongue *are given in vain*" (3:306–8). While cats get claws and bees get stings to fight back, and while leopards get swift feet and eagles get wings to flee from danger, humans get "Hands" to lift in battle and "Tongues" to talk and reason their way out of danger. The political conclusion flows from these empirical facts about both humanity and beasts. "Nature's just Argument from this is plain": "'tis as Nat'ral still, and full as just, / That what he [man] must not bear, he may resist" (3:327–28). Doctrines of passive obedience are unjust and unnatural, and Defoe's poetic argument against them is clinched by close attention to animals.[48] It is even posed as "Nature's" argument, only given voice by the poet.

Throughout his poem, Defoe respects this possibility of learning political lessons from nature by featuring an enormously complex understanding of human agency and the progress of history. He recognizes that people act against kings but that their individual actions are prompted by divinely created human nature (reason, instinct, the urge to self-preservation) and sanctioned by the nature of things (in general and in particular). Defoe enacts this complexity in his very syntax. Parts of his poem offer the kind of conjectural history featured in this chapter, but the last six books also contain more straightforwardly historical investigations of the "slow" progress of human history. Actual people from the past get agency in determining the course of human societies. For example, book 8 opens by featuring the seventh-century BC tyrant King Sardanapalus and the rebel Arbaces, initially "General of the *Medes*, under *Sardanapalus*" (8:65n).[49] These men act in history: the king performs "*Unnatural Crimes*," "With horrid Scenes provok[ing] the Peoples Rage," and the rebel "in Arms for Liberty appear[ed]," lifting "the First Sword against Oppression" (8:30–31, 67, 99). Yet, throughout this passage, nature retains agency as well. As in Pope's *Essay*, "She" performs active verbs and communicates truths. Against Sardanapalus's crimes and spurious claims to divine right, "*Instructing Nature* made the People Wise, / *Instructing Nature* shew'd the weak Disguise" (8:19–20). Nature points "the People" away from Sardanapalus's corruption of true government. Defoe continues, however, to render this "*Instructing*" process with real nuance. First, Sardanpalus's "Crimes" themselves had forced people to pay attention to his tyrannical power, and human nature almost forced them to act: "Tir'd with Oppression, Nature acts by Sense, / And makes their Reason guard their Innocence" (8:58–59). Then, Arbaces uses his natural capabilities—his "fierce Hand"—to stand up for the people and for truth. Arbaces's action is at once individual (one man who bravely "durst" raise his "fierce Hand" against a "Murth'rer") and on behalf of forces much larger than him ("The Laws of Nature thus o'er Power prevail'd") (8:117, 127). Defoe purposefully alludes to his "*Instructing Nature*" lines as he invites readers to see a real link between nature and Arbaces: "To" his "Great Soul instructed Nations owe, / The First Example what they ought to do" (8:86–87). Nations are "instructed" by both human actors and nature, and agency is convoluted here on purpose. Defoe insists that "Both Heaven and Nature mov'd *the Hand* of War" (8:53). Human hands—and Arbaces's "fierce Hand" in particular—act of their own volition even as they act in accordance with heaven and reason and nature. They were created to be lifted, Defoe suggests (and we could perhaps think of our poet working in parallel to Arbaces, using that other God-given gift, his "Tongue," to resist tyranny). Defoe's poem displays a nuanced sense of how nature and humanity collaborate in the unfolding of history.

In the world of *Jure Divino*, people are emphatically in charge. The whole poem is pitted against any sense that kings get direct divine guidance or that people should quietly submit to things as they are. People make the "Rules of Politie" for themselves and should, Arbaces-like, firmly resist any power that tries to usurp this right. Yet, human political agency is always exerted in a larger cosmic scheme. Individuals should heed God-given morality, and they should not infringe on the tenets of reason and nature. God might have left humanity "wholly to their own Choice" in questions of government, but he is always there, using nature to prompt and guide them. Arbaces himself acts after the exemplary model of an animal with claws.

These arguments are not merely local flourishes in this poem. The central idea that Defoe takes from the meditative empiricism—that humans have power to shape their world but that they ought to heed God's providential, analogical natural clues in so doing—is crucial to his thought more generally. Fascinatingly, Defoe's nonfictional writings often explicitly depict the same careful cooperation among God, nature, and humanity that *Jure Divino* features.[50] For example, like Locke (and Addison), Defoe offers a version of the origins of economic society that foregrounds human agency exerted in accordance with natural, providential hints. In a 1713 essay in his *Review*, Defoe claims: "Providence concurrs in, and seems to have prepared the World for Commerce; assists us in the Diligent Pursuit of needful Improvement, and seems to expect Trade should be Preserved, Encouraged, and Extended by all Honest and Prudent Methods, as a stated Provision, made for the Support and Maintenance, Employment and Improvement of his Creatures."[51] Providence has "prepared the World" for economic societies—Defoe cites many particular geographical and biological facts to support this point—but humans have to realize this order.[52] They must work "Diligent[ly]," and they must use "Honest and Prudent Methods." But if they succeed in "Preserving," "Encouraging," and "Extending" the nascent providential clues that prompt trade arrangements, they will have realized God's order and reap his rewards. Trade was designed to enrich everyone's quality of life and instill familial and global harmony. This worldview requires meditative-empiricist observation of creation.

Defoe's *General History of Discoveries and Improvements in Useful Arts* (1725–26) actually narrates the origin story outlined in the *Review* with particularized detail. For instance, Defoe's account "Of the first Discovery of Shipping and Navigation" prefigures Pope's interest in the nautilus fish by insisting that technological innovations are prompted by animals: an eagle's way of managing its flight through the air suggested "the use of a *Rudder* or *Helm* to steer or guide the Boat, in her Motion from place to place," and ships were built "exactly form'd after the model of a Swan's" "Breastbone."[53] Nature plays a key role, here, as an object of painstaking attention and as a prompt to human creation. The rudder's invention happened when "an Ingenious" and "Curious Observer . . . took notice" of the particular way an eagle uses his wings to "steer" his flight, and Defoe describes this process in a long passage full of empirical particulars. But Defoe also continues to foreground the hard human work required to actualize the natural prompt: the "Curious Observer" applied this principle and refined it through "daily Experiment, and great Application."[54] Defoe's sense of the progress of global commerce and technology intriguingly resonates with the logic of his political origin story (and of the meditative empiricism more generally):

"Navigation was founded in Reason, and the Nature of Things, and discover'd by slow degrees."[55] "The Nature of Things" prompts and models; humans diligently observe, "Reason," "Experiment," and try to approximate; and by "slow degrees" people to progress from technological innovation to a global connectedness that realizes navigation's (and therefore trade's) "inexpressible advantage to Mankind."[56]

Locke and Defoe are celebrated today for providing some of the intellectual and literary underpinnings of the modern individual. They privilege human agency and feature stories of social contract, but I argue that their versions of contract depict people deploying the meditative empiricism's brand of close attention to nature. Like Pope, they suggest that our conjectural ancestors were "Curious Observers" who scrutinized nature as they constructed societies in humble approximations of divine order.

Empiricist Methodologies, Empiricist Selves

We should, of course, remind ourselves about the very real political differences between Whiggish Locke and Defoe and Tory Pope and Bolingbroke (and even between the two thinkers from each party). We should also remember that there were other models of the political individual available at the time: following in the footsteps of Filmer and Hobbes, respectively, Charles Leslie vigorously defended divine right doctrines, and Bernard Mandeville voiced a controversial skepticism as he argued that calculating politicians created morality and social structures for their own ends. The meditative empiricism did not structure all political thought. Still, unexpected similarities in the most basic assumptions of Locke and Bolingbroke or Pope and Defoe show that writers across the political spectrum—Whig and Tory, "modern" and "nostalgic" alike—engaged with the meditative empiricism. Pope, Locke, and Defoe all propose that close attention to nature helped our conjectural, "observant" ancestors get into society. Scrutiny of fish feet, swan breastbones, beehives, and bits of bullion pointed to new kinds of technology and new forms of community. In this final section, I argue that, in addition to dramatizing the meditative empiricism's brand of close attention in their origin stories, these writers deployed it as a methodology for their writings more generally. Second, I argue that their stories and their methods turn on an understanding of the human self that complicates influential commonplaces about "modern" subjects (empiricist and political).

At a few provocative moments in the texts we have been exploring, these writers suggest that this distinctive brand of close attention accessed meaningful information about the society in the past and that it could *still* glimpse truths. For instance, Defoe's treatment of animal defense mechanisms is somewhat separate from his origin story. He uses the empirical facts to encourage reform of problematic political beliefs in the contemporary political scene: animal claws and human hands suggest that Tory notions of passive obedience and nonresistance are perversions from a natural order. Bolingbroke actually theorizes the possibility of contemporary access to such truths, as he exhorts people in his moment to try to act according to the larger plan: "By employing our reason to collect the will of God from the fund of our nature, physical and moral, and by contemplating seriously and frequently the laws that are plainly, and even necessarily deducible from these." It is this possibility that underwrites Locke's methodology on economic issues and, in a rather more complex way, his famous fascination with the possibility of an empirically demonstrable ethics.[57] These writers confirm that eighteenth-century people could still continue the pious empiricist practice of their conjectured ancestors.

Pope's *Essay on Man* seems problematic in this context, for it is often read as dogmatic, rationalist, or totalizing.[58] Yet, I argue that Pope's method is empiricist in just the tradition this book has been recovering. Certainly, Pope understood himself to be proceeding from empirical particulars. His comments on the "Design" of his *Essay* are startlingly similar to Locke's understanding of a "workmanship"-inspired methodology. Where Locke seeks to "uncover God's intentions in making man by seeing what purposes man's natural attributes embody" and "what ends man and other natural phenomena can be seen to be designed to serve" (Tully's summary), Pope suggests that "to prove any moral duty, to enforce any moral precept, or to examine the perfection or imperfection of any creature whatsoever, it is necessary first to know what *condition* and *relation* it is placed in, and what is the proper *end* and *purpose* of its *being*."[59] Like Locke, Pope starts figuring out what man is supposed to do in the world by focusing on what man and his world are, how they were created. Pope's poem enacts this process of knowing. He begins with observable facts of nature (especially "Man" and his "station here," his "*condition*" and "*relation*"), and Pope then proceeds "from" and "refer[s]" to these empirical facts as he aims to answer larger questions about "the proper *end* and *purpose*" of human life (1:18–20). The first and second epistles of the *Essay* focus on nature and human nature, the perceived universe and the psychology of man. Only after establishing these empirical givens does Pope venture to turn in the third epistle to humans in society: people learn social ethics by quite literally "taking" instructions from creatures, and they find in the "Union" order of the universe a model for the ideal social order. Pope's fourth epistle merely continues this project, exploring nature's dictates for human happiness: concisely summarized, "LOVE of GOD, and LOVE of MAN"—or, "Union" further extrapolated (4:340). Knowledge about the particulars in nature conduces to knowledge about society, ethics, and even happiness.

In his critique of Lucretius, Pope deploys an even more specific methodology that begins from natural particulars. As Miriam Leranbaum shows, Pope's sense that empirical knowledge conduces to ethical truth resonates with Lucretius's method.[60] For Lucretius, however, this works because nature's flaws and imperfections—predatory animals, zones of intemperate heat, tornadoes, and human hunger—prove that there is no God (in the Christian sense). The Lucretian ethical system proceeds from this lack. If there is no God, there is no providence, no immaterial human souls, and no afterlife; and it is therefore silly to worry oneself with superstitious religions, moral bugbears, or fear of death.[61] Pope begins his critique of Lucretius's system by countering his predecessor's understanding of problematic natural objects, and he manages this by cultivating one of the meditative empiricism's distinctive attitudes—close attention to nature that accesses analogical meaningfulness even while remaining skeptically aware of the limits of human knowledge.

Pope starts in the first epistle by focusing on natural evils like "earthquakes" and "tempests." He postulates ways that these particular evils *might* relate to a larger whole. His solutions are many, sometimes incompatible but always posed skeptically, without making firm claims about the always inaccessible whole. As Pope summarizes his point(s) later in the poem:

> God sends not ill; if rightly understood,
> Or partial Ill is universal Good,
> Or Change admit, or Nature lets it fall. . . . (4:113–15)[62]

With all these "or's," Pope suggests that there may be many possible ways the particulars make sense in a larger whole, and it does not matter if the possibilities are incompatible or overlapping. What matters, Pope argues, is that it is wrong, presumptuous, and narrow minded to condemn God for allowing a specific evil without considering the ways it might be related to the whole. He then reasons analogically from these hypotheses about natural evils to speculations about harder-to-understand moral evils: "If plagues or earthquakes break not Heav'n's design, / Why then a Borgia, or a Cataline?" (1:155–56). The parts that relate to the whole in ways we can sort of comprehend can help us conjecture about the parts whose relation to God's plan is harder to see. Pope counters Lucretius by trying to glimpse how particulars relate to wholes; he conjectures analogically between spheres of experience; and he ends with a skeptical, provisional trust. Pope's engagement with natural particulars buttresses his provisional belief that all parts have a place in this plan: "whatever wrong we call, / May, must be right, as relative to all" (1:51–52). The hypothetical "may" precedes the belief expressed by "must"—it actually plays a crucial role in licensing this belief.

The confidence suggested by this "must" might seem akin to Pope's oft-cited (and oft-misunderstood) conclusion to his treatment of evil: "Whatever IS, is RIGHT" (1:294).[63] When excerpted as a stand-alone proposition, this claim seems extremely problematic (rather Leibnizian or Panglossian, and surely not empiricist), and I am not interested in defending Pope against those who insist that he insufficiently understood the implications of this claim on its own terms. Rather, I want to point out that, in the context of the poem, Pope is not naively affirming a perfect world and a perfect God. Pope prefaces this concluding line with a much more humble empiricist exhortation: "Know thy own point" (1:283). And his reasoning toward the final line privileges negatives whose real force is too often ignored: we can "know" our "own point," but the whole is "unknown," "not see[n]," and "not understood." Still, Pope also does not say we can never know. Instead, his *faith* in the good of the whole and his strong assertion of the limits of human knowledge motivate his focus on parts. He explains, with a somewhat common use of the clock figure: we may not understand the purpose of a seeming evil or imperfection, but perhaps it "Touches some wheel, or verges to some goal; / 'Tis but a part we see, and not a whole" (1:59–60).[64] Pope's simultaneous affirmation of the goodness of God's whole and the human inability to comprehend it leads to richly creative but never finally demonstrable conjecturing about how the particulars we do have access to might conduce to the larger good. The *Essay on Man* does not proceed downward from a massive rationalist claim. Instead, Pope scrutinizes particulars, conjectures possible explanations, and analogizes from one realm of experience to another: in short, Pope engages the meditative empiricism as he thinks creatively and skeptically from particulars.[65]

Thus, Pope unfolds his ethical positions from empirical facts and licenses even his biggest claims with a skeptical engagement with particulars. It is in a similar spirit that Locke outlines an economics with a "Foundation in

Nature" and hopes for an empirically demonstrable ethics. Bolingbroke turns to human nature, and Defoe to animals. These are empiricist moralities—attempts to enact the pious empirical practice of the ancestors depicted in their origin stories. Importantly, the entire project of occasional reflection and the meditative empiricism was premised on the same possibility. Boyle, Flavel, Austen, Hooke, and Hervey meditated—empirically and earnestly—on the meanings of particular things, and Berkeley, Cheyne, Hodges, Gildon, and Addison looked to nature for hints on how to behave in their here-and-now. Like the political systems of Pope and Defoe's conjectural ancestors, the moral lessons glimpsed by these eighteenth-century writers were derived from nature but only glimpsed and approximated by humans.

The political origin stories, moreover, help us understand the stakes of this epistemological posture. By showing that close attention to particular things played a formative role in society, Bolingbroke, Pope, Locke, and Defoe guarded against the worrying prospect that social and moral conventions are humanly constructed and thus have no sanction more ultimate than self-interest or force. On the other hand, they guarded against dangerous enthusiastic claims of immediate access to God. They acknowledged a divine ideal while closing off what in a different context has been called "the many hot lines to God" professed by jure divino patriarchalism or by enthusiastic dissenters possessed by the spirit.[66] They embraced human autonomy and remained skeptical about the infallibility of any human construct even as they insisted that nature (and the God who stands just behind it) anchors human societies. The meditative empiricism more broadly similarly grounded ethical truths in a larger order. Since all knowledge comes from nature, which comes from God, not just society but systems of ethics and religion have a kind of supra-human sanction. Yet, these conclusions were never dogmatically certain; humans are fallible and should proceed from humble empiricist skepticism. Each writer's moral conclusions represented, then, his or her (always only approximate) attempt to unfold the truths inherent in the universe that God created.

These empiricist methodologies evince a discomfort with human agency and human constructions that is rather surprising, given how we usually think about social contract stories and the emergence of modern science. For one, it is a commonplace of political philosophy that social contract theories fundamentally uphold "the idea that political legitimacy, political authority, and political obligation are derived from the consent of the governed, and are the artificial product of the voluntary agreement of free and equal moral agents."[67] These "free and equal moral agents" are not bound to others with all sorts of reciprocal ties; they are autonomous, capable of reasoning, promising, choosing, creating political authority. Such assumptions are further bolstered by the influential notion that the modern autonomous individual emerged in eighteenth-century England. This involves, of course, a new kind of political individualism. The process of modernization is said to involve a fundamental shift from status to contract: people emerged from the hierarchal and communal structures that bound them and took on the responsibility and freedom to construct governments and choose representatives for themselves. These modern individuals were equal by nature and under the law, and their rationality and their rights were fundamental to morality and government. In true Enlightenment spirit, they reasoned themselves to secular moral tenets, and their politics reached its apotheosis with the age of revolutions and the rise of democratic governments. Indeed, our usual stories about most of the cultural forces that *Empiricist Devotions* explores involve shifts toward human autonomy: the new consumer economy licensed human constructions and human self-interest, and science empowered the individual who no longer existed *in* nature so much as acted *on* it.

Of course, in one sense, the writers in this chapter endorsed a "modern" notion of the individual: human agents came together to construct governments and make laws. None of them, however, wanted to argue that the resulting moral and social arrangements were merely "artificial," arbitrary products of human construction. Instead, they maintained that the consenting subject exists in vital relationship with nature. The heroes of their origin stories were not autonomous subjects who mastered nature, who were eager to construct institutions based solely on their ideas. Instead, their stories of social contract featured people heeding prompts in their own bodies and following hints in particular things as they attempt to approximate a divinely ordained, naturally manifest order. Their heroes were eager to respect and even subordinate political decision making to a natural order, anxious to ground consent in something larger than the human mind even as they were aware of the difficulty of ever doing so perfectly. This shared understanding opens up provocative possibilities for our understanding of "modern" individuals in early eighteenth-century England. It suggests that—even in social contract theory and new science—the individual's autonomy involved an epistemological posture that is rather more complicated than we usually allow. In fact, it suggests that even the process of constructing governments "by the people, and for the people" often involved empiricist attention to the providential natural world.

Therefore, the eighteenth-century individual is misunderstood if we recognize only autonomous subjects who break with nature: confident scientists, self-interested economic men, liberal citizens, and secular systematizers. If the heroes of the origin stories of Bolingbroke, Pope, Locke, and Defoe were eager to respect and even subordinate political decision making to an empirically glimpsed order, so too were Bolingbroke, Pope, Locke, and Defoe themselves. So too were all the other occasional reflectors and Christian empiricists in this moment. These individuals acted in the world—they constructed societies and governments for themselves, and they made moral decisions in accordance with the systems their minds, hands, and pens had formalized. But they did not think of these institutions and moralities as *merely* human constructions. Far from embracing their total autonomy, eighteenth-century individuals wanted to subordinate themselves to nature, providence, and God. They looked closely at the world, and they grappled thoughtfully with the impossibility of accessing unmediated truths as they tried earnestly to approximate a supra-human plan in their institutions and moralities. They were political and moral agents, but they were also empiricists, skeptics, Christians, and products of God's workmanship.

Georgic Realism, an Empirical-Devotional Poetics

GEORGIC POETRY became massively popular in early eighteenth-century England. Important poems like *Windsor Forest* (1713) and *The Seasons* (1728–44) featured the genre, but the fascination with georgic went far beyond these canonical works. There were original English georgics on breeding animals, making beer, and getting proper exercise, satirical georgics on predicting the weather and using the restroom, and translated georgics on gardening and raising silkworms. There were poems featuring georgic set pieces and georgic-inflected topographical poems on places from Burley Hill (east of London) to Phoenix Park (in the Irish West). Georgic verses were penned by gentlemen writers but also by women, physicians, clergymen, and soldiers.[1]

Scholars often explain this popularity by pointing out that georgic's themes resonate with the modernizing currents transforming the eighteenth-century world: these are poems about labor, science, commerce, nation, and empire.[2] This is quite true, but it is only one part of the story. Early eighteenth-century writers understood georgic as more than a set of themes (which, after all, could be treated in poetry or prose). Georgic was also a way of presenting those themes: the poetic genre contains long, elaborate nature descriptions full of personifications and periphrases, and it revels in allusion, digression, and complex structural patterning. It is these formal traits that link the otherwise quite different poems mentioned above—poems set in hunting grounds, urban alehouses, or public parks and featuring prescription, description, encomium, learning, or mockery. To understand georgic's popularity, then, we need to understand not only why poems about science and commerce were attractive in a moment being transformed by these cultural forces but also why *poems* about such topics were attractive. Why the elaborate diction and complex structuring? This chapter aims to provide an answer. I contend that these features of georgic form crucially contributed to its popularity in the moment, for they made the genre an apt vehicle for the tradition of meditative empiricism. Georgic became the mode, par excellence, for empiricist devotions.

For early eighteenth-century writers, georgic offered a mode of realist description, characterized by highly referential language and the accumulation of sensed particulars. Because of the elaborate, patterned ways that georgic pursues referential particularity, however, its realist description actually helped access nature's fraught meaningfulness. It helped people understand both nature's minute workings and its broadest moral and religious implications. Further, this link between georgic and meditative empiricism helps us better understand the genre's formal workings. Challenging influential assumptions about the genre's "heightening" language, I insist that its personifications, metaphors, and periphrases constituted a serious engagement with nature and science and that particularized description and poetic troping were both part of georgic's *realist* project.

This chapter's first section traces the development of the distinctive early eighteenth-century understanding of georgic from the very different approaches available at the end of the seventeenth century. The rest of the chapter then dwells on the contours of the eighteenth-century tradition. The second section details georgic's close relationships with the meditative empiricism. Georgic enacts this empiricism's logic: it is a genre intent on scrutinizing particulars, considering likenesses, and seeking their larger meanings. Then, in a section focused on John Gay's *Rural Sports* (1713, 1720), I show that georgic's mode of realist description troubles some pervasive critical assumptions about literary particularity. The fourth section, on John Philips's *Cyder* (1708), contends that eighteenth-century georgic's empiricist commitments motivate even its attitude to poetic form. Throughout, my understanding of georgic is informed not only by the canonical texts I read—including Addison's *Essay on the Georgics* (1697) and Pope's *Epistle to Burlington* (1731)—but also by a large archive of contemporary poems, even anonymous and ephemeral works.

Reading Georgic

Early eighteenth-century writers valued georgic as a way of pursuing empiricist devotions, a way of scrutinizing nature and seeking its larger meanings. This understanding of the genre involved an active recasting of two very different earlier approaches to the genre. At the end of the seventeenth century, readers tended to focus on either georgic's words or its things, either its poetry or its agricultural praxis, either its metaphors or its material facts. Eighteenth-century writers, however, realized that Virgilian georgic is rather stranger than these partial approaches allowed, for it has a slippery way of straddling dichotomies. For early eighteenth-century poets, georgic was about metaphor *and* materiality. It developed meditations on nature's agency and import through minutely particular descriptions of agricultural facts. This section traces how early eighteenth-century poets brought together the two earlier conceptions of the genre, and it suggests that much recent scholarship on georgic is more adequate to the partial approaches than to the distinctive dichotomy-straddling of eighteenth-century georgic.

The two seventeenth-century approaches to georgic were quite different, almost opposite. On the one hand, a tradition of learned gentleman poets highlighted the least practical, most exciting bits of Virgil's poem: prodigies and mythical history, the idyllic "happy husbandman," the force of love, the Orpheus story, and the mini-epic battle of the bees.[3] When such poets took on the whole poem, as John Dryden did in his masterful 1697 translation of Virgil, they were interested in the culture of the soil primarily as a metaphor for the culture of the human being, and they privileged the poem's tropes, its intertextual allusions, and its play with the epic tradition.[4] For Dryden, Virgil's *Georgics* was "the best Poem of the best Poet"—a poetic masterpiece in an ancient learned tradition that invites readers to chase down its allusions, to allegorize and moralize its contents, and not to get bogged down in anything so base as the actual soil.[5] On the other hand, a tradition of English husbandry manuals read Virgil's text *as* a husbandry manual, as chock full of pragmatic advice that one might put into action. Historians of agriculture like Joan Thirsk, G. E. Fussell, and Andrew McRae explain: the *Scriptores Res Rusticae*, an influential collection of ancient agrarian texts including both prose treatises and the *Georgics*, were received eagerly upon their first print publication in 1470 by (then, often negligent) English landlords who read them as a pragmatic resource for agricultural improvement, as well as an ancient sanction for the dignity of such work. In the following centuries, these classical texts sparked English translations, imitations, and original prose treatises on husbandry. While developing new, sophisticated approaches to farming, agricultural writers well into the eighteenth century continued to conceive of their work in parallel to the practical project of the *Georgics*.[6] When the Royal Society convened a group to research cutting-edge agricultural topics, they dubbed it the "Georgicall Committee." Virgil's poem was not *like* science—it was science. Georgic was "*an exact Art of Husbandry,*" which "might be as well deliver'd in *Prose,* and without any Ornament."[7]

Both of these approaches found some license in Virgil's slippery, hybrid text. For example, when Virgil insists that the husbandman must carefully consider the nature of his soil, he urges attention to "*quid quaeque ferat regio et quid quaeque recuset*"—what the region will bring forth and what it will refuse. He also urges consideration of the surrounding climate and the soil's special nature, its "*patrios*" and "*habitus*": roughly, its agricultural antecedents or ancestors and its habits.[8] There is a hint of personification: soil gets agency to affect the kinds and qualities of the plants it produces, and this agency is described in terms associated with human life (ancestors, habits). Dryden's translation revels in this hint, imagining a soil's natural inclination as a force that can be personified—its "Genius." The "Genius" of one kind of ground "loads the Trees with happy Fruits," while another "with Grass, unbidden, decks the Ground." The power of this "Genius" goes well beyond the decorative. India, motherlike, "bears" ebon and ivory, and Arabian ground "weeps her od'rous Tears."[9] Dryden uses "Genius" with a full sense of its pagan prehistory. Roman mythology assigned tutelary genii to houses, institutions, trees, and rivers. This makes for a magical, animated world, resplendent with fairies and natural actors: *genius* comes from the Greek verb "to beget." In the world of Dryden's *Georgics,* soil, trees, calves, and bees have "genius"—the power to act or beget, to smile or weep or love.

While Virgil offers Dryden an anthropomorphic hint, the Roman poet also seriously instructs the husbandman to adjust himself, his labor, and his choice of seed to suit the soil's inherent tendencies. Late seventeenth- and early eighteenth-century husbandry manuals took this as agricultural truth, ignoring the possibilities for personification while refining Virgil's precept with hundreds of recipes and experiments adjusted to particular soils.[10] One writer even drew directly on this husbandry manual tradition as he condemned Dryden's "Genius." Luke Milbourne was one of Dryden's noisiest critics, and he had more than one quarrel to pick; however, his critique of Dryden's *Georgics* proceeded from husbandry-manual assumptions about the poem's pragmatic treatment of agricultural precept.[11] Milbourne criticizes Dryden's personifications for departing from Virgil's text in ways that falsify fact: he argues that it is utter nonsense to have soil "weep[ ]" gums and that, where Dryden has one kind of soil good for fruit trees and another good for grass, Virgil mentions only one kind that is good for both trees and grass. Milbourne strengthens his case by appealing to the kind of natural fact he assumes that georgics deal in—"*Land* which is good for *Fruit-Trees,* is good for *Grass* too, tho the *spreading* of the *Trees* sour the *Grass* in time" (112). Milbourne measures Dryden's translation against scientific truth and proceeds to refine the poetry's natural facts, as scientific engagements with georgic often did. At the end of the seventeenth century, georgic was understood to feature either personifications and allusions *or* pragmatic agricultural fact.

These two approaches involved very different understandings of the relationship between nature and language. For the gentlemen-poet tradition, the *Georgics* was first and foremost a poem. Dryden assumed that Virgil was not really good at agriculture—Virgil "has shewn more of Poetry than Skill" in farming, Dryden says.[12] Thereby freed from factual material reference, Dryden allows "genius" agency to make things available as actors in object lessons. He famously renders Virgil's battle of the king-bees as a transparent allegory for the events of 1688, and throughout he opens up his natural descriptions to human relevance in more local ways. For example, Virgil follows the "Genius" passage by advising that barren soil should lie fallow every other year. In rendering this advice, Dryden makes the soil both an agent and a figure. The husbandman should only use each field in "alternate Years," so "the spent Earth may gather heart again" (1:107–8): "sweet Vicissitudes of Rest and Toyl / Make easy Labour, and renew the Soil" (1:116–17). During the fallow, the soil is "not idle, though at rest" (1:121). Vacillating cycles of rest and toil are good for the soil, and—with talk of the soil's "heart"—Dryden hints at the human application of this agricultural truth: a larger lesson about moderation, about how alternating hard work and well-deserved (but not slothful) rest is good for people too. Dryden confirms the human moral relevance of this passage, echoing it in his later rendering of Virgil's praise of the life of the "happy husbandman": "ev'ry sev'ral Season is employ'd: / Some spent in Toyl, and some in Ease enjoy'd" (2:749–50). For Dryden, the soil provides an occasion for personifying and metaphorizing.

Unsurprisingly, Milbourne objects. Drawing on the fundamental assumptions about georgic made by the husbandry-manual tradition, he critiques such object lessons as *mere* figures in a "*Catechrestical*" translation (167). Catechresis, dubbed by George Puttenham "the Figure of Abuse," involves the improper application of words or tropes. Milbourne condemns what he sees as the problematic introduction of irrelevant figures in a text that needs to show farming "Skill"; as he puts it, "*Virgil*'s true *sence* is not to be understood *Morally,* but *Physically*" (158).[13] (Tellingly, Milbourne's own stubbornly practical translation of the fallowing advice owes something to past agricultural writers' occasional use of mnemonic verse: a field "recovers best / When left unplow'd each other Year to rest" [210].) Dryden metaphorizes, and Milbourne rejects metaphor as inappropriate, departing from agricultural reality.

Early eighteenth-century poets, however, were intrigued by both the "genius" and the soil composition. They brought together the two opposing traditions of reading georgic. More than the gentleman-poet tradition, early eighteenth-century georgic engages actual rural things. While these writers manifest varying degrees of interest in agricultural praxis, they all register the influence of the husbandry-manual approach in their sharpened focus on empirical particulars. Yet, this close attention to the material does not preclude metaphor and personification, and eighteenth-century poets draw on the meditative empiricism as they allow real natural things to act, beget, *mean.* After all, Dryden's recovering of a prompt to moderation and rest in the soil works in a way strikingly similar to Boyle's various object lessons (a fire that teaches something about sin), and Boyle's occasional meditations firmly locate the source of meaning in the real world. Contemporary discourse about georgic makes explicit the link between these modes. In a 1722 edition of Oppian's georgic on fishing, for example, William Diaper and John Jones use the empiricist tradition to claim that georgic object lessons have ontological purchase, some intriguing link with the real. They license the georgic technique of drawing human morals from natural fact by explaining that the structure of nature contains layers of likeness ("there is a regular Gradation of created Beings from Man down to the lowest Vegetable") and by nodding to that oft-cited piece of scripture: "The *Wisest of Men* . . . bids the *Sluggard go to the Ant, consider her ways, and be wise.*"[14] Another early eighteenth-century georgic poet, Henry Needler, uses this empiricism to make truth claims for "genius" personifications. Needler dismisses the old Roman idea that rural places were "haunted" by "Rural Deities," but he insists that the superstition approximates a fundamental truth: "tho' there are . . . no Marks" in nature of "Chimerical Divinities" and genii, "an attentive and considering Mind may find there many Tokens and Signatures of the real Presence and Operation of the true God."[15] Early eighteenth-century poets believed that the natural world really contains lessons from its Creator and that "genius" personifications are licensed by natural fact and providential design. In this way, early eighteenth-century georgic brings together two competing traditions: georgic is about the metaphorical *and* the material, the active *and* the actual. This poetry pays empiricist attention to objects understood to contain, in themselves, agency and meaning beyond the projections of the human mind.

Alexander Pope's interest in "Genius" provides a rich instance of this eighteenth-century approach to georgic. Pope borrows the word from Dryden's *Georgics,* a poem that he admired: Pope praised Dryden's Virgil project as "the most noble and spirited Translation I know in any Language."[16] Interestingly, Pope picks up on something more complicated than Milbourne allows in Dryden's handling of "Genius" personifications. The *Oxford English Dictionary* confirms that Dryden's is one of the earliest uses of the word to refer to "the natural character, inherent constitution or tendency" of a material thing; and, at its least fanciful, Dryden's "genius" is linked to natural realities. For instance, Dryden describes osiers "Sprung from the watry Genius of the Ground"—"genius" referring both to the soil's natural inclination á la India "bearing" Ebon as well as to its capacity, taken seriously, for spontaneous generation (2:16). The soil's "genius" is a personification, but one grounded more realistically and *almost* non-figuratively in natural fact. (Interestingly, John Evelyn, a member of the Royal Society's "Georgicall Committee," uses this word similarly in a late seventeenth-century scientific text.)[17] Pope's earliest application of "genius" to a natural object, in his translation of Homer's *Odyssey* (1725–26), marks his debt to Dryden by borrowing the phrasing of the osier line: plants are "Sprung from the fruitful genius of the ground."[18] Like Dryden's and Evelyn's, this "genius" works on a different register than the mythical or allegorical genii to which it alludes—it refers to the soil's natural (and realistic, if idealized) propensity to produce.

Similarly, Pope's "Genius of the Place" in the *Epistle to Burlington* (1731) is licensed by the land's real-life productivity. Pope's "Genius" partakes in the possibilities of personification that this productivity opens up: it laughs, commands, and plays artist. Yet, Pope also registers the influence of the husbandry-manual tradition of reading georgic, as he respects "Genius" as a topographical reality in a way Dryden never did. The "Genius" precept of the *Burlington* poem is a riff on the Virgilian exhortation to consider the nature of the soil:

> Consult the Genius of the Place in all;
> That tells the Waters or to rise, or fall;
> Or helps th' ambitious Hill the heav'n to scale,
> Or scoops in circling theatres the Vale. . . .[19]

Pope insists that there is a special natural force in the ground. Where Virgil suggests that some soil is best for grapes while some encourages grain to thrive, Pope imagines stretches of land being fit for falling waters or for rising hills, some bits encouraging the open prospect and some the sublime terrain. This is more than poetic conceit. Before the "Genius of the Place" became a personified force in his poem, Pope offered the basic Virgilian advice as a pragmatic principle of landscape design, advice that could have been taken straight from the pages of a husbandry manual. Joseph Spence records Pope's advice to Lord Bathurst on improving his estate: "In laying out a garden, the first and chief thing to be considered is the genius of the place."[20] Because Bathurst's land is very flat, Pope observes, it requires "two or three mounts" to bring out its natural beauty. Consulting "Genius," in other words, requires the dirty manual labor of bringing heaps of soil into the proper places. Pope thus combines two quite different approaches to georgic. As Pope develops "*habitus*" / "*patrios*" personification possibilities, he sharpens his focus on agricultural reality and respects the real-world efficacy of Virgilian advice. The result of these georgic borrowings is a materially sensitive brand of personification, a way of approaching the real natural world that brings out the animation inherent in it.

Pope also uses "Genius" to figure the way that objects contain moral or social relevance, à la occasional reflection, and he makes a kind of truth claim for this possibility too. We saw in chapter 4 that, in the *Essay on Man*'s "Great Nature" monologue, Pope turns to Oppian's georgic for a concrete example of how particularized attention to things yields productive knowledge: the nautilus fish's shell and feet helped people refine technologies for navigation. Pope follows this with the language of "genius." He revels in the way that Virgil's ants and bees are simultaneously actual natural creatures and richly relevant analogues for humans: the "voice of Nature" exhorts humans to "Learn each small People's genius, policies, / The Ant's republic, and the realm of Bees" (3:183–84). For Pope, "genius" stands for the (georgic) way that animate and relevant actual things offer humanity clues and prompts.

In a 1724 commentary exuberantly developing this new approach to georgic, William Benson manages at once to out-Dryden Dryden and out-husbandry-manual the husbandry manuals. Benson translates Virgil's precepts into up-to-date farming terminology and channels contemporary agricultural writers as he details Dryden's agricultural errors and offers empirical notes about the particular objects Virgil describes.[21] Benson makes rather enormous claims for Virgilian georgic as a workable agricultural system.[22] While Virgil's precepts very clearly "relate to" their ostensible agricultural subjects, however, Benson also insists that "It is impossible not to perceive" that they also "relate to something else besides the Soil."[23] Benson here follows Dryden in insisting that the soil's force makes it available as a moral agent and actually faults Dryden for "pass[ing] by so many beautiful Metaphors, by which *Virgil* gives Life, Sence, Hope, Fear, Love, Hatred, Oblivion, Ambition, Avarice, and, in short, all sorts of Passions, to Trees and Plants, and to the very Soil."[24] Benson rewrites some of Dryden's passages, highlighting Virgil's moral valences with italics and commentary. Benson believes that georgic enables real natural facts to open into a rich simultaneity of meaning. Beyond underscoring specific morals, he proposes that the poem explicates the best kind of political organization (a "Republic governed by a Monarch"); rehearses the stages of human life through a complex allegory; and more generally encourages sobriety, patriotism, and religion. Importantly, Benson maintains throughout a kind of ontological claim: "the Foundation of the whole is TRUTH."[25]

Benson's commentary illuminates the eighteenth-century understanding of georgic, as well as recent critical *mis*understandings of it. Benson argues that Dryden's assumptions about the poem's metaphoricity and the husbandry manuals' privileging of its material praxis each comprehend only part of the genre's functioning, and both require that other parts of the *Georgics* be misread or ignored. Interestingly, some scholarly treatments of georgic replicate what Benson sees as the seventeenth century's partial readings. Scholars attentive to the generic form, like Dryden, tend to follow the poems' digressions and allusions away from agricultural objects and processes that are seen as pretense, trope, or the boring bits between set-pieces.[26] On the other hand, those interested in themes of labor, science, and commerce in georgic often ignore the formal and figurative aspects of the genre altogether, like latter-day agricultural writers. Georgic becomes a set of themes or "an attitude towards life," as manifest in husbandry manuals and economic treatises as in ornate verse.[27] By focusing on either the poetry or the agriculture, critics miss the ways that early eighteenth-century georgic brings these together. In short, these scholarly approaches work better for the seventeenth century than for the eighteenth.

The genre's best readers have offered a more promising way to understand eighteenth-century instantiations. John Chalker dwells on georgic's "outward-turning" form, its omnivorous appetite for metaphor, allusion, digression, and panegyric. He suggests that this form sometimes was used as a "mechanism" or "means of apprehension," a way of understanding the world.[28] Kevis Goodman posits a fundamental interaction between the genre, whose "complex, non-mimetic practice of reference" functions as an "epistemological instrument," and "the real," which it "amplifi[es]" or "intensif[ies]."[29] Chalker and Goodman contend that the genre engages with and works on "the real." They help us see georgic's metaphors and personifications as tools for exploring nature's fraught complexity.

I want to pursue this insight, with a real focus on the genre's specific dirty rural things. Early eighteenth-century poets describe agricultural objects and processes in acute detail, while simultaneously reveling in metaphors and personifications—figures that are understood as not simply imaginative but able to illuminate nature. The poetry mediates between things and words, the agricultural and the "*Catachrestical*." As Benson exclaims, "the Foundation" is "TRUTH."

An Empirical-Devotional Mode

I have already outlined some intersections and parallels between georgic and the meditative empiricism. Pope and Benson used materially sensitive modes of figuration that work like those in Boyle's occasional meditations, and Needler, Diaper, and Jones explicitly appealed to Christian empiricist tenets to give georgic's metaphors and personifications some ontological warrant. In this section, I argue for an even more fundamental relationship: early eighteenth-century English poets understood georgic as an especially apt generic vehicle for the meditative empiricism. I explore the many ways that georgic resonates with the empiricist project.[30] Then, focusing on Joseph Addison's influential writings on the genre, I demonstrate that his contemporaries privileged georgic as an exciting way of pursuing empiricist devotions.

Early eighteenth-century georgic grapples with contemporary agricultural science. Following Virgil's detailed descriptions of soil composition, grafted plants, and livestock and following the husbandry manuals' painstaking emphasis on English particulars, georgic poems dwell knowingly on the lowest and meanest natural things. They privilege empiricist attention and description, and they feature good science, up-to-date knowledge about agriculture. Where Dryden doubted Virgil's agricultural "Skill," these poets insist that georgics communicate practical knowledge. They draw on cutting-edge scientific discoveries as they offer real advice on how crops and animals should be treated, and they assume that their readers would, Milbourne-like, measure the poems against agricultural fact.[31] They reference and commend science: for instance, one anonymous georgic poet cites Newtonian lectures and describes using his microscope to "pursue a Particle / Of Matter thro' th' untold Varieties / Of infinite Divisibility."[32] Early eighteenth-century georgic is empiricist in its particular descriptions, practical payoffs, and concern for up-to-date information.

In both empiricism and georgic, moreover, knowledge of particular objects and processes is never an end in itself. Things are signs, object lessons, or clues to a providential order. For Virgil, all of nature is a great book, full of signs that can help the attentive husbandman. The way soil crumbles indicates its proper uses; certain animal behaviors infallibly presage big storms; and the appearance of the sun and moon provides guidance about the right moments to plant and to reap.[33] Things are prompts to action. Further, the world of georgic is full of plants and animals that act in ways that parallel human action. Like early modern empiricists, Virgil foregrounds the fundamental similarities that make this possible. For instance, he asserts that "amor omnibus idem" and shows love's effects on a spectrum of creatures from birds to boars to people.[34] When a bull fights a rival for his mistress, the animal is not a proxy for humanity but is acting out feelings shared between the species. Virgil's emphases on nature's signs and the significance of animal actions thus resonated with eighteenth-century ideas about the Book of Nature. Accordingly, in the hands of early eighteenth-century poets, georgic becomes a fit place to pursue both practical and moral applications of facts. It encourages both description and meditation on meaningfulness.[35] Also relevant is the genre's fascination with questions of cosmogony and theodicy. These themes have roots in Hesiod's *Works and Days*, and Virgil offers an account of humankind from the golden to the iron age.[36] Eighteenth-century georgic poems take up these possibilities as they try to situate contemporary agricultural reality in the still-unfolding sweep of a divine plan. Like eighteenth-century empiricism, georgic encourages people to scrutinize particulars as they try to understand what they mean—practically, morally, and providentially.

For both empiricism and georgic, an emphasis on nature's meaningfulness leads to a distinctive model of the human agent. Everywhere in occasional meditation and meditative empiricism, writers insist that people need to subordinate themselves to hints and lessons encoded in nature. A similar logic is crucial to georgic: as David Fairer explains, "Tyranny and mastery over the environment won't work, and Virgil repeatedly aims to curb human pride. To work with the forces of Nature is crucial."[37] Pope actually dramatizes this in his *Burlington* poem. When humans respect natural demands, the "Genius" potential of things collaborates with them, but—disrespected or neglected—it can also act *against* them. Timon, the butt of the poem's satire, ignores nature's hints and logics, and in the end "Deep harvests bury all his pride has plann'd."[38] Like the meditative empiricism's own careful attention to the animation inherent in nature, Pope's georgic awareness of the agency of things serves to chasten the self. Individual human actions should seek to attain provisional harmony with what we can glimpse about nature and God. Like empiricism, georgic subordinates the human individual to the larger order.

To state these resonances in a more fundamental way: both early eighteenth-century meditative empiricism and georgic work to articulate relationships between the particular and the larger patterns. We have seen that empiricist writers interrogate the relationships between things, trying to trace particular things' relations to an entire material world and a broader cosmic scheme that is only ever glimpsed. Georgic works similarly, situating its agricultural particulars in the center of patterns of meaning that the poem tries to recover. Georgic describes each natural thing in manifold relationships: it is considered in terms of its practical payoffs, its moral meaningfulness, its relationship to humanity, and its place in the cosmos. Soil composition contains information about what to plant in it, how to behave in society, and how God designed the world.

Significantly, georgic's very form furthers this project. Fairer's work is helpful here, as—going even further than Chalker and Goodman—he suggests that the genre's formal features serve its engagement with "the real." Fairer explains, georgic depicts a profoundly "mixed" nature and advises the husbandman to forward such "mixtures"—to engraft, to manure, to put labor into the soil. Further, Fairer argues, georgic *enacts* such productive mixture formally, as it embraces ("mixes") very different objects, themes, tropes, and registers.[39] Georgic's "interest in how adaptation and co-ordination can be made to work in any mixed economy" pertains to the farm, the "society," *and* the "poem" itself.[40] For Fairer, georgic's formal complexity is part of its serious concern with its theme (and—we can now see—is closely related to a fundamental empiricist logic): formal complexity and mixture provide a way of making sense of how particulars fit into "mixed economies," complex patterns.

In other words, georgic's form furthers its tendency to arrange particulars in meaningful patterns. Georgic poems progress through comparison and contrast (one kind of soil does this, while another does that), and they set up a richly realized series of point/counterpoint relationships that gesture to natural patterns: advice on what not to do precedes advice on proper technique, and the pleasure of harvest time succeeds a summer of labor.[41] As his eighteenth-century readers recognized, Virgil also structures his poem around an overlapping set of natural patterns. Each book treats natural phenomena of increasing complexity—soil, plants, animals, bees. There are central thematic contrasts, as well: Virgil's first and third books offer a more violent, pessimistic view of farming while his second and fourth are more optimistic and peaceful. His first pair of books depicts people more separate from nature, whereas in the second pair issues of sex, death, and community integrate them into it.[42] Georgic is a profoundly mixed genre, so a related kind of patterning happens in its shifts of registers and modes. Philosophical digression balances mock-heroic, and idyllic scene-painting stands in tension with social critique; a theme stated in terms of agriculture will be restated as a political point, then as philosophical truth.[43] Georgic is also highly allusive, situating each natural thing in relationship to an entire poetic tradition.[44] Georgic considers each thing in terms of not only its practical payoffs and moral or cosmic meaningfulness but its opposites and analogues, its role in natural patterns, and its links to textual tradition. It puts particular objects amid multiple and overlapping patterns.

But this is not all. In addition to connecting the particular and the pattern, georgic highlights links between the local and the global. The genre underscores the importance of specific rural places and things to the well-being of the nation and the empire. Virgil helped early eighteenth-century writers regard agriculture as a force for commercial prosperity, for national peace and imperial hope. What happens in local fields has quite real national and international effects. John Dyer's 1757 poem on the wool industry encapsulates a georgic logic that had fascinated his predecessors in the first half of the century: "What bales, what wealth, what industry, what fleets! / Lo, from the simple fleece how much proceeds."[45] These poems follow the implications of "simple" rural things from specific British places: products that travel, "wealth" that accumulates, "industries" that flourish, and ships that carry English objects and influence to every corner of the globe. The particular is global, in georgic.

Scholarship on the politics of eighteenth-century georgic helpfully identifies other ways that it forges links between specific English places and larger sociopolitical orders. Pat Rogers explores how Pope embraces and reworks "a kind of thematic synecdoche" at the heart of georgic, "by which the destiny of a tribe or clan is made to stand for the fate of an entire people."[46] Rachel Crawford further develops the possibilities of such synecdoche, as she shows how English poets used georgic to understand particular plots of land in relation to the time and space of empire: georgic offered an "image of the world that issued from a single English center" and a way of conceiving "a present which expands backward into an archaic British past" and "simultaneously presumes the eschaton of a British future."[47] Georgic approaches particulars as synecdoches (or signs, prompts, object lessons, emblems). It links them with larger patterns, including the national, the imperial, and the world-historical.

As Chalker explains, the eighteenth-century poet "enjoyed, and made the most of" the way that georgic offered an "opportunity to expand, to dilate on the ramifications of a given theme," "to develop a large range of implications and to place his central preoccupation in a wide literary, social and historical context."[48] The genre focuses on particulars while forging links and glimpsing patterns. It makes sense of one thing in terms of other things and of parts in terms of wholes. It situates the agricultural object in relationships with natural patterns, causes and effects, a textual tradition, a cosmic plan, a sociopolitical order, and all sorts of human moods and meanings. The genre, therefore, was especially apt for the meditative empiricism. The genre also shares with this empiricism an attitude toward meaning. These poems try to uncover and articulate broader patterns that they know can never be fully grasped. They proceed with a kind of trust dedicated to opening up meanings and an awareness of such meanings' provisional and approximate truth status. They offer multiple meanings for each particular thing (practical, moral, religious, political, economic), and the correspondence between an object and its frames of reference are shifting and ephemeral.[49] In sum, georgic provides textual space and classical sanction for empiricist devotions.

Joseph Addison's *Essay on the Georgics* (published as a preface to Dryden's 1697 translation) theorized georgic in this spirit. Addison helped contemporaries think about the formal traits of Virgil's georgic—its language, its materially sensitive personifications, its digressive reflecting, and its exuberant connection-making—as tools for better apprehending nature. For Addison, georgic conjures up the presence of objects in readers' imaginations and, by using the slippery resources of the Virgilian genre to unfold more than sensory meaning, actually encourages meditation on their meaningfulness.

Addison's *Essay* was widely influential in helping contemporaries understand georgic, but its influence is, I think, often misunderstood today.[50] Addison's definition of the genre is oft cited: "*some part of the Science of Husbandry put into a pleasing Dress, and set off with all the Beauties and Embellishments of Poetry.*"[51] Lifted out of its context, this statement has encouraged misleading critical assumptions about georgic. The idea that a georgic poet "*Dresses*" and "*Embellishes*" agricultural subject matter has led scholars to assume that the poet's big words and ornate periphrases "heighten" mundane, meaningless matter. Georgic becomes a stylistic challenge, and the poet a word master with little interest in things.[52] While this notion of georgic as a rhetorical feat removed from "the real" might be appropriate for some instantiations of the seventeenth-century gentleman-poet tradition, it is not appropriate for early eighteenth-century georgic. In fact, Addison clearly states that georgic poetry does not simply lift or decorate the natural world: mere metaphrasis—"a modern Almanack in Verse"—does not a georgic make (150). Even if Addison's language of "*Dress*" invites confusion, the rest of his *Essay* propounds a more complex relationship between the poem's words and things. "*Dress*" does not involve embellished metaphrastic versification so much as an "Address" that unfolds the multivalent meanings of things (145). It involves a real engagement with agricultural things that tries to access the relevance they already contain.

Interestingly, Addison explains Virgil's poem in terms of landscape painting. The *Essay* says that Virgil's poem "raises in our Minds a pleasing variety of Scenes and Landskips," and in Addison's later *Spectator* essays on imagination he says it is "a Collection of the most delightful Landskips that can be made out of Fields and Woods, Herds of Cattle, and Swarms of Bees" (146).[53] Landscape painting is a strange, oddly static way to understand a didactic genre that works through precepts and digressions. Georgic, a prescriptive genre, is reimagined as a descriptive one. Addison even argues that "*Virgil*'s Master-piece," the distinctive triumph of his georgic style, is the way that georgic description conjures the presence of things. It enables an object to "immediately present it self, and rise up to the Reader's view" (149). Georgic is realist: one of its special attractions is the way it "presents" natural objects to the reader.

Addison continues to make the striking claim that the object "presented" is somehow richer and truer than an object merely seen with human eyes: "we receive more strong and lively *Ideas* of things from his words, than we cou'd have done from the Objects themselves: and find our Imaginations more affected by his Descriptions, than they wou'd have been by the very sight of what he describes" (149). Georgic "presents" natural objects with a special density or complexity of meaning. Accordingly, Addison's precepts on the poet's "Address" focus on how georgic poetry not only conjures objects but actually helps readers perceive them in their fraught entirety. Addison praises georgic descriptions for opening objects up to larger kinds of relevance. He notes that Virgil digresses from agricultural objects out to meditations on their social, political, or historical relevance: "his Husbandman" is "concern'd even in what relates to" battles and imperial politics. Addison also depicts Virgil as a kind of occasional meditator: he describes things and then offers "Moral Reflection" (148). Further, for Addison, Virgil excels at achieving "significancy of Expression"—using "Metaphors" and "Circumlocutions" to bring out the human relevance of natural descriptions (151, 149). He also uses personifications, so that bees illuminate "the most important Concerns of Mankind" and "an Inanimate Plant" evinces "Humane Thoughts and Passions" (152, 151). In Addison's account, georgic offers "more strong and lively *Ideas* of things" because it conjures both their material realities and their larger kinds of meaningfulness.

In his own neo-Latin georgic poetry, Addison locates such meaningfulness *in* nature. As Estelle Haan demonstrates, Addison's georgic poem on the barometer takes science quite seriously. It uses cutting-edge meteorological instruments to extend and particularize Virgil's understanding of nature as full of signs and "secrets" that people can access.[54] Throughout his *Essay on the Georgics,* Addison more subtly suggests that the poet captures meaning that is located in and emanating from the agricultural scene. He explains that georgic enables objects to "shew themselves in the best and most advantagious Light" (146). Reflections and digressions should have "a remote alliance at least to the Subject," and "We shou'd never quite lose sight of the Country, tho' we are sometimes entertain'd with a distant prospect of it" (148). He also emphasizes the poetry's correspondence with nature. Transitions and metaphors are articulated through a "Natural unforc'd Method," and digressions and reflections proceed from the object: they are "not brought in by force, but naturally rise out of" a poem's central concerns (146, 148). Georgic helps objects "shew themselves" in their full complexity: the poems capture their material realities but also the pragmatic information they contain, the moral "Reflections" they prompt, and the philosophical and historical digressions they encourage. The "Address" of the georgic poet demonstrates these "important Concerns" unfolding from agricultural realities.

More fundamentally still, Addison's explanation of Virgil's distinctive

"Address" seems to presuppose a poet engaged with an inherently meaningful natural world. Virgil "loves to suggest a Truth indirectly, and without giving us a full and open view of it: To let us see just so much as will naturally lead the Imagination into all the parts that lie conceal'd. This is wonderfully diverting to the Understanding, thus to receive a Precept, that enters as it were through a By-way, and to apprehend an Idea that draws a whole train after it" (147–48). The georgic poet describes some small part of a "Truth," leaving the reader imaginatively to chase down the "whole train" of "conceal'd" meanings. Addison here shares a critical ground with Dryden. In the dedication to his translation, Dryden praises Virgil's characteristic technique: "having said what he thought convenient, he always left somewhat for the imagination of his Readers to supply," and readers only "think they had added to his thought, when it was all there beforehand."[55] Addison learned much from Dryden's discussions of Virgil, but he reworks the synecdochal principle away from Dryden's linguistic or oral model ("having said") to a *visual* one that implies some contact with "the real."[56] Virgil "lets us see just so much" and refuses to give "a full and open view." In Addison's insistence that georgic conjures presence *and* allows readers to perceive wholes from parts, we glimpse his conviction that georgic objects are the tips of icebergs. Virgil describes a small part of a thing, showing "just so much as will naturally lead the Imagination into all the parts that lie conceal'd." Importantly, the "hint[s]" that Addison says readers take from georgic poetry are naturally related to the objects and processes described—they "lie conceal'd" under things or are "drawn" along behind them (148). Georgic mimics the "very sight" of "the Objects themselves," and, by using its slippery formal resources to unfold more than sensory meaning, it actually improves our "*Ideas* of things." As its best readers suggest, it works as a "mechanism of apprehension" or an "epistemological instrument." It provides a lens through which readers can look at soil and explore the moral imperatives it contains or the serious reflection it encourages. Nature is richly meaningful, and georgic is uniquely adequate to this meaningfulness.

Addison enabled his contemporaries to think about georgic as a tool, a way of conjuring up and better understanding nature. For example, Benson echoes Addison as he explains that Virgil "paint[ed]" each natural thing "to the Life," "spread[ ]" it "before" the reader's "Eyes," and "describe[d] it strongly to the Imagination." Tellingly, Benson praises such conjuring up specifically in a description in which Virgil avoids "expressing the Thing it self in the common Phrases," instead using a materially sensitive personification.⁵⁷ Elsewhere, Benson even pointedly uses the language of occasional meditation to make sense of Virgil's procedure in moving from materiality to meaningfulness: he offers an "Application," "points out" a "Moral," or "makes a solid Reflection."⁵⁸ Similarly, Pope explains georgic as a form that presents particulars and meditates on their meaningfulness. He describes John Denham's *Cooper's Hill* (1642), a poem that he read as a prototype for eighteenth-century georgic (and for his own *Windsor Forest* in particular), in Addisonian terms: "the Descriptions of Places, and Images rais'd by the Poet, are still tending to some Hint, or leading into some Reflection, upon moral Life or political Institution: Much in the same manner as the real Sight of such Scenes and Prospects is apt to give the Mind a compos'd Turn, and incline it to Thoughts and Contemplations that have a Relation to the Object."⁵⁹ For Pope, georgic works "Much in the same manner" as the "real Sight" of objects—it is related to empiricist attention. Further, close attention to nature opens outward into larger relevance, and Pope gives these meanings some ontological basis. They "have a Relation to the Object." His syntax dictates that, as in occasional reflection, natural things actually change one's mindset and "incline it to thoughts and Contemplations." They, in themselves, "tend" or "lead" to "Hints," "moral" and "political."

Eighteenth-century georgic appeals to a tradition of meditative empiricism. It works like this empiricism, and it works *for* this empiricism. It provides a generic vehicle for close observation and description of the richly meaningful natural world.

Georgic's Realist Description

John Gay's *Rural Sports* (1713, 1720) is the kind of eighteenth-century georgic that managed to be simultaneously scientifically serious *and* exuberant about nature's meaningfulness. Gay links georgic to science and religion (even drawing on the tradition of Christian Newtonianism) and evinces a fascination with the way that georgic situates particular objects in complex larger patterns.⁶⁰ He foregrounds both practical and moral ways that people can learn from nature. They should mimic it exactly in making bait for fish, and they should also follow its analogical prompts as they try to live happily: "As in successive course the seasons roll, / So circling pleasures recreate the soul" (1:121–22). Gay also stages how close attention to nature opens into meditation—"Sweet contemplation elevates my sense, / While I survey the works of providence" (1:113–14). He follows Addison in depicting georgic as a descriptive genre ("In ev'ry page I see new landscapes rise") and its descriptions as opportunities for close attention *cum* "contemplation" (1:69). When he digresses from sport to describe himself reading Virgil's georgic, he emphasizes its most anthropomorphic and analogical animal descriptions. Gay's poem itself provides a typical—but tour de force—example of georgic description. This section uses *Rural Sports* to explore georgic's distinctive descriptive techniques. I argue that georgic offered contemporaries a brand of realist description that complicates many assumptions about how literary particularity worked in the moment.

Gay's poem privileges particulars, but these do not work as our usual accounts of scientific and novelistic particularity teach us to expect. Influential stories about the "rise of the novel" have long taught that the Royal Society's plain style shaped realist description in literature. Famously, Ian Watt's *Rise of the Novel* proposed that the early novel "develop[s] a more factual prose" and "embod[ies]" an empiricist "apprehension of reality" that is concerned with "the discrete particular, the directly apprehended sensum, and the autonomous individual."[61] In the half century since Watt's book, scholars have developed and extended this account of realist particularity. They often start from Thomas Sprat's ideal for scientific writing ("so many things almost in an equal number of words") as they argue that realist description serves the epistemological ideal of one-to-one correspondence between a word and its referent. Such reference conjures up concrete places and things, and the world in which it functions no longer believes in ghosts, occult qualities, or traditional correspondences. According to more recent work on the novel, empiricism helped to engender a new kind of subject who could "taxonomize, manipulate, and objectify a newly secular world."[62] "Rise of the novel" accounts assume that particularized description distances the world from the observer, fixing the meanings of things as it empowers human subjects. Empiricist particularity and realist prose are thought to presuppose inert, unmeaning things and autonomous, meaning-generating subjects.

This account of realist particularity—developed from the early novel—structures influential assumptions about poetry. Blanford Parker, for example, offers an account of poetry's descriptive precision that parallels Watt's claims for novelistic prose: eighteenth-century poetry features "sophisticated and minute poetic observations," but this very minuteness marks what Parker calls "the invention of the literal," a break with traditional emblematizing in favor of the factual. Inasmuch as the poetry is particular, we're told, it serves "to break down structures of allegoresis," and "the observing power seems to override any moral purpose." The rise of realist particularity spells the advent of a world of cold hard facts and the death of allegorizing and moralizing. Approached through such assumptions, the moral applications that are everywhere evident in eighteenth-century poetry become residuals, *mere* figures. As Parker puts it, they are the "shriveled offspring" of older ways of finding truths in the Book of Nature, here "reduced" to the only imaginative "relation of tenor and vehicle."[63]

This might be true for the personifications and metaphors of the gentleman poets who treated georgic as a stylistic challenge, but it does not apply to the early eighteenth-century writers who approached the genre through the meditative empiricism. Throughout *Empiricist Devotions*, I have shown that this tradition offers another way of engaging particulars. Instead of limiting meaning to a one-to-one ratio, particularity helps access the multiple meanings prompted by things. And instead of exerting control over an emptied-out world, empiricist subjects search nature in an attempt to subordinate themselves to a supra-human order. Where scholars of novelistic realism privilege "the discrete particular" and "the autonomous individual," I have recovered the densely and multiply meaningful particular and the pious, modest empiricist individual. Georgic poets embrace this tradition. The cultivation of particulars does not mean the death of the moral or allegorical, nor does it exist in some kind of awkward tension with such meaningfulness. Particularity *enables* the meaningfulness.

In fact, the epistemological ideal of one-to-one correspondence between word and thing—what Parker terms "the literal"—is not as relevant to georgic particularity as another epistemological concept crucial to the period's empiricism: taxonomic classification. Seventeenth- and eighteenth-century natural histories describe things precisely but do not isolate them or limit their meanings. Rather, empiricists strive for language to define a thing even as they set it in relationships with other things and with a larger metaphysical order. In *The Language of Natural Description in Eighteenth-Century Poetry,* John Arthos describes the logic of taxonomic language:

> Those things which share common qualities or properties must be classified—that is, arranged in groups, since in nature, it is the postulate of science, things exist in relation to each other. Terms must be found to name classes of things in such a way that the distinctive characteristics of those classes are exactly indicated, and so that the members of each class and the classes themselves may be known in their various relationships.[64]

In other words, the best scientific language defines things not only in themselves "but also" in relationship "to the scheme of things in which these phenomena have existence," as well as to the broader "philosophies of nature" that structure them.[65] Taxonomy's concern with language thus reflects the energies that led Boyle to scrutinize twigs to learn about both fire and hellfire and Hooke to connect bee stings with nettles, syringes, and warfare.

The best-known eighteenth-century taxonomy is the Linneaean, which uses two words—*genus* and *species*—to indicate relation *and* distinction. Even before Linneaus, though, English empiricists used words in somewhat similar ways: soil could be "Sandy, Gravelly, Stony, Clayie, Chalky, Lightmould, Heathy, Marish, Boggy, Fenny"—the adjectives here crucially marking the relationships of different kinds of soil to other objects (sand, gravel, stone, clay), as well as to one another (since they all share the noun *soil*).[66] Accumulating particulars cultivate descriptive precision at the same time as they situate things in broader contexts and relationships. They offer *more* factual information than a "literal," precise word-to-thing correspondence would.

As Arthos's book points out, the logic of taxonomy structures a distinctive technique of eighteenth-century poetic description: periphrasis. Periphrasis is a trope that uses "many words to express the sense of one" (as Samuel Johnson put it).[67] In its most basic form, it loosely mimics taxonomy's two-part descriptions: a particularizing adjective modifies a general noun. Gay's georgic is full of periphrases, like the "finny race" for fish (1:253). Such phrasings have often been dismissed as artificial or bloated—the "shriveled offspring" of a language that used to have real purchase on nature or examples of the ugly and overly conventional "stock diction" from which Romanticism would save poetry. Such dismissals miss the way that these phrases are imagined in crucial contact with the natural world. These phrases emblematize the logic at the heart of Gay's poem and the georgic project generally: they are quite particular, in their way, and they enable accumulated details to open up possibilities for meaningfulness.

Above all, Gay's periphrases work like taxonomy to situate a particular thing in complex patterns. A phrase like the "finny race" links together particular fish—"the roving trout" and "the golden carp" mentioned elsewhere in the poem—into a general category or species (1:152, 263). Each such phrase, in itself, also serves to mediate between the particular and general. The direct articles are crucial in such phrases, for there is a kind of deixis about them—the trout, *that* one over there. Yet, as David Parker points out, articles can be used in more general ways, as well. Behind their usage are phrases like "the fish is an amphibious animal," "the carp is golden." Parker suggests that periphrases thereby prompt "a synthesizing state of mind, in which we see the specific as a manifestation of general order, the general as an extrapolation from specific experience."[68] Georgic descriptors also ask readers to bring such a "synthesizing state of mind" to relations *between* species. By calling these fish the "finny race," Gay invites comparison with the "insect race" and "the circling race" (hares) that he mentions elsewhere (1:192, 2:292). Readers must think about how fish, bugs, and hares are *like,* and the poem provides an answer: they are all depicted as creatures hunted. While highlighting this similarity, though, these phrases also feature particularizing modifiers that distinguish one "race" from the other. Hares run in circles; fish have fins. Periphrases forge relationships—between the particular and the general and between different particulars.

Of course, the fact that these "races" are linked most compellingly by their shared status as game requires us to consider humanity's destructive role in the natural ecosystem. This particular theme, moreover, resonates with the work periphrases do more generally. As fascinating recent work by John Sitter, Heather Keenleyside, and Tobias Menely shows, periphrases often provoke consideration of the relationships between nature and humanity.[69] Because the general noun *race* applies to both humans and animals, it highlights likeness among people, bugs, hares, and fish. As Sitter explains, such general nouns "soften[ ] the boundary between human and animal."[70] They prompt us to consider what kind of "race" we are: nonfinny, often sedentary. Are we, like fish, sometimes hunter and sometimes hunted? Do we too circle quickly in our attempts to escape inescapable fate? Gay underscores the relationship set up between races, human and animal, as he closes his poem by praising the "rural maid": "With secret joy she sees her little race, / Hang on her breast, and her small cottage grace" (2:429–30). All kinds of "races" flourish in the countryside, and human children exist in a spectrum that also includes hares and fish.

Gay embraces the connection-making abilities of poetic periphrasis, making much of how these phrases require readers to pay attention to multiple, overlapping relationships. For example, his description of "the feather'd prey" works similarly to his "circling race" periphrasis: it evokes "the scaly prey" already victimized in the poem (2:302, 258). But this is not the only complex pattern in which Gay situates the "feather'd" victim. He continues to depict the death of another avian "prey" by gunshot: the "death in thunder" is relatively quick and painless (2:338, 342). This stands in stark contrast to the earlier death of one member of the "circling race": the greyhound "tears with goary mouth the screaming prey" (2:294, 298). In using "prey," the poem sets up a spectrum of violence and pain. The modifier sets up other relationships still: "the feather'd prey" relates to "the feather'd choir" depicted in an earlier, nonhunting scene. Gay proposes that birds can be "prey" to humans, or we can let them exist in a harmonious relationship with us—a relationship that can actually *generate* choral harmony. Further relations are suggested by the poetic context in which we are introduced to these singing birds. At the end of a long day, "No warbling chears the woods; the feather'd choir / To court kind slumbers to their sprays retire" (1:95–96). The phrase "the feather'd choir" refers to songbirds, but it also complicates their place in a natural scheme. As Geoffrey Tillotson explains in his reading of a related moment in Thomson's *Seasons* (where sheep freezing in a winter scene are called "The bleating kind"): "The diction is parcel of the meaning. . . . 'Bleating kind' is anything but an unthinking substitute for 'sheep.' Thomson is saying: we think of sheep as creatures who bleat, but they are silent enough in the snow."[71] Gay's line works similarly: songbirds sing, but they are silent enough when exhausted, needing sleep. These periphrases force readers to think about the functions of things and their failures. As the "choir" lines immediately follow description of a "ploughman . . . trudging homeward" at the end of a long day, the poem points out that humans also feel exhaustion and that we too do not always perform the actions that should define us. The "ploughman" manages to "whistle[ ] on the way" despite his day's work, mimicking and replacing bird music (1:91–92). Gay's periphrases promote awareness of relationships between humans and animals, as well as between universal truths (songbirds sing) and circumstance and context. In other words, it is actually by avoiding "the literal" that Gay invites readers to think like meditative empiricists—drawing connections between things and discovering complex patterns.

Of course, periphrases are common to eighteenth-century poetic diction beyond the georgic. They are paradigmatic of a central impulse in the period's poetry: in the words of Patricia Meyer Spacks, "The particularities of early eighteenth-century verse locate objects in a universe of significance and enmesh readers in a web of meanings."[72] But periphrases have a special import in georgic, because the trope shares a fundamental impetus with georgic form more generally. By forging relationships between the particular and the general, between different natural things, between nature and humanity, and between circumstances and universals, periphrastic descriptions actually enact, writ small, georgic's pattern-making, analogy-forging structures. Georgic's special relation to the most fundamental logics of eighteenth-century verse helps further explain the popular appeal of the genre in the moment. It is the quintessential form for "particularities" in "webs of meaning." It takes dirty rural things seriously, providing a brand of realism wherein accumulating "particularities" lead to accumulating "significances." (Provocatively, Spacks's formulation also helps us see that—in its privileging of "particularities" in "webs"—*all* early eighteenth-century poetry might stand in productive relationship to the meditative brand of empiricism.)

Periphrasis is not the only descriptive technique that georgic uses to situate particular things in its "web." Many periphrases contain active present participles that work through the kind of materially sensitive personification of Pope's "Genius." These participles are often not even personifications, if we think of personifications as involving the projection or addition of human qualities: "the roving trout," "the circling race," "the screaming prey," "the mounting lark," "the trembling hare" (2:354, 381). Gay has animals act as animals do, but he also sees that their actions make them available as agents in object lessons with human implications.

Georgic is an apt vehicle for empirical devotions. The link between modes is unmistakable in Gay's poem, for in his first edition he deliberately deploys the logic and structures of occasional meditation. For instance, he exhorts his fisherman that the best way to catch "the disporting Fish" is to "tempt their Hunger with the Curious Fly."[73] He offers minute advice about how bait ought to move across the surface of the water (following the water's rippling movements and subtly resisting them as the fisherman mimics the "Nat'ral Motion" of an insect at "play"), and he offers a description of the effect of such successful "Motion": "The sporting Fish leaps at the floating Bait, / And in the dainty Morsel seeks his Fate."[74] Gay's periphrases give the fish agency (it is "disporting" and "sporting," adjectives that imply agency while echoing the human action of the poem's title, *Rural Sports*). Like a good occasional meditator, then, Gay highlights the moral possibilities suggested by the hint of personification as he makes a turn to explicit application: "Thus the nice *Epicure*, whom Lux'ry sways," heeds his "vicious Palate" and "In ev'ry Bit sucks in a new Disease."[75] Close attention to the fish prompts a parallel moral lesson for humans: beware "Lux'ry," and don't overeat. The moral application is warranted by the basic fact that both people and fish eat food and by the insight that the epicure is acting out his most corporeal, animalistic instincts ("Who ev'ry Craving of his Taste obeys").[76] Gay uses periphrases, personification, and occasional meditation to articulate the natural facts, the pragmatic rules, and the moral stakes involved in fish behavior.

In his thoroughgoing revision of *Rural Sports* in 1720, Gay refines his techniques for articulating the natural and moral possibilities of particular natural things. He shows that he has learned from Virgil's distinctive descriptive techniques. We have seen that Virgil uses *habitus* and *patrios* to suggest at once personification and pragmatic information. He does this throughout his poem, choosing words that in themselves mediate between the material and the metaphorical: *laetas* indicates that land is richly fertilized but also happy, and *arma* refers to agricultural equipment or weapons.[77] In the revised version of *Rural Sports*, Gay foregrounds this quieter, more indirect way of indicating moral and social applications. He no longer needs to point the moral explicitly, for the power of georgic description is its way of pursuing precise natural fact at the same time as its figurative implications. Tellingly, in the second edition of *Rural Sports*, Gay cuts out many of his explicitly moralized passages, including that on the epicure's "Lux'ry."

Still, the moral about luxurious consumption does not go away. Gay keeps many passages that invoke this moral through the descriptive language itself. For instance, Gay follows a truncated version of his advice about how to "tempt" the fish with an extended description of a salmon taking the bait:

> If an enormous salmon chance to spy
> The wanton errors of the floating fly,
> He lifts his silver gills above the flood,
> And greedily sucks in th'unfaithful food;
> Then downward plunges with the fraudful prey,
> And bears with joy the little spoil away.
> Soon in smart pain he feels the dire mistake,
> Lashes the wave, and beats the foamy lake. . . . (1:225–32)

The fish, eventually, "Stretches his quivering fins" as he is pulled into "the sick'ning air," where he "gasping dies" (1:250, 252). There is empirical precision here: Gay observes the salmon's body, its appearance, and its movements, even noting its gills in a flash of color as the fish "lifts" himself above the water. The fish's mouth opens to take the "floating fly" that is moving across the surface of the water with just that prescribed "nat'ral motion" that Gay recommends to the fisherman (1:214). The fish acts realistically, while Gay quietly but unmistakably foregrounds the moral implications of its actions: it dies a painful death in punishment for its luxurious consumption. In true georgic form, descriptive precision discloses the moral meaning. The food's movement is "wanton" (tempting, frivolous). The adverb and verb, "greedily sucks," give us very real information about the fish's movements and motivations even as they highlight the human relevance, the problem of "greed." The fish's rich "silver" color and upward motions suggest that, even at the height of success and happiness, misfortune and punishment await, and its quick motion to get away—its only partial success in "downward plunging"—shows that we cannot truly escape the effects of our choices. The poem insists on an awareness of this natural action in a "web" that contains other actions, including human ones. Just after the fish sees the fly ("chance to spy") and shows "greed" in treating it as a "little spoil," Gay depicts the fisherman's greed (his "longing eyes") and willingness to treat his object as "spoil"—"prize" is used twice (1:241–22, 247). As Diane Dugaw points out, the male pronoun slides throughout this passage between fish and man.[78] For both, greed is bad. Gay uses the Virgilian technique of mediating between the material and the metaphorical in ways that resonate with the essential logic of taxonomy (and the meditative empiricism more generally): the more particulars about the fish's actions and contexts he offers, the more relationships and meanings readers can take from the description.

Therefore, while georgic's descriptive techniques may seem to us ornate or artificial (a kind of imposition on nature), their links to scientific description involve them with natural fact. Gay deploys a kind of realism, a language of description that pays close attention to particular things and even conjures the presence of objects. To rephrase Watt's influential formulation about the realist novel, we might say georgic "embod[ies]" an empiricist "apprehension of reality." Yet, it "embodies" the meditative empiricist "apprehension," and so its realism does not involve a one-to-one correspondence between word and thing. Far from signaling the advent of a world of cold, hard facts and the death of allegorizing and moralizing, its particularized description energizes (and is energized by) the search for the moral meaningfulness of things. Gay's georgic descriptive techniques help readers see particular natural things in relationships with other things and with themselves; they help readers understand practical questions involved in angling but also larger ethical questions.

Georgic's realist description also had lively implications for contemporary ways of apprehending "reality" more broadly. The descriptive techniques of georgic realism *suggest* relationships and meanings, without explicitly stating them. The poem does not exactly say, fish are like hares and children, and Gay does not even say the names of these things, speaking around them in ways that require readerly engagement. Periphrases are like taxonomies but also like riddles. Similarly, Gay revises his poem away from the explicit moralizing of occasional meditation. Instead, he requires certain kinds of readerly work to access the broader meanings—moving between the particular and the general, collating the different kinds of "races," attending to a thing's contexts, considering how a fish's appetites illuminate human morality. Georgic descriptions prompt (as David Parker said) "a synthesizing state of mind" that considers relationships between particulars and more general, more human kinds of truth. Remember, too, that Addison praises georgic style for the way it "let[s] us see just so much as will naturally lead the imagination into all the parts that lie conceal'd." In these ways, georgic descriptions do more than depict or reflect nature's particulars. They enact a way of engaging those facts that requires readers to participate. By forcing this kind of readerly work, asking readers to follow certain "leads," georgic teaches a way of appreciating our relationships to animals and approaching nature as full of rich object lessons. The language itself fosters a way of understanding nature's meaningfulness—a "synthesizing" or meditative "state of mind"—that might be taken out of the library and into the world.[79] Suggestively, when Gay's narrator depicts himself reading Virgil's *Georgics*, he is outside under an oak in the hot sun of the countryside, appreciating the poetry about nature and the poetry of nature.

Georgic Realism and Poetic Form: *Cyder*

John Philips's *Cyder* (1708)—with its nearly fifteen hundred blank verse lines describing the Herefordshire landscape and the processes of cider production in locally and scientifically precise detail—is part of a georgic realist tradition, a tradition that uses georgic's particularizing techniques to explore the densely meaningful natural world. Philips's poem is significant in the history of the genre: as one of the earliest original English georgics, it helped spark the trend for georgic and influenced its future directions.[80] It is also significant, for our purposes, for the way it depicts the relationship between a particularizing poet and the landscape. Philips understands his interaction with the natural world in a way similar to the scenes and sites of digging that *Cyder* repeatedly dramatizes: he excavates sediments of meaning from the soil. His emphasis on the soil is fitting, because soil in the period was an especially fraught part of the material world. It was not uncommon to find Roman artifacts in the English ground; Philips himself probably had personal experience digging relics out of the soil.[81] Philips accordingly imagines his poem in real contact with the dirty soil. He digs into the Herefordshire soil that is his theme, unearthing ever more meanings. Indeed, he excavates a coherent moral and political vision *from* a highly specific and local natural world.

We have seen that georgic descriptive techniques foster glimpses of truths encoded in the world and that georgic is invested in complex patterns and "mixed economies" at the level of both theme and form. In this section, I expand on the latter possibility. I show how the georgic realist project, taken seriously, renders even poetic structure part of an empiricist search for meaning in nature. Georgic form offers an approximation of an order only glimpsed through natural particulars. Philips means it when he asserts, at the beginning of his poem, that his "Native Soil / Invites" him to write.[82] The soil informs the very shape of his poem: he imaginatively digs into it and, by accumulating particulars, accumulates meanings.

Cyder's soil is densely meaningful. For one, it contains history. Philips deliberately dramatizes the process by which this happened. Throughout the poem, Philips returns almost obsessively to Virgil's single short mention of blood in the Roman soil. Near the end of his first book, Virgil digresses from a discussion of how to read signs in the sky to recount a set of marvelous prognostics reported to have occurred after Caesar's murder, and these culminate in a divine punishment fulfilled on the battlefields of Phillipi. In Dryden's translation:

> For this, th'*Emathian* Plains once more were strow'd
> With *Roman* Bodies, and just Heav'n thought good
> To fatten twice those Fields with *Roman* Blood.
> Then, after length of Time, the lab'ring Swains,
> Who turn the Turfs of those unhappy Plains,
> Shall rusty Piles from the plough'd Furrows take,
> And over empty Helmets pass the Rake:
> Amaz'd at Antick Titles on the Stones,
> And mighty Relicks of Gygantick Bones (1:659–67)

Philips is interested in this passage for some of the same reasons as Addison, who praised it as an example of how Virgil "made his Husbandman concern'd even in what relates to the Battel" (148). Virgil tells a history focused on the soil of "those unhappy Plains." The soil is cursed, blood soaked, and finally made into an archeological site loaded with "Relicks" of these events. Further, Virgil hints that the way in which soil contains history affects its agricultural productivity: he uses versions of the same word (*pinguis*) to describe the richness of the soil in this passage and his later soil classification tests.[83] Blood acts as a fertilizer in the soil that absorbs it, and this was confirmed agricultural fact in Philips's time.[84] Virgil locates history in the soil.

Cyder brings Virgil's passage together with the contemporary fact that relics lurked in English ground. Philips thereby develops a way of understanding how the soil contains and embodies history. He then uses this principle to explore the history that Herefordshire's soil contains in one of the poem's most extended and bloody excavations—its description of the fall of Ariconium, a pre-Roman and then Roman settlement in what is now Herefordshire. From the beginning of his retelling of the fall of Ariconium, Philips portrays ways in which soil came to contain relics of historical events: the story is of "How our Fore-fathers" were "ingulft / By the wide yawning Earth" and "in one sad Sepulchre enclos'd" (1:170–72). He describes the history of the Ariconium settlement—it was established by ancient Britons and then conquered by the Romans—and, channeling Milton, he offers a dramatic account of the earthquake that destroyed it: "The Ground adust her riven Mouth disparts," and the entire city "sinks" into this "Horrible Chasm, profound!" Finally, "her rav'nous Jaws th' Earth satiate clos'd" (1:227–29, 234). Before even turning to his Virgilian precedent, Philips dramatizes several ways in which history gets buried in the densely fraught soil. The ground is a tomb that holds bodies, as well as a nightmarish "Mouth" that swallows them. Bodies bleed and die, and the ground absorbs, entombs, digests.

Continuing to foreground that basic principle of soil as archeological site, Philips then follows Virgil's fast-forward. Nothing remains of Ariconium now,

> save Coins, and mould'ring Urns,
> And huge unweildy Bones, lasting Remains
> Of that Gigantic Race; which, as he breaks
> The clotted Glebe, the Plowman haply finds,
> Apall'd. . . . (1:238–42)

Philips draws on Virgil's passage to establish the basic principle in a nearly identical way: there are relics, bones, "gigantic" ancestors, and the swain, shocked while furrowing his fields. Like Virgil, Philips has an unassuming swain view the archeological site, but the English poet places this swain in a present—not a future—of agricultural productivity; the plowman "breaks" and "finds." Philips also rearranges the Virgilian passage to emphasize a somewhat linear move toward a climax in the present. While Virgil describes the swain's work before the relics, Philips first depicts the relics, allowing them to act as physical markers from the past that persist into the present of the swain who finds them.

Philips treats bloody soil similarly. While his initial description of the soil as "clotted Glebe" is at once a literal description of soil and a quiet recognition of past blood soaking, he diverges from Virgil by postponing his fully fledged treatment of this theme until after he has described the "Apall'd" swain.[85] Philips then repeats a movement from the Ariconian past into the present:

> . . . Upon that treacherous Tract of Land,
> She whilome stood; now *Ceres,* in her Prime,
> Smiles fertile, and, with ruddiest Freight bedeckt,
> The Apple-Tree, by our Fore-fathers Blood
> Improv'd. . . . (1:242–46)

The "treacherous Tract of Land" where Ariconium once was now boasts grain and apple trees. By placing this *after* the mention of Roman relics, by staging once more the soil's absorption of the events of history, Philips reinforces the dense history his soil contains. Philips also emphasizes the direct effect of the blood of the past on agricultural products. The blood shed in the terrible earthquake must have "fattened" the soil. "Our Fore-fathers Blood" has actually "Improv'd"—with all of that word's connotations of agricultural and commercial development—the apple tree. As Rachel Crawford points out, the "ruddy" apples declare the persisting efficacy of indelible Roman blood in their very appearance.[86] History inheres in the apples.

At this point, Philips's muse is reminded of agricultural topics by the "Improv'd" tree and moves on to treat techniques for improvement. Philips is not yet done with blood-soaked soil, though. The poem features it no fewer than five times (and dwells on free-flowing blood in at least four more passages), as the soil's capacity to absorb and retain blood motivates the poem's frequent historical digressions. In these digressions, Philips heeds his own instruction to "the Planter," who must "with Discretion meet, / The Force and Genius of each Soil explore" (1:41–42). For instance, Philips is highly detailed about the grounds that are good for apples. He specifies particular parishes that have this soil, such as Sutton-Acres in Hereford. These particulars, however, point him to new stories—he must mention that Ethelbert, an Anglo-Saxon king of the eighth century, was treacherously deceived and bled into the soil of Sutton-Acres (1:70–77). Expanding on the Virgilian insight that the soil persists into its products, Philips has the past persist materially into a place and its products. Philips thus renders extremely literal the genius loci's traditional role as a historian. The "Genius of each soil" actually contains history. As he says, his "Native Soil / Invites" him to write: it motivates his historical excurses, as he digresses from natural fact to account for the history it contains.

This is not all. Philips is also attuned to the moral applications of a soil's "Genius." For example, he insists that the best soils for apples are those in which "full-ear'd Sheaves of Rye / Grow wavy"; the worst are "miry" soils of a "rich Mold" (1:60–61, 46–47). This is agricultural truth, confirmed by contemporary agricultural manuals. But agricultural fact does not preclude moral lesson: "rich" soil produces apples with attractive outsides but corrupted insides, and there is an obvious application to rich people, "in outward Lineaments / Elaborate; less, inwardly, exact" (1:51–52). The analogy between people and apples plays up its own literariness; there is a Miltonic allusion, to a passage about Eve's outsides.[87] The allusion, however, is not merely ornamental: it forges a relationship between apples in Herefordshire and Eden, while implicitly proposing an explanation for human in-"exact"-ness more generally. Neither is the analogy only allusive. It is licensed by the poem's pervasive sense that nature evinces moral traits: at one point Philips programmatically explains that "not to Man alone, / But all the wide Creation, Nature gave / Love, and Aversion" (1:249–51). The analogy is also encouraged by almost periphrastic linkages among the "Race of Birds," "of Men," and even of inanimate things: the cider pressed from apples will be "racy" with the mark of its soil (1:395, 627, 297). Throughout his poem, Philips carefully describes the natural world and constantly digresses to account for the fraught meanings he can dig out of it: the soil contains relics of the past as well as hints to morality from its creator.

Bloody soil is relevant here too, for it quite literally provides the ground for a sustained analogy that structures much of the two-book poem: a fundamental congruence between natural processes and social ones. Simply put, intemperance both natural and social ends in bloody soil. The Ariconium episode is introduced into the poem to illustrate this as a quite specific natural fact: "the Sun's intemp'rate Force" is dangerous (1:167). Philips opens the section by countering his recognition of the sun's productive effects—"the great Light of Heav'n . . . quickens all things"—with an awareness of its deadly possibilities. The intemperate sun can be "Noxious to planted Fields," as well as to "Virgins, in their Flower" (1:137–39, 156). True to his sense that nature is full of meaningful analogues, Philips underscores continuity between the sun's destruction of flowers and the flowers of human youth with his metaphorical language for women. The Ariconium history comes in here as the logical completion of his spectrum, from fields to flowers to people to entire cities. The spectrum climaxes at the end of the Ariconium passage with even the "fabled Gods, / Who with their Vot'ries in one Ruin shar'd" (1:215–16).[88] Philips takes pains to underscore that his powerful narrative episode (which is also a clever revisiting of the plague in Virgil's third georgic and the battles in *Paradise Lost*) has a foundation in natural fact. In the spirit of his Virgilian precedent, he credits a divine mandate for the destruction of Ariconium, but Philips describes this divine punishment working through the natural relationships between sun and soil: a particularly hot summer without rain parched the soil, which became increasingly full of "Sulphur, and nitrous Spume," before these underground "unctuous Vapours" burst, causing the earthquake (1:192, 199). Philips unearths historical and spiritual relevance by attending to natural fact.

Cyder's treatment of the sun's intemperance as a natural (albeit resonant) fact downplays the element of personification involved in attributing a moral vice to a celestial object. In the second half of the poem, the sun's intemperance gets a potent analogue as the poet treats *human* intemperance. Philips maintains this analogy by situating the two passages, roughly equivalent in length, as bookends: he begins to treat the sun's intemperance approximately 140 lines into the poem and concludes his treatment of human intemperance 140 lines from its end.[89] Further, he structures the passages in parallel ways. Just as he turned to the sun's deadly effects only after treating its salubrious workings as "the great Light of Heav'n," Philips treats human intemperance only after examining *its* salubrious opposite. He concludes his precepts on cider making with a happy rustic scene of peasants enjoying cider: "Gladsome they quaff, yet not exceed the Bounds / Of healthy Temp'rance" (2:380–81). He warns, though, that the scene of cider drinking remains happy only within these "Bounds," "within / The Golden *Mean* confin'd" (2:444–45). Beyond is "Intemperance" with its concomitant, bloody destruction (2:472). Just as the sun's intemperance wreaked disaster for a spectrum from plants and people to cities and gods, Philips has this moral lesson apply to incidents on a vast spectrum of importance, from the everyday dystopia of a pub fight to the toppling of governments. As he treats this spectrum, Philips finds once more that bloody soil is the result of intemperance. First, Philips's idyll turns into a drunken battle: "Bottles with Bottles clash / In rude Encounter," and "Mixt Gore, and Cyder flow" (2:459–60, 462). Then, invoking heaven—"nor let Civil Broils / Ferment from Social Cups"—Philips continues to add to his layers of meaning the instance of blood in soil that his contemporary readers surely had in mind when hearing of regal blood-soakings: the English Civil War (2:481–82). The poet's slow climb up a spectrum of importance finally reaches its pinnacle with that "Fact / Unparallel'd": "Apostate, Atheist Rebells!" committed the ultimate act of intemperance, as they "Abstain'd not from Imperial Bloud . . . O *Charles*! O Best of Kings!" (2:507–8, 501). For Philips, Cromwell and the regicides are the perfect emblems of intemperance, not to mention the second book's answer to the pagans that were justly punished at Ariconium.

Philips has taught us to expect that blood will persist into the present. The blood of Charles I and the Royalists (and, in his partisan laments, it is as if only they fell) soaks into the soil to enrich its layered history. This blood also persists to improve the present. Here again, Philips articulates the disaster of human intemperance that was the war, in his telling of it, in a meaningful analogy with the sun's intemperance. While the destruction wreaked in Ariconium by unallayed heat is redeemed somewhat by the "improvement" of Herefordshire's apple trees, Royalist deaths are salved only by the fact that Philips can see "Their Virtues yet surviving in their Race!" (2:497). Sons, like apple trees "Improv'd" by past blood spilling, retain and reincarnate the virtues of their fathers. Charles's bloodline, too, lingers in Queen Anne, and Philips's recounting of all this bloodshed climaxes in an endorsement of Stuart rule: "mighty ANNA[ ]" now successfully "Quell[s] the Ambitious" and "restrains / The Rage of Kings" (such energies imagined as akin to the "infuriate" heat of the sun's intemperance) (2:525, 530, 527–28). Intemperance both physical and moral results in bloody soil, which provides the ground for Philips's extended analogy. The analogy is posed as more than a figure spun out by the poet's mind. Philips suggests that physical excesses are naturally congruent to human ones, and careful attention to nature's processes—the destruction wreaked by the sun—is the first step in excavating the truth of Anne-like moderation.

Of course, Philips's poem features a naturalized, loaded political vision: the furious heat of Commonwealth Puritanism is naturally "Noxious," and the triumphant Tory future will be as productive as the soil. These are heady claims, the Royalist exuberance surely influenced by the contemporary political situation and the fact that Philips seems anxious about his relationship with Milton (his poetic predecessor and political enemy).[90] Further, Philips's interest in blood and the soil, in racial and political imperatives embedded in national ground, bears an uncanny resemblance to Nazi mantras of "Blut und Boden"—a resemblance that urgently highlights the importance of remembering that representations of nature have real political effects. But it is inadequate to assume, as many scholars do, that Philips merely uses "heightening" language to make meaningful a neutral nature. We're told, for example, that he "smuggl[es]" in politics and ideology as he metaphrastically ornaments information lifted from contemporary husbandry manuals.[91] Such an account requires an interpretative procedure that returns us to problematic and limiting assumptions about subjects and objects: it requires that we posit a manipulative distance between a meaning-generating poet and an inert, unmeaning landscape, and it assumes that the poem's meaning—including its formal order—comes from a feat of imagination or ideological projection that makes a neutral natural world meaningful.[92] While of course the poet generates meaning, we need not assume that he or she is the source of *all* meaning. Such interpretations fail to account for the seriousness with which Philips's politics and histories respect the natural workings of fertilizers, nitrous vapors, and intense heat.

My reading takes seriously the possibility that Philips understands real links to pertain among reality, morality, and poetry, among nature, meaning, and form. We can respect Philips's own sense of what he was doing—excavating meaning from the soil—without uncritically accepting his claims in the name of nature. And we can see that Philips naturalizes his own high Toryism without missing the fascinating ways that he unfolds this vision *from* the natural world. Nature, he assumes, is a complex network of relationships that georgic's realist techniques can help articulate and explicate.

Since this georgic understanding of poetic form is often overlooked or misunderstood, I want to linger over its complexities. In some ways, its workings were recognized by an older tradition of scholarship that affirmed georgic's richly ordered and inherently moral landscapes. Scholars like Earl Wasserman, Maynard Mack, Martin Price, and Martin Battestin argued that eighteenth-century poets tried to capture a meaning that was out in the world, not only in their minds. Such an aim is said to have shaped poets' attitudes toward both particulars (which had their place in an entire universal order or *concordia discors*) and poetic form more generally. Poets tried to recapitulate the balance, order, and symmetry of God's world in their work: a poem itself constituted a *concordia discors*, and the poet's art mimicked his creator's.[93] For all its insight, though, this interpretation also poses its own problems. For one, it privileges a confidently totalizing notion of order—of a perceivable unity or wholeness on every level of experience. These venerable literary critics often presume the poet's grasp of the entire scheme: Wasserman even insists that poets can only engage the inherent meanings in nature so long as they believe they can glimpse the whole *concordia discors*. The realization that "the totality of things must forever elude" human knowledge signified the end of the poet's access to meaning in nature (a condition Wasserman represents by Tristram Shandy's frustration).[94] Yet, John Barrell and Harriet Guest rightly question whether eighteenth-century poets share such a privileging of the general order over the particulars, whether "the concern with unity and consistency, was as important to Pope . . . as it was (for example) to Wasserman."[95]

Both older and more recent readings, in fact, are totalizing in their way: either the poet can hope for total access to God's order, or he or she is totally in control of an order forged by the human mind or imagination. And, I suggest, both readings are inadequate to eighteenth-century georgic precisely insofar as they privilege total order. Recent suspicious readings recognizing only the poet's ordering capacities go against the very logic of a genre that chastens the human and affirms the dense meaningfulness of nature. And Wasserman's emphasis on the poet's confident access to an ordered "totality of things" is also inappropriate for the empiricist tradition I have been tracing—a tradition that privileged particulars and humbly acknowledged the limits of human knowledge.

But both of these readings also get something right, and I want to use the older scholarship to moderate the claims of recent criticism, without importing its own problematic assumptions. Work like Wasserman's helps us see that the poets explored in this chapter affirmed very real links among reality, morality, and poetry (links that recent scholarship ignores or obscures). The poets understood their work as an attempt to capture—not create—the truth of things. Yet, these poets were also more empiricist than work like Wasserman's allows. Their own (re)ordering capacities were important, and they approached links among reality, morality, and poetry in humble, partial, speculative, and creative ways. They began from the conviction that "the totality of things must forever elude" and that human knowledge is at best limited and fragmented. They nonetheless believed that there were moral meanings in nature, available only in glimpses and fragments, and they embraced their own limits as a necessary condition for their empiricist search for such meanings. Fairer's emphases are salutary: georgic depicts nature as a "mixed economy," "an endlessly varied process that takes different forms." It allows for "a nature that is less comprehensible and supportive than any benevolent system might suggest."[96] The search for order does not presuppose the ability to wholly grasp it. Poetry—especially georgic poetry, focused as it is on patterns and interconnections—is a privileged site for apprehending nature and seeking to glimpse its hints and clues.

Philips asserts that his "Native Soil / Invites" him to write. Later in the poem, he makes a related claim: the apple tree is "the copious Matter of" his "Song" (1:526). *Cyder* takes these claims quite seriously. Though Philips works to write the poem (spending hours "in Meditation deep"), he insists that it is "Matter" itself—not his imagination—that is "copious" (1:366). He imaginatively digs into this "copious Matter" and the soil that nourishes it: the more particular details he collects concerning the natural workings of seeds, fertilizers, and nitrous vapors, the more the "Soil / Invites" him to say. Georgic's generic resources not only help him depict nature's "copiousness": they help him enact the meditative process that unfolds such "copiousness" from particulars. The soil informs the very shape of his poem. The past it materially contains points him to historical excurses, and its relationships with other natural objects direct his analogies. His two-book structure helps illuminate one kind of congruence between natural and social processes, one way particulars might fit into a larger pattern. Philips does not have access to a total scheme, but his georgic aims, empirically, to glimpse patterns and seek larger meanings.

Why, then, did georgic poetry find such a wide, enthusiastic audience in early eighteenth-century England? Yes, the genre was popular because it celebrated much of what is supposed to be "rising" or modernizing in the period: commerce, empire, science, and the particularized detail. But it celebrated thus while affirming a providential natural world by which humans could direct their behavior. Georgic poetry was popular in the early eighteenth century because its descriptive techniques and formal structures offered a compelling way of apprehending nature in its fraught complexity. It offered, in other words, just the promise and the excitement of the meditative empiricism. People wrote and read poems about animal breeding, beer making, weather predicting, and silkworm raising because they were fascinated by the dense meaningfulness of God's great book.

Maynard Mack once suggested that eighteenth-century poems have the "habit of opening out vistas while seeming to be looking at something close at hand."[97] *Empiricist Devotions* has argued that this formal density corresponds with the nature of the world as understood by many of the period's writers. For poets, Protestant meditators, and natural philosophers alike, empiricist observation and description enabled things "close at hand" to "open out vistas."

My story ends here, though the meditative empiricism does not. I have focused on tracing this tradition's emergence in the late seventeenth century and its flourishing in the early eighteenth, but I do not mean to suggest that it disappears as a cultural influence after the 1730s. Certainly, I do not read the meditative empiricism as merely a blip or quick detour on the way to scientific modernity, nor do I only want to postdate by a few decades the usual stories about autonomous subjects, unmeaning objects, separations between words and reality. These tame interpretations are belied by the meditative empiricism's influence on modernizing currents—on science's popularity, proto-capitalist notions, and social contract stories—and by the endurance of its logics: for instance, Philo-Naturae exhorted women to meditation in the mid-1740s, and Hervey's *Meditations* were popular well into the later decades of the century. More fundamentally, I resist reinscribing the meditative empiricism within the too-tidy sweep of influential modernization narratives—for *Empiricist Devotions* is, among many other things, a polemic against the ways "modern" categories have structured and blinkered our scholarship and an exemplification of the productive insights that we can reach only by provisionally setting these categories aside.

Rather, my story ends in the 1730s because the following decades saw important changes in science, religion, and literature that altered the role and functioning of the meditative empiricism in interesting ways. For instance, popular Newtonianism started to take seriously very different, aetherial explanations for gravity, and the contours of the scientific scene changed with new work on electricity, chemistry, and taxonomy. The increasing popularity of evangelical and mystical Christian traditions affected the way people thought (or worried) about the human self in relation to God. And the literary landscape for both poetry and prose was transformed by the emerging visibility and influence of the novel.[98] The question of *how* such cultural changes impacted the meditative empiricism is too big to take up here, and I should not like to foreclose future investigation into the rich persistences and afterlives of its modes of observation and description. I suspect that my study of the early eighteenth-century tradition sheds light on continuities or influences at the heart of, say, the use of analogy in vitalist science and later traditions of "natural religion"; at the heart of Thomas Gray's poetic diction, Charlotte Smith's attitude to mixed forms, and Erasmus Darwin's scientific poetry.[99] I also suspect that there's much to be said about another question outside the scope of this project: How did meditative-empirical modes migrate and mutate outside of England? (Clearly, they influenced Cotton Mather in America, for example.) Indeed, I suspect that—if we set aside our old truisms about secularization and modernization, as well as our penchant for suspiciously seeing *through* nature descriptions—we would find many other ways still that eighteenth-century empiricist observation and description enabled things "close at hand" to "open out vistas." This is fitting, for the meditative empiricism's fundamental wager was that there were ever more "Physical," "Theological," "Moral," "Political," and "Oeconomical" truths to be glimpsed in nature.

Notes

Introduction

1. Boyle, *Usefulness of Experimental Natural Philosophy*, in vol. 3 of *Works*, 200–201.
2. For one example of a pervasive interpretation, see McKeon, *Origins of the English Novel*, 66.
3. K. L. Edwards, *Milton and the Natural World*, 45.
4. Boyle, *Usefulness of Experimental Natural Philosophy*, 232.
5. Picciotto, *Labors of Innocence*, 280.
6. Black, *Of Essays*, chap. 3. See also K. L. Edwards, *Milton and the Natural World*, 46.
7. Boyle, *Occasional Reflections*, in vol. 5 of *Works*, 39.
8. Boyle, *Usefulness of Experimental Natural Philosophy*, 262.
9. The best recent work on eighteenth-century poetic personification is helpful here: Sitter, *Cambridge Introduction*, chaps. 9–12; and Keenleyside, "Personification for the People."
10. Boyle, *Usefulness of Experimental Natural Philosophy*, 233.
11. *Oxford English Dictionary*, s.v. "abstruse."
12. In emphasizing the meditative empiricism's simultaneous embrace of skepticism and trust, I build on a tradition of work by Barbara Shapiro and Douglas Lane Patey, for example, that underscores probability, uncertainty, and contingency in the period's thought.
13. Locke, *Locke on Money*, 2: 403.
14. On science and the plain style, see the work of R. F. Jones, Svetlana Alpers, and Peter Dear. For discussions of this tradition, see Vickers, "Royal Society and English Prose Style"; and Markley, *Fallen Languages*, 1–33.
15. Sprat, *History of the Royal Society*, 113.
16. R. F. Jones, *Seventeenth Century*, 83–84.
17. Jones's thesis receives influential affirmation in Shapiro, *Probability and Certainty*, chap. 7. More specifically, on religious writing and the "plain style," see Fisch, "Puritans and the Reform"; and Auski, *Christian Plain Style*, 306–9. On novelistic style, see Watt, *Rise of the Novel*, 101, and the many works it has influenced.
18. Tita Chico, "Quantum Physics / *Gulliver's Travels*" (paper presented at the annual meeting for the American Society for Eighteenth-Century Studies, Williamsburg, VA, Mar. 2014). "Structure of belatedness," used below, is also from Chico's excellent

paper. NB: Scholars of seventeenth- and eighteenth-century religion have made a related point about accounts tracing the influence of science on religion; they argue, by contrast, that Protestant "plain style" *preceded* its scientific counterpart.

19. Cf. Kroll, *Material Word*, 5: "The very determination to move *from* 'science' *to* 'language' in Jones's argument . . . constructed 'science' as the prior and privileged category of the two."

20. The *locus classicus* of scholarship on "virtual witnessing" is Shapin and Schaffer, *Leviathan and the Air-pump*. See also work by John T. Harwood and Michael Wintroub.

21. Bender and Marrinan, *Culture of Diagram*.

22. Stalnaker, *Unfinished Enlightenment*, 103.

23. *Charters and Statutes*, 48, quoted in R. F. Jones, *Seventeenth Century*, 84; and Vickers, "Royal Society and English Prose Style," 14.

24. These various possibilities—and the scholarship that explores them—will be treated at greater length in chapter 1. "The analogical poetics of ontological speculation" is from J. Rogers, *Matter of Revolution*, xi.

25. Starr, "Defoe's Prose Style," 286.

26. Boyle, *Essay on the Great Effects*, 4–5.

27. Ibid., 27, 29, 2.

28. Ibid., 30 (wind), 31 (water on sugar), 34 (animal spirits), 32–33 (spirit of wine), 36–37 (blow pipes).

29. Gentner and Jeziorski, "Shift from Metaphor," 457, make a related point, though see my comments on their reading, below.

30. Boyle, *Essay on the Great Effects*, 31, 36–37.

31. All references to the fire meditation are to Boyle, *Occasional Reflections*, 85.

32. Finch, "Upon the Hurricane," ll. 178–86.

33. Gentner and Jeziorski, "Shift from Metaphor," 451, 448, 454.

34. J. P. Hunter, "Robert Boyle and the Epistemology," 285, 276, 283.

35. This phrasing is from the critique of a pervasive tendency in scholarly treatments of religion in Anderson, *Imagining Methodism*, 27.

36. B. Parker, *Triumph of Augustan Poetics*, 148, 154.

37. For more on the use of Romantic categories, see my "Anne Finch's Descriptive Turn."

38. "False consciousness" is from another critique of scholarly treatments of religion, offered in K. Jackson and Moretti, "Turn to Religion," 168.

39. Merton, *Science, Technology and Society*; and Webster, *Great Instauration*.

40. Henry, "Religion and the Scientific Revolution," 46, 47. See also M. Jacob and Jacob, "Anglican Origins."

41. Funkenstein, *Theology and the Scientific Imagination*, 11.

42. P. Harrison, *Bible, Protestantism*; and Picciotto, *Labors of Innocence*.

43. The best work on science and language (discussed above) has not yet fully appreciated the crucial role of religion and especially providential understandings of nature. More generally, I take as symptomatic of the emerging field the recent *Routledge Companion to Literature and Science*, in which religion features in only a few, short, and

scattered discussions—and in which it is tellingly absent from a list of disciplines relevant to the study of ecology offered by Stacy Alaimo and cited approvingly and more generally by the editors (100–101, 3). (It is, I think, a testament to how well situated eighteenth-century studies is to contribute here that the most thoughtful and extended of the extant discussions of religion in the Routledge volume is in Lucinda Cole's account of the period from "Newton to Laplace.")

44. Derham, *Physico-Theology*. Interesting scholarship on physico-theology includes Brooke, *Science and Religion*, chap. 6; Markley, *Fallen Languages;* Mandlebrote, "Uses of Natural Theology"; Jager, *Book of God;* P. M. Harman, *Culture of Nature*, chap. 2; and Gaukroger, *Collapse of Mechanism*, chap. 1.

45. P. Harrison, "Sentiments of Devotion," 114. See also M. L. Jones, *Good Life;* and Corneanu, *Regimens of the Mind.*

46. Girten, "Unsexed Souls," 64.

47. The meditative empiricism I feature is allied closely with physico-theology. I refrain from describing it straightforwardly as part of that tradition throughout the book, however, because scholars have emphasized, almost exclusively, physico-theology's use of arguments from design (with "contrivance," "purposeful," "wisdom," and "benevolence" as its keywords). Quite right, but I worry that such privileging of design leads us too often to overlook a sustained fascination in the period with *what else* nature teaches about God's will for humanity, including lessons about morality, society, and politics. Still, the tradition I recover *is* physico-theology by Samuel Johnson's *Dictionary* definition—"Divinity enforced or illustrated by natural philosophy"—and my work can be seen as a salutary reminder of physico-theology's capaciousness, even beyond the design argument.

48. Vickers, "Analogy versus Identity," 95.

49. Foucault, *Order of Things*, 134, 43, 63.

50. I cite and discuss versions of this modernization narrative throughout the book. A sampling of representative works in the categories mentioned here might include Bethell, *Cultural Revolution;* Greenleaf, *Order, Empiricism and Politics;* Abrams, *Mirror and the Lamp;* Foucault, *Order of Things;* and Taylor, *Secular Age.*

51. Vickers, "Analogy versus Identity," 95, 115, 122.

52. Ibid., 116

53. Boyle, *Occasional Reflections*, 30.

54. Wasserman, "Nature Moralized," 40–41.

55. Ibid., 40, 68, 40, 75.

56. Ibid., 42, 42, 54.

57. Ibid., 40, 44, 59. Wasserman thus contradicts his own insight that eighteenth-century analogizing fit the "skeptical, empirical" worldview. I am indebted to the scattered moments when he develops this (now ruled-out) possibility. For example, he points out that, "because analogy claims to yield nothing more definitive than probable and proportionate truth, it did not pretend that man can have full and absolute knowledge of divinity, but only what is sufficient for his mortal career" (53). And in discussing George Cheyne—a Royal Society fellow also featured in my study—Wasserman underscores an empiricist impulse at the core of such analogizing: humans have "the

task of seeing things spiritual by the indirect, but only available means of sensory experience" (43).

58. Ibid., 71.

59. Ibid., 70.

60. Schmidgen, "Undividing the Subject," 87–88, 98.

61. Work like Wasserman's helps license assumptions about the poetry's backward-looking values. For other challenges to such contrasts, see K. Parker and Smith, *Eighteenth-Century Poetry*.

62. This formulation of a pervasive assumption is from its critique in H. Thompson and Meeker, "Empiricism, Substance, Narrative," 183.

63. Wahrman, "God and the Enlightenment," 1058. For representative work participating in a "theological turn" or "postsecular" criticism, see Holsinger, *Literary History*; and Rivett, "Early American Religion." A related project of recovering older forms' impact on modernity motivates groundbreaking arguments—by Frances Yates, Betty Jo Teeter Dobbs, William Newman, and others—for the importance of older alchemical traditions to the history of modern science.

64. Boyle, *Free Enquiry into the Vulgarly Receiv'd Notion of Nature*, 32, 31, 33, 32.

65. Latour, *We Have Never Been Modern*, 9, 115.

66. Morton, *Hyperobjects*, 174, 10, 112, 174, 104.

67. G. Harman, "Well-Wrought Broken Hammer," 184.

68. Johnson, *Dictionary*, s.v. "nature." Morton, *Ecology without Nature*, 18, dramatizes the vacillations between specific and general in "nature" talk today: "Nature is . . . animals, tree, the weather . . . the bioregion, the ecosystem. It is both the set and the contents of the set. It is the world and the entities in that world. It appears like a ghost at the never-arriving end of an infinite series: crabs, waves, lightning, rabbits, silicon . . . Nature" (original ellipses).

69. Johnson, *Dictionary*, s.v. "natural" (sense 5), "naturalness" (sense 2), and "nature" (sense 10).

70. Daston and Park, *Wonders and the Order of Nature*, 363.

71. Ricoeur, *Freud and Philosophy*, 9.

72. Latour, *We Have Never Been Modern*, 35.

73. Latour, "Why Has Critique," 237, 239, 238.

74. Sontag, "Against Interpretation," 5.

75. Daston and Vidal, "Introduction," 3.

76. Anderson, *Imagining Methodism*, 27, 16.

77. K. Jackson and Moretti, "Turn to Religion," 168.

78. For more on how such reading strategies distort our understanding of eighteenth-century poetry in particular, see also my "Anne Finch's Descriptive Turn."

79. For instance, Corneanu's otherwise excellent *Regimens of the Mind* treats Boyle's "emblem-book type of investigation of" the natural world as part of his early devotional interests and sharply distinguishes it from the properly "natural philosophical" type of investigation that would "supersede" it (120).

80. Latour, *We Have Never Been Modern*, 99–100, suggests that such a strategy is another way of reinforcing the ontological bifurcation: "The internal partition between

humans and nonhumans [crucial to the modern mindset] defines a second partition—an external one this time—through which the moderns have set themselves apart from the premoderns. For Them, Nature and Society, signs and things, are virtually coextensive. For Us they should never be. . . . We believe our duty is to extirpate ourselves from those horrible mixtures as forcibly as possible by no longer confusing what pertains to mere social preoccupations and what pertains to the real nature of things."

81. Vickers, "Analogy versus Identity," 150, 151. His treatment of Johannes Kepler is symptomatic. Vickers cites Kepler describing "analogies" as his "most faithful masters, acquainted with all the secrets of nature," but then simply insists, in spite of his source's syntax and overarching point, that the figures are "subordinate" and separate from the "scientific argument." He cites Kepler, *Gesammelte Werke*, ed. Max Casper et al. (Munich, 1937–), 2: 92.

82. Just as anachronistic—but somewhat closer to the spirit of the meditative empiricism—are recent challenges to the hermeneutics of suspicion and recent work in the new materialisms. Though *Empiricist Devotions* differs from these in important ways, my methodological commentary has been energized by this work's refusal of tidy boundaries between active people and inert things, between language and reality. For experiments in reading, see Sedgwick, "Paranoid Reading"; M. Warner, "Uncritical Reading"; Felski, *Uses of Literature*, and "Context Stinks!"; Marcus and Best, "Surface Reading"; and Love, "Close but Not Deep." See also my gestures to the new materialisms in notes 84–86, below.

83. My commentary here addresses some of the methodological questions emerging from the "theological turn." See Rivett, "Early American Religion," 993, 990: "What are the tools necessary for reading religious texts, for understanding how a literary-critical hermeneutic rooted in secular epistemology can approach a mode of 'uncritical reading'" and offer "more synchronic accounts of history and human experience"? For an intriguing, different way of forging a method responsive to empiricism's own interpretative dynamics, see Silver, "Locke's Pineapple."

84. My methodology shares energy with recent work in the new materialisms. For instance, Latour encourages, instead of demystifying critique, close, sociological attention to complex assemblages of hybrid, human and nonhuman actants that do things and mean things outside of our intentions and interpretations. My willingness to take seriously the ontological purchase of literary figurations also resonates with an interest in anthropomorphism-as-tool evident in Bennett, *Vibrant Matter*, 99; and Plumwood, "Nature in the Active Voice." I would suggest that eighteenth-century texts could offer resources to help add conceptual nuance to such work.

85. Here too my interpretive stance resonates with the new materialisms. Cf. Coole and Frost, "Introducing the New Materialisms," 27: "It is entirely possible, then, to accept social constructionist arguments while also insisting that the material realm is irreducible to culture or discourse."

86. For a related approach to interpretation, see Daston, "Introduction," 12, 15. Acknowledging that "talk of talk with respect to things" might be merely "metaphoric" or imaginative but also "accept[ing] these doubts for the sake of argument," Daston fosters a provisional trust that allows her to pursue usable implications: "There is still

the stubborn persistence of the illusion, if illusion it be. If we humans do all the talking, why do we need things not only to talk about but to talk with?" Daston is not usually grouped with the new materialisms, but her work has much to offer.

1. Occasional Meditation, an Empirical-Devotional Mode

1. Boyle, *Occasional Reflections*, 20. These quotes are from Boyle's description of his readers, but—as he encourages each of his readers to turn occasional meditator—it follows that he wanted this diverse readership to scrutinize nature. All further references are given parenthetically in the text.

2. Daston, "Empire of Observation," 99, 99, 100, 101.

3. NB: Boyle's long opening commentary explains and encourages the process in many different ways. I draw on this entire commentary as I piece together the logic of his how-to guide.

4. Huntley, *Bishop Joseph Hall*, 43. For humanist traditions of reading and rhetoric, see Black, *Of Essays*, chap. 3; for the humanist tradition of moralized natural history, see Ogilvie, "Natural History," esp. 89.

5. Boyle underscores the multiplicity and capaciousness of occasional meditation's lessons by offering in his introductory discourse a virtuosic demonstration of many possible applications for the moon (43–45) and a tree (45–50), by dedicating the entire second section of meditations to "Accidents of an Ague" that he experienced, and by deploying an innovative use of dialogue among multiple characters in his fourth section on angling.

6. Coolahan, "Redeeming Parcels of Time," 124. In addition to the work of scholars mentioned in the text (and cited in the bibliography), some older treatments of the genre remain useful: Williams, *Prophetic Strain;* Huntley, Bishop *Joseph Hall;* Lewalski, *Protestant Poetics*, 162–73; and Kauffman, *Pilgrim's Progress*.

7. In addition to the texts I cite in this chapter, there were published meditations for professions from shepherds to soldiers and many, many miscellaneous collections. Coolahan, "Redeeming Parcels of Time," compiles manuscript evidence for the popular practice of the genre.

8. Anselment, "Robert Boyle, Izaak Walton," 129, and "Robert Boyle and the Art of Occasional Meditation," 75; Black, *Of Essays*, 79, 82; and Lewalski, *Protestant Poetics*, 201.

9. J. P. Hunter, *Before Novels*, 202, 207.

10. For scholars on the Book of Nature belief, see Anselment, "Robert Boyle and the Art of Occasional Meditation," 75–76, and "Robert Boyle, Izaak Walton," 126; Coolahan, "Redeeming Parcels of Time," 125; J. P. Hunter, *Before Novels*, 203, 206–7; Williams, *Prophetic Strain*, 52–54; and Lewalski, *Protestant Poetics*, 185.

11. Ranew, *Solitude Improved*, 379; and Calamy, *Art of Divine Meditation*, 15.

12. These exemplary formulations are taken from Williams, *Prophetic Strain*, 56; Girten, "Unsexed Souls," 65; and Picciotto, *Labors of Innocence*, 276.

13. J. P. Hunter, *Before Novels*, 206. See, for instance, Hunter's talk of the genre's "premises of empiricism and individuation cum subjectivity," of its functioning

through "free associat[ion]," of its "making the world into a series of interlocking subjective texts" (200, 207, 201).

14. Picciotto, *Labors of Innocence*, 278.

15. Ibid., 278, 276.

16. This formulation of the assumptions of pervasive modernization narratives is taken from McKeon, *Origins of the English Novel*, 66. See also Thomas, *Man and the Natural World*, 67.

17. J. Hall, *Works*, 105.

18. Lewalski, *Protestant Poetics*, 148; and Picciotto, *Labors of Innocence*, 274–76. For the practice of Ignatian meditation, see Martz's classic *Poetry of Meditation*.

19. Bury, *Husbandmans Companion;* and Collinges, *Weavers Pocket-Book*.

20. K. L. Edwards, *Milton and the Natural World*, 45.

21. Austen, *Dialogue*, "Epistle," sig.*2r.

22. Austen, *Spirituall Use*, "Preface," sig.†3r, †2v, †3v-†4r. (Throughout, I cite the expanded 1657 versions of the *Treatise* and *Spirituall Use*.)

23. Isaiah 1:2–4; Jeremiah 8:7; Luke 12:24, 27–28. Also often cited are the frequent biblical agricultural analogies.

24. Steele, *Husbandman's Calling*, 25. In my understanding of Steele's phrasing, I am indebted to conversations with Natalie Spar.

25. J. R. Jacob, *Robert Boyle and the English Revolution*, 98.

26. Ibid., 104, 6. M. Hunter, *Boyle*, chaps. 4 and 5, details Boyle's familiarity with hermetic thought and Comenius's work in the period during which he composed the *Occasional Reflections*. Comenius was a Czech philosopher influential among members of Samuel Hartlib's circle, which Boyle was participating in by 1647.

27. Kaufmann, *Pilgrim's Progress*, 183, makes this point in a way applicable to all practitioners in some degree but especially the more radical: "The talent for spiritualizing was emphatically not the gift of ingenuity, as it must appear to many a modern reader, but an indication that grace was operative within the meditator."

28. See my introduction.

29. Anselment, "Introduction," 27.

30. Flavel, *Husbandry Spiritualized*, 165–66. All further references are given parenthetically in the text.

31. J. P. Hunter, *Before Novels*, 206, 207; and Picciotto, *Labors of Innocence*, 277.

32. Wall, *Prose of Things*, 77. Other examples of such work will be discussed over the course of this section.

33. Picciotto, *Labors of Innocence*, 280. See also ibid., 274, 275, 277; Huntley, *Bishop Joseph Hall*, 33; J. P. Hunter, *Before Novels*, 197–99, 202, 204; Black, *Of Essays*, 82; Anselment, "Introduction," 23–26, 34; Girten, "Unsexed Souls," 60–65; Coolahan, "Redeeming Parcels of Time," 129; and Wintroub, "Looking Glass of Facts," 128–29.

34. Bury, *Husbandmans Companion*, 75, 76, 84, 76, 81.

35. Rich, *Occasional Meditations*, 52, 85; Spurstowe, *Spiritual Chymist*, 11; Flavel, *Husbandry Spiritualized*, 258; and Delaval, *Meditations*, 77.

36. This possibility was central to occasional meditation from the practice's very

origins. Huntley, *Bishop Joseph Hall*, 33, points out that Hall's genre-forging volume "show[ed] an interest in the growing science of his day," featuring several astronomical meditations (on solar eclipses, a "gliding starre," and a "milkie Circle in the firmament"). See J. Hall, *Occasional Meditations*, 1–4, 7–12, 97–99.

37. By (implicitly here) arguing that Rich's brand of occasional meditation *shared* energies with her brother's empiricist project, I depart from the otherwise intriguing analyses of Bowerbank, "Of Mice and Women," and *Speaking for Nature*, chap. 3. Bowerbank's contrast between Rich and Boyle (as emblematic of female and male ways of knowing nature) precludes the possibility of female occasional meditators being active in empiricist enquiries. Yet, meditation provided a site where both men and women expressed their curiosity about how the world works. In fact, as piety, open-mindedness, and a habit of particularized attention were as fundamental as traditional learning in the pursuit of such truth, this empiricist practice allowed women to take on real authority unheard of in other venues: the authority to speculate on what and how nature means.

38. Rich, *Occasional Meditations*, 71–72, 124; and Purchas, *Theatre of Politicall Flying-Insects*, 293, 315–16. On the glass hive, see Raylor, "Samuel Hartlib."

39. Blair, "Natural Philosophy," 401.

40. Daston and Park, *Wonders and the Order of Nature*, 236–37.

41. Ibid., 237. Daston and Park say "grainy with facts, full of experiential particulars conspicuously detached from explanatory or theoretical moorings," but I worry that "detached" is misleading. The interpretations are separate from the particulars—detached—but they nonetheless often remain *there*.

42. Swinnock, *Christian-Mans Calling*, 374; and Purchas, *Theatre of Politicall Flying-Insects*, 303. A related sense of the relationship between science and meditation underwrites frequently repeated praises of the occasional meditator as a "divine," "spiritual," or "heavenly Alchymist."

43. For the originality of this move, see Anselment, "Robert Boyle and the Art of Occasional Meditation," 77.

44. For Boyle's intellectual trajectory, see M. Hunter, *Boyle*, and "How Boyle Became a Scientist"; and Principe, "Virtuous Romance and Romantic Virtuoso."

45. Principe, "Virtuous Romance and Romantic Virtuoso," 394; and M. Hunter, *Boyle Papers*.

46. Boyle, *Correspondence*, 2: 486. The text in question is a new, post-Restoration edition of Ralph Austen's *Treatise of Fruit-Trees* (originally published 1653); Boyle discusses his advice to Austen in *Correspondence*, 2: 530.

47. Boyle, *Correspondence*, 2: 486–87, does note a distinction between meditative and experimental practices but also discusses their relations. M. Hunter, *Boyle Papers*, 42, points out that, for Boyle, "distinctions" such as those between the "Theological" and the "Philosophical . . . were never very watertight."

48. Cf. Shapin and Schaffer, *Leviathan and the Air-Pump*, 298–310; and M. Hunter, *Science and Society*. It is a well-established truism of the history of science that the Royal Society's appeal to "things themselves" constituted a powerful reaction against Commonwealth radicalism and dissenting enthusiasm in the wake of the Restoration of the monarchy in 1660 and the politically turbulent decades that had preceded it.

49. J. Rogers, *Matter of Revolution*, 3. Schmidgen, *Exquisite Mixture*, 96, 100, points out that *Occasional Reflections* contains "one of the few sustained . . . political meditations in Boyle's oeuvre" but also that his more canonical scientific writings themselves articulate a "political ontology" that "contributed to the growing acceptance of a mixed body politic."

50. Hunter and Davis, "Introductory Notes," xi, xiii.

51. Black, *Of Essays*, 79. See also Anselment, "Robert Boyle and the Art of Occasional Meditation," 87.

52. Principe, "Virtuous Romance and Romantic Virtuoso," 393, 394.

53. Mulligan, "Robert Boyle, 'Right Reason,'" 250. See Markley, *Fallen Languages*, chaps. 1 and 3, for Boyle's views on biblical language.

54. For a helpful survey of these themes throughout Boyle's career and in the *Christian Virtuoso* in particular, see Mulligan, "Robert Boyle, 'Right Reason.'"

55. M. Hunter, *Science and Society*, 91.

56. Collinges, *Weavers Pocket-Book*, 49, 60–61.

57. Boyle, "Of the Study of the Booke of Nature," in vol. 13 of *Works*. Though this text does represent something of a turning point for Boyle, I strongly disagree with Michael Hunter's claim that it "bears no resemblance at all to the sets of brief meditations that Boyle" published as *Occasional Reflections* (*Boyle*, 74). "Of the Study of the Booke of Nature" not only shares fundamental themes, logics, and even phrases with *Occasional Reflections*—it contains occasional meditations (167–68, 170).

58. Boyle, *Correspondence*, 1: 82–83.

59. Webster, *Great Instauration*, 478.

60. Ibid., 508.

61. Austen, *Treatise of Fruit-Trees*, 100; and Austen, *Spirituall Use*, 71. ("Twenty yeares" is from the subtitle of the *Treatise*.)

62. Girten, "Unsexed Souls," 64.

63. Power, *Experimental Philosophy*, 25. All citations from the ant description refer to this page. For Power's connections to the Royal Society, see Johns, "Power."

64. Hooke, *Micrographia*, 164. All further references are given parenthetically in the text.

65. For more on playful and explanatory analogies, see, respectively, Wall, *Prose of Things*, 70–76; and Wragge-Morley, "'Vividness.'" For more on machine analogies, see my chapter 2. I treat Hooke's analogical applications in the discussion below.

66. For a sustained discussion of Vickers's work, see the introduction.

67. Reill, *Vitalizing Nature*, 8, 55, 36, 35.

68. McGuire, "Atoms and the 'Analogy of Nature,'" 30, 10, 37, 43.

69. Wragge-Morley, "'Vividness.'"

70. Elkins, "On Visual Desperation," 34.

71. Bono, "Science, Discourse, and Literature," 61, 81. For further discussion of the roles that figurative language plays in science today, see Crane, "Analogy, Metaphor and the New Science"; Boyd, "Metaphor and Theory Change"; and Lakoff and Johnson, *Metaphors We Live By*.

72. W. Lynch, *Solomon's Child*; Preston, *Thomas Browne*; and Cantor, "Weighing Light."

73. W. Lynch, *Solomon's Child*, 115.

74. J. Rogers, *Matter of Revolution*, 3; M. Jacob, *Newtonians and the English Revolution*; M. Jacob and Jacob, "Anglican Origins"; Schmidgen, *Exquisite Mixture*.

75. Newton, "Third Rule of Philosophizing," quoted in McGuire, "Atoms and the 'Analogy of Nature,'" 3.

76. McGuire, "Atoms and the 'Analogy of Nature,'" 31. Cantor's work on the fluid theory of optics emphasizes the Christian—even biblical—nature of such ontological beliefs: "It was by the word that God had created the universe. It was through language too that the divine plan was revealed." Thus, "metaphors of flow and fountain" that occur in both the Bible and contemporary scientific thought were not understood as "fanciful analogies but . . . [as] tropes which revealed the underlying similarities between" physical and spiritual "forms of light" ("Weighing Light," 131).

77. W. Lynch, *Solomon's Child*, 77–78, is an especially interesting case of the tendencies I explore in the introduction: Lynch provocatively mentions that Hooke uses "imaginative metaphors designed to make sense of the structure of observed natural and artificial objects," suggesting something creative or rhetorical about Hooke's analogizing. Yet Lynch immediately follows this possibility by undermining it; in sum, Hooke's analogizing is *not* "unbridled and unmethodological speculation" but a "systematic" and "disciplined" mode of generating empirically verifiable conjecture (77–78).

78. Walmsley, *Locke's "Essay,"* 117, 102–3. Walmsley quotes Locke, *Essay Concerning Human Understanding*, 4: 16.12.

79. Elkins, "On Visual Desperation," 39.

80. *Oxford English Dictionary*, s.v. "analogy." *Similitude* also had an interesting range of contemporary meanings. It could refer to "a comparison drawn between two things or facts"—a relationship posed by a human agent. Alternatively, it could refer to "the quality or state of being like"—a relationship in objects without a human agent (*OED*).

81. Stalnaker, *Unfinished Enlightenment*, 90, illuminates possible further resonances between new scientific and vitalist practice: Jacques-Henri Bernadin de Saint-Pierre's figurative descriptions are at once explanatory (helping readers understand a phenomenon); aesthetic (proceeding from a subjective appreciation of the world's beauty and provoking a related response in the reader); and crucial in performing scientific work, "reveal[ing] hidden affinities and the underlying natural laws that motivated them."

82. Cf. Coolahan, "Redeeming Parcels of Time," and note 16, above. For the related assumption that a tradition of moralized natural history declines sharply at the turn of the eighteenth century, see the otherwise excellent work by Ogilvie, "Natural History," 89.

83. J. P. Hunter, *Before Novels*, 384. Cf. also J. P. Hunter, *Reluctant Pilgrim*, 95–96: "unable to utilize" the totalizing analogies of Renaissance thought, the Puritans approached nature's "book" as "not a reproduction of the spiritual world nor an exact index of the attributes of God but, rather, an imperfect emblem of the spiritual world—an emblem which needed careful interpretation but which led equally surely, if not equally easily, to truth."

84. The story, as told by Lady Betty Germaine to Lady Lambert, her "intimate," is recounted in Sheridan, *Life*, 42–45.

85. Flavel's *Husbandry Spiritualized* was republished in London in 1693, 1705, 1714, 1724, and 1732, and his *Navigation Spiritualized* in 1690, 1698, 1698, 1708, 1721, and 1733. Both texts were included in *The Whole Works of Reverend Mr. John Flavel*, which was first published in London, 1701, and had reached its fourth edition by 1740. (NB: The second edition was published in 1716, but I have been unable to locate a third London edition; there was a third edition published in Edinburgh in 1731.)

86. Anon., *Young Man's Guide* [subtitle, *Travelling Spiritualized*]; Anon., "Dialogue III., Between Eutocus and Fidelius, About Natural Things Spiritualized"; and Watts, *Reliquae Juveniles*, 91–94, 120–22 (see also 285–88).

87. Bunyan's book was first published as *Book for Boys and Girls: or Country Rhimes for Children* (1686); then as *A Book for Boys and Girls: or Temporal Things Spiritualized* (1701); and, increasingly throughout the century, under the title *Divine Emblems: or Temporal Things Spiritualized*. While all the edition dates are not known, the latter title had reached its ninth edition by 1724 and was still being reprinted in the 1790s. See Murray, "Book for Boys and Girls."

88. On Hervey's literary forms, borrowings, and allusions, see Kearney, *James Hervey*.

89. For the book's influence, see Rivers, "Hervey"; Kearney, *James Hervey*, 41, 43; and McKillop, "Nature and Science." Hervey's cemetery meditations are often cited as an influence on the "graveyard school" and William Blake, and his nature meditations also inspired imitations and riffs.

90. Hervey, *Meditations and Contemplations*, 1: 219, 185, 249, 186. For helpful background on the "Sensitive Plant," see Webster, "Recognition of Plant Sensitivity."

91. Haywood, *Female Spectator*, 3: 153, 148, 153, 155–56; Girten, "Unsexed Souls," 64.

92. Haywood, *Female Spectator*, 3: 156.

93. Hervey, *Meditations and Contemplations*, 2: 210–14.

94. Boyle's introductory treatment of the "differing Reflections, and Similitudes" prompted by the moon nicely illustrates this range (43). At various times, the moon is rendered as active, passive, male, female, an ideal, and a negative object lesson. Also, Boyle's tour de force demonstration of copious possibilities for application here stands in rich tension with a particular moral likening the moon to the human mind: "For as the Light of the Moon is sometimes Increasing, and sometimes in the Wane, and not onely is sometimes totally Eclips'd, but even when she is at the Full, is never free from dark Spots; so the mind of Man, nay, even of a Christian, is but partly enlighten'd, and partly in the dark, and is sometimes more, and sometimes less, Illustrated by the Beams of Heavenly Light, and Joy, and not alone now and then quite Eclipsed by disconsolate Desertions, but even when it receives the most Light, and shines the brightest, knows but in part, and is in part blemish'd by its native Darknesses, and Imperfections" (44–45).

2. Deus *in* Machina

1. Tiffany, *Toy Medium*, 5, 49.
2. M. Jacob, *Scientific Culture*; M. Jacob and Dobbs, *Newton and the Culture of New-*

tonianism; M. Jacob and Jacob, "Anglican Origins"; M. Jacob, "Newtonianism and the Origins"; M. Jacob, *Newtonians and the English Revolution;* and M. Jacob and Guerlac, "Bentley, Newton and Providence."

3. Curiously, the assumption that the clock is compatible only with a rationalized universe and a distant God is crucial to arguments for Newton both as the triumph of the clock figure and as the death of it. For more cautious statements of a tension perceived (or pressed) by contemporaries, see Yolton, *Thinking Matter;* Force, *William Whiston,* chap. 5; and Des Chene, *Spirits and Clocks,* 95–102.

4. For an example of the distortions caused by the positivist/progressive version of Newtonianism that dominates general scholarship, see Zakai, "Jonathan Edwards and the Language of Nature." Zakai describes Edwards's interest in reenchanting the world as a "radical departure" from Newtonianism, when it shares much common ground with early Newtonianism.

5. M. Jacob, *Newtonians,* 271. Jacob's work consistently emphasizes the world's "stability and order" over God's activity. Of course, Jacob recognizes that Newton praises an interventionist God and adds forces to his ontology, but she plays up her keywords *regular* and *uniform* to make God's providence seem more static and ordered than many of the formulations she reads actually suggest. See James Force's discussion of Jacob's argument in *William Whiston,* 3–8.

6. Koyre, *From the Closed World,* and *Newtonian Studies;* Shapin, "Of Gods and Kings"; Brooke, *Science and Religion;* Force, *William Whiston;* Force, "Linking History and Rational Science"; Force, "Newton's 'Sleeping Argument'"; and Force, "Providence and Newton's Pantokrator." See also Viner, *Role of Providence,* 16–17; Dahm, "Science and Apologetics"; and Metzger, *Attraction universelle.* Historians like Herbert Odum, Arnold Thackray, and Robert Schoefield have also recognized something unexpectedly religious happening in early Newtonianism.

7. Recent work on the Leibniz-Newton debates emphasizes these contexts: Meli, "Newton and the Leibniz-Clarke Correspondence," and "Caroline, Leibniz and Clarke"; Shapin, "Of Gods and Kings"; Stewart, "Samuel Clarke, Newtonianism, and the Factions"; and R. A. Hall, *Philosophers at War.*

8. Leibniz's first letter, in Leibniz and Clarke, *Collection of Papers,* 1: 4. All further references to this edition, given parenthetically in the text, indicate letter and section number.

9. Even the best readers of the Leibniz/Clarke correspondence suggest that Newtonians were uncomfortable with the clock figure. Cf. Shapin, "Of Gods and Kings," 193: he "note[s] that it is Leibniz who introduced the notion of a clockwork universe" and suggests that the Newtonians were prepared only "to *defend* the less satisfying notion of God as clock repairer."

10. Cheyne, *Philosophical Principles,* part I, 143, 186, 144, 159. All further references, given parenthetically in the text, indicate part and page number. Cheyne's early Newtonian text was "translated into Dutch, French, and Italian" and became "a recommended text in both natural and moral philosophy at Oxford and Cambridge" (Guerrini, "Cheyne").

11. Motion and dust were other unpredictable factors. For information on seven-

teenth- and eighteenth-century clockwork, see the work of David Landes, Samuel Macey, Carlo M. Cipolla, Samuel Guye, and Henry Michael.

12. Mayr, *Authority, Liberty and Automatic Machinery*, 101. See also Schoen, "Clocks, God and Scientific Realism," 564–65.

13. "Eminently nonpopular" is from Gillespie, "Natural History," 37. (Gillespie also describes Newtonian natural theology as "esoteric" and "mathematically demanding" [37].) Relatedly, Young, *Religion and Enlightenment*, emphasizes the most difficult, a priori apologetic arguments offered by Newtonians. However, early Newtonians like Clarke were at their least Newtonian when they resorted to a priori argumentation.

14. A footnote to Leibniz's letter indicates the source of his accusation: Clarke's English gloss of his own Latin translation of the *Opticks*.

15. For God as maintenance man and Newton's (millenarian) belief that the universe was "unwinding," see Odum, "Estrangement of Celestial Mechanics and Religion"; Kubrin, "Newton and the Cyclical Cosmos"; and Shapin, "Of Gods and Kings."

16. Newton, *Mathematical Principles*, 388–90.

17. Newton, "[Newton to Editor of *Memoirs of Literature*]," in *Philosophical Writings*, 115, 117. This text, while never published, lays bare a logic that is evident throughout Newton's works.

18. I. B. Cohen, "Newton's Concepts of Force and Mass"; and Janiak, "Newton and the Reality of Force."

19. See McGuire and Rattansi, "Newton and 'the Pipes of Pan'"; McGuire, "Force, Active Principles"; McMullin, *Newton on Matter and Activity;* Gaukroger, *Collapse of Mechanism*, chap. 2; and especially Dobbs, *Janus Faces of Genius*.

20. Newton, MS 3965.6, f. 266v, quoted in Westfall, *Never at Rest*, 509.

21. This divide is enacted in M. Jacob and Dobbs, *Newton and the Culture of Newtonianism*. Dobbs, *the* expert on Newton's alchemy, treats the influence of alchemy on Newton's science in sophisticated detail in the "Newton" chapter, while Jacob's "Newtonianism" chapter emphasizes order and commercial/technological improvement.

22. Fatio is quoted in Dobbs, "Newton's Alchemy," 58; Whiston, *Collection of the Authentick Records*, 1073.

23. Boyle, *Free Enquiry into the Vulgarly Receiv'd Notion of Nature*, 7–8. These scientists also needed recourse to spiritual agencies to explain mysterious phenomena like animal motion, cohesion, and elasticity. For more on this, see Henry, "Occult Qualities"; and Gillespie, "Natural History."

24. Brooke, *Science and Religion*, 137: "Newton's philosophy of nature is sometimes discussed as if his conception of God were a mere appendage—a hypothesis to explain what his science could not, a god-of-the-gaps. But this is a superficial view, for Newton was deeply concerned with the action of God in human history."

25. Harris, *Lexicon Technicum*, s.v. "gravity."

26. Newton, *Opticks*, 372–73.

27. Chambers, *Cyclopaedia*, s.v. "gravity."

28. Whiston, *Astronomical Principles of Religion*, 45–46.

29. Whiston, *Collection of the Authentick Records*, 1073–74.

30. Bentley, *Folly and Unreasonableness*, sermon 7, 30. All further references to this

edition, given parenthetically in the text, indicate sermon and page number. For the history of the Boyle lectureship, see M. Jacob, *Newtonians and the English Revolution*.

31. S. Clarke, *Rohault's System*, 2: 98.

32. Newton to Bentley, Dec. 10, 1692, in vol. 3 of *Correspondence of Isaac Newton*, 233.

33. Harris, *Lexicon Technicum*, s.v. "gravity."

34. Chambers, *Cyclopedia*, s.v. gravity."

35. This "Recourse" interpretation of Newtonian gravity had a surprisingly long and influential afterlife (even after the rise of aetherial explanations). Quincy, *Lexicon Physico-Medicum*, applied more generally what Harris said of Halley, and Johnson cited Quincy in his *Dictionary*, s.v. "gravity."

36. See Vailati, "Introduction," ix–xxxi; Gascoigne, "Clarke"; Pfizenmaier, *Trinitarian Theology*; and Ferguson, *Philosophy of Dr. Samuel Clarke*. I follow recent work in assuming that Clarke is a thinker in his own right and not a cover or pseudonym for Newton, as older scholarship would have it.

37. For the debate's influence, see Sharpe, *Defence of the Late Dr. Samuel Clarke*, ix; and Samuel Johnson's comments on the debate quoted in Boswell, *Journal of a Tour to the Hebrides*, 356.

38. Leibniz's clockwork paradigm has been recognized and explored in detail, but Clarke's competing clock paradigm is usually ignored or denied. In fact, for Mayr, *Authority, Liberty, and Automatic Machinery*, 91–101, and Schoen, "Clocks, God and Scientific Realism," 564–65, it was Clarke who killed the clock figure. I am indebted, though, to insightful readings that identify providence as a central issue: Reventlow, *Authority of the Bible*; Force, "Providence and Newton's Pantokrator"; and Vailati, *Leibniz and Clarke*.

39. S. Clarke, *Discourse concerning the Being and Attributes of God*, 17–18. For a version of the "fill in the non fingo," see S. Clarke, *Third Defence of an Argument*, 79–80.

40. See Henry, "'Pray do not Ascribe'"; and Janiak, "Newton and the Reality of Force," 133–35.

41. See Clarke's discussion in Leibniz and Clarke, *Collection of Papers*, 5: 83–91, 110–16. Clarke describes Leibniz's *praestabilita harmonia* as a "two clocks" theory: God designed his machine of the material world to exactly correspond to the workings of a system of souls that He knows perfectly in advance, without the soul ever actually influencing the body, as two clocks might be designed to "*go alike*, without at all affecting each other" (5: 110–16). Clarke then focuses on what seems to him like the familiar atheist reduction of the material world and human bodies to mere mechanism.

42. See Clarke's discussion in Leibniz and Clarke, *Collection of Papers*, 4: 15, 5: 103. Especially telling is Clarke's claim that Leibniz makes God "(as it were *Mechanically*) always determined by things extrinsick" (3: 7–8). Clarke's point is that a God constrained by the Principle of Sufficient Reason is like a mere machine determined to act in specific ways. But "as it were mechanically"—God determined by mere matter and motion even in his creation of matter and motion? This is a strange thought that relies on Clarke's sense of a relationship between God's free will and man's.

43. Harris, *Lexicon Technicum*, s.v. "frame." Clarke similarly balances divine action and mechanism even as he approaches the problem from the opposite extreme. In his

treatment of occasionalists like Malebranche, Clarke argues that—while God does act constantly—a denial of the clockwork nature of the world is a wrongheaded denial of physics. See *Rohault's System*, 41–42.

44. Whiston, *Historical Memoirs*, 132, quoted in Mayr, *Authority, Liberty, and Automatic Machinery*, 243. For Caroline's comment, see Leibniz to Wolff, Dec. 23, 1715, in *Leibniz-Clarke Correspondence*, 188.

45. Worster, *Compendious and Methodical Account*, 9–10; Warburton, *Dunciad*, 4: 641n; and Gurdon, *Pretended Difficulties*, 173, 175. In addition to texts I have discussed elsewhere, see also Keill, *Introduction to Natural Philosophy*, 136; Woodward, *Essay Toward a Natural History*, 52; Colliber, *Impartial Enquiry*, 117–19; Morgan, *Philosophical Principles of Medicine*, 32–33; Hales, *Vegetable Staticks*, 2; and Browne, *Essay on the Universe*, 365–66.

46. For the implied other option—that God might have superadded the extramaterial power gravity to matter in the beginning—see Henry, "'Pray do not Ascribe.'" Bentley never forecloses this possibility (as other early Newtonians do), but I suspect that it would have brought to contemporary minds the firestorm around Locke's suggestion that God might have superadded thought to matter; Yolton's *Thinking Matter* helpfully shows how this would have smacked of atheism.

47. Cf. Yolton, *Thinking Matter*, 194: "The mechanism of the body matches the mechanism of nature." He means that, for the early Newtonians, thought "matches" gravity as a natural phenomenon that seems to exceed mechanism, and many of the key players are the same in both debates. For instance, Baxter's *Enquiry into the Nature of the Human Soul* brings out the Newtonian clock figure that we might understand as implicit in Clarke's formulation of the relation between soul and body: the immaterial soul spontaneously "set[s] the mechanism [of the body] at work" (65). Baxter's reworked version of clock man, however, has an extra layer of complexity. Where God is the immediate cause of gravity that moves the clock world, God concurs with and continues man's free will in the motion of clock bodies. See Baxter's detailed example of what happens when a man shoots a bow (78–79).

48. Addison, *Spectator* #120, in Addison and Steele, The *Spectator*, 1: 492–93.

49. I. B. Cohen, "Newton and the Social Sciences," provides a fascinating survey of "the use of Newtonian physics in social theory" (60).

50. In understanding these explorations, I have found helpful Striner, "Political Newtonianism"; I. B. Cohen, *Science and the Founding Fathers;* M. Jacob and Jacob, "Anglican Origins"; McKillop, *Background of Thomson's Seasons*, chap. 1; and Kinsley, "Physico-Demonology."

51. For the social context of Berkeley's essay, see Breuninger, *Recovering Bishop Berkeley*, 35–39. For verifications of his authorship, see Luce, "Berkeley's Essays"; and Berman, *George Berkeley*, 72–77.

52. Berkeley, *Guardian* #126, 152. All further references are given parenthetically in the text. On Berkeley's understanding of the providential world, see T. Jones, *Pope and Berkeley*, 57: "The visual world is, as it were, a series of clues from God that lead the attentive person towards ways of behaving that are good for him or her, and the attentive person may learn to understand these clues by accumulating experience of the world."

53. Breuninger, *Recovering Bishop Berkeley*, 40, suggestively links this aspect of Berkeley's analogy to "the Stoic notion of *oikeiosis*."

54. Fissell and Cooter, "Exploring Natural Knowledge," 135, argue that Desaguliers "helped to forge the new occupation of natural philosophy lecturer." See also Fara, "Desaguliers."

55. Desaguliers, *Newtonian System of the World*, p. iv. All further references, given parenthetically in the text, indicate line number.

56. Desaguliers also foregrounds the ways that the sun's gravitational power is an analogue to the king's power, and contemporaries familiar with deeply traditional links among God, the sun, and the king would have, I think, happily allowed for a divine force at the center of this system.

57. The best scholars of Newtonian natural theology have only begun the work of understanding this renegotiation of the natural world: see especially Koyré, *Newtonian Studies;* and Metzger, *Attraction universelle*.

58. On Whiston's life, see Force, *William Whiston;* and Snobelen, "William Whiston, Isaac Newton, and the Crisis."

59. Whiston, *Astronomical Principles*, 109–10. All further references are given parenthetically in the text.

60. Snobelen, "William Whiston, Isaac Newton, and the Crisis," 588. On Whiston's coffeehouse lectures, see Nicolson and Rousseau, *"This Long Disease, My Life,"* 141–49; and Force, "Holy Grail," 118–20.

61. Clarke's second letter, in Leibniz and Clarke, *Collection of Papers*, 2: 12; Bentley, *Folly and Unreasonableness*, 2.1; and Newton, *Mathematical Principles*, 390. See also Whiston, *Astronomical Principles*, 173; Gurdon, *Pretended Difficulties*, 205; and Cheyne, *Philosophical Principles*, 2: 116–17.

62. On Mather's contacts with the Royal Society and indebtedness to Ray and Derham, see Solberg, "Introduction," xix–cxxxiv; and Jeske, "Cotton Mather."

63. Mather, *Christian Philosopher*, 88. All further references are given parenthetically in the text.

64. Andrew Baxter's *Enquiry* features the reworked Newtonian clock figure with determined deliberateness, and he continued using this figure even as the popularity of the tradition waned: the 1733 *Enquiry* was published in new editions in 1737 and 1745, and his 1750 *Appendix to the First Part of the Enquiry* addresses the aether, as it was presented in Colin Maclaurin's *Account of Sir Isaac Newton's Philosophical Discoveries* (London, 1750). For the influence of Baxter's book, see Yolton, *Thinking Matter*, 111–12, 121–22, 149–50, 190–91; and Bracken, *Early Reception*, chap. 5.

65. A. Baxter, *Enquiry*, 67. All further references are given parenthetically in the text. Baxter also wonderfully translates Newton's bracketed gravity-cause into a concrete set of parentheses: "a system of matter so disposed, that the fixed or immoveable parts of it may direct the motion impressed (by the power) on the moveable parts, that it may be by them communicated, to the weight, or thing designed to be moved" (58).

66. A. Baxter, *Matho*, vol. 1, 233. For the discussion of gravity, see vol. 1, pp. 18–34, 163–233.

67. For insightful treatments of Newtonian tropes of deification and (sexual) dom-

ination of nature, see Markley, *Fallen Languages*, 185; W. P. Jones, *Rhetoric of Science*, 96–105; and Nicolson, *Newton Demands the Muse*.

68. Thomson, "Poem Sacred to the Memory," in *Seasons, A Hymn, A Poem*, ll. 39, 73, 26, 28. All further references, given parenthetically in the text, indicate line number. Though much scholarship on this poem focuses on order and design or on God and nature tearing asunder, a few scholars have recognized Thomson's use of a gravity-god argument: see Sambrook's comments on "Poem Sacred to the Memory," l. 15n (in Sambrook, *Liberty, The Castle of Indolence*), and on "Summer," ll. 32–42n (in Sambrook, *Seasons*); Drennon, "James Thomson's Contact with Newtonianism"; and McKillop, *Background of Thomson's Seasons*, 31–34.

69. Colliber, *Impartial Enquiry*, 218.

70. For Shaftesbury's influence on the "Hymn," see Inglesfield, "Thomson and Shaftesbury," 81, 69; and Connell, "Newtonian Physico-Theology." Without denying Shaftesbury's influence, I recover a different *Newtonian* source for Thomson's receptivity to spirit or divine agency.

71. Thomson, "Hymn on the Seasons," in *Seasons, A Hymn, A Poem*, ll. 31–34.

72. Ibid., ll. 2–3, 43–44, 57–58, 36, 116.

73. Bowden, "Poem Sacred to the Memory," ll. 31–32. All further references, given parenthetically in the text, indicate line number.

74. Brereton, "On the Bustoes," 10.

75. Early Newtonian dramatizations of the active order repeat in popular form one of the most intriguing ideas that scholars have recovered from Newton's alchemical manuscripts. McGuire and Rattansi, "Newton and the 'Pipes of Pan,'" reconstruct Newton's belief that the ancients understood true gravitation, though the knowledge was then corrupted through the centuries. Newton cites, as proof, a coded classical reference to gravity: the ancients, Newton asserts, explained gravity correctly by describing God as "harmony and comparing him & matter (the corporeal part of the Universe) to the God Pan and his Pipe" (108). Pan produced the harmony in the world by playing his pipe, and Newton reads this as a reference to the now scientifically verifiable way in which God produces order by, as it were, "playing" his planets. Order is emphatically not a static, in-the-beginning product. Rather, it is the ordered harmony of a celestial sonata: God's breath enlivens his instrument and produces, in time, perfect chord progressions.

76. Fontenelle, *Discourse of the Plurality of Worlds*, 5.

3. Money, Meaning, and a "Foundation in Nature"

1. Locke, *Locke on Money*, 2: 403. All further references to Kelly's edition of Locke are given parenthetically in the text.

2. These influential narratives underpin the scholarship I explore for the rest of this chapter.

3. Schabas, *Natural Origins of Economics*, 2. See also Schabas and de Marchi, *Oeconomies in the Age of Newton;* and Wennerlind, *Casualties of Credit*, chaps. 1–2.

4. Hutchinson, *Before Adam Smith*, 56.

5. My treatment of the recoinage is indebted throughout to the work of Thomas J. Sargent and Francis R. Velde, Patrick Hyde Kelly, John Brewer, P. G. M. Dickson, Ming-Hsun Li, J. Keith Horsefield, and A. E. Feavearyear.

6. See, for example, Baker, *On Demand;* Ogborn, *Indian Ink;* Markley, *Far East;* and Sudan, "Mud, Mortar, and Other Technologies."

7. Kelly, "Introduction," 36–67, provides a thoughtful overview of England's silver problem, its wartime commitments, and the disruptions of English trade caused by both the Nine Years War and the conflict with the Mughal empire.

8. Scoryer, *Corrupted Coin made Good,* 1. For estimates about the composition and lightness of the circulating coin, see Lowndes, *Report Containing an Essay,* 102–8; and Li, *Great Recoinage,* 31. On the price of gold, see the accessible price chart in Li, *Great Recoinage,* 10–11.

9. Lowndes, *Report Containing an Essay,* 115. All further references are given parenthetically in the text.

10. NB: I depart from the usual assumption that there were two basic positions on the recoinage. Traditional scholarship reads these debates as a confrontation between John Locke and William Lowndes. More recent work—like Kelly's excellent "Introduction," 12–39, 106–9—cogently challenges the centrality of these two figures. Still, it remains standard to think of two basic positions, for and against devaluation. I believe that the complexities of the historical moment are better served by distinguishing various arguments for devaluation: Lowndes's position is different in spirit and intent from that of Barbon and Hodges.

11. Markley, "Recent Studies," 638.

12. J. Thompson, *Models of Value,* 43; Sherman, *Finance and Fictionality;* Nicholson, *Writing and the Rise of Finance;* Ingrassia, *Authorship, Commerce and Gender;* Woodmansee and Osteen, *New Economic Criticism;* Mitchell, "'Beings that have Existence.'"

13. Pocock, *Machiavellian Moment,* chaps. 11–14; and *Virtue, Commerce and History,* chaps. 3 and 6.

14. Pocock, *Machiavellian Moment,* ix; and Kramnick, *Bolingbroke and His Circle.*

15. Both Ingrassia, *Authorship, Commerce, and Gender,* 9, and J. Thompson, *Models of Value,* 83, thoughtfully invoke this language of "residual" and "emergent."

16. Sherman, *Finance and Fictionality,* 25–26, illustrates how appeals to the material are situated using these binaries.

17. For more about the government's decision regarding the recoinage, see Kelly, "Introduction," 12–39.

18. "Fundamental Axiom" is from Anon., *Review of the Universal Remedy,* 5. This letter and its companion, *Some Considerations,* are anonymous. Horsefield, *British Monetary Experiments,* 308, convincingly challenges a spurious attribution to William Paterson, one of the founders of the Bank of England.

19. Anon., *Some Considerations,* 46–52.

20. Ibid., 30.

21. Anon., *Review of the Universal Remedy,* 12.

22. Ibid., 12.

23. Markley, "'Land Enough in the World,'" 832.

24. Anon., *Review of the Universal Remedy*, 12, 17; and Anon, *Some Considerations*, 30.

25. Locke, *Some Considerations*, 30.

26. NB: Locke is speaking here of silver as well as other precious metals like gold. Locke has a complicated understanding of gold that we need not go into here.

27. Viner, *Role of Providence;* and Landa, "Of Silkworms."

28. Anon., *Some Observation's*, 23. All further references are given parenthetically in the text. Though most sources have this book as anonymously authored, a copy in the Rare Book and Manuscript Library at Columbia University in the City of New York suggests an intriguing, though unconfirmed, attribution: Sir Edward Ward, the lawyer who was made lord chief baron of the exchequer in 1695.

29. It bears acknowledging that, while widely available, such an appeal to nature was not made by all advocates of restoring the coin.

30. Torre, *Political Economy of Sentiment*, 12.

31. Levenson, *Newton and the Counterfeiter*, 118. Notwithstanding the caveats discussed here, Levenson provides a nuanced and accessible treatment of economic issues.

32. Pratt, *Regulating Silver Coin*, 6. While sharing Lowndes's understanding of value—try as governments might, money passes for what "it is *really*, not *Extrinsically* or Imaginarily, worth"—Pratt has a different plan to solve the problem (39). De Quehen, "Pratt," notes that the Treasury paid for the publication of Pratt's pamphlet.

33. Kelly, "Introduction," 106–9; and Hanham, "Lowndes."

34. Briscoe, "Discourse of Money," in *Historical and Political Essays*, 158. All further references are given parenthetically in the text.

35. Lowndes, *Report Containing an Essay*, 30. See also Evelyn, *Numismata*, 228: "Nor is there a more fatal Symptom of Consumption in a State, than the Corruption and Diminution of the Coin."

36. Hodges, *Present State of England*, 262. All further references are given parenthetically in the text. Little information is available about Hodges, but Goldie, *Reception of Locke's Politics*, 6: viii, voices the general consensus that he was among Locke's "most cogent" critics.

37. "Slumlord" is from Markley, *Far East*, 221. For an overview of Barbon's rather colorful career, see Finkelstein, *Harmony and the Balance*, 205–6; and Sheldon, "Barbon."

38. Barbon, *Discourse concerning Coining*, 18. All further references are given parenthetically in the text.

39. Finkelstein, *Harmony and the Balance*, 212, 215, 213. Markley, *Far East*, 221–22, complements this argument by focusing particularly on how Barbon's notion of "infinite productivity" structures his thinking about stock and credit.

40. These are Barbon's words, quoted in Finkelstein, *Harmony and the Balance*, 212.

41. Wennerlind, *Casualties of Credit*, 59, chap. 2 generally.

42. Ingrassia, *Authorship, Commerce, and Gender*, 21.

43. Carey, "Introduction," 3, makes a similar point. For another counterintuitive aspect of these positions, see Desan, *Making Money*, chap. 9: Locke's understanding of money "broke with tradition," whereas arguments for devaluation proceeded from a more usual understanding of "commodity money" (346).

44. See the useful bibliography in Bellamy, "It-Narrators and Circulation."

45. Gildon, *Golden Spy*, 14, 9. All further references are given parenthetically in the text.

46. Addison, *Tatler* #249, in Addison and Steele, *The Tatler*, 3: 271, 270. All further references are given parenthetically in the text.

47. Flint, "Speaking Objects," 216, 220, 223. See also Douglas, "Britannia's Rule"; Bellamy, *Commerce, Morality and the Eighteenth-Century Novel*, and "It-Narrators and Circulation"; and D. Lynch, *Economy of Character*.

48. Douglas, "Britannia's Rule," 71.

49. Festa, *Sentimental Figures*, 118. Festa, Wolfram Schmidgen (*Eighteenth-Century Fiction*), and Christina Lupton further challenge commodity readings by showing that *other* contemporary understandings of object agency play a role in different it-narratives—demonstrating, respectively, the influence of the sentimental projection of human emotions onto objects in Helenus Scott's *Adventures of a Rupee* (1781), of mercantile movement across heterogeneous spaces on *The History and Adventures of a Lady's Slippers and Shoes* (1754), and of an awareness of how a booming print culture materializes ideas on "Adventures of a Quire of Paper" (1779). My work supplements these readings.

50. Lamb, *Things Things Say*, 201, 200, xxix.

51. Ibid., xviii, 206, 213, 224.

52. Ibid., xiv, 219, xvi, 206, 219.

53. Interestingly, Lamb, *Things Things Say*, also discusses Gildon's text and Charles Johnstone's *Chrysal; or, The Adventures of a Guinea* (1760) in relation to a contemporary crisis in monetary value. He notes that "belief in the intrinsic value of coin was powerful" and even suggests that *Chrysal* might be read as "erecting a human standard of candor or ingenuousness analogous to that of the British guinea . . . a coin so pure" that it "exhibit[ed] a perfect match of face value and intrinsic value" (223, 222). Lamb insists, however, that Gildon's book "has little in common with this project": "The sense of things" in the *Golden Spy* "is starkly opposed to the reliability and trust which Locke and Newton wished to foster by means of coin which honestly stated what it was for purposes of exchange" (223, 224). Lamb gets to this conclusion by linking intrinsic value with a stable public "trust" and downplaying the role of the intrinsic itself; he reasons that the golden spies' "Confidence"-destroying secret explicitly counters this ideal. But this conclusion only follows if intrinsic value is somehow undercut by the collapse of public trust, whereas I am suggesting that, for contemporaries, intrinsic values and natural meanings persist *in spite of* human deviations from them. They become all the more pressing to assert in a society that has deviated so far from nature that unveiling the deviations threatens the very fabric of "human Society."

54. Addison, *Spectator* #69, in Addison and Steele, *The Spectator*, 1: 294–95.

55. For Gildon's treatment of heterodox, materialist thought, see Nowka, "Talking Coins." NB: In *Deist's Manual* (1708)—which contains his argument *against* thinking matter—Gildon also demonstrates an interest in something quite like the meditative empiricism: he affirms the idea that "right reason" can access the basic laws of nature. Moral rules are accessible to all, even coded into the world.

56. J. Jackson, *New Translation of Aesop's Fables*, 278.

57. Ibid., 278.

58. Gildon's book repeats this point about the sun and gold's natural "aversion" to misers, underscoring its importance—cf. 15–16.

59. Austen, *Dialogue*, 73. NB: There is evidence that this book was still being read in the eighteenth century, by one reader at least. The copy of the text available on *Early English Books Online* (*EEBO*) is autographed, "William Clarke His Book 1778."

60. Austen, *Dialogue*, 1, A1v. Austen makes a similar set of points in the opening pages of the *Spirituall Use of an Orchard*.

61. Often the trees state some feature of their natural reality, and the husbandman moralizes on it (citing scripture, at times, for additional verification)—here things provoke interpretations, which they sometimes then explicitly affirm. At other times, however, the trees themselves make the analogical application or state the moral truth, and sometimes there is a kind of back and forth as the husbandman holds his meditative conclusions accountable to the facts that the trees articulate.

62. Anon., *Sermon on the Restoring*, 1–2.

63. Ibid., 15.

64. Ibid., 16.

65. The human narrator's closing meditations on corruption underscore the centrality of "value" and valuations to the coins' stories—cf. Gildon, *Golden Spy*, 276–77.

66. For "Base," see ibid., 64, 292, 96. (The last example is complicated by being spoken by someone who corruptly misvalues things.) For "Talent," see ibid., 295; in the lines immediately following "Talent," I also hear a slight punning on "Tale"—both story and flipside of coin.

67. The Italian coin offers another corrupt reading of nature's dictates on the second night, when he tries to justify those who break "Moral Rules" (45–46).

68. I find it productive to ruminate on contemporaneous meanings of *matter* and *material*. Samuel Johnson defined *material* as the "corporeal" but also as that which is "momentous, essential." The material was at once corporeal and consequential—it was consequential *because* corporeal (and created). *Matter* is "body"—including "body" that is "subject to particular consideration." To "matter," as a verb, can mean "to be of importance" or to "generate matter"—as in a wound that oozes. The impossible dream of many of the writers I study, I think, is a matter that oozes meanings without the "particular consideration" that it was of course "subject to." Cf. Johnson, *Dictionary*, s.v. "material" and "matter."

69. My formulation here—"in the active voice"—is a nod to Plumwood, "Nature in the Active Voice." My work on personification in this chapter resonates with intriguing attempts, by scholars working in the new materialisms, to propose that literary techniques like personification might help us better understand the complexity of the real. See also Bennett, *Vibrant Matter*, 99.

4. Empiricist Subjects, Providential Nature, and Social Contracts

1. Kahn, *Wayward Contracts;* and S. Macpherson, *Harm's Way*. My rethinking of the eighteenth-century self also resonates with H. Thompson, *Ingenuous Subjection;* and Powell and Swenson, *Sensational Subject*.

2. Kramnick, *Bolingbroke and His Circle*, 98, 193, 217.

3. Ibid., 188, 194.

4. Boucher and Kelly, "Social Contract," 1, argues against the idea "that there is a single unified tradition or a single model or definition of the contract." I try to respect such complexity throughout.

5. Schonhorn, *Defoe's Politics*, 2, offers an argument against the older notion that Defoe was only "proselytiz[ing] for Locke in mediocre verse." Also, the apocryphal story that Pope merely versified a prose outline by his friend has been disproved, and scholars now agree that the influence was more reciprocal—see note 8, below. NB: My strategy of pairing poets and philosophers is also a corrective to what Walker, "Pocock," 86, recently diagnosed as "a conspicuous *lack* of dialogue between the history of political thought and literary criticism"—a "*lack*" especially "conspicuous" in regard to literary critics' use of outdated assumptions about Locke.

6. More generally, the verse essay was a genre crucial in bringing philosophical ideas to a general audience in the period. For example, Backscheider, "Verse Essay," 119: Defoe's *Jure Divino* "sold far better than" Locke's *Two Treatises*.

7. Gerrard, *Patriot Opposition*, 86. See also P. Rogers, *Political Biography*, and Erskine-Hill, *Poetry of Opposition*.

8. Pope, *Essay on Man*, in vol. 3.1 of *Poems*, 4: 390; and Bolingbroke, *Fragments*, in *Philosophical Works*, 3: 334. All further references to Pope's *Essay*, given parenthetically in the text, indicate book and line number. All further references to Bolingbroke's *Fragments*, also given parenthetically in the text, indicate volume and page number. Pope completed his drafts of the *Essay on Man*'s first three epistles while at Bolingbroke's house in April and May of 1731.

9. On Pope's philosophical seriousness and influence, see Hammond, *Pope and Bolingbroke*, 57–58, 69–79; and Solomon, *Rape of the Text*, 1, 23.

10. Hammond, *Pope and Bolingbroke*, 87. The whole discussion surrounding this claim elucidates the rich relationship between the two origin stories (86–91).

11. Ibid., 89.

12. Erskine-Hill, "Pope on the Origins," 89. See also Hammond, *Pope and Bolingbroke*, 89, 138, 153–55; F. Parker, *Scepticism and Literature*, 109–17; and Ellenzweig, *Fringes of Belief*, conclusion.

13. Erskine-Hill, "Pope on the Origins," 91, 82. (I will return to the problematic assumptions about Locke affirmed in this otherwise perceptive reading.)

14. Leranbaum, *Alexander Pope's "Opus Magnum,"* 60; and Nuttall, *Pope's "Essay on Man,"* 112–28.

15. T. Jones, *Pope and Berkeley*, 186.

16. Kramnick, *Bolingbroke and His Circle*, chap. 4 (though see below for my reservations of Kramnick's treatment of Locke).

17. Bolingbroke, *Fragments*, recognizes his common ground with Locke as he notes at least one way in which Locke emphasizes the naturalness of society to humanity: Locke tries to "acknowledge" that "paternal government" "preceded civil" (4: 66). Yet, Bolingbroke worries that the overarching tendency of Locke's

argument—to demonstrate "that all political societies began from a voluntary union"—makes civil laws mere products of "voluntary" human agreement and makes government itself a human construct (4: 71). He associates Locke with the Hobbesian position that society and even morality are "nominal natures, dependent on the will of men."

18. See Creech's translation of *De natura rerum*, 50–52.

19. Besides Erskine-Hill's own contribution, the situation has not changed appreciably since Erskine-Hill lamented the scarcity of scholarship on this portion of the poem in "Pope on the Origins of Society," 79. For condemnations of this passage as "childish," "unsatisfying," and silly, see, respectively, Elwin and Courthope's edition of Pope's *Works*, 416; Leranbaum, *Alexander Pope's "Opus Magnum,"* 60; and T. Edwards, *This Dark Estate*, 36.

20. Lucretius, *De Rerum Natura*, 3: 931–64. Pope's *Essay* as a whole can be read as a Christianizing of Lucretius. For example, Pope's history of society reworks *De Rerum Natura*, 5: 963–66, 1012–23; for other links, see Leranbaum, *Alexander Pope's "Opus Magnum,"* chap. 2.

21. Bacon, *Of the Advancement*, 221–22.

22. Erskine-Hill, "Pope on the Origins," 83–85.

23. Brower, *Pope*, 228, notes that Pope's ants and bees have ancestors in another text in this tradition, Virgil's *Georgics*.

24. Montaigne, "Apology for Raymond Sebond," in *Complete Essays*, 489–683, 508–9.

25. I here refute the assumption that the *Essay*'s careful empiricism contradicts its analogical reasoning. As A. D. Nuttall puts it, the fundamental empiricist premise is "that we are restricted to knowledge of human affairs and that any attempt to reason beyond the range of our information is absurd." In his account, then, analogical reasoning proceeds from a diametrically opposite premise, "that we may draw certain inferences about God and man from the knowledge we possess" (*Pope's "Essay,"* 58, 61). See also White, *Pope and the Context of Controversy*, 80; and Solomon, *Rape of the Text*, 165–75. (Solomon questionably disavows Pope's relationship with "the camp of the analogists" even as he insightfully treats analogy in my sense under the category of "regulatory metaphors.") I draw on T. Jones, *Pope and Berkeley*, chap. 4, which insightfully allows for empiricism *and* analogizing.

26. This is from Erskine-Hill, "Pope on the Origins," cited earlier. For other contrasts between Pope and Locke—even in the best work on Pope—see T. Jones, *Pope and Berkeley*, 157–60; and Hammond, *Pope and Bolingbroke*, 89, 138, 153–55 (though note his insightful comments on some methodological similarities). For the broader ideological contrast, see Kramnick, *Bolingbroke and His Circle*, 98, 193, 217. Another influential argument for Locke's individuals as quintessential "modern" subjects is found in C. B. Macpherson, *Political Theory of Possessive Individualism*, 208–11.

27. Sim and Walker, *Discourse of Sovereignty*, 80. I adopt this more modest formulation of Locke's influence instead of recently challenged commonplaces about Locke's intention to justify 1688 and his absolute centrality to Whig thought.

28. On Defoe's politics, see Schonhorn, *Defoe's Politics;* Furbank and Owens, *Political Biography;* Kay, *Political Constructions,* 47–66; and Backscheider, *Daniel Defoe.*

29. Tully, *Discourse on Property,* 11, 4. For links among political individuals, nature, and God, see works cited in bibliography by the authors mentioned, as well as by J. B. Schneedwind, Francis Oakley, Alex Tuckness, and Jeremy Waldron.

30. Locke, *Two Treatises on Government,* 2: 77. All further references, given parenthetically in the text, refer to treatise and paragraph number.

31. Tully, *Discourse on Property,* 166, 168. NB: The most important critique of "workmanship" interpretations of Locke's property chapter—Waldron, *Right to Private Property,* chap. 6—does not challenge Locke's sense of humanity and nature as God's creations.

32. Furbank and Owens, *Political Biography,* 53.

33. Schonhorn, *Defoe's Politics,* 151, 129. He cites Kramnick, *Bolingbroke and His Circle,* 99.

34. Defoe, *Jure Divino,* 2: 195, 197, 194n. All further references, given parenthetically in the text, indicate book and line number (unless otherwise noted).

35. NB: Bolingbroke, *Fragments,* 3: 404, uses the same phrase: "Nature directed them [humans] to unite in societies."

36. Defoe, *Jure Divino,* p. 33.

37. For Defoe's other intriguing accounts of such "Necessity," see *Jure Divino,* 2: 211–12, and *Review,* Sept. 10, 1706.

38. Clark, *Daniel Defoe,* 62.

39. See C. B. Macpherson, *Political Theory of Possessive Individualism,* 208–11; Tully, *Discourse on Property,* 146–54; and Caffentzis, *Clipped Coins.*

40. Locke, *Locke on Money,* 374, 1: 323. See my more extended discussion of Locke's economic thought in chap. 3.

41. Locke, *Questions concerning the Law of Nature,* 211.

42. Defoe, *Jure Divino,* p. 35.

43. For a lucid overview of the political doctrines Defoe reacts against, see Furbank, "Introduction," 1–3, 16–21.

44. Locke's discussion of William Barclay's understanding of a right to self-defense provides a precedent for Defoe's argument. See *Two Treatises,* 2: 232–33.

45. See also "*Confounds the Order* Nature fix'd at first" and "*Inverts the World,* and Crosses Providence" (3: 441, 439).

46. Derham, *Physico-Theology,* 240–44, makes the same point in his Boyle Lectures, just a few years after Defoe's poem.

47. Defoe further notes that people widely agree that "'Tis fair" for animals to resist meddling humans; if a human gets hurt, "We blame *the Blockhead,* never blame *the Beast*" (3: 268, 272).

48. Cf. Defoe's later uses of analogies with worms, load-bearing animals, and water (*Jure Divino,* 5: 643, 7: 659–71, 5: 28–29, 6.15).

49. Furbank's edition points out that Sardanapulus is "otherwise known as Asurbanipal (c. 670–650 BC), a king of Assyria, noted for his extravagant debauchery" (378).

Defoe's footnotes offer extensive information about Sardanapalus and Arbaces (8: 47n, 98n, 134n, 136n).

50. Also relevant, here, is work on Defoe's fiction that emphasizes his fascination with both human agency and providence's power: Starr, *Defoe and Spiritual Autobiography;* Damrosch, *God's Plot and Man's Stories;* J. P. Hunter, *Reluctant Pilgrim;* Battestin, *Providence of Wit;* and Kay, *Political Constructions,* chap. 2.

51. Defoe, *Review,* Feb. 3, 1713, vol. 9.1, 213.

52. Ibid., 212–13. Relevant in this context is the fascinating argument about Defoe's understanding of providential "scattering and gathering" offered in Wolfram Schmidgen, "The Metaphysics of *Robinson Crusoe*" (forthcoming in *ELH*).

53. Defoe, *General History,* 30, 33–34.

54. Ibid., 31. Defoe's description, 30–31, is noteworthy for its minute detail: the "Observer" noticed "how a great Eagle, which us'd the Shore thereabouts, soaring, and as it were sailing aloft in the Air, in a calm Evening, turn'd her Tail from a Horizontal to a perpendicular or polar Situation, as she had occasion to guide herself this way, or that in her Flight, by which turning of her Tail, the Wind which always blows Horizontal, pushing against the Feathers, whose flat Side lay then towards it, forced the Tail forward, and that again turn'd the Body of the Eagle the contrary way. For Example, If the Eagle flew North, and the Wind blew from the East, the Eagle turning the flat Side of her Tail towards the Wind, and the Wind pushing the Tail, on that occasion due West, the Head of the Bird would necessarily be turn'd to the other way Easy." He then makes the application explicit: it works "by the same Rule."

55. Ibid., 31.

56. Ibid., 32.

57. For Locke's demonstrable ethics, see Schneedwind, "Locke's Moral Philosophy"; and Colman, "Locke's Empiricist Theory."

58. For Pope as systematizer—sometimes-Leibnizean, advocate of the Chain of Being, spokesperson for total world harmony, or complacent "cosmic Tory" (defending "Things as They Are")—see, respectively, Crousaz, *Examination;* Lovejoy, *Great Chain of Being;* M. Mack's Twickenham edition of the poem; and Willey, *Eighteenth-Century Backgrounds,* 48.

59. Tully, *Discourse on Property,* 45; and Pope, *Essay on Man,* "The Design," 7.

60. Leranbaum, *Alexander Pope's "Opus Magnum,"* chap. 2. After demonstrating relations between *De Rerum Natura* and Pope's first three books, Leranbaum notes that Pope's fourth book departs from this paradigm (and is more indebted to Juvenal or Boethius). I see no need to distinguish the fourth book in this way, for it merely continues Pope's project, contra Lucretius, of unfolding an ethical system from Christianized particulars.

61. Lucretius, *De Rerum Natura,* 5: 195–235, 1: 146–48, 2: 59–61, 3: 91–93, 6: 39–41.

62. The *Essay*'s more extended treatment of evil (1: 141–232) furthers Pope's everything-but-the-kitchen-sink mode of explanation.

63. My reading complements recent attempts to (in Fairer's words) "put[ ] a more discomfiting emphasis on statements which can in isolation sound complacent and optimistic" (Fairer, "Pope, Blake, Heraclitus," 178). For instance, James Force finds in

Pope's poem a "cautious empirical methodology" indebted to Newtonianism ("Holy Grail," 109). See also Sitter, "Eighteenth-Century Ecological Poetry," 128.

64. A contemporary example of this clock figure can be found in a text that Pope draws on in his treatment of evil: King, *Essay on the Origin of Evil*, 133.

65. My reading draws on the best recent work on Pope's poem, which underscores the skeptical and provisional nature of the poem's philosophical postures; see books by Fred Parker, Helen Vendler, James Laverty, and Patricia Meyer Spacks. For an older take on the poem that shares some of the spirit of recent work, see Tuveson, "*Essay on Man*," 371–72.

66. Brooke and Cantor, *Reconstructing Nature*, 145.

67. Riley, "Social Contract Theory," 347.

5. Georgic Realism, an Empirical-Devotional Poetics

1. The poems I mention comprise a very partial bibliography of interesting contemporary georgics: Tickell, "Fragment"; Churchill (a soldier), *October;* J. Armstrong (a physician), *Art of Preserving Health;* Swift, "Description of a City Shower," in *Tatler* #248; Anon., "A Description in Imitation of Milton"; Gardiner (a clergyman), *Rapin of Gardens;* Anon., *Silk-worms;* Chudleigh, "Happy Man"; Wright, *Burley Hill;* and Ward, *Phoenix-Park*.

2. Such explanations usually draw on Low, *Georgic Revolution*, 12, which argues that the "revolution" that made georgic popular was not only "literary" but "social, ideological, economic, and technological."

3. See the georgics featured in the Dryden-Tonson miscellanies (including those by Knightly Chetwood, Thomas Creech, Henry Sacheverill, and Richard Maitland, Earl of Lauderdale).

4. Recent work shows that Dryden's most original contributions to a tradition of metaphorizing and moralizing georgic processes are his politicizing moves, which further shift his translation's focus from agricultural topics: Winn, *John Dryden*, 479–89; and Zwicker, "Reading Vergil in 1690s."

5. Dryden, *Dedication to Virgil's Georgics*, in vol. 5 of *Works*, 137.

6. See the work of G. E. Fussell, Andrew McRae, and Joan Thirsk.

7. Milbourne, *Notes on Dryden's Virgil*, 108. All further references are given parenthetically in the text.

8. Virgil, *Georgics*, 1: 53, 52.

9. Dryden, *Virgil's Georgics*, in vol. 5 of *Works*, 1: 82–83, 85–86. All further references to the *Georgics* translation, given parenthetically in the text, indicate book and line number.

10. Worlidge, *Systema Agriculturae*, 31–32; and Lister, "Ingenious Proposal."

11. Milbourne's approach to Virgil has been read as offering a literalist understanding of translation against Dryden's tendencies to imitate: Bottkil, "Dryden's Latin Scholarship"; and Frost, *John Dryden*, 195.

12. Dryden, *Notes and Observations*, in vol. 6 of *Works*, 813–14.

13. For Puttenham's definition, see *Oxford English Dictionary*, s.v. "catachresis."

14. Diaper and Jones, *Oppian's Halieuticks*, 9.

15. Needler, "On the Beauty of the Universe," 95–96. Needler features georgic themes throughout this essay and his entire volume.

16. Pope, "Preface" to *Iliad of Homer*, in vol. 7 of *Poems*, 22.

17. Evelyn, *Sylva*, 3.

18. Pope, *Odyssey*, in vol. 9 of *Poems*, book 9, l. 152.

19. Pope, *Epistle to Burlington*, in vol. 3.2 of *Poems*, 123–51, ll. 57–60.

20. Spence, *Observations*, 195.

21. Benson, *Virgil's Husbandry* (1724), xxi (for critique of Dryden), 2n (for detailed description). The following year, Benson published, under the same short title, a translation of and commentary on the first georgic; for clarity of reference, all citations will indicate the date. Benson had a varied career that included engagement in Whig politics and architecture (and an appearance in Pope's *Dunciad*). Benson and Pope provide evidence that this understanding of georgic spanned ideological divides.

22. Benson, *Virgil's Husbandry* (1724), xvi. In his otherwise smart series of articles, Frans De Bruyn somewhat misleadingly has Benson represent the "scientific reading" that "approached the *Georgics* as a compendium of axioms" about agriculture.

23. Benson, *Virgil's Husbandry* (1724), 18n.

24. Ibid., 15n.

25. Ibid., xi, iii.

26. The following are excellent treatments of georgic's form (even if they tend to neglect the status of the dirty rural things at the genre's heart): Durling, *Georgic Tradition;* Fowler, "Georgic and Pastoral"; and Pellicer, "Georgic."

27. Low, *Georgic Revolution*, 7. The following are thoughtful treatments of the politics and social stakes of georgic (even if they tend to neglect the genre's formal structures): Barrell, *English Literature;* Chambers, "'Wild Pastorall Encounter'"; McRae, *God Speed the Plough;* London, *Women and Property;* O'Brien, "Imperial Georgic"; and Van Sant, "Crusoe's Hands."

28. Chalker, *English Georgic*, 67, 169–70.

29. Goodman, *Georgic Modernity*, 22, 42, 28.

30. I build on scholarship highlighting eighteenth-century georgic's physicotheological themes: Patey, "Finch, Dyer and the Georgic Syntax"; R. Cohen, "Innovation and Variation"; and Chalker, *English Georgic*, 141–63.

31. For an intriguing example, see Fairer, "Caribbean Georgic," 21–22; or Johnson, "PHILIPS," 4: 16. (Samuel Johnson describes John Philips's English georgic *Cyder* as "at once, a book of entertainment and of science." The latter is confirmed "by Miller, the great gardener and botanist, whose expression was, *that there were many books written on the same subject in prose, which do not contain so much truth as that poem.*")

32. Anon., *Il Penseroso*, 164, 166. This poem is a georgic filtered through Milton. For another interesting example of a poet referencing scientific writings, see Mounsey, "Botanical Source."

33. Virgil, *Georgics*, 2: 226–58 (on soil composition), 1: 204–58, 374–89 (on natural signs).

34. Ibid., 2: 244.

35. For interesting eighteenth-century examples of these themes, see Somervile, *Chace*, ll. 135–38; and Anon., *Innocent Epicure*, 52.

36. Virgil, *Georgics*, 1: 118–59. Actually *two* of Virgil's Greek models—Hesiod's *Works and Days* and Aratus's *Phenomena*—deal directly with fundamental questions about God(s) and the origins of the world, mankind, and mankind's need to labor; see Nelson, *God and the Land*. In a similar spirit (though with a different set of theological assumptions), eighteenth-century georgic writers often feature serious Christian theodicies and/or more playful myths of origins.

37. Fairer, "'Where Fuming Trees,'" 210. See also Erin Drew, "'Iron War' as 'Daily Care': Sustainability and the Dialectic of Care in Dryden's *Georgics*" (forthcoming in *1650–1850: Ideas, Aesthetics, and Inquiries*).

38. Pope, *Epistle to Burlington*, 175.

39. Fairer, "Caribbean Georgic," 24. See also Fairer, "'Where Fuming Trees,'" and *English Poetry*, chap. 5.

40. Fairer, "'Where Fuming Trees,'" 205.

41. Ross, *Virgil's Elements*, x, 7–8, offers a supple sense of what he calls "Virgil's weave, with one detail connected to so many others in his patterns."

42. On Virgil's structural patterning, see Otis, "New Study," 45, 57–59.

43. Spacks, *Poetry of Vision*, 39, makes a point that applies to all eighteenth-century georgic: *The Seasons* evinces Thomson's "almost obsessive effort to reveal the patterns he perceives as he 'sees' the world. . . . Each kind of language [including anthropomorphic, scientific, and generalizing] points to a distinct way of perceiving; the juxtaposition of varied dictions insists that many different modes of perception must merge to express even approximate truths about nature."

44. For Virgil's allusiveness and intertextuality, see Farrell, *Vergil's "Georgics"*; and Gale, "Virgil's Metamorphoses." For an eighteenth-century analogue, see Goodman, *Georgic Modernity*, 28.

45. Dyer, *Fleece*, 3: 631–32. See also Low, *Georgic Revolution*; and O'Brien, "Imperial Georgic."

46. P. Rogers, "John Philips, Pope and Political Georgic," 442.

47. Crawford, *Poetry, Enclosure*, 25. See also Genovese, "Organic Commerce."

48. Chalker, *English Georgic*, 64.

49. Batstone, "Virgilian Didaxis," 140.

50. For Addison's influence, see Tickell, *De Poesi Didactica*; Trapp, *Lectures on Poetry*; and Moréri, *Continuation of Mr. Collier's supplement*, s.v. "georgic," 306.

51. Addison, *Essay on the Georgics*, 146. All further references are given parenthetically in the text.

52. See the otherwise quite astute discussions by Chalker, *English Georgic*, 30–33; and Crawford, *Poetry, Enclosure*.

53. Addison, *Spectator* #417, in Addison and Steele, *The Spectator*, 3: 565.

54. Addison, "Barometri Descriptio," l. 55 (in Haan's translation). Haan's excellent chapter on the barometer poem makes the case for its scientific seriousness.

55. Dryden, *Dedication to Virgil's Georgics*, in vol. 5 of *Works*, 139.

56. For Addison's debts to Dryden, see Salter, "Dryden and Addison."

57. Benson, *Virgil's Husbandry* (1724), 2n; Benson, *Virgil's Husbandry* (1725), vi.

58. Benson, *Virgil's Husbandry* (1724), 41n, 27n, 42n.

59. Pope, *Iliad of Homer,* in vol. 8 of *Poems,* book 16, l. 466n. For an insightful reading of Denham's poem that situates him in a providential tradition, see O'Hehir, *Expans'd Hieroglyphicks.*

60. Gay, *Rural Sports,* engages Christian Newtonianism at book 1, ll. 111–20. All further references to the revised, 1720 edition, given parenthetically in the text, indicate book and line number. Also, Gay's fascination with georgic patterning led him to toy profoundly with the poem's way of managing this in his revisions: compare Chalker, *English Georgic,* 142 (on the 1713 structure), and Aden, "1720 Version."

61. Watt, *Rise of the Novel,* 101, 15, 62.

62. This formulation of a pervasive assumption is from the intriguing discussion in H. Thompson and Meeker, "Empiricism, Substance, Narrative," 183–86.

63. B. Parker, *Triumph of Augustan Poetics,* 149, 136, 149, 149, 148, 154.

64. Arthos, *Language of Natural Description,* 36.

65. Ibid., 23, viii.

66. Anon., "Enquiries Concerning Agriculture," 92. Arthos discusses this passage in *Language of Natural Description,* 33.

67. Johnson, *Dictionary,* s.v. "periphrasis."

68. D. Parker, "Periphrasis in Eighteenth-Century Verse," 151, 153.

69. Sitter, *Cambridge Introduction,* chaps. 9–12; Keenleyside, "Personification for the People"; and Menely, "Animal Signs." I am indebted throughout my discussion of periphrasis to these very smart readings.

70. Sitter, *Cambridge Introduction,* 202.

71. Tillotson, *Augustan Studies,* 42.

72. Spacks, *Reading Eighteenth-Century Poetry,* 40.

73. Gay, *Rural Sports* (1713), ll. 105, 108.

74. Ibid., ll. 112–13, 115–16.

75. Ibid., ll. 117, 121–22.

76. Ibid., l. 118.

77. Batstone, "Virgilian Didaxis," 130, offers a rich reading of such slippery reference in Virgil's opening line.

78. Dugaw, *"Deep Play,"* 99.

79. Rothstein, *Restoration and Eighteenth-Century Poetry,* xiii, 53, 55: early eighteenth-century poems "bob[ ] between the particular and the general, perception and interpretation, given objects and the analogues they suggest but clearly differ from." Rothstein provocatively argues that such bobbing is staged *in* the poem but also solicited *from* the reader: these poems "encourage" a similarly "synecdochic, scenic habit of reading."

80. Philips's poem was immediately popular, provoking exuberant panegyric as well as fierce satire. For its continuing importance, see Johnson, "PHILIPS"; Dunster's edition of *Cyder;* and P. Rogers, "John Philips, Pope and Political Georgic."

81. On the frequency of such discoveries and the "archeological economy" of early eighteenth-century England generally, see Woolf, *Social Circulation.*

82. John Philips, *Cyder*, book 1, ll. 5–6. All further references, given parenthetically in the text, refer to book and line number.

83. Virgil, *Georgics*, 1: 492, 2: 184.

84. Blood is an often recommended, albeit a mildly atypical, fertilizer associated with the cultivation of vines: Evelyn, *Philosophical Discourse*, 126, 131; and Switzer, *Nobleman, Gentleman, and Gardener's Recreation*, 134.

85. The double meaning of "clotted" is certainly intended. See Philips, *Bleinheim*, p. 8: "Th'ensanguin'd Field" where "mangled Limbs," "Brains and Gore / Lie clotted."

86. Crawford, *Poetry, Enclosure*, 131.

87. The allusion is to *Paradise Lost*, book 8, 537–39. For Philips's Miltonic borrowings more generally, see Griffin, "Bard of Cyder-Land."

88. The transition from precepts about the sun into the Ariconium digression has an intertextual as well as a physical foundation: see Chalker, *English Georgic*, 37–39.

89. He treats the sun's intemperance in ll. 139–247 of book 1 (which has 796 lines) and human intemperance in ll. 445–530 of book 2 (which has 669 lines).

90. On the political situation, see Pellicer, "Introduction"; and P. Rogers, "John Philips, Pope and Political Georgic," and *Pope and the Destiny*. For the fraught relationship between Milton and Philips, see Philips's wicked suggestion that, if Milton had "like his *Abdiel* been / 'Mong many faithless, strictly faithful found," he would not have *deserved* his blindness (book 1, ll. 784–95).

91. Crawford, *Poetry, Enclosure*, 126. (Apart from ascribing to the frustratingly pervasive, "heightening" theory of the genre, Crawford offers a rather brilliant reading of Philips's *Cyder*—"an ur-narrative that idealized native English character as issuing from the sheltered apple orchards of Herefordshire.") Other recent work on *Cyder* similarly privileges the meaning-generating poet at the expense of nature, and a similar procedure dominates much recent work on georgic more generally.

92. See my introduction. Menely, "Animal Signs," makes a related point, specifically about animals.

93. Wasserman, *Subtler Language*, chaps. 3–4; Price, *To the Palace of Wisdom;* and Battestin, *Providence of Wit*.

94. Wasserman, *Subtler Language*, 169–70.

95. Barrell and Guest, "On the Uses of Contradiction," 135.

96. Fairer, "'Where Fuming Trees,'" 209, 207. Interestingly, classicist Stephanie Nelson, *God and Land*, 169, discusses Virgil in a way that suggests that eighteenth-century poets could have found in the *Georgics'* very different theological and formal assumptions a kind of analogue to their approach to meaning. In contrast to Hesiod's more confident articulation of cosmic order, Virgil's poem is "a composition not of objects, but of perspectives. Each perspective, each individual part of the whole, is uncomplicated. The whole, however, can be grasped only momentarily, before it dissolves again into mutually exclusive parts."

97. M. Mack, "1946: On Reading Pope," 104.

98. I am not alone in sensing a fundamental change in English culture in this moment. For instance, the *Cambridge Companions to English Literature* of the period divide

the eighteenth century into two parts, with the break at 1740. The scholarship on the big changes I mention here is vast, but good places to start include R. Porter, *Cambridge History of Science*, vol. 4; P. Mack, *Heart Religion;* Young, *Religion and Enlightenment*, chap. 4; W. Warner, *Licensing Entertainment;* Richetti, *Cambridge Companion;* and Sitter, *Literary Loneliness*.

99. These possibilities are motivated by my reading of the following intriguing works: Reill, *Vitalizing Nature;* Stalnaker, *Unfinished Enlightenment;* Brooke, "Science and Religion"; Eddy, "Nineteenth-Century Natural Theology"; Terry, "Gray and Poetic Diction"; Goodman, "Conjectures on *Beachy Head*"; and D. Porter, "Scientific Analogy."

Bibliography

Abrams, M. H. *The Mirror and the Lamp: Romantic Poetry and the Critical Tradition.* Oxford: Oxford University Press, 1953.
Addison, Joseph. "Barometri Descriptio." In *Vergilius Redivivus: Studies in Joseph Addison's Latin Poetry,* edited and translated by Estelle Haan, 148–51. Philadelphia: American Philosophical Society, 2005.
———. *An Essay on the Georgics.* In vol. 5 of *The Works of John Dryden,* edited by William Frost and Vinton A. Dearing, 145–53. Berkeley and Los Angeles: University of California Press, 1987.
Addison, Joseph, and Richard Steele. *The Spectator.* Edited by Donald F. Bond. 5 vols. Oxford: Clarendon Press, 1965.
———. *The Tatler.* Edited by Donald F. Bond. 3 vols. Oxford: Clarendon Press, 1987.
Aden, John M. "The 1720 Version of Rural Sports." *MLQ* 20, no. 3 (1959): 228–32.
Alpers, Svetlana. *The Art of Describing: Dutch Art in the Seventeenth Century.* Chicago: University of Chicago Press, 1983.
Anderson, Misty. *Imagining Methodism in Eighteenth-Century Britain: Enthusiasm, Belief and the Borders of the Self.* Baltimore: Johns Hopkins University Press, 2012.
Anon. "Amor omnibus idem." In *Examen Poeticum: Being the Third Part of Miscellany Poems,* 335–42. London, 1693.
Anon. "A Description in Imitation of Milton. Humbly Inscribed to the late Translator of Virgil." In vol. 2 of *A Miscellaneous Collection of Poems, Songs, Epigrams,* 54–58. Dublin, 1721.
Anon. "Dialogue III., Between Eutocus and Fidelius, About Natural Things Spiritualized." In *Christian Conversation; in Six Dialogues,* 33–53. London, 1720.
Anon. "Enquiries Concerning Agriculture." *Philosophical Transactions* 1, no. 92 (1665): 91–94.
Anon. *Il Penseroso.* In *A Miscellany of Poems by Several Hands. Publish'd by J. Husbands,* 161–69. Oxford, 1731.
Anon. *The Innocent Epicure: Or, the Art of Angling.* London, 1697.
Anon. *A Review of the Universal Remedy for all Diseases Incident to Coin.* London, 1696.
———. *Some Considerations about the Raising of Coin In a Second Letter.* London, 1696.
Anon. *Sermon on the Restoring of the Coyn.* London, 1697.
Anon. *Some Observation's on Our Trade, and on the Use of a Standard.* London, 1701(?).

Anon. *The Young Man's Guide in His Journey to Heaven; or, Travelling Spiritualized*. London, 1700.

Anon., trans. *Silk-worms. A Poem . . . Written Originally in Latin by Marc. Hier. Vida*. London, 1723.

Anselment, Raymond. "Introduction." In *The Occasional Meditations of Mary Rich, Countess of Warwick*, 1–39. Tempe: Arizona Center for Medieval and Renaissance Studies, 2009.

———. "Robert Boyle and the Art of Occasional Meditation." *Renaissance and Reformation* 32, no. 4 (2009): 73–94.

———. "Robert Boyle, Izaak Walton, and the Art of Angling." *Prose Studies* 30, no. 2 (2008): 124–41.

Armstrong, John. *The Art of Preserving Health*. London, 1744.

Armstrong, Nancy. *Desire and Domestic Fiction: A Political History of the Novel*. New York: Oxford University Press, 1987.

———. *How Novels Think: The Limits of British Individualism, 1719–1900*. New York: Columbia University Press, 2005.

Arthos, John. *The Language of Natural Description in Eighteenth-Century Poetry*. Ann Arbor: University of Michigan Press, 1949.

Ashcraft, Richard. *Revolutionary Politics and Locke's Two Treatises of Government*. Princeton: Princeton University Press, 1986.

Auski, Peter. *Christian Plain Style: The Evolution of a Spiritual Ideal*. Montreal: McGill-Queen's University Press, 1995.

Austen, Ralph. *A Dialogue (or Familiar Discourse) and Conference between the husbandman and fruit-trees*. Oxford, 1676.

———. *The Spirituall Use of an Orchard*. Oxford, 1657.

———. *A Treatise of Fruit-Trees*. Oxford, 1657.

Backscheider, Paula. *Daniel Defoe: Ambition and Innovation*. Lexington: University Press of Kentucky, 1986.

———. "The Verse Essay, John Locke, and Defoe's Jure Divino." *ELH* 55, no. 1 (1988): 99–124.

Bacon, Francis. *Of the Advancement and Proficience of Learning*. London, 1640.

Baker, David. *On Demand: Writing for the Market in Early Modern England*. Palo Alto: Stanford University Press, 2010.

Barbon, Nicholas. *Discourse concerning Coining the New Money Lighter. In Answer to Mr. Lock's Considerations about Raising the Value of Money*. In vol. 6 of *The Reception of Locke's Politics*, edited by Mark Goldie, 7–56. London: Pickering & Chatto, 1999.

Barrell, John. *English Literature in History: An Equal, Wide Survey*. New York: St. Martin's Press, 1983.

Barrell, John, and Harriet Guest. "On the Uses of Contradiction: Economics and Morality in the Eighteenth-Century Long Poem." In *The New Eighteenth Century: Theory, Politics and English Literature*, edited by Felicity Nussbaum and Laura Brown, 121–43. London: Methuen, 1987.

Batstone, William. "Virgilian Didaxis: Value and Meaning in the Georgics." In *The

Cambridge Companion to Virgil, edited by Charles Martindale, 125–44. Cambridge: Cambridge University Press, 1997.

Battestin, Martin. *The Providence of Wit: Aspects of Form in Augustan Literature and the Arts*. Oxford: Clarendon Press, 1974.

Baxter, Andrew. *Appendix to the First Part of the Enquiry . . .* London, 1750.

———. *An Enquiry into the Nature of the Human Soul*. London, 1733.

———. *Matho: Or, the Cosmotheoria Puerilis*. 2 vols. London, 1740.

Baxter, Richard. *The Saints Everlasting Rest*. 8th ed. London, 1659.

Bellamy, Liz. *Commerce, Morality and the Eighteenth-Century Novel*. Cambridge: Cambridge University Press, 1998.

———. "It-Narrators and Circulation: Defining a Subgenre." In *The Secret Life of Things: Animals, Objects, and It-Narratives in Eighteenth-Century England*, edited by Mark Blackwell, 117–46. Lewisburg: Bucknell University Press, 2007.

Bender, John, and Michael Marrinan, *The Culture of Diagram*. Stanford: Stanford University Press, 2010.

Bennett, Jane. *Vibrant Matter: A Political Ecology of Things*. Durham: Duke University Press, 2009.

Benson, William. *Virgil's Husbandry, or an Essay on the Georgics: Being the Second Book Translated into English Verse*. London, 1724.

———. *Virgil's Husbandry, or an Essay on the Georgics: Being the First Book Translated into English Verse*. London, 1725.

Bentley, Richard. *The Folly and Unreasonableness of Atheism*. London, 1693.

Berkeley, George. *Guardian #126*. In vol. 2 of *The Guardian*, 152–55. London, 1714.

———. *Philosophical Works*. Edited by M. R. Ayers. London: Dent, 1975.

Berman, David. *George Berkeley: Idealism and the Man*. Oxford: Clarendon Press, 1994.

Bethell, S. L. *The Cultural Revolution of the Seventeenth Century*. London: Dennis Dobson, 1951.

Black, Scott. *Of Essays and Reading in Early Modern Britain*. Houndsmills: Palgrave, 2006.

Blair, Ann. "Natural Philosophy." In vol. 3 of *The Cambridge History of Science*, edited by Katherine Park and Lorraine Daston, 365–406. Cambridge: Cambridge University Press, 2006.

Bolingbroke, Henry St. John, Viscount. *Bolingbroke: Political Writings*. Edited by David Armitage. Cambridge: Cambridge University Press, 1997.

———. *The Philosophical Works*. 5 vols. London, 1754–77.

Bono, James J. "Science, Discourse, and Literature: The Role/Rule of Metaphor in Science." In *Literature and Science: Theory and Practice*, edited by Stuart Peterfreund, 59–89. Boston: Northeastern University Press, 1990.

Boswell, James. *Journal of a Tour to the Hebrides*. 2nd ed. London, 1785.

Bottkil, J. McG. "Dryden's Latin Scholarship." *Modern Philology* 40, no. 3 (1943): 241–54.

Boucher, David, and Paul Kelly. "The Social Contract and Its Critics: An Overview." In *The Social Contract from Hobbes to Rawls*, 1–34. London: Routledge, 1994.

Bowden, Samuel. "A Poem Sacred to the Memory of Sir Isaac Newton." In vol. 2 of *Poetical Essays on Several Occasions*, 1–16. London, 1733–35.

Bowerbank, "Of Mice and Women: Early Modern Roots of Ecological Feminism." *Women and Environments International Magazine* 52–52 (2001): 27–9.

———. *Speaking for Nature: Women and Ecologies of Early Modern England*. Baltimore: Johns Hopkins University Press, 2004.

Boyd, "Metaphor and Theory Change: What Is 'Metaphor' a Metaphor For?" In *Metaphor and Thought*, edited by Andrew Ortony, 356–408. Cambridge: Cambridge University Press, 1979.

Boyle, Robert. *The Correspondence of Robert Boyle*. Edited by Michael Hunter, Antonio Clericuzio, and Lawrence M. Principe. 6 vols. London: Pickering & Chatto, 2001.

———. *An Essay on the Great Effects of Even Languid and Unheeded Motion*. London, 1685.

———. *A Free Enquiry into the Vulgarly Receiv'd Notion of Nature*. London, 1686.

———. *The Works of Robert Boyle*. Edited by Michael Hunter and Edward B. Davis. 14 vols. London: Pickering & Chatto, 1999–2000.

Bracken, Harry. *The Early Reception of Berkeley's Immaterialism, 1710–1733*. The Hague: Martinus Nijhoff, 1965.

Brereton, Jane. "On the Bustoes in the Royal Hermitage." In *Merlin*, 13–16. London, 1735.

Breuninger, Scott. *Recovering Bishop Berkeley: Virtue and Society in the Anglo-Irish Context*. New York: Palgrave Macmillan, 2010.

Brewer, John. *Sinews of Power: War, Money and the English State, 1688–1783*. New York: Alfred A. Knopf, 1989.

Briscoe, John. *Historical and Political Essays or Discourses on Several Subjects*. London, 1698.

Brooke, John Hedley. "Science and Religion." In vol. 4 of *The Cambridge History of Science*, edited by Roy Porter, 741–61. Cambridge: Cambridge University Press, 2003.

———. *Science and Religion: Some Historical Perspectives*. Cambridge: Cambridge University Press, 1991.

Brooke, John, and Geoffrey Cantor. *Reconstructing Nature: The Engagement of Science and Religion*. Oxford: Oxford University Press, 2000.

Brower, Reuben. *Alexander Pope: Poetry of Allusion*. Oxford: Clarendon Press, 1959.

Browne, Moses. *An Essay on the Universe*. In *Poems on Various Subjects*, 291–390. London, 1739.

Bunyan, John. *Book for Boys and Girls: or Country Rhimes for Children*. London, 1686.

———. *A Book for Boys and Girls: or Temporal Things Spiritualized*. London, 1701.

———. *Divine Emblems: or Temporal Things Spiritualized*. 9th ed. London, 1724.

Bury, Edward. *The Husbandmans Companion*. London, 1677.

Caffentzis, Constantine George. *Clipped Coins, Abused Words and Civil Government: John Locke's Philosophy of Money*. New York: Autonomedia, 1989.

Calamy, Edward. *The Art of Divine Meditation*. London, 1680.

Cantor, Geoffrey N. "Weighing Light: The Role of Metaphor in Eighteenth-Century

Optical Discourse." In *The Figural and the Literal: Problems of Language in the History of Science and Philosophy, 1630–1800*, edited by Andrew E. Benjamin, Geoffrey N. Cantor, and John R. R. Christie, 124–46. Manchester: Manchester University Press, 1987.

Carey, Daniel. "Introduction: Money and Political Economy in the Era of the Enlightenment." In *Money and Political Economy in the Enlightenment*, edited by Daniel Carey, 1–29. Oxford: Voltaire Foundation, 2014.

Carmichael, Gershom. *Natural Rights on the Threshold of the Scottish Enlightenment: The Writings of Gershom Carmichael*. Edited by James Moore and Michael Silverthorne. Indianapolis: Liberty Fund, 2002.

Chalker, John. *The English Georgic: A Study in the Development of a Form*. Baltimore: Johns Hopkins University Press, 1969.

Chambers, Douglas. "'Wild Pastorall Encounter': John Evelyn, John Beale, and the Renegotiation of Pastoral in the Mid-Seventeenth Century." In *Culture and Cultivation in Early Modern England: Writing and the Land*, edited by Michael Leslie and Timothy Raylor, 173–94. Leicester: Leicester University Press, 1992.

Chambers, Ephraim. *Cyclopaedia*. 2 vols. London, 1728.

Chetwood, Knightly. "The Praises of Italy, out of Virgil's Second Georgic." In *Miscellany Poems . . . By the most Eminent Hands*, 310–13. London, 1684.

Cheyne, George. *Philosophical Principles of Religion: Natural and Reveal'd*. London, 1715.

Chudleigh, Mary. "The Happy Man." In *Poems on Several Occasions . . . By the Lady Chudleigh*, 35–36. London, 1703.

Churchill, William. *October, a Poem*. London, 1717.

Cipolla, Carlo M. *Clocks and Culture*. London: Collins, 1967.

Clark, Katherine. *Daniel Defoe: The Whole Frame of Nature, Time, and Providence*. London: Palgrave Macmillan, 2007.

Clarke, Bruce, and Manuela Rossini, eds. *The Routledge Companion to Literature and Science*. London: Routledge, 2011.

Clarke, Samuel. *Discourse concerning the Being and Attributes of God, the Obligations of Natural Religion, and the Truth and Certainty of the Christian Revelation*. 3rd ed. London, 1711.

———, ed. *Rohault's System of Natural Philosophy, Illustrated with Dr. Samuel Clarke's notes taken mostly out of Sir Isaac Newton's Philosophy*. London, 1723.

———. *A Third Defence of an Argument made use of in a Letter to Mr. Dodwell*. London, 1708.

Cohen, I. Bernard. "Newton and the Social Sciences, with Special Reference to Economics, or, the Case of the Missing Paradigm." In *Natural Images in Economic Thought: "Markets Read in Tooth and Claw,"* edited by Philip Mirowski, 55–90. Cambridge: Cambridge University Press, 1994.

———. "Newton's Concepts of Force and Mass." In *The Cambridge Companion to Newton*, edited by I. Bernard Cohen and George E. Smith, 57–84. Cambridge: Cambridge University Press, 2002.

———. *Science and the Founding Fathers: Science in the Political Thought of Thomas*

Jefferson, Benjamin Franklin, John Adams, and James Madison. New York: Norton, 1995.

Cohen, Ralph. "Innovation and Variation: Literary Change and Georgic Poetry." In *Literature and History: Papers Read at a Clark Library Seminar, March 3, 1973,* 3–42. Los Angeles: University of California Press, 1974.

Colliber, Samuel. *Impartial Enquiry into the Existence and Nature of God.* London, 1718.

Collinges, John. *The Weavers Pocket-Book: or, Weaving Spiritualized.* 2nd ed. London, 1695.

Colman, John. "Locke's Empiricist Theory of the Law of Nature." In *The Philosophy of John Locke: New Perspectives,* edited by Peter R. Anstey, 106–26. London: Routledge, 2003.

Connell, Philip. "Newtonian Physico-Theology and the Varieties of Whiggism in James Thomson's *The Seasons.*" *Huntington Library Quarterly* 72, no. 1 (2009): 1–28.

Coolahan, Marie-Louise. "Redeeming Parcels of Time: Aesthetics and Practice of Occasional Meditation." *Seventeenth Century* 22, no. 1 (2007): 124–43.

Coole, Diana, and Samantha Frost. "Introducing the New Materialisms." In *New Materialisms: Ontology, Agency, and Politics,* edited by Diana Coole and Samantha Frost, 1–43. Durham: Duke University Press, 2010.

Corneanu, Sorana. *Regimens of the Mind: Boyle, Locke, and the Early Modern Cultura Animi Tradition.* Chicago: University of Chicago Press, 2011.

Cottret, Bernard. *Bolingbroke's Political Writings: The Conservative Enlightenment.* Houndsmills: Macmillan, 1997.

Crane, Mary Thomas. "Analogy, Metaphor and the New Science: Cognitive Science and Early Modern Epistemology." In *Introduction to Cognitive Cultural Studies,* edited by Lisa Zunshine, 103–14. Baltimore: Johns Hopkins University Press, 2010.

Crawford, Rachel. *Poetry, Enclosure and the Vernacular Landscape, 1700–1830.* Cambridge: Cambridge University Press, 2002.

Creech, Thomas. "Part of Virgil's 4th. Georgick." In *Sylvae, or the Second Part of Poetical Miscellanies,* 145–54. London, 1685.

———, trans. *T. Lucretius Carus the Epicurean philosopher his six books De natura rerum done into English verse, with notes.* Oxford, 1682.

Crousaz, J. P. de. *An Examination of Mr. Pope's Essay on Man.* London, 1739.

Dahm, John. "Science and Apologetics in the Early Boyle Lectures." *Church History* 39, no. 2 (1970): 172–86.

Damrosch, Leopold. *God's Plot and Man's Stories: Studies in the Fictional Imagination from Milton to Fielding.* Chicago: University of Chicago Press, 1985.

Daston, Lorraine. "The Empire of Observation, 1600–1800." In *Histories of Scientific Observation,* edited by Lorraine Daston and Elizabeth Lunbeck, 81–113. Chicago: University of Chicago Press, 2011.

———. "Introduction." In *Things That Talk: Object Lessons from Art and Science,* edited by Lorraine Daston, 7–24. New York: Zone Books, 2004.

Daston, Lorraine, and Fernando Vidal. "Introduction: Doing What Comes Naturally." In *The Moral Authority of Nature,* 1–20. Chicago: University of Chicago, 2004.

Daston, Lorraine, and Katherine Park. *Wonders and the Order of Nature, 1150–1750*. New York: Zone Books, 1998.

Davis, Lennard. *Factual Fictions: The Origins of the English Novel*. New York: Columbia University Press, 1983.

De Bruyn, Frans. "Eighteenth-Century Editions of Virgil's Georgics: From Classical Poem to Agricultural Treatise." *Lumen: Selected Proceedings from the Canadian Society for Eighteenth-Century Studies* (2005): 149–63.

———. "From Virgilian Georgic to Agricultural Science: An Instance in the Transvaluation of Literature in Eighteenth-Century Britain." In *Augustan Subjects*, edited by Albert J. Rivero, 47–67. Newark: University of Delaware Press, 1997.

———. "Reading Virgil's Georgics as a Scientific Text: The Eighteenth-Century Debate between Jethro Tull and Stephen Switzer." *ELH* 71, no. 3 (2004): 661–89.

De Quehen, Hugh. "Pratt, Samuel (1658–1723)." In *Oxford Dictionary of National Biography*. Oxford University Press, 2004. doi:10.1093/ref:odnb/22709.

Dear, Peter. "Totius in Verba: Rhetoric and Authority in Early Royal Society." *Isis* 76, no. 2 (1985): 145–61.

Defoe, Daniel. *A General History of Discoveries and Improvements in Useful Arts*. London, 1725–26.

———. *Jure Divino*. Vol. 2 of *Satire, Fantasy and Writings on the Supernatural by Daniel Defoe*. Edited by P. N. Furbank. London: Pickering & Chatto, 2003–4.

———. *Review of the Affairs of France*. 9 vols. Edited by John McVeagh. London: Pickering and Chatto, 2004.

Delaval, Elizabeth. *The Meditations of Lady Elizabeth Delaval, Written between 1662 and 1671*. Edited by Douglas Greene. Gateshead: Northumberland Press, 1978.

Derham, William. *Physico-Theology: Or, a Demonstration of the Being and Attributes of God, from his Works of Creation*. 2nd ed. London, 1714.

Desaguliers, J. T. *The Newtonian System of the World, the Best Model of Government*. London, 1728.

Desan, Christine. *Making Money: Coin, Currency, and the Coming of Capitalism*. Oxford: Oxford University Press, 2014.

Des Chene, Dennis. *Spirits and Clocks: Machine and Organism in Descartes*. Ithaca: Cornell University Press, 2001.

Diaper, William, and John Jones, trans. *Oppian's Halieuticks of the Nature of Fishes and Fishing of the Ancients*. Oxford, 1722.

Dickson, P. G. M. *The Financial Revolution in England: A Study in the Development of Public Credit, 1688–1756*. New York: St. Martin's Press, 1967.

Dobbs, Betty Jo Teeter. *Janus Faces of Genius: The Role of Alchemy in Newton's Thought*. Cambridge: Cambridge University Press, 1991.

———. "Newton's Alchemy and His 'Active Principle' of Gravitation." In *Newton's Scientific and Philosophical Legacy*, edited by P. B. Sheurer and G. Debrock, 55–80. Dordrecht: Kluwer Academic Press, 1988.

Douglas, Aileen. "Britannia's Rule and the It-Narrator." *Eighteenth-Century Fiction* 6 (1993): 65–83.

Drennon, Herbert. "James Thomson's Contact with Newtonianism." *PMLA* 1 (1934): 71–80.
Dryden, John. *The Works of John Dryden.* Edited by H. T. Swedenberg Jr., George R. Guffey, Alan Roper, and Vinton A. Dearing. 20 vols. Berkeley and Los Angeles: University of California Press, 1956–2002.
Dugaw, Diane. *"Deep Play"—John Gay and the Invention of Modernity.* Newark: Delaware, 2001.
Dunn, John. *The Political Thought of John Locke: An Historical Account of the Argument of the "Two Treatises of Government."* Cambridge: Cambridge University Press, 1969.
Dunster, Charles, ed. *Cyder, A Poem . . . with Notes Provincial, Historical and Classical.* London, 1791.
Durling, Dwight. *Georgic Tradition in English Poetry.* New York: Columbia University Press, 1935.
Dyer, John. *The Fleece.* London, 1757.
Eddy, Matthew D. "Nineteenth-Century Natural Theology." In *The Oxford Handbook of Natural Theology,* edited by Russell Re Manning, 100–117. Oxford: Oxford University Press, 2013.
Edwards, Karen L. *Milton and the Natural World: Science and Poetry in "Paradise Lost."* Cambridge: Cambridge University Press, 1999.
Edwards, Thomas. *This Dark Estate: A Reading of Pope.* Berkeley: University of California Press, 1963.
Elkins, James. "On Visual Desperation and the Bodies of Protozoa." *Representations* 40 (1992): 33–56.
Ellenzweig, Sarah. *The Fringes of Belief: English Literature, Ancient Heresy, and the Politics of Freethinking, 1660–1760.* Stanford: Stanford University Press, 2008.
Elwin, Whitwell, and William John Courthope, eds. *The Works of Alexander Pope.* 10 vols. London: J. Murray, 1871–89.
Erskine-Hill, Howard. *Poetry of Opposition and Revolution: Dryden to Wordsworth.* Oxford: Clarendon Press, 1996.
———. "Pope on the Origins of Society." In *The Enduring Legacy: Alexander Pope Tercentenary Essays,* edited by G. S. Rousseau and Pat Rogers, 79–93. Cambridge: Cambridge University Press, 1988.
Evelyn, John. *Numismata.* London, 1697.
———. *A Philosophical Discourse of Earth.* London, 1676.
———. *Sylva.* 2nd ed. London, 1670.
Fairer, David. "A Caribbean Georgic: James Grainger's *The Sugar-Cane.*" *Kunapipi* 25, no. 1 (2003): 21–8.
———. *English Poetry of the Eighteenth Century 1700–1789.* London: Longman, 2003.
———. "Pope, Blake, Heraclitus and Oppositional Thinking." In *Pope: New Contexts,* edited by David Fairer, 169–88. New York: Harvester Wheatsheaf, 1990.
———. "'Where Fuming Trees Refresh the Thirsty Air': The World of Eco-Georgic." *Studies in Eighteenth-Century Culture* 40 (2011): 201–18.

Fara, Patricia. "Desaguliers, John Theophilus (1683–1744)." In *Oxford Dictionary of National Biography*. Oxford University Press, 2004. doi:10.1093/ref:odnb/7539.

Farrell, Joseph. *Vergil's "Georgics" and the Traditions of Ancient Epic: The Art of Allusion in Literary History*. Oxford: Oxford University Press, 1991.

Feavearyear, A. E. *The Pound Sterling: A History of English Money*. Oxford: Oxford University Press, 1931.

Felski, Rita. "Context Stinks!" *New Literary History* 42, no. 4 (2011): 573–91.

———. *Uses of Literature*. Malden: Blackwell, 2008.

Ferguson, James. *The Philosophy of Dr. Samuel Clarke and Its Critics*. New York: Vantage Press, 1974.

Festa, Lynn. *Sentimental Figures of Empire in Eighteenth-Century Britain and France*. Baltimore: Johns Hopkins University Press, 2006.

Finch, Anne. "Upon the Hurricane." In *Eighteenth Century Poetry: An Annotated Anthology*, edited by David Fairer and Christine Gerrard, 26–33. 2nd ed. Malden: Blackwell, 2004.

Finkelstein, Andrea. *Harmony and the Balance: An Intellectual History of Seventeenth-Century English Economic Thought*. Ann Arbor: University of Michigan Press, 2000.

Fisch, Harold. "The Puritans and the Reform of Prose Style." *ELH* 19, no. 4 (1952): 229–48.

Fissell, Mary, and Roger Cooter, "Exploring Natural Knowledge: Science and the Popular." In vol. 4 of *The Cambridge History of Science*, edited by Roy Porter, 129–58. Cambridge: Cambridge University Press, 2003.

Flavel, John. *Husbandry Spiritualized: Or, The Heavenly Use of Earthly Things*. London, 1669.

———. *Navigation Spiritualized: Or, a New Compass for Sea-Men*. London, 1677.

Flint, Christopher. "Speaking Objects: The Circulation of Stories in Eighteenth Century Prose Fiction." *PMLA* 113, no. 2 (1998): 212–26.

Fontenelle, Bernard de. *A Discourse of the Plurality of Worlds*. Translated by W. D. Knight. Dublin, 1687.

Force, James E. "Holy Grail, (Almost) Wholly Newton: Revisiting the Newtonian Elements in Alexander Pope's *Essay on Man*." *Enlightenment and Dissent* 25 (2009): 106–34.

———. "Linking History and Rational Science in the Enlightenment." In *Astronomical Principles of Religion, Natural and Reveal'd*, 1–71. Hildscheim: Georg Olms Verlag, 1983.

———. "Newton's 'Sleeping Argument' and the Newtonian Synthesis of Science and Religion." In *Standing on the Shoulders of Giants*, edited by Norman J. W. Thrower, 109–27. Berkeley: University of California Press, 1990.

———. "Providence and Newton's Pantokrator." In *Newton and Newtonianism: New Studies*, 65–92. Dordrecht: Kluwer Academic Publishers, 2004.

———. *William Whiston: Honest Newtonian*. Cambridge: Cambridge University Press, 1985.

Foucault, Michel. *The Order of Things: An Archeology of the Human Sciences*. New York: Vintage Books, 1973.

Fowler, Alastair. "Georgic and Pastoral." In *Culture and Cultivation in Early Modern England*, edited by Michael Leslie and Timothy Raylor, 81–88. Leicester: Leicester University Press, 1992.

Frost, William. *John Dryden: Dramatist, Satirist, Translator*. New York: AMS Press, 1988.

Funkenstein, Amos. *Theology and the Scientific Imagination from the Middle Ages to the Seventeenth Century*. Princeton: Princeton University Press, 1986.

Furbank, P. N. "Introduction." In *Jure Divino*. Vol. 2 of *Satire, Fantasy and Writings on the Supernatural by Daniel Defoe*, edited by P. N. Furbank, 1–29. London: Pickering & Chatto, 2003–4.

Furbank, P. N., and W. R. Owens. *A Political Biography of Daniel Defoe*. London: Pickering & Chatto, 2006.

Fussell, G. E. *Old English Farming Books from Fitzherbert to Tull, 1523 to 1730*. London: Crosby, Lockwood & Son, 1947.

Gale, Monica R. "Virgil's Metamorphoses: Myth and Allusion in the *Georgics*." In *Oxford Readings in Classical Studies: Vergil's Georgics*, edited by Katharina Volk, 94–127. Oxford: Oxford University Press, 2008.

Gardiner, James. *Rapin of Gardens*. London, 1718.

Gascoigne, "Clarke, Samuel (1675–1729)." In *Oxford Dictionary of National Biography*. Oxford University Press, 2004. doi:10.1093/ref:odnb/5530.

Gaukroger, Stephen. *The Collapse of Mechanism and the Rise of Sensibility: Science and the Shaping of Modernity, 1680–1760*. Oxford: Oxford University Press, 2010.

Gay, John. *Rural Sports. A Georgic*. In vol. 1 of *Poems on Several Occasions. By Mr. John Gay*, 3–25. London, 1720.

———. *Rural Sports. A Poem*. London, 1713.

Genovese, Michael. "An Organic Commerce: Sociable Selfhood in Eighteenth-Century Georgic." *Eighteenth Century Studies* 46, no. 2 (2013): 197–221.

Gentner, Dedre, and Michael Jeziorski, "The Shift from Metaphor to Analogy in Western Science." In *Metaphor and Thought*, edited by Andrew Ortony, 447–80. 2nd ed. Cambridge: Cambridge University Press, 1993.

Gerrard, Christine. *The Patriot Opposition to Walpole: Politics, Poetry, and National Myth, 1725–1742*. Oxford: Clarendon Press, 1994.

Gildon, Charles. *Deist's Manual*. London, 1708.

———. *The Golden Spy: Or, a Political Journal of the British Nights Entertainment*. London, 1709.

Gillespie, Neal C. "Natural History, Natural Theology, and Social Order: John Ray and the 'Newtonian Ideology.'" *Journal of the History of Biology* 20, no. 1 (1987): 1–49.

Girten, Kristen. "Unsexed Souls: Natural Philosophy as Transformation in Eliza Haywood's *Female Spectator*." *Eighteenth-Century Studies* 43, no. 1 (2009): 55–74.

Goldie, Mark, ed. *The Reception of Locke's Politics*. 6 vols. London: Pickering & Chatto, 1999.

Goodman, Kevis. "Conjectures on *Beachy Head:* Charlotte Smith's Geological Poetics and the Grounds of the Present." *ELH* 81, no. 3 (2014): 983–1006.

———. *Georgic Modernity and British Romanticism: Poetry and the Mediation of History.* Cambridge: Cambridge University Press, 2004.
Greenleaf, W. H. *Order, Empiricism and Politics: Two Traditions of English Political Thought, 1500–1700.* London: Oxford University Press, 1964.
Griffin, Dustin. "The Bard of Cyder-Land: John Philips and Miltonic Imitation." *Studies in English Literature* 24 (1984): 441–60.
Guerrini, Anita. "Cheyne, George (1671/2–1743)." In *Oxford Dictionary of National Biography.* Oxford University Press, 2004. doi:10.1093/ref:odnb/5258.
Gurdon, Brampton. *The Pretended Difficulties in Natural or Reveal'd Religion no Excuse for Infidelity.* London, 1723.
Guye, Samuel, and Henry Michel. *Time and Space: Measuring Instruments from the Fifteenth to the Nineteenth Centuries.* New York: Praeger Publishers, 1970.
Hales, Stephen. *Vegetable Staticks.* London, 1727.
Hall, Joseph. *Occasionall Meditations.* London, 1630.
———. *The Works of Joseph Hall.* London, 1625.
Hall, Rupert A. *Philosophers at War: The Quarrel between Newton and Leibniz.* Cambridge: Cambridge University Press, 1980.
Hammond, Brean. *Pope and Bolingbroke: A Study of Friendship and Influence.* Columbia: University of Missouri Press, 1984.
Hanham, A. A. "Lowndes, William (1652–1724)." In *Oxford Dictionary of National Biography.* Oxford University Press, 2004. doi:10.1093/ref:odnb/17099.
Harman, Graham. "The Well-Wrought Broken Hammer: Object-Oriented Literary Criticism." *New Literary History* 43, no. 2 (2012): 183–202.
Harman, P. M. *The Culture of Nature in Britain, 1680–1860.* New Haven: Yale University Press, 2009.
Harris, John. *Lexicon Technicum.* 2 vols. 2nd ed. London, 1708.
Harrison, Peter. *The Bible, Protestantism, and the Rise of Natural Science.* Cambridge: Cambridge University Press, 1998.
———. "Sentiments of Devotion and Experimental Philosophy in Seventeenth-Century England." *Journal of Medieval and Early Modern Studies* 44, no. 1 (2014): 113–33.
Harrison, Ross. *Hobbes, Locke, and Confusion's Masterpiece: An Examination of Seventeenth-Century Philosophy.* Cambridge: Cambridge University Press, 2003.
Harwood, John T. "Rhetoric and Graphics in *Micrographia*." In *Robert Hooke: New Studies,* edited by Michael Hunter and Simon Schaffer, 119–47. Woodbridge: Boydell, 1989.
Haywood, Eliza. *Female Spectator.* 4 vols. London, 1745–6.
Heimann, P. M., and J. E. McGuire. "Newtonian Forces and Lockean Powers." *Historical Studies in the Physical Sciences* 3 (1971): 233–306.
Henry, John. "Occult Qualities and the Experimental Philosophy: Active Principles in Pre-Newtonian Matter Theory." *History of Science* 24 (1986): 335–81.
———. "'Pray do not Ascribe that Notion to Me': God and Newton's Gravity." In *The Books of Nature and Scripture,* 123–48. Dordrecht: Kluwer Academic, 1994.
———. "Religion and the Scientific Revolution." In *The Cambridge Companion to*

Science and Religion, edited by Peter Harrison, 39–58. Cambridge: Cambridge University Press, 2010.

Hervey, James. *Meditations and Contemplations*. 2 vols. London, 1748.

Hodges, James. *The Present State of England, as to Coin and Publick Charges*. London, 1697.

Holsinger, Bruce, ed. *Literary History and the Religious Turn*. Special issue, *English Language Notes* 44, no. 1 (2006).

Hooke, Robert. *Micrographia*. London, 1665.

Horkheimer, Max, and Theodor Adorno. *Dialectic of Enlightenment: Philosophical Fragments*. 1944. Edited by Gunzelin Schmid Noerr. Translated by Edmund Jephcott. Stanford: Stanford University Press, 2002.

Horsefield, J. Keith. *British Monetary Experiments, 1650–1710*. Cambridge: Cambridge University Press, 1960.

Hunter, J. Paul. *Before Novels: The Cultural Contexts of Eighteenth-Century English Fiction*. New York: Norton, 1990.

———. *The Reluctant Pilgrim: Defoe's Emblematic Method and Quest for Form in Robinson Crusoe*. Baltimore: Johns Hopkins University Press, 1966.

———. "Robert Boyle and the Epistemology of the Novel." *Eighteenth-Century Fiction* 2, no. 4 (1990): 275–91.

Hunter, Michael. *Boyle: Between God and Science*. New Haven: Yale University Press, 2009.

———. *The Boyle Papers: Understanding the Manuscripts of Robert Boyle*. Aldershot: Ashgate, 2007.

———. "How Boyle Became a Scientist." *History of Science* 33 (1995): 59–103.

———. *Science and Society in Restoration England*. Cambridge: Cambridge University Press, 1981.

Hunter, Michael, and Edward B. Davis. "Introductory Notes: *Occasional Reflections upon Several Subjects* (1665)." In vol. 5 of *The Works of Robert Boyle*, edited by Michael Hunter and Edward B. Davis, xi–xv. London: Pickering & Chatto, 1999.

Huntley, Frank Livingstone. *Bishop Joseph Hall and Protestant Meditation in Seventeenth-Century England*. Binghamton: Center for Medieval and Early Renaissance Studies, 1981.

Hutchinson, Terence. *Before Adam Smith: The Emergence of Political Economy, 1662–1776*. Oxford: Blackwell, 1988.

Inglesfield, Robert. "Thomson and Shaftesbury." In *James Thomson: Essays for the Tercentenary*, edited by Richard Terry, 67–91. Liverpool: Liverpool University Press, 2000.

Ingrassia, Catherine. *Authorship, Commerce and Gender in Early Eighteenth Century England: A Culture of Paper Credit*. Cambridge: Cambridge University Press, 1998.

Jackson, Joseph. *A New Translation of Aesop's Fables*. London, 1708.

Jackson, Ken, and Arthur Moretti. "The Turn to Religion in Early Modern English Studies." *Criticism* 46, no. 1 (2004): 167–90.

Jacob, J. R. *Robert Boyle and the English Revolution: A Study in Social and Intellectual Change*. New York: Burt Franklin & Co, 1977.

Jacob, Margaret. "Newtonianism and the Origins of the Enlightenment: A Reassessment." *Eighteenth Century Studies* 11, no. 1 (1977): 1–25.

———. *The Newtonians and the English Revolution, 1689–1720*. Ithaca: Cornell University Press, 1976.

———. *Scientific Culture and the Making of the Industrial West*. Oxford: Oxford University Press, 1997.

Jacob, Margaret, and Betty Jo Teeter Dobbs. *Newton and the Culture of Newtonianism*. Highlands: Humanities Press, 1995.

Jacob, Margaret, and Henry Guerlac. "Bentley, Newton and Providence (The Boyle Lectures Once More)." *Journal of the History of Ideas* 30, no. 3 (1969): 307–18.

Jacob, Margaret, and James R. Jacob. "The Anglican Origins of Modern Science: The Metaphysical Foundations of the Whig Constitution." *Isis* 71, no. 2 (1980): 251–67.

Jager, Colin. *The Book of God: Secularization and Design in the Romantic Era*. Philadelphia: University of Pennsylvania Press, 2007.

Janiak, Andrew. "Newton and the Reality of Force." *Journal of the History of Philosophy* 45, no. 1 (2007): 127–46.

Jeske, Jeffrey. "Cotton Mather: Physico-Theologian." *Journal of the History of Ideas* 47, no. 4 (1986): 583–94.

Johns, Adrian. "Power, Henry (c. 1626–1668)." In *Oxford Dictionary of National Biography*. Oxford University Press, 2004. doi:10.1093/ref:odnb/22665.

Johnson, Samuel. *Dictionary of the English Language*. 2nd ed. London, 1755–6.

———. "PHILIPS." In vol. 4 of *Prefaces, Biographical and Critical, to the Works of the English Poets*, 1–16. London, 1779.

Johnston, Freya. "Little Lives: An Eighteenth-Century Sub-Genre." *Cambridge Quarterly* 32, no. 2 (2003): 143–60.

Jones, Matthew L. *The Good Life in the Scientific Revolution: Descartes, Pascal, Leibniz and the Cultivation of Virtue*. Chicago: University of Chicago Press, 2006.

Jones, R. F. "Science and English Prose Style in the Third Quarter of the Seventeenth Century." *PMLA* 45 (1930): 977–1009.

———. *The Seventeenth Century: Studies in the History of English Thought and Literature from Bacon to Pope*. Stanford: Stanford University Press, 1951.

Jones, Tom. *Pope and Berkeley: The Language of Poetry and Philosophy*. London: Palgrave Macmillan, 2005.

Jones, William Powell. *The Rhetoric of Science*. Berkeley: University of California Press, 1966.

Kahn, Victoria. *Wayward Contracts: The Crisis of Political Obligation in England, 1640–1674*. Princeton: Princeton University Press, 2004.

Kauffman, U. Milo. *The Pilgrim's Progress and Traditions in Puritan Meditation*. New Haven: Yale University Press, 1966.

Kay, Carol. *Political Constructions: Defoe, Richardson, and Sterne in Relation to Hobbes, Hume and Burke*. Ithaca: Cornell University Press, 1988.

Kearney, Flora McLaughlin. *James Hervey and Eighteenth-Century Taste*. Muncie: Ball State University, 1969.

Keenleyside, Heather. "Personification for the People: On James Thomson's *The Seasons*." *ELH* 76, no. 2 (2009): 447–72.
Keill, John. *An Introduction to Natural Philosophy: or, Philosophical Lectures Read in the University of Oxford Anno Dom 1700*. London, 1726.
Kelly, Patrick Hyde. "Introduction." In vol. 1 of *Locke on Money*, edited by Patrick Hyde Kelly, 1–121. Oxford: Clarendon Press, 1991.
King, William. *An Essay on the Origin of Evil . . . Translated from the Latin*. London, 1731.
Kinsley, William. "Physico-Demonology in Pope's *Dunciad* IV. 71–90." *Modern Language Review* 70, no. 1 (1975): 20–31.
Koyré, Alexander. *From the Closed World to the Infinite Universe*. Baltimore: Johns Hopkins University Press, 1957.
———. *Newtonian Studies*. Cambridge: Harvard University Press, 1965.
Kramnick, Isaac. *Bolingbroke and His Circle: The Politics of Nostalgia in the Age of Walpole*. Cambridge: Harvard University Press, 1968.
Kroll, Richard W. F. *The Material Word: Literate Culture in the Restoration and Early Eighteenth Century*. Baltimore: Johns Hopkins University Press, 1991.
Kubrin, David. "Newton and the Cyclical Cosmos: Providence and the Mechanical Philosophy." *Journal of the History of Ideas* 28, no. 3 (1967): 325–46.
Lakoff, George, and Mark Johnson. *Metaphors We Live By*. 1980. Chicago: University of Chicago Press, 2003.
Lamb, Jonathan. *The Things Things Say*. Princeton: Princeton University Press, 2011.
Landa, Louis A. "Of Silkworms and Farthingales and the Will of God." In *Studies in the Eighteenth Century II*, edited by R. F. Briseenden, 259–77. Toronto: University of Toronto Press, 1973.
Landes, David. *Revolution in Time*. Cambridge: Belknap Press of Harvard University Press, 1983.
Latour, Bruno. *We Have Never Been Modern*. Translated by Catherine Porter. Cambridge: Harvard University Press, 1993.
———. "Why Has Critique Run Out of Steam? From Matters of Fact to Matters of Concern." *Critical Inquiry* 30, no. 2 (2004): 225–48.
Laudan, Laurens. "The Clock Metaphor and Probabilism: The Impact of Descartes on English Methodology Thought, 1650–65." *Annals of Science* 22, no. 2 (1966): 73–104.
Laverty, James. *Pope, Print, and Meaning*. Oxford: Oxford University Press, 2001.
Leibniz, Gottfried, and Samuel Clarke. *A Collection of Papers, Which Passed between the Late Learned Mr. Leibnitz, and Dr. Clarke, In the Years 1715 and 16. Relating to the Principles of Natural Philosophy and Religion*. London, 1717.
———. *The Leibniz-Clarke Correspondence*. Edited by H. G. Alexander. Manchester: Manchester University Press, 1956.
Leranbaum, Miriam. *Alexander Pope's "Opus Magnum," 1729–1744*. Oxford: Clarendon Press, 1977.
Leslie, Charles. *The Finishing Stroke. Being a Vindication of the Patriarchal Scheme of Government, in Defence of the Rehearsals*. London, 1711.

Levenson, Thomas. *Newton and the Counterfeiter: The Unknown Detective Career of the World's Greatest Scientist.* Boston: Houghton Mifflin Harcourt, 2009.

Lewalski, Barbara Kiefer. *Protestant Poetics and the Seventeenth-Century Religious Lyric.* Princeton: Princeton University Press, 1979.

Li, Ming-Hsun. *The Great Recoinage of 1696 to 1699.* London: Weidenfeld and Nicolson, 1963.

Lister, Martin. "An Ingenious Proposal for a new sort of Maps of Countrys." *Philosophical Transactions* 14, no. 164 (1684): 739–46.

Locke, John. *Locke on Money.* Edited by Patrick Hyde Kelly. 2 vols. Oxford: Clarendon Press, 1991.

———. *Questions concerning the Law of Nature.* Edited and translated by Robert Horwitz, Jenny Strauss Clay, and Diskin Clay. Ithaca: Cornell University Press, 1990.

———. *Some Considerations of the Consequences of the Lowering of Interest and Raising the Value of Money.* London, 1692.

———. *Two Treatises of Government.* Edited by Peter Laslett. 2nd ed. Cambridge: Cambridge University Press, 1967.

London, April. *Women and Property in the Eighteenth-Century English Novel.* Cambridge: Cambridge University Press, 1999.

Love, Heather. "Close but Not Deep: Literary Ethics and the Descriptive Turn." *New Literary History* 41, no. 2 (2010): 371–91.

Lovejoy, Arthur. *The Great Chain of Being: A Study in the History of an Idea.* 1936. Reprint, Cambridge: Harvard University Press, 2001.

Low, Anthony. *The Georgic Revolution.* Princeton: Princeton University Press, 1985.

Lowndes, William. *A Report Containing an Essay for the Amendment of the Silver Coins.* London, 1695.

Luce, A. A. "Berkeley's Essays in *The Guardian.*" *Mind* 52, no. 207 (1943): 247–63.

Lucretius. *De Rerum Natura.* Translated by Martin Ferguson Smith. Indianapolis: Hackett Publishing, 2001.

Lupton, Christina. "The Knowing Book: Authors, It-Narratives, and Objectification in the Eighteenth Century." *Novel* 39, no. 3 (2006): 402–20.

Lynch, Deidre. *The Economy of Character.* Chicago: University of Chicago Press, 1998.

Lynch, William. *Solomon's Child: Method in the Early Royal Society.* Palo Alto: Stanford University Press, 2001.

Macey, Samuel. *Clocks and the Cosmos.* Hamden: Archon Books, 1980.

Mack, Maynard. "1946: On Reading Pope." *College English* 22, no. 2 (1960): 99–107.

Mack, Phyllis. *Heart Religion in the British Enlightenment: Gender and Emotion in Early Methodism.* Cambridge: Cambridge University Press, 2011.

Macpherson, C. B. *The Political Theory of Possessive Individualism: Hobbes to Locke.* Oxford: Clarendon Press, 1962.

Macpherson, Sandra. *Harm's Way: Tragic Responsibility and the Novel Form.* Baltimore: Johns Hopkins University Press, 2010.

Maitland, Richard, Fourth Earl of Lauderdale. "The First Book of Virgil's *Georgicks.*" In *The Annual Miscellany for the Year 1694. Being the Fourth Part of Miscellany Poems,* 217–53. London, 1694.

Mandeville, Bernard. *The Fable of the Bees.* London, 1714.

Mandlebrote, Scott. "The Uses of Natural Theology in Seventeenth-Century England." *Science in Context* 20, no. 3 (2007): 451–80

Marcus, Sharon, and Stephen Best. "Surface Reading: An Introduction." *Representations* 108 (2009): 1–21.

Markley, Robert. *Fallen Languages: Crises of Representation in Newtonian England, 1660–1740.* Ithaca: Cornell University Press, 1993.

———. *The Far East and the English Imagination, 1600–1730.* Cambridge: Cambridge University Press, 2006.

———. "'Land Enough in the World': Locke's Golden Age and the Infinite Extension of 'Use.'" *South Atlantic Quarterly* 98, no. 4 (1999): 817–37.

———. "Recent Studies in Restoration and Eighteenth-Century Literature." *SEL* 37, no. 3 (1997): 637–67.

Martz, Louis. *The Poetry of Meditation: A Study in English Religious Literature of the Seventeenth Century.* New Haven: Yale University Press, 1954.

Mather, Cotton. *The Christian Philosopher: The Best Discoveries in Nature, with Religious Improvements.* London, 1721.

Mayr, Otto. *Authority, Liberty and Automatic Machinery in Early Modern Europe.* Baltimore: Johns Hopkins University Press, 1986.

McGuire, J. E. "Atoms and the 'Analogy of Nature': Newton's Third Rule of Philosophizing." *Studies in the History and Philosophy of Science,* Part A 1, no. 1 (1970): 3–58.

———. "Force, Active Principles, and Newton's Invisible Realm." *Ambix* 15, no. 3 (1968): 154–208.

McGuire, J. E., and P. M. Rattansi, "Newton and 'the Pipes of Pan.'" *Notes and Records of the Royal Society of London* 21, no. 2 (1966): 108–43.

McKeon, Michael. *The Origins of the English Novel, 1600–1740.* Baltimore: Johns Hopkins University Press, 1987.

McKillop, Alan Dugald. *The Background of Thomson's Seasons.* Minneapolis: University of Minnesota Press, 1942.

———. "Nature and Science in the Works of James Hervey." *University of Texas Studies in English* 28 (1949): 124–38.

McMullin, Ernan. *Newton on Matter and Activity.* Notre Dame: University of Notre Dame Press, 1978.

McRae, Andrew. *God Speed the Plough: The Representation of Agrarian England, 1500–1660.* Cambridge: Cambridge University Press, 1996.

———. "Husbandry Manuals and the Language of Agrarian Improvement." In *Culture and Cultivation in Early Modern England,* edited by Michael Leslie and Timothy Raylor, 35–62. Leicester: Leicester University Press, 1992.

Meli, Bertolini D. "Caroline, Leibniz and Clarke." *Journal of the History of Ideas* 60, no. 3 (1999): 469–86.

———. "Newton and the Leibniz-Clarke Correspondence." In *The Cambridge Companion to Isaac Newton,* edited by I. Bernard Cohen and George E. Smith, 455–64. Cambridge: Cambridge University Press, 2002.

Menely, Tobias. "Animal Signs and Ethical Significance: Expressive Creatures in the British Georgic." *Mosaic* 39, no. 4 (2006): 111–27.

Merton, Robert K. *Science, Technology and Society in Seventeenth Century England*. 1938. Reprint, New York: Fertig, 1970.

Metzger, Helene. *Attraction universelle et religion naturelle chez quelques commentateurs anglais de Newton*. Paris: Hermann & cie, 1938.

Milbourne, Luke. *Notes on Dryden's Virgil in a letter to a friend: with an essay on the same poet*. London, 1698.

Milton, John. *Paradise Lost*. Edited by Alastair Fowler. Rev. 2nd ed. Harlow: Longman, 2007.

Mitchell, Robert. "'Beings that have Existence only in ye Minds of Men': State Finance and the Origins of the Collective Imagination." *Eighteenth Century: Theory and Interpretation* 49, no. 2 (2008): 117–39.

Montaigne, Michel De. *The Complete Essays*. Translated by M. A. Screech. London: Penguin Books, 1991.

Moréri, Louis. *Continuation of Mr. Collier's supplement to the great historical dictionary*. London, 1705. .

Morgan, Thomas. *Philosophical Principles of Medicine*. London, 1725.

Morton, Timothy. *Ecology without Nature: Rethinking Environmental Aesthetics*. Cambridge: Harvard University Press, 2007.

———. *Hyperobjects: Philosophy and Ecology after the End of the World*. Minneapolis: University of Minnesota Press, 2013.

Mounsey, Chris. "A Botanical Source for Christopher Smart." *Notes and Queries* 44, no. 2 (1997): 197–200.

Mulligan, Lotte. "Robert Boyle, 'Right Reason,' and the Meaning of Metaphor." *Journal of the History of Ideas* 55, no. 2. (1994): 235–57.

Murray, Shannon. "A Book for Boys and Girls: Or, Country Rhimes for Children: Bunyan and Literature for Children." In *The Cambridge Companion to Bunyan*, edited by Anne Dunan-Page, 120–35. Cambridge: Cambridge University Press, 2010.

Needler, Henry. "On the Beauty of the Universe." In *The Works of Mr. Henry Needler*, 94–107. London, 1724.

Nelson, Stephanie. *God and the Land: The Metaphysics of Farming in Hesiod and Vergil*. New York: Oxford University Press.

Newman, William. *Atoms and Alchemy: Chymistry and the Experimental Origins of the Scientific Revolution*. Chicago: University of Chicago Press, 2006.

Newton, Isaac. *The Correspondence of Isaac Newton*. Edited by H. W. Turnbull et al. 7 vols. Cambridge: Cambridge University Press, 1959–77.

———. *The Mathematical Principles of Natural Philosophy*. Translated by Andrew Motte. 2 vols. London, 1729.

———. *Opticks*. 2nd ed. London, 1718.

———. *Philosophical Writings*. Edited by Andrew Janiak. Cambridge: Cambridge University Press, 2004.

Nicholson, Colin. *Writing and the Rise of Finance: Capital Satires of Early Eighteenth Century*. Cambridge: Cambridge University Press, 1994.

Nicolson, Margaret Hope. *Newton Demands the Muse: Newton's Opticks and the Eighteenth-Century Poets.* Hamden: Archon, 1946.

Nicolson, Marjorie, and G. S. Rousseau. *"This Long Disease, My Life": Alexander Pope and the Sciences.* Princeton: Princeton University Press, 1968.

Nowka, Scott. "Talking Coins and Thinking Smoke-Jacks: Satirizing Materialism in Gildon and Sterne." *Eighteenth-Century Fiction* 22, no. 2 (2009): 195–222.

Nuttall, A. D. *Pope's "Essay on Man."* Winchester: Allen and Unwin, 1984.

Oakley, Francis. "Locke, Natural Law and God—Again." *History of Political Thought* 18, no. 4 (1997): 624–51.

O'Brien, Karen. "Imperial Georgic, 1660–1789." In *Country and the City Revisited: England and the Politics of Culture, 1550–1850,* edited by Gerald Maclean, Donna Landry, and Joseph P. Ward, 160–80. Cambridge: Cambridge University Press, 1999.

Odum, Herbert. "The Estrangement of Celestial Mechanics and Religion." *Journal of the History of Ideas* 27, no. 4 (1966): 533–48.

Ogborn, Miles. *Indian Ink: Script and Print in the Making of the English East India Company.* Chicago: University of Chicago Press, 2007.

Ogilvie, Brian W. "Natural History, Ethics, and Physico-Theology." In *Historia: Empiricism and Erudition in Early Modern England,* edited by Gianna Pomata and Nancy G. Siraisi, 75–103. Cambridge: MIT Press, 2005.

O'Hehir, Brendan. *Expans'd Hieroglyphicks: A Critical Edition of Sir John Denham's "Coopers Hill."* Berkeley: University of California Press, 1969.

Otis, Brooks. "A New Study of the Georgics." *Phoenix* 26, no. 1 (1972): 40–62.

Parker, Blanford. *The Triumph of Augustan Poetics: English Literary Culture from Butler to Johnson.* Cambridge: Cambridge University Press, 1998.

Parker, David. "Periphrasis in Eighteenth-Century Verse and the Function of the Direct Article." *Neophilologus* 59, no. 1 (1975): 147–56.

Parker, Fred. *Scepticism and Literature: An Essay on Pope, Hume, Sterne and Johnson.* Oxford: Oxford University Press, 2003.

Parker, Kate, and Courtney Weiss Smith. *Eighteenth Century Poetry and the Rise of the Novel Reconsidered.* Lewisburg: Bucknell University Press, 2014.

Patey, Douglas Lane. "Anne Finch, John Dyer and the Georgic Syntax of Nature." In *Augustan Subjects,* edited by Albert J. Rivero, 29–46. New York: University of Delaware Press, 1997.

———. *Probability and Literary Form: Philosophic Theory and Literary Practice in the Augustan Age.* Cambridge: Cambridge University Press, 1984.

Pellicer, J. C. "The Georgic." In *A Companion to Eighteenth-Century Poetry,* edited by Christine Gerrard, 403–16. Oxford: Blackwell Publishing, 2006.

———. "Introduction: The Politics of Cyder." In *Cyder: A Poem in Two Books,* i–xvi. Cheltenham: Cyder Press, 2001.

Pfizenmaier, Thomas. *The Trinitarian Theology of Dr. Samuel Clarke.* Leiden: Brill, 1997.

Philips, John. *Bleinheim, A Poem.* London, 1705.

———. *Cyder.* London, 1708.

Picciotto, Joanna. *Labors of Innocence in Early Modern England*. Cambridge: Harvard University Press, 2010.

Plumwood, Val. "Nature in the Active Voice." *Australian Humanities Review* 46 (2009): 113–29.

Pocock, J. G. A. *The Machiavellian Moment: Florentine Political Thought and the Atlantic Republican Tradition*. 1975. Reprint, Princeton: Princeton University Press, 2003.

———. *Virtue, Commerce and History: Essays on Political Thought and History, Chiefly in the Eighteenth Century*. Cambridge: Cambridge University Press, 1985.

Pope, Alexander. *The Twickenham Edition of the Poems of Alexander Pope*. Edited by John Butt. 11 vols. London: Methuen & Co., 1939–69.

Porter, Dahlia. "Scientific Analogy and Literary Taxonomy in Darwin's *Loves of the Plants*." *European Romantic Review* 18, no. 2 (2007): 213–21.

Porter, Roy, ed. *Eighteenth-Century Science*. Vol. 4 of *The Cambridge History of Science*. Cambridge: Cambridge University Press, 2003.

Powell, Manushag, and Rivka Swenson, eds. *The Sensational Subject*. Special issue, *The Eighteenth Century: Theory and Interpretation* 54, no. 2 (2013).

Power, Henry. *Experimental Philosophy*. London, 1664.

Pratt, Samuel. *The Regulating Silver Coin, Made Practicable and Easie to the Government and Subject*. London, 1696.

Preston, Claire. *Thomas Browne and the Writing of Early Modern Science*. Cambridge: Cambridge University Press, 2005.

Price, Martin. *To the Palace of Wisdom: Studies in Order and Energy from Dryden to Blake*. Garden City: Doubleday, 1964.

Principe, Lawrence M. "Virtuous Romance and Romantic Virtuoso: The Shaping of Robert Boyle's Literary Style." *Journal of the History of Ideas* 56, no. 3 (1995): 377–97.

Purchas, Samuel. *A Theatre of Politicall Flying-Insects*. London, 1657.

Quincy, John. *Lexicon Physico-Medicum*. 3rd ed. London 1726.

Ranew, Nathanael. *Solitude Improved by Divine Meditation*. London, 1670.

Raylor, Timothy. "Samuel Hartlib and the Commonwealth of Bees." In *Culture and Cultivation in Early Modern England*, edited by Michael Leslie and Timothy Raylor, 91–129. Leicester: Leicester University Press, 1992.

Reill, Peter Hanns. *Vitalizing Nature in the Enlightenment*. Berkeley: University of California Press, 2005.

Reventlow, Henning Graf. *The Authority of the Bible and the Rise of the Modern World*. Translated by John Bowden. Philadelphia: Fortress Press, 1985.

Rich, Mary. *The Occasional Meditations of Mary Rich, Countess of Warwick*. Edited by Raymond A. Anselment. Tempe: Arizona Center for Medieval and Renaissance Studies, 2009.

Richetti, John, ed. *Cambridge Companion to the Eighteenth-Century Novel*. Cambridge: Cambridge University Press, 1996.

Ricoeur, Paul. *Freud and Philosophy: An Essay on Interpretation*. Translated by Denis Savage. New Haven: Yale University Press, 1970.

Riley, Patrick. "Social Contract Theory and Its Critics." In *The Cambridge History of*

Eighteenth-Century Political Thought, edited by Mark Goldie and Robert Wokler, 347–75. Cambridge: Cambridge University Press, 2006.

Rivers, Isabel. "Hervey, James (1714–58)." In *Oxford Dictionary of National Biography*. Oxford University Press, 2004. doi:10.1093/ref:odnb/13113.

Rivett, Sarah. "Early American Religion in a Postsecular Age." *PMLA* 128, no. 4 (2013): 989–96.

Rogers, John. *The Matter of Revolution: Science, Poetry and Politics in the Age of Milton*. Ithaca: Cornell University Press, 1996.

Rogers, Pat. "John Philips, Pope and Political Georgic." *MLQ* 66 (2005): 411–42.

———. *A Political Biography of Alexander Pope*. London: Pickering & Chatto, 2010.

———. *Pope and the Destiny of the Stuarts*. Oxford: Oxford University Press, 2005.

Ross, David O., Jr. *Virgil's Elements: Physics and Poetry in the Georgics*. Princeton: Princeton University Press, 1987.

Rothstein, Eric. *Restoration and Eighteenth-Century Poetry 1660–1780*. Boston: Routledge and Kegan Paul, 1981.

Royal Society of London. *The Charters and Statutes of the Royal Society of London, For Improving Natural Knowledge*. London, 1728.

Sacheverill, Henry. "From Virgil's 1st Georgick." In *Examen Poeticum: Being the Third Part of Miscellany Poems*, 413–17. London, 1693.

Salter, C. H. "Dryden and Addison." *Modern Language Review* 69, no. 1 (1974): 29–39.

Sambrook, James, ed. *Liberty, The Castle of Indolence, and Other Poems*. By James Thomson. Oxford: Clarendon Press, 1986.

———, ed. *The Seasons*. By James Thomson. Oxford: Clarendon Press, 1981.

Sargent, Thomas J., and Francis R. Velde. *The Big Problem of Small Change*. Princeton: Princeton University Press, 2002.

Schabas, Margaret. *The Natural Origins of Economics*. Chicago: University of Chicago Press, 2005.

Schabas, Margaret, and Neil de Marchi, eds. *Oeconomies in the Age of Newton*. Durham: Duke University Press, 2003.

Schmidgen, Wolfram. *Eighteenth-Century Fiction and the Law of Property*. Cambridge: Cambridge University Press, 2002.

———. *Exquisite Mixture: The Virtues of Impurity in Early Modern England*. Philadelphia: University of Pennsylvania Press, 2013.

———. "Undividing the Subject of Literary History: From James Thomson's Poetry to Daniel Defoe's Novels." In *Eighteenth Century Poetry and the Rise of the Novel Reconsidered*, edited by Kate Parker and Courtney Weiss Smith, 87–104. Lewisburg: Bucknell University Press, 2014.

Schneedwind, J. B. "Locke's Moral Philosophy." In *The Cambridge Companion to John Locke*, edited by Vere Chappell, 199–225. Cambridge: Cambridge University Press, 1994.

———. "Pufendorf's Place in the History of Ethics." *Synthese* 72, no. 1 (1987): 123–55.

Schochet, Gordon J. *Patriarchalism in Political Thought: The Authoritarian Family and Political Speculation and Attitudes Especially in Seventeenth-Century England.* Oxford: Basil Blackwell, 1975.

Schoefield, Robert. "An Evolutionary Taxonomy of Eighteenth-Century Newtonianisms." *Studies in Eighteenth-Century Culture* 7 (1978): 175–92.

Schoen, Edward. "Clocks, God and Scientific Realism." *Zygon* 37, no. 3 (2002): 555–80.

Schonhorn, Manuel. *Defoe's Politics: Parliament, Power, Kingship, and Robinson Crusoe.* Cambridge: Cambridge University Press, 1991.

Scoryer, Richard. *Corrupted Coin made Good by Caesar, Corrupted Man made Good by Christ.* London, 1696.

Sedgwick, Eve. "Paranoid Reading and Reparative Reading, or, You're So Paranoid, You Probably Think This Essay Is About You." In *Touching Feeling: Affect, Pedagogy, Performativity*, 123–51. Durham: Duke University Press, 2003.

Shapin, Steven. "Of Gods and Kings: Natural Philosophy and Politics in the Leibniz-Clarke Disputes." *Isis* 72, no. 2 (1981): 187–215.

Shapin, Steven, and Simon Schaffer. *Leviathan and the Air-Pump: Hobbes, Boyle and the Experimental Life.* Princeton: Princeton University Press, 1989.

Shapiro, Barbara. *Probability and Certainty in Seventeenth-Century England.* Princeton: Princeton University Press, 1983.

Sharpe, Gregory. *A Defence of the Late Dr. Samuel Clarke.* London, 1744.

Sheldon, R. D. "Barbon, Nicholas (1637/40–1698/9)." In *Oxford Dictionary of National Biography.* Oxford University Press, 2004. doi:10.1093/ref:odnb/1334.

Sheridan, Thomas. *The Life of the Rev. Dr. Jonathan Swift.* London, 1784.

Sherman, Sandra. *Finance and Fictionality in the Early Eighteenth Century: Accounting for Defoe.* Cambridge: Cambridge University Press, 1996.

Silver, Sean. "Locke's Pineapple and the History of Taste." *Eighteenth Century: Theory and Interpretation* 49, no. 1 (2008): 43–65.

Sim, Stuart, and David Walker. *The Discourse of Sovereignty, Hobbes to Fielding: The State of Nature and the Nature of the State.* Aldershot: Ashgate, 2003.

Sitter, John. *The Cambridge Introduction to Eighteenth-Century Poetry.* Cambridge: Cambridge University Press, 2011.

———. "Eighteenth-Century Ecological Poetry and Ecotheology." *Religion and Literature* 40, no. 1 (2008): 11–37.

———. *Literary Loneliness in Mid-Eighteenth-Century England.* Ithaca: Cornell University Press, 1982.

Smith, Courtney Weiss. "Anne Finch's Descriptive Turn." *Eighteenth Century: Theory and Interpretation* 57, no. 2 (2016).

Snobelen, Stephen David. "William Whiston, Isaac Newton, and the Crisis of Publicity." *Studies in the History and Philosophy of Science* 35 (2004): 573–603.

Solberg, Winton U. "Introduction." In *The Christian Philosopher*, by Cotton Mather, xix–cxxxiv. Urbana: University of Illinois Press, 1994.

Solomon, Harry. *The Rape of the Text: Reading and Misreading Pope's "Essay on Man."* Tuscaloosa: University of Alabama Press, 1993.

Somervile, William. *The Chace.* 3rd ed. London, 1735.

Sontag, Susan. "Against Interpretation." In *Against Interpretation and Other Essays*, 3–14. New York: Picador, 1964.
Spacks, Patricia Meyer. *An Argument of Images: The Poetry of Alexander Pope*. Cambridge: Harvard University Press, 1971.
———. *The Poetry of Vision: Five Eighteenth-Century Poets*. Cambridge: Harvard University Press, 1967.
———. *Reading Eighteenth-Century Poetry*. Maldan: Wiley-Blackwell, 2009.
Spence, Joseph. *Observations, Anecdotes, and Characters of Books and Men*. London, 1820.
Sprat, Thomas. *The History of the Royal Society of London, for the Improving of Natural Knowledge*. London, 1667.
Spurstowe, William. *The Spiritual Chymist*. London, 1666.
Sreenivasan, Gopal. *The Limits of Lockean Rights in Property*. Oxford: Oxford University Press, 1995.
Stalnaker, Joanna. *The Unfinished Enlightenment: Description in the Age of the Encyclopedia*. Ithaca: Cornell University Press, 2010.
Starr, G. A. *Defoe and Spiritual Autobiography*. Princeton: Princeton University Press, 1965.
———. "Defoe's Prose Style: 1. The Language of Interpretation." *Modern Philology* 71, no. 2 (1974): 277–94.
Steele, Richard. *The Husbandman's Calling*. London, 1668.
Stewart, Larry. "Samuel Clarke, Newtonianism and the Factions of Post-Revolutionary England." *Journal of the History of Ideas* 42, no. 1 (1981): 53–72.
Striner, Richard. "Political Newtonianism: The Cosmic Model of Politics in Europe and America." *William and Mary Quarterly* 52, no. 4 (1995): 583–608.
Sudan, Rajani. "Mud, Mortar, and Other Technologies of Empire." *Eighteenth Century: Theory and Interpretation* 45, no. 2 (2004): 147–69.
Swinnock, George. *The Christian-Mans Calling*, Part 3. London, 1665.
Switzer, Stephen. *The Nobleman, Gentleman, and Gardener's Recreation*. London, 1715.
Taylor, Charles. *A Secular Age*. Cambridge: Belknap Press of Harvard University Press, 2007.
Terry, Richard. "Gray and Poetic Diction." In *Thomas Gray: Contemporary Essays*, edited by W. B. Hutchings and William Ruddick, 73–110. Liverpool: Liverpool University Press, 1993.
Thackray, Arnold. *Atoms and Powers*. Cambridge: Cambridge University Press, 1970.
Thirsk, Joan. "Agricultural Innovations and their Diffusion." In vol. 5 of *The Agrarian History of England and Wales*, 533–89. Cambridge: Cambridge University Press, 1985.
———. "Making a Fresh Start: Sixteenth-Century Agriculture and the Classical Inspiration." In *Culture and Cultivation in Early Modern England*, edited by Michael Leslie and Timothy Raylor, 15–34. Leicester: Leicester University Press, 1992.
———. "Plough and Pen: Agricultural Writers in the Seventeenth Century." In *Social Relations and Ideas: Essays in Honor of RH Hilton*, 295–318. Cambridge: Cambridge University Press, 1983.

Thomas, Keith. *Man and the Natural World: A History of the Modern Sensibility.* New York: Pantheon, 1983.

Thompson, Helen. *Ingenuous Subjection: Compliance and Power in the Eighteenth-Century Domestic Novel.* Philadelphia: University of Pennsylvania Press, 2005.

Thompson, Helen, and Natania Meeker. "Empiricism, Substance, Narrative: An Introduction." *Eighteenth Century: Theory and Interpretation* 48, no. 3 (2007): 183–86.

Thompson, James. *Models of Value: Eighteenth-Century Political Economy and the Novel.* Durham: Duke University Press, 1996.

Thomson, James. *The Seasons, A Hymn, A Poem to the Memory of Sir Isaac Newton and Britannia, a Poem.* London, 1730.

Tickell, Thomas. *De Poesi Didactica.* Translated by J. L. Austin. In *Thomas Tickell and the Eighteenth Century Poets 1685–1740*, edited by Richard Eustace Tickell, 198–209. London: Constable, 1931.

———. "A Fragment of a Poem upon Hunting." In *Poetical Miscellanies. . . published by Mr. Steele*, 177–86. London, 1714.

Tiffany, Daniel. *Toy Medium: Materialism and Modern Lyric.* Berkeley: University of California Press, 2000.

Tillotson, Geoffrey. *Augustan Studies.* London: Athlone Press, 1961.

Torre, Jose. *The Political Economy of Sentiment: Paper Credit and the Scottish Enlightenment in Early Republic Boston, 1780–1820.* London: Pickering & Chatto, 2007.

Trapp, Joseph. *Lectures on Poetry Read in the Schools of Natural Philosophy at Oxford.* Translated by William Bowyer and William Clarke. London, 1742.

Tuckness, Alex. "The Coherence of a Mind: John Locke and the Law of Nature." *Journal of the History of Philosophy* 37, no. 1 (1999): 73–90.

Tully, James. *A Discourse on Property: John Locke and his Adversaries.* Cambridge: Cambridge University Press, 1980.

Tuveson, Ernest. "*An Essay on Man* and 'The Way of Ideas.'" *ELH* 26, no. 3 (1959): 368–86.

Vailati, Ezio. "Introduction." In *A Demonstration of the Being and Attributes of God*, by Samuel Clarke, ix–xxxi. Cambridge: Cambridge University Press, 1998.

———. *Leibniz and Clarke: A Study of the Correspondence.* Oxford: Oxford University Press, 1997.

Van Sant, Ann. "Crusoe's Hands." *Eighteenth-Century Life* 32, no. 2 (2008): 120–37.

Vendler, Helen. *Poets Thinking: Pope, Whitman, Dickinson, Yeats.* Cambridge: Harvard University Press, 2006.

Vickers, Brian. "Analogy versus Identity: The Rejection of Occult Symbolism, 1580–1680." In *Occult and Scientific Mentalities in the Renaissance*, edited by Brian Vickers, 95–163. Cambridge: Cambridge University Press, 1984.

———. "The Royal Society and English Prose Style: A Reassessment." In *Rhetoric and the Pursuit of Truth*, 3–76. Los Angeles: William Andrews Clark Memorial Library, 1985.

Viner, Jacob. *The Role of Providence in the Social Order: An Essay in Intellectual History.* Philadelphia: American Philosophical Society, 1972.

Virgil. *Eclogues, Georgics, Aeneid I-VI*. Edited by H. Rushton Fairclough. Cambridge: Harvard University Press, 1999.

Wahrman, Dror. "God and the Enlightenment." *American Historical Review* 108, no. 4 (2003): 1057–60.

Waldron, Jeremy. *God, Locke, and Equality: Christian Foundations in Locke's Political Thought*. Cambridge: Cambridge University Press, 2002.

———. *The Right to Private Property*. Oxford: Clarendon Press, 1988.

Walker, William. "J. G. A. Pocock and the History of British Political Thought: Assessing the State of the Art." *Eighteenth-Century Life* 33, no. 1 (2009): 83–96.

Wall, Cynthia. *The Prose of Things; Transformations of Description in the Eighteenth Century*. Chicago: University of Chicago Press, 2006.

Walmsley, Peter. *Locke's "Essay" and the Rhetoric of Science*. Lewisburg: Bucknell University Press, 2003.

Warburton, William, ed. *The Dunciad, Complete in Four Books*. By Alexander Pope. London, 1749.

Ward, James. *Phoenix-Park*. In *Poems on Several Occasions by His Grace the Duke of Buckingham . . . and other eminent hands*, 8–19. London, 1717.

Warner, Michael. "Uncritical Reading." In *Polemic: Critical or Uncritical*, edited by Jane Gallop, 13–38. New York: Routledge, 2004.

Warner, William. *Licensing Entertainment: The Elevation of Novel Reading in Britain, 1684–1750*. Berkeley: University of California Press, 1998.

Wasserman, Earl. "Nature Moralized: The Divine Analogy in the Eighteenth Century." *ELH* 20, no. 1 (1953): 39–76.

———. *The Subtler Language: Critical Readings of Neoclassical and Romantic Poems*. Baltimore: Johns Hopkins University Press, 1959.

Watt, Ian. *The Rise of the Novel*. 1957. Reprint, Berkeley: University of California Press, 2000.

Watts, Isaac. *Reliquae Juveniles*. London, 1734.

Webster, Charles. *The Great Instauration: Science, Medicine and Reform, 1626–60*. New York: Holmes and Meier Publishers, 1976.

———. "Recognition of Plant Sensitivity by English Botanists in the Seventeenth Century." *Isis* 57, no. 1 (1966): 5–23.

Wennerlind, Carl. *Casualties of Credit: The English Financial Revolution, 1620–1720*. Cambridge: Harvard University Press, 2011.

Westfall, Richard. *Never at Rest: A Biography of Isaac Newton*. Cambridge: Cambridge University Press, 1980.

Whiston, William. *Astronomical Principles of Religion, Natural and Reveal'd*. 1717. Facsimile edition, with an introduction by James Force. Hildesheim: Georg Olms Verlag, 1983.

———. *A Collection of the Authentick Records Belonging to the Old Testament*. 2 vols. London, 1727–8.

———. *Historical Memoirs of the Life of Dr. Samuel Clarke*. London, 1730.

———. *A Scheme of the Solar System with Orbits of the Planets and Comets Belonging Thereto*. London, 1712.

White, Douglas. *Pope and the Context of Controversy: The Manipulation of Ideas in "An Essay on Man."* Chicago: University of Chicago Press, 1970.
Willey, Basil. *Eighteenth-Century Backgrounds: Studies on the Idea of Nature in the Thought of the Period.* London: Chatto & Windus, 1940.
Williams, Anne. *Prophetic Strain: The Greater Lyric in the Eighteenth Century.* Chicago: University of Chicago Press, 1984.
Winn, James Anderson. *John Dryden and His World.* New Haven: Yale University Press, 1987.
Wintroub, Michael. "The Looking Glass of Facts: Collecting, Rhetoric and Citing the Self in the Experimental Natural Philosophy of Robert Boyle." *History of Science* 35, no. 108 (1997): 189–217.
Woodmansee, Martha, and Mark Osteen, eds. *The New Economic Criticism: Studies at the Intersection of Literature and Economics.* London: Routledge, 1999.
Woodward, John. *An Essay Toward a Natural History of the Earth.* London, 1702.
Woolf, Daniel. *The Social Circulation of the Past: English Historical Culture 1500–1730.* Oxford: Oxford University Press, 2003.
Worlidge, John. *Systema Agriculturae; Being the Mystery of Husbandry Discovered and Layd Open.* London, 1669.
Worster, Benjamin. *A Compendious and Methodical Account of the Principles of Natural Philosophy.* London, 1722.
Wragge-Morley, Alexander. "'Vividness' in English Natural History and Anatomy, 1650–1700." *Notes and Records of the Royal Society of London* 66, no. 4 (2012): 341–56.
Wright, James. *Burley Hill.* In *Farther Additions to the History and Antiquities of the County of Rutland*, 3–7. London, 1714.
Yates, Frances. "Hermetic Tradition in Renaissance Science." In *Art, Science, and History*, edited by Charles Singleton, 255–74. Baltimore: Johns Hopkins University Press, 1967.
Yolton, John. *Thinking Matter: Materialism in Eighteenth-Century Britain.* Minneapolis: University of Minnesota Press, 1983.
Young, Brian. *Religion and Enlightenment in Eighteenth-Century England: Theological Debate from Locke to Burke.* Oxford: Clarendon Press, 1998.
Zakai, Avihu. "Jonathan Edwards and the Language of Nature." *Journal of Religious History* 26, no. 1 (2002): 15–41.
Zwicker, Steven. "Reading Vergil in 1690s." In *Vergil at 2000*, edited by John D. Bernard, 281–302. New York: AMS Press, 1986.

Winners of the Walker Cowen Memorial Prize

Elizabeth Wanning Harries
The Unfinished Manner: Essays on the Fragment in the Later Eighteenth Century

Catherine Cusset
No Tomorrow: The Ethics of Pleasure in the French Enlightenment

Lisa Jane Graham
If the King Only Knew: Seditious Speech in the Reign of Louis XV

Suvir Kaul
Poems of Nation, Anthems of Empire: English Verse in the Long Eighteenth Century

Richard Nash
Wild Enlightenment: The Borders of Human Identity in the Eighteenth Century

Howard G. Brown
Ending the French Revolution: Violence, Justice, and Repression from the Terror to Napoleon

Jewel L. Spangler
Virginians Reborn: Anglican Monopoly, Evangelical Dissent, and the Rise of the Baptists in the Late Eighteenth Century

Theresa Braunschneider
Our Coquettes: Capacious Desire in the Eighteenth Century

James D. Drake
The Nation's Nature: How Continental Presumptions Gave Rise to the United States of America

Francesca Saggini
Backstage in the Novel: Frances Burney and the Theater Arts
Translated by Laura Kopp

Scott R. MacKenzie
Be It Ever So Humble: Poverty, Fiction, and the Invention of the Middle-Class Home

Denver Brunsman
The Evil Necessity: British Naval Impressment in the Eighteenth-Century Atlantic World

Jacob Sider Jost
Prose Immortality, 1711–1819

Christopher J. Tozzi
Nationalizing France's Army: Foreign, Black, and Jewish Troops in the French Military, 1715–1831

Courtney Weiss Smith
Empiricist Devotions: Science, Religion, and Poetry in Early Eighteenth-Century England

Index

Addison, Joseph, 2, 86, 87, 94, 170, 187; *Essay on the Georgics*, 31, 174, 186–89, 199; *Tatler* #249, 30, 108, 126, 128–29, 133–35
Adorno, Theodor, 20
aether, 76, 79, 84, 96, 209. *See also* gravity
agency. *See* human mind and human agency; personification; voice of nature
alchemy, 16, 76, 122, 130
alienation, 127
allegory, 76, 175, 177, 191–92
allusion, 103, 164, 173, 175, 181–82, 185, 203
analogy: as crucial tool, 2, 4–5, 8–13, 16, 34–35, 36, 47, 49, 52–53, 57–64, 128; examples of, 44, 86, 133–35, 136, 150, 168–69, 203; in nature, 61, 89, 130, 178; as structural principle of poetry, 203–5; traditional accounts of, 15, 17, 26, 233n25. *See also* figurative language
Anderson, Misty, 25
angels, 82, 85
animals: design of, 99, 116, 168; in georgic poetry, 183, 185, 194–95; instincts of, 144; as models for humanity, 128, 150–52, 161–63, 165–66; relationship to humans, 4–5, 34, 183, 194. *See also* ants; bees; instinct
Anne, Queen, 205
Anselment, Raymond, 36, 45

ants, 48, 56–57, 150–51, 178, 180. *See also* animals
application and use: in georgic poetry, 183, 190, 192, 197; in meditative empiricism, 4, 33–34, 47, 49, 51; —, examples of, 44, 58, 63–64, 70, 177; as part of the appeal of new science, 55; in sermons, 39. *See also* meditative empiricism
Arianism, 76
Aristotelianism, 8, 49, 50
Armstrong, Nancy, 18
Arthos, John, 192–93
atheism, 74, 79, 85
attention. *See* observation
Augustinianism, 144, 162
Austen, Ralph, 40, 52, 56, 132–33, 149, 170
autonomy: meditative empiricism's understanding of, 141–43, 155, 160–61, 170–72; traditional accounts of, 17, 18, 20, 24, 26, 140, 191, 209. *See also* human mind and human agency; individualism

Bacon, Francis, 14, 54, 56, 151
Barbon, Nicholas, 110, 120–22, 125
Barrell, John, 207
Bathurst, First Earl of (Allen Bathurst), 180
Battestin, Martin, 206
Baxter, Andrew, 92, 99–100
Baxter, Richard, 37

bees, 48–49, 54, 57–58, 63–64, 66, 150–51, 175, 177, 180, 185. See also animals
Bender, John, 7
Benson, William, 180–82, 189–90
Bentley, Richard, 73, 79–80, 84, 85, 97, 101
Berkeley, George, 86–89, 170
Bible, the: 46, 48, 63, 134, 162, 219n53, 220n76; Acts, 97, 99, 104; biblical hermeneutics, 14; 2 Corinthians, 136; Ecclesiastes, 115; Jeremiah, 135; Job, 40, 132; Proverbs, 48, 56–57, 149, 178. See also parables
Black, Scott, 3, 36, 53
blood, 200–201, 202–5
Bolingbroke, First Viscount (Henry St. John), 30, 111, 141–48, 155, 156, 158, 167
Bono, James, 60, 61
book of nature, 1–5, 16, 28–29, 33, 37–38, 39–40, 41, 49, 53, 65, 71, 183, 192, 208. See also nature; providence; voice of nature
Bowden, Samuel, 102–3
Boyle, Robert, 1–5, 14, 16, 25, 41–42, 51–53, 55, 77, 112, 151, 170; *Christian Virtuoso*, 53; *Essay of the Great Effects of Even Languid and Unheeded Motion*, 9–10, 12–23; *Free Enquiry into the Vulgarly Receiv'd Notion of Nature*, 20–21, 75; *Occasional Reflections*, 10–11, 12–13, 28, 33–35, 38, 40–45, 49, 51, 52, 54, 60–61, 65, 131–32, 140, 149, 178, 193; "Of the Study of the Booke of Nature," 55, 219n57; *Some Considerations touching the Usefulness of Experimental Naturall Philosophy*, 1–5
Boyle Lectures, 29, 79–80, 81, 85, 93
Brereton, Jane, 104
Briscoe, John, 118–19
Brooke, John, 71
bullion, 107, 108–13, 118, 120, 121, 134. See also money

Bunyan, John, 66
Bury, Edward, 48, 56

Calamy, Edward, 37
Cambridge Platonism, 76
Campanella, Tommaso, 130
Cantor, Geoffrey, 60
capitalism, 18, 30, 117. See also economic thought; international trade; money
Caroline, Princess, 84, 87
Cartesianism, 72, 78, 79, 81, 91, 104
catachresis, 178, 182
Catholicism, 39, 137
Chalker, John, 182, 184, 186
Chambers, Ephraim, 80
Charles I, 205
chemistry, 10, 54, 55, 209
Cheyne, George, 69, 72, 78, 86, 89–90, 98, 104–5, 170
Chico, Tita, 6–7
children, 57, 143–45, 156, 194
children's literature, 66
Cicero, 151
circulation: 109; in it-narratives, 126, 129, 130–31, 133–34
Clark, Katherine, 158
Clarke, Edward, 125
Clarke, Samuel, 29, 73–74, 77, 80, 81–86, 87, 97, 98, 102
clipping (coins), 109, 113, 119, 134
clocks, 73, 75, 93; clock metaphors, 58, 61, 69–86, 93, 98, 104–5, 116, 169
coffeehouses, 90, 93–94
Colliber, Samuel, 84
Collinges, John, 55
Collins, Anthony, 81
Comenius, J. A., 41, 217n26
comets, 74, 94
commodity: commodity value of money, 110, 118, 121; Marx's notion of, 30, 107, 126–27, 138
concordia discors, 206–7. See also harmony; order

272 · Index

conjectural history, 2, 30, 143–45, 147–55. *See also* origins
consent, 114–15, 145, 146–47, 157–58, 159–61, 170–72. *See also* social contract
conservation of force, 82–83
consumer culture, 18, 19, 20, 106, 126–27, 173–74, 181. *See also* economic thought
Coolahan, Marie-Louise, 36
Corneanu, Sorana, 14
corpuscularianism, 9, 11, 36, 44, 49, 67, 77, 78, 101
correspondences, 4, 15, 16, 17, 43, 46, 87, 130. *See also* harmony; patterns
corruption, 99, 111, 119, 126, 135, 147, 157, 158, 161
cosmogony, 183
Crawford, Rachel, 186
credit, 106–7, 111, 122
Creech, Thomas, 148
Cromwell, Oliver, 205

Darwin, Erasmus, 209
Daston, Lorraine, 23, 25, 34, 43, 49, 50
Davis, Lennard, 18
debt, 106–7, 111
Defoe, Daniel, 2, 65, 111, 165–66, 170–72; *Jure Divino*, 2, 30, 141–42, 155–56, 157–58, 161–64
deixis, 193–194
Denham, John, 190
Derham, William, 14, 98
Desaguliers, J. T., 86, 90–92
description, 4, 5, 6, 7–11, 15, 16, 46, 48, 57, 182, 187–99. *See also* figurative language
design. *See* book of nature; design arguments; order; providence; voice of nature
design arguments, 4, 71, 79, 86, 94, 99, 104, 116, 160
devaluation, 110, 112, 117–25, 228n10
devil, 10, 44–45, 138

Diaper, William, 178, 182
diction, 19, 174, 193, 195. *See also* figurative language; periphrasis
didacticism, 18, 128, 187
digression, 173, 181–82, 186, 188, 202–3
disenchantment, 17, 20, 21, 67, 87
divine activity, 22, 122; in Newtonian texts, 29, 71, 73, 76–77, 79, 81–82, 84–85, 95–102. *See also* miracles; providence
divine right, 147, 156, 166, 170
Douglas, Aileen, 127
Dryden, John, 175–81, 183, 186, 189, 200
Dugaw, Diane, 198
Dunn, John, 159
Dyer, John, 185

East India Company, 108
economic thought, 5, 29–30, 51, 106–25, 159–61. *See also* money; international trade
Eden, 38, 203
Edwards, Karen, 3, 40
electricity, 79, 209
Elizabeth I, 119, 129
Elkins, James, 60, 63
emblem, 12, 35, 48, 57, 65
empire, 173, 185–86
empiricism: relationship between meditative and Royal Society sponsored brands of, 35–36, 47, 49, 50–65; Royal Society sponsored brand of, 9–10, 14, 34, 52. *See also* meditative empiricism; new science; observation; particularity
enargeia, 44, 48
enthusiasm, 90, 170, 218n48
epistemology: meditative empiricism's account of, 1–2, 5, 10, 26, 37–38, 47, 59, 169–72; other accounts of, 12, 62–63, 182, 191. *See also* empiricism; fallibility; meditative empiricism; modesty; observation; provisionality; trust
Erskine-Hill, Howard, 145

Index · 273

evangelicalism, 209
Evelyn, John, 48, 179
evil, 64, 90, 161, 168–69. *See also* devil; sin
experiments, 8, 14, 22, 38, 50, 70, 100, 176; in meditative empiricism, 3, 4, 8, 10, 43–44, 47, 48, 52, 55, 56, 66, 165–66. *See also* empiricism; Royal Society

fables, 130–31
Fairer, David, 184, 200, 207
fallibility, 43, 47, 62, 147, 149, 152–53, 170. *See also* epistemology; modesty; provisionality; trust
Fatio, Nicolas, of Duillier, 76
Festa, Lynn, 127
fiction, 111, 117, 121, 127; in the it-narrative form, 128–39
figurative language: in meditative empiricism, 2, 3–5, 8–9, 12–13, 16, 17, 19, 30, 69–70, 192; —, characteristics of, 57–64, 131–33; —, in georgic poetry, 174, 178, 187, 197; traditional accounts of, 6–7, 12, 15, 17, 18, 26. *See also* analogy; diction; metaphor; personification; periphrasis; puns; synecdoche
Filmer, Robert, 145, 146–47, 149, 158, 166
Finch, Anne, 11–13, 25
Finklestein, Andrea, 121
Flavel, John, 46, 66, 170
Flint, Christopher, 126–27
Force, James, 71
Foucault, Michel, 15, 17
free will, 83–84, 224n42
Funkenstein, Amos, 14
Fussell, G. E., 175

Gay, John, 2, 31, 174, 190–99
genius of the soil, 176, 178–80, 184, 203
Gentner, Dedre, 12, 26, 60, 62
georgic poetry, 2, 19, 31, 152, 173–208. *See also* meditative empiricism

georgicall committee, 54–55, 176, 179. *See also* Royal Society
George II, 91–92
Germain, Elizabeth (*née* Berkeley), 65
Gildon, Charles, 30, 108, 126–33, 135–38, 170
Girten, Kristen, 14, 36, 66–67
Glanvill, Joseph, 14
God. *See* book of nature; design; divine activity; harmony; order; providence; voice of nature
gold, 106, 109, 114, 115, 130–31, 160–61. *See also* bullion; money
Goodman, Kevis, 182, 184, 189
grafting, 182, 184
gravity, 70–71, 74–105, 209; cause of, 74–76, 78, 79–80, 81–82, 85, 93, 102–3. *See also* aether; Newton; Newtonianism
Gray, Thomas, 209
Gregory, David, 98
Guest, Harriet, 207

Haan, Estelle, 188
Hales, Stephen, 84
Hall, Joseph, 39, 51, 56
Halley, Edmund, 80, 98
Hammond, Brean, 143, 145
harmony, 89, 154, 164, 184, 195, 227n75; between truths, 16, 41–42, 46, 62, 112. *See also* book of nature; correspondences; order; patterns; providence
Harris, John, 80
Harrison, Peter, 14
Harrison, Ross, 156
Hartlib, Samuel, 48, 56
Harvey, William, 61
Haywood, Eliza, 2, 66–67, 209
Henry VIII, 119
Henry, John, 14
hermeneutics of provisional trust, 27–28, 206, 209–10
hermeneutics of suspicion, 24–27, 206, 207, 209
Hervey, James, 66, 170, 209

Hesiod, 183
hierarchy, 70, 142, 171
Hobbes, Thomas, 77, 117, 146–47, 149, 158, 166
Hodges, James, 110, 120, 121, 122–25, 128, 139, 170
Homer, 179
Hooke, Robert, 35–36, 56, 57–65, 151, 170, 193
Hooker, Richard, 146
Horkheimer, Max, 20
humanism, 35, 53
human mind and human agency: meditative empiricism's account of, 34, 47, 171–72; —, anxiety about, 112, 126–27, 138, 141, 146, 148, 157, 170; —, and nature, 113–15, 121; modernization stories' privileging of, 15–16, 17, 26, 38–39, 107. *See also* autonomy; individualism
human nature, 22, 128, 144–45, 147, 148, 156–57, 167. *See also* fallibility; reason
Hunter, J. Paul, 18, 36–38, 42, 46, 65
Hunter, Michael, 54–55, 219n57
husbandry manuals, 175–78, 180, 203, 206
Huygens, Christaan, 75
hypothesis, 4, 5, 11, 14, 35, 43, 49, 55, 62; *hypothesis non fingo*, 74, 75–77, 80, 82, 85, 169. *See also* empiricism; Royal Society

ideology, 12, 25, 28, 206
Ignatian meditation, 39. *See also* meditation
imagination, 8, 35, 62–63, 94, 114, 186–89; not the sole source of meaning, 12–13, 17, 25, 38, 47. *See also* human mind and human agency; subjectivity
improvement, 51, 55, 66, 122, 144, 165, 175, 180, 202, 205
individualism, 18, 19, 20, 30, 171–72. *See also* autonomy; human mind and human agency

induction, 8, 26, 34, 75. *See also* empiricism
instinct, 86, 143–45, 147–48, 152, 154, 156–58, 162–63. *See also* animals
intellectualism, 84
international trade, 106, 108, 112, 123, 185; providential arguments for, 115, 129, 165
intrinsic value, 112–17, 119, 120–21, 122–23, 135, 230n53. *See also* economic thought
it-narratives, 2, 30, 31, 108, 126–39, 149

Jackson, Joseph, 130–31
Jacob, J. R., 41–42, 52
Jacob, Margaret, 52, 61, 70, 71, 79, 86
Jacobitism, 143
Jeziorski, Michael, 12, 26, 60, 62
Johnson, Samuel, 23, 231n68
Jones, John, 178, 182
Jones, Katherine, Lady Ranelagh, 55
Jones, Matthew, 14
Jones, R. F., 6–7, 8
Jones, Tom, 145, 157

Kahn, Victoria, 140–41
Kant, Immanuel, 21, 143
Keenleyside, Heather, 194
Keill, John, 84, 98
Koyré, Alexander, 71
Kramnick, Isaac, 111, 141–42, 146, 157

Lamb, Jonathan, 127–28, 230n53
land, 111, 159–60, 161, 177, 179–80, 186, 199, 202
Landa, Louis, 115
landscape painting, 187, 189, 190
language. *See* description; figurative language; literal language
Latour, Bruno, 21, 24, 214n80
laws: activity required, 91–92, 103–4; of motion, 22, 77; of nature, 22, 80, 87, 144, 146–47, 152, 156–57, 159–61; static order implied, 71

Leibniz, G. W., 29, 49, 72–75, 81–84, 86, 97, 169
Leranbaum, Miriam, 168, 235n59
Leslie, Charles, 166
Levenson, Thomas, 117
Lewalski, Barbara, 39
Linneaus, Carl, 193
literal language, 6, 15, 16, 45, 191–93. *See also* description; plain style
literature and science. *See* science and literature
Locke, John, 62, 125, 160, 167; economic writings, 2, 110, 111–15, 116, 160, 228n10; *Two Treatises of Government*, 30, 141–42, 145, 146, 155–61, 166–67, 169–72
love, 88–89, 143–45, 152–53, 168, 175, 183; in nature, 154–55
Lowndes, William, 2, 109, 117–19, 228n10
Lucretius, 147–48, 149, 151, 168–69
Lynch, William, 60, 62

machines. *See* clocks; mechanism
Mack, Maynard, 206, 208
Macpherson, C. B., 159
Macpherson, Sandra, 140–41
Mandeville, Bernard, 166
Markley, Robert, 113, 121, 219n53
Marrinan, Michael, 7
Marxism, 107, 126–27
materialism, 73–74, 77. *See also* new materialism
mathematics, 29, 63, 70, 74, 76, 104, 146; model for prose, 6, 59. *See also* measurement; new science
Mather, Cotton, 92, 98–99, 209
McGuire, J. E., 59, 60, 61, 62
McKeon, Michael, 18, 19
McRae, Andrew, 175
measurement, 76, 97, 112
mechanism, 59, 61, 69–70, 77–80, 81–83, 87, 92. *See also* clocks
meditation, 2, 14–15, 39. *See also* design arguments; meditative empiricism; occasional meditation
meditative empiricism, 1–5, 9–12, 22–24, 29, 47–53, 65, 209–10; and economic policy, 106–8, 109–10, 115–17, 124; and georgic, 174, 178–79, 182–90, 192–95, 207–8; and it-narratives, 128, 130–35; and Newtonianism, 71, 86–92; and political thought, 140–43, 148–49, 158–66, 168–69; model of human agency, 145, 146–47, 166, 170–72, 183–84; modernization narratives troubled by, 12–13, 14–15, 20, 27. *See also* empiricism; epistemology; observation; particularity
Menely, Tobias, 194
Merton, Robert K., 13
metaphor: as crucial tool, 16, 62, 69; in poetry, 175, 177, 181–82, 188, 203–4. *See also* analogy; clocks; figurative language
microscopy, 2, 47, 56–59, 60, 64, 66, 183. *See also* new science
Milbourne, Luke, 176–78, 183
millenarianism, 13, 223n15
Milton, John, 66, 201, 203, 204, 205
Mint, the, 109, 117
miracles, 75, 83, 84, 86. *See also* divine activity
mnemonic verse, 178
modernization narratives, 13–20, 26, 36, 65, 67, 110–11, 141–42, 171–72, 208, 209; turned on their heads, 20, 30, 107, 111, 125
modesty: examples of, 10, 11, 44, 106–7, 147, 152; in hermeneutics of provisional trust, 28; meditative empiricism's understanding of, 1–3, 5, 17, 22, 42, 49–50, 62, 170
money, 106, 108–39, 159–61. *See also* bullion; clipping; gold; silver
Montaigne, Michel de, 152
morality: relationship to empiricism, 5, 23, 27, 36, 49, 51, 61, 169–71, 198,

207; —, examples of, 41, 55, 86–90, 167–69, 180, 203, 207. *See also* origins
Morton, Timothy, 21
Mulligan, Lotte, 53

natural theology, 14, 72, 73, 209. *See also* design arguments
nature: as guide, 41, 128, 147, 162–64, 170; definitions of, 20–24, 67, 206–7; endowed with agency, 157, 164; contains hints, 1–5, 128–29, 131, 149, 151, 153–55, 160–61, 165–66, 183, 189, 207; gendered, 22, 67; uniform, never acts in vain, 61, 96–97. *See also* book of nature; correspondences; harmony; order; providence; voice of nature
navigation, 115, 165–66, 180
Needler, Henry, 178, 182
neostoicism, 76
new materialisms, 21, 215nn84–86
new science, 20, 47–48, 55, 173–74, 176, 182–83, 198; and language, 6, 15, 17, 59, 198. *See also* empiricism; measurement; observation; Royal Society; taxonomy
Newton, Isaac, 2, 29, 59, 63, 70–71, 73, 75–79, 81, 84, 93, 97, 100, 117. *See also* gravity; Newtonianism
Newtonianism, 2, 29, 70–105, 183, 190, 209
Nicholson, Colin, 111
Nine Years' War, 108–9
novels, 6, 18–19, 209. *See also* rise of the novel

object narratives. *See* it-narratives
observation: and divine activity, 92, 98–100; in georgic poetry, 182, 190–91; in meditative empiricism, 2–3, 5, 15, 34–35, 47, 132; —, examples of, 9–11, 43–44, 48, 106, 114, 152, 161–62, 165–66. *See also* empiricism; meditative empiricism; particularity
occasional meditation, 14–15, 28–29, 33–43, 47, 65–68, 170; as brand of empiricism, 47–65; examples of, 10–11, 43–46, 87–89, 110, 123–24, 141, 148–49; and georgic, 183–84, 188, 190, 196; and it-narratives, 128, 134–36, 138; practiced by women, 33, 39, 48–49, 218n37. *See also* meditation
occult qualities, 49, 75, 77, 191
occult science, 15, 16, 26, 59, 130
Oppian, 152, 178
order, 23, 72, 103–5, 206, 207. *See also* pattern
origins: of monetary value, 114–15, 119, 121, 122–23; of morality, 140, 146; of religion, 152–53; of society, 140–41, 143–55, 165. *See also* conjectural history
Orpheus, 175
orrery, 101–4

paper money, 106–7, 111. *See also* money
parables, 41. *See also* Bible, the
Paracelsianism, 16
Park, Katherine, 23, 50
Parker, Blanford, 191–92
Parker, David, 193–94, 199
particularity: in georgic, 174, 178, 182–85, 192–98, 199–200; in meditative empiricism, 3, 13, 33–34, 50; —, examples of, 9–11, 43, 46, 48, 57, 152, 166, 168–69, 235n53; traditional accounts of, 6, 8, 18–19, 191. *See also* empiricism; observation
passive obedience, 156, 161–64
patriarchal government, 142, 152, 157
patterns, 34, 49, 64, 173–74, 184–86, 190, 194, 195, 200, 208. *See also* correspondences; harmony; order; providence
periphrasis, 2, 9, 173, 193–99, 203. *See also* diction; figurative language
personification: as crucial tool, 2, 4–5, 9, 12, 131–32, 196–97, 231n69; in it-narratives, 128–29, 131–34, 137; in poetry, 149–50, 173, 176, 177–80, 186, 188–89, 196–97, 204. *See also* figurative language; voice of nature

Philips, John, 31, 174, 199–208
physico-theology, 14, 98, 116, 213n47. *See also* design arguments; natural theology
Picciotto, Joanna, 3, 36, 38, 39, 46–47
plain style, 6–9, 47. *See also* description; literal language
planets, 67, 75, 88–89, 91, 94–98, 154
plants, 4–5, 64, 66, 121, 150, 154, 177, 179, 181, 183, 185, 188, 203–4. *See also* trees
Plumwood, Val, 231n69
Pocock, J. G. A., 111
political thought, 19, 30, 51, 52, 61, 90–92, 140–66, 181. *See also* autonomy; consent; social contract
poetry, 12–13, 17–19, 142, 173–74, 195–96, 208. *See also* figurative language; georgic poetry
Pope, Alexander, 31, 87, 94, 173, 190; *Essay on Man*, 2, 30, 141–45, 147–56, 158, 165, 166–69, 180; *Epistle to Burlington*, 174, 179–80, 182, 184
Power, Henry, 56–57
Preston, Claire, 60
Price, Martin, 206
pride, 35, 54, 67, 134, 184
Principe, Lawrence, 51, 53
property, 111, 119, 127, 159–61
providence: central to the new science, 73–74, 82, 86–87, 93, 90, 101, 138; meaning in nature, 3, 5, 9, 20, 42, 208; —, examples of, 113–16, 122–23, 128–29, 156–57, 161–62, 165–66, 178–79, 190. *See also* book of nature; correspondences; design arguments; divine activity; harmony; voice of nature
provisionality: in meditative empiricism, 5, 9, 34–35, 49, 62–63; —, examples of, 10, 11, 45, 106–7, 138, 169, 236n65. *See also* hermeneutics of provisional trust
puns, 134, 136–37. *See also* figurative language

Purchas, Samuel, 48–49, 54, 56
Puttenham, George, 178
Pythagoras, 76

Ranew, Nathaneal, 37
Ray, John, 98
readers, 57, 189, 194–95, 198–99, 239n79
realism, 18–19, 174, 187–89, 191–99. *See also* novels
reason, 5, 76, 144, 156, 157, 162–63, 166, 171
recoinage crisis, 29–30, 108–25, 134–35, 155
Reill, Peter, 59, 63
religion. *See* angels; Bible, the; devil; divine activity; evil; miracles; natural theology; occasional meditation; providence; sin
relics, 199–202, 203
Renaissance, the, 12, 17, 42, 130
resemblances. *See* analogy; correspondences
rhetoric. *See* description; figurative language; literal language
Rich, Mary, 2, 48–49, 54, 218n37
Ricoeur, Paul, 24
riddles, 198
rise of the novel, 6, 18–20, 191–92. *See also* novels; realism
Rogers, John, 52, 61
Rogers, Pat, 186
Romans, 176, 200–202
Romanticism, 12–13, 17, 193
Rousseau, Jean-Jacques, 143
royal prerogative, 119, 120, 122
Royal Society, 1–2, 13–14, 54–55, 94; and language, 6, 7, 8, 26, 191; methodologies of, 47, 48, 49, 51–52. *See also* empiricism; georgicall committee

sailing, 40, 151–52
Schabas, Margaret, 107
Schaffer, Simon, 7
Schmidgen, Wolfram, 18, 52, 61, 219n49

Schonhorn, Manuel, 157
science and literature, 6–13, 14, 38
secularization, 13–16, 19–20, 36, 65, 209. *See also* modernization narratives
self-defense, 156, 161–63
self-interest, 88, 111, 148
self-love, 143–44
Senex, John, 94
sentimentalism, 127
sex, 136, 137, 143–44, 156, 185
'sGravesand, William James, 80
Shaftesbury, First Earl of (Anthony Ashley Cooper), 155
Shaftesbury, Third Earl of (Anthony Ashley Cooper), 101
Shapin, Steven, 7, 71
Sherman, Sandra, 111
silver, 106, 108–10, 112–16, 118–21, 123–24, 128–29, 160–61. *See also* bullion; money
similitudes. *See* analogy; correspondences
sin, 10–11, 45, 46, 54, 158
Sitter, John, 194
skepticism, 152; in meditative empiricism, 35, 47, 166, 168, 211n12, 236n64. *See also* fallibility; provisionality
Smith, Charlotte, 209
social contract, 20, 30, 126, 140–47, 151–63, 170–72. *See also* consent; origins
Somers, John, 125
Sontag, Susan, 25
soul, 168, 224n41; associated with the divine, 86, 157, 225n47; in occasional meditations, 54, 55, 88
Spacks, Patricia Meyer, 195–96, 238n43
Spence, Joseph, 180
Spinoza, Baruch, 49
Sprat, Thomas, 6, 191
Sreenivasan, Gopal, 156
Stalnaker, Joanna, 8, 220n81
Steele, Richard (minister), 41
Steele, Richard (writer), 87

Sterne, Laurence, 207
subjectivity: not the sole source of meaning, 12–13, 25, 38, 42–43, 47. *See also* human mind and human agency; imagination
sun, 91, 96–97, 130–31, 203–4
Swift, Jonathan, 65, 87, 128
Swinnock, George, 50
synecdoche, 186, 189, 239n79. *See also* figurative language

taxonomy, 192–93, 198, 209
technology, 10, 64, 151–52, 165–66
Thales, 76
thinking matter, 130, 133, 225n87
Thirsk, Joan, 175
Thompson, James, 111
Thomson, James, 66, 100–102, 103, 173, 195, 238n43
Tiffany, Daniel, 69
Tillotson, Geoffrey, 195
Toland, John, 85
Torre, Jose, 117
Tory, 125, 141–42, 143, 161, 166, 167, 205–6
trades, 40, 54–55, 116
Treasury, 109–10, 117, 118
trees, 40–41, 56, 132, 176–77, 181, 202, 205, 208. *See also* plants
trust, 5, 29, 35, 37, 42–43, 45–46, 62, 149, 169, 186. *See also* epistemology; hermeneutics of provisional trust
Tully, James, 156–57, 159, 167
tyranny, 153, 157, 161–64, 184

use. *See* application and use
use value, 113–14, 159. *See also* economic thought

Vickers, Brian, 15, 16, 17, 26, 59
Vidal, Fernando, 25
Viner, Jacob, 115
Virgil, 175–90, 197, 199, 200–201, 204. *See also* georgic poetry

virtual witnessing, 7–8, 44, 46. *See also* description
vitalism, 59, 209
Vitruvius, 151
voice of nature, 40–41, 67, 132–33, 149–52, 180. *See also* book of nature; nature; personification; providence
Voltaire, 143, 169
voluntarism, 84

Wahrman, Dror, 20
Wall, Cynthia, 36, 47
Walmsey, Peter, 62
Walpole, Robert, 143
Warburton, William, 85

Wasserman, Earl, 17–18, 206–7
Watt, Ian, 7, 18, 19, 20, 191–92, 198
Watts, Isaac, 66
weaving, 40, 55, 150
Webster, Charles, 13
Wennerlind, Carl, 121–22
Whig, 70, 125, 141–42, 143, 155–57, 166
Whig history, 20, 107
Whiston, William, 78, 92–98
William III, 155
Worster, Benjamin, 85
Wragge-Morley, Alexander, 59–60

Young, Edward, 66

www.ingramcontent.com/pod-product-compliance
Lightning Source LLC
Chambersburg PA
CBHW031801220426
43662CB00007B/487